THE TRANSITION IN CENTRAL AND EASTERN EUROPEAN POLITICS

J. William Derleth

University of the Pacific

PRENTICE HALL, Upper Saddle River, New Jersey 07458

Library of Congress Cataloging-in-Publication Data

Derleth, J. William (James William)
    The transition in Central and Eastern European politics
/ J. William Derleth.
        p.   cm.
    Includes index.
    ISBN 0-13-756453-8
    1. Europe, Eastern—History—20th century.   2. Post-communism—
Europe, Eastern.   I. Title.
DJK49.D47   2000
947'.0009'04—dc21   99-24870
                                                                CIP

Editorial Director: Charlyce Jones Owen
Editor in Chief: Nancy Roberts
Senior Acquisitions Editor: Beth Gillett Mejia
Editorial Assistant: Brian Prybella
Project Manager: Merrill Peterson
Prepress and Manufacturing Buyer: Ben Smith
Cover Director: Jayne Conte
Cover Designer: Bruce Kenselaar
Marketing Manager: Christopher DeJohn

This book was set in 10/12 Palatino by Stratford Publishing
Services and was printed and bound by Courier Companies, Inc.
The cover was printed by Phoenix Color Corp.

© 2000 by Prentice-Hall, Inc.
Upper Saddle River, New Jersey 07458

Printed in the United States of America

10   9   8   7   6   5   4   3   2   1

ISBN 0-13-756453-8

PRENTICE-HALL INTERNATIONAL (UK) LIMITED, *London*
PRENTICE-HALL OF AUSTRALIA PTY. LIMITED, *Sydney*
PRENTICE-HALL CANADA INC., *Toronto*
PRENTICE-HALL HISPANOAMERICANA, S.A., *Mexico*
PRENTICE-HALL OF INDIA PRIVATE LIMITED, *New Delhi*
PRENTICE-HALL OF JAPAN, INC., *Tokyo*
PEARSON EDUCATION ASIA PTE. LTD., *Singapore*
EDITORA PRENTICE-HALL DO BRASIL, LTDA., *Rio de Janeiro*

CONTENTS

3   HUNGARY   *194*

4   POLAND   255

CONCLUSION   321

PREFACE

The genesis for this manuscript grew out of a Fulbright Lectureship at the American University in Bulgaria between 1992 and 1994. Responding to students' desire to learn about the economic, political, and social systems in other former socialist states, we created a course called "Central and Eastern European Comparative Politics." Since there were no texts that compare and contrast the polities of the states in the region since the fall of the Berlin Wall in 1989, I had my students write one!

Although Central and Eastern Europe no longer dominate the headlines as they did in 1989, the economic, political, and social problems of the region continue to present students with a broad array of interesting phenomena. The decade since the fall of the Berlin Wall has seen the collapse of authoritarian regimes, the enactment of market economic reforms, the reestablishment of democratic institutions, and significant social and demographic changes. Since these states are still struggling to create a new polity and their success or failure will have global and regional significance, it is vital to explain these events and their ramifications to students.

How can we do this? Most existing works on Central and Eastern Europe are overly specialized—that is, either they focus on theoretical issues or they focus on a single country or single issue such as economic transformation. In other words, they are either too specialized for undergraduates or lack a broad comparative perspective. Although I have experimented with a number of these textbooks, my students—most of whom know little about the contemporary Russian polity, let alone Bulgaria, Hungary, or Poland—have told me that neither of these approaches makes the events in the region accessible to them.

As a result, I have used an organizational framework that allows students to learn about the political history, political culture, economic situation, governmental and nongovernmental elite, policy making, and other features of each state—Bulgaria, Hungary, Poland, and Russia—included in the book. To introduce students to some of the larger political issues as well as facilitating comparative analysis, the book also examines the success or failure of the states in reaching their stated goals of creating a civil society, democratic institutions/political rights, a market economy, and a law-based society.

Though not in vogue with the ever-increasing emphasis on quantitative analysis and microspecialization, this interdisciplinary approach has numerous benefits. It gives students a general introduction to the region, helps them understand why states that shared a common political legacy for forty-five years can be so different today, and, most important, helps them draw comparative conclusions. In summary, we use the detailed country studies to help students understand events that are simultaneously occurring in very different countries.

The layout of the book is straightforward. The first chapter introduces the analytical framework through which all the states are examined. The next four chapters are country case studies that help students identify the differences and similarities between the states. The concluding chapter integrates these comparisons in order to shed light on the profound changes occurring throughout Central and Eastern Europe.

Because of a dearth of library resources, the first draft of this manuscript was based on student interviews with businesspeople, embassy officials, and other sources. The insights gained from talking with policy makers and people directly affected by the regime change greatly enhanced the students' work, and thus this manuscript. Therefore, a special note of recognition goes to Galina Chuleva, "Jimmy" Dimitrov, Olya Egorova, Vesselina Kolcheva, Ivanka Lakova, Velina Nedialkova, Maria Spirova, Nadia Tisheva, Vessala Todorova, and Deniz Toro, who wrote the "first draft" of this book. While working on subsequent versions, I was fortunate to have four very conscientious research assistants, Dawn Jones, Mike Hutchinson, Leah Thayer, and Marjorie Tillinghast. They not only helped with bibliographic research, fact checking, proofreading, and preparing the country chronologies, but also helped to ensure that the book was "student friendly," that the tone, style, and concepts were appropriate for their peers.

I would also like to thank the Institute of International Education for their generous support. In 1995, I was fortunate enough to be awarded an IIE Professional Development Fellowship. As a junior scholar who teaches at a small liberal arts university with limited resources, IIE's support was crucial. Thus I am very grateful to the IIE. The fellowship allowed me to spend time in the region speaking with government officials, academics, business people, and political leaders. Although space prevents me from naming them all, I am especially indebted to Antal Disztl, Counsellor at the Hungarian Embassy in Sofía; Dr. Peter Hack, MP for the Hungarian Alliance of Free Democrats; Professor Andrzej Bryk, Institute of History and Law, Jagellonian

University—Krakow; and Ognyan Avramov, chief-of-staff to Bulgarian President Zhelyu Zhelev. Their insight was especially helpful.

Academically, I am indebted to two professors who stimulated my interest in Central and Eastern Europe and have been mentors ever since: Jack Oster, now retired from the University of Wisconsin—Stevens Point, and Karen Dawisha at the University of Maryland—College Park.

I also wish to thank the reviewers of the manuscript: James W. Peterson, Valdosta State University; and Nayef H. Samhat, Centre College.

Finally, I must thank all my students and friends from Wisconsin and elsewhere who not only suffered through lectures and discussions about the region and politics in general but also stimulated my interest by asking me questions and, more importantly, supporting my efforts in the numerous ways it takes to bring a project like this to fruition.

J. William Derleth

INTRODUCTION

Events in recent years have dramatically changed the political landscape in Central and Eastern Europe (CEE). The disintegration of the Soviet Union, the collapse of centrally planned economies, the unraveling of the post–World War II geopolitical balance, and the appearance of newly independent states have combined to plunge the region into an uncertain phase of historical transformation. The effects of these changes will have significant regional and global repercussions.

BACKGROUND

Starting with the 1917 Bolshevik Revolution in Russia and continuing with the liberation and then occupation of the region by the Soviet Army at the end of World War II, the CEE states were forced to create Soviet-style regimes. Commonalities included authoritarian political systems and centrally planned economies. Although most would regard these as negative attributes, the regimes also provided many benefits to their citizens. State control over most aspects of life provided social mobility, universal education, health care, and greatly improved living standards for the vast majority of the population. In other words, people saw tangible benefits in communist rule. Therefore, it should come as no surprise that in an era of rapid economic, political, and social change, many people long for the benefits of the past.

Sharing a common political legacy, Central and Eastern European states also have common problems in the 1990s. Economically, they have to deal with the thousands of people who have lost their jobs as a result of economic restructuring and the closing of inefficient state factories. Politically, they must create new political structures that not only reflect the people's will, but also have the authority and legitimacy to act.

Despite the similarities among CEE states, they have reacted to the end of the old regime in several different ways. The states in the region have adopted distinct economic, foreign, political, and social policies. These divergent policies have had varying consequences. Some countries, such as Hungary and Poland, have managed to build relatively stable, pluralistic political systems and are well on their way to creating market economies. In contrast, states like Bulgaria and Russia have been largely unsuccessful in the transformation of their political and economic systems.

COMPARATIVE POLITICS

Identifying the similarities and differences between states and, even more important, describing *why* they occur, is the goal of comparative politics. This branch of political science examines the factors shared by political systems around the world, delineating the relationship between government and society, identifying the economic and political elite, and describing the institutions and processes of politics and government—how they operate and the outcomes of these interactions. In other words, political scientists try to explain what is happening and predict what the results of these processes will be in order to discover what is universal and what is incidental.

To organize our evaluation of different political systems systematically and determine cause-and-effect relationships, political scientists develop theories to test their ideas. For example, prior to 1989, most texts that examined Central and Eastern Europe used *statism theory* to describe the political processes in the region. This theory is based on the idea that the state is a integrated administrative, legal, bureaucratic, and coercive system that helps determine the relationships between society and the state. In other words, in authoritarian regimes, the state structure dominates the political process.

As the rapid collapse of the communist regimes showed, however, this theory was no longer relevant. We saw instead that the state is not a truly autonomous actor and that economic, political, and social conditions have a dramatic effect on the polity. As this example illustrates, political science has not had much success in creating a generally applicable theory that describes political interactions across cultures. Without proposing a new model of politics, we can nonetheless devise a comparative framework that can help us better organize our thinking about this subset of politics.

All of the states in the CEE region are in the process of stumbling away from a single-party regime in which the communist party dominated the economy, political system, and society. But stumbling toward what? Each has declared its intention to create a polity based on a civil society, democratic institutions and political rights, a market economy, and the rule of law. By tracing the development of these features in the various states, we can accomplish several goals. First, we will gain a general understanding of political patterns and trends and in CEE states themselves. Second, we can begin to identify the factors that explain the differences between them. Third, since we will be examining how people deal with certain universal economic, political, and social problems (here associated with the creation of new polities), our comparative study should help students understand their own country better. Finally, although the goal of this study is not to elaborate and test theory, we hope our observations and conclusions will provide the foundations for future theoretical development.

FACTORS

Since a key goal of this book is to help students understand the similarities and differences among various political systems, let us elaborate upon and define the variables we will use to compare them.

Civil Society

The notion of a civil society is not discussed much in the United States because Americans take its existence for granted. A *civil society* consists of the aggregate of networks and institutions that exist and act independently of the state and are capable of developing their own spontaneous views on state and local issues. In effect, these groups limit the power of the state. Hence the emergence of a civil society in CEE states will have a crucial impact on the development of the polity. The existence of a civil society can be determined by the freedom of individuals to develop views, institutions, and personal autonomy separate from the state.[1] To lessen the subjectivity of our analysis, we use the Freedom House's *Comparative Survey of Freedom—Civil Liberties* to rank each state.[2] On their ranking scale, 1 represents the most free and 7 the least free.

Political Rights

Political rights are the people's ability to freely participate in the political process. In contrast to nondemocratic states, members of the governmental bodies in democratic states are selected through competitive elections and enact policies that broadly reflect the wishes of a significant portion of the population. In addition, the power of governmental institutions over people is limited either through law or tradition.

This factor will be measured by the ability of people to participate in meaningful elections and to choose the type of the political system as well as its leaders.[3] The Freedom House's *Comparative Survey of Freedom—Political Rights* is used to measure the level of democratic institutional development and political rights in each state. It shares the same ranking scale as the survey for civil liberties: 1 is the most free and 7 the least free.

Market Economy

A *market economic system* is one in which market forces determine prices, which in turn allocate scarce resources among competing uses. In contrast, the states we will be discussing had command economies. As the name implies, *command economies* are based on governmental control over all sectors of the economy.

To compare the progress of CEE states in creating a market economy, we use the European Bank for Reconstruction and Development's (EBRD) *Progress in Transition in Eastern Europe: 1997.* This report measures four basic aspects of a market economy: privatization and restructuring of enterprises, the competitiveness and openness of the market, the ability of financial institutions to collect and channel savings to productive investments, and the extensiveness and effectiveness of legal rules on investment.

Rule of Law

The *rule of law* has numerous features. In addition to guaranteeing basic individual freedoms, such as speech, press, association and personal security, rule of law prevents or limits corruption, tax evasion and customs fraud, police brutality, and extralegal judicial procedures. In other words, a society based on the rule of law has clearly stated, universally applied, and impartially administered legal sanctions for behavior (e.g., contract law).

Interestingly, there is no international measurement of the rule of law. Therefore, we have decided to use Transparency International's *Corruption Perceptions Index* to rank the states.[4] This index is used by the World Bank to measure effective governance and lack of corruption, two key features of a system governed by the rule of law.

Although the goals of each state are clear, how they can be reached is not as obvious. The swift disintegration of the communist regimes after almost fifty years of apparent invincibility created a general euphoria that led people to believe the establishment of a new polity would be a simple matter. Although all the new regimes proclaimed themselves to be democratic, their travails since then show that it is one thing to create a new polity and quite another to sustain one. Since some states have been more successful than others, one of the goals of this book is to discern *why* this is the case. In other words, which factors—cultural, economic, historical, political, and so forth—have most affected the transition?

CASE STUDIES

Now that we have defined the factors we will examine in comparing the various states, we need a common framework through which we can identify basic similarities and differences.

To make sense of events in a changing environment like Central and Eastern Europe, students must have a basic understanding of the polity—the economic situation, history, political culture, governmental structures, elites, and so forth. This foundation not only facilitates comparative analysis, it also allows students to examine the larger issues of political science. Therefore each state is described and evaluated using this framework:

1. National data—geographic, resource, demographic, and economic features
2. Political history—the influence of history on the polity
3. Informing political ideas—ideology, traditions, culture, and political socialization
4. Formal governmental institutions
5. Elites—governmental and nongovernmental elites and their influence on the polity
6. General public—composition, political recruitment, and influence
7. Policy making and implementation—actors, process, effectiveness
8. Conclusion

Although there are many possible variables that affect political change, one of the goals of this book is to identify the key ones. Thus students will gain insight into which variables are country specific, which are regional specific, and which have universal significance.

However, a couple of notes of caution must be added. First, we cannot think in terms of either/or. Although Russia has formal democratic institutions, politics is in fact dominated by a narrow elite. Thus whether or not Russia has elections and a parliament is not as important as understanding the degree to which people actually have a say in politics. Second, because political science is an inexact science, we can never eliminate the random or idiosyncratic events that affect politics. For example, what would have happened in Russia if Boris Yeltsin had not climbed on top of an armored personnel carrier in 1991 to rally the opposition against the attempted coup against President Mikhail Gorbachev?

CHOICE OF STATES

Until 1989, the states of Central and Eastern Europe were considered part of a single entity, the Soviet bloc. Despite minor differences, their political and economic systems were modeled on, and closely controlled by, the USSR. The end of the Soviet Union caused the bloc to split into several smaller groups. Although imprecise, they can be roughly divided into the following: Central European states (the Czech Republic, Hungary, Poland, Slovakia, and Slovenia); the Balkan states (Bosnia, Bulgaria, Croatia, Macedonia, Romania, and Yugoslavia); and Russia and the former soviet republics.

The Central European group is at the forefront of political and economic reforms. With the exception of Slovakia, these states have managed to build relatively stable political systems and overcome the post-1989 transitional economic recession. In contrast, these Balkan states have lagged behind their former allies or neighbors from the north. Attempts at reform in these Balkan states have met with only limited success. As a result, their polities have been marked by economic and political instability. The wars of

Yugoslavian succession have also had a destabilizing effect on states in this region.

The final group, Russia and the fourteen former Soviet republics, has made even less progress. With the exception of the Baltic states (Estonia, Latvia, Lithuania), their polities have been characterized by poor economic performance, unsettled relations between the branches of government, and, in several of them, regional and ethnic problems. A detailed examination of each of the twenty-six CEE states is beyond the scope of this text. Therefore, we will focus on one or two examples from each group.

Hungary and Poland represent the Central European group. Although they are at similar stages in their postcommunist development, they have taken very different paths to get there. In contrast to Poland, Hungary has achieved a peaceful and orderly transition from an authoritarian regime to a democratic one. Constitutional safeguards, such as a restrictive German-type electoral law, have created working coalitions and brought Hungary political stability. Economically, as a result of reforms initiated prior to 1989, the Hungarian economy is well on its way to becoming a market economy. Furthermore, central bank discipline has kept inflation low and encouraged foreign investment; between 1990 and 1996, Hungary received half of all foreign investment in the region.

In contrast, the Polish polity has been dominated by political instability. In an attempt to break away with the legacy of centralized control, Poland at first adopted a very liberal electoral law. This resulted in a fragmented parliament with twenty-nine parties. Although a new electoral law ended parliamentary fragmentation, ongoing battles between the executive and legislative branches have slowed reforms. Perhaps surprisingly, although major political reforms have been blocked or slowed, economic growth has not. In 1996, Poland had the fastest economic growth rate of any European state, east or west. This is the result of a broad consensus on the need to restructure the economy.

Bulgaria represents the Balkan countries. As in Poland, the postcommunist period has been characterized by revolving door governments—eight since 1989. However, in contrast to Poland, the Bulgarian polity has suffered from inconsistent economic policies. Although attempts have been made to enact economic reforms, until massive street demonstrations in 1997 led to early elections, there has been little progress. As a result, living standards have plummeted.

Russia, our case study from the third group, has even more problems than the Balkan states. Fifteen years after Gorbachev launched his policy of *perestroika*, Russia continues to face the same problems it did in 1985. In contrast to Bulgaria, Hungary, and Poland, where the major political actors have accepted pluralist systems and acted mostly within them, the Russian polity has been dominated by continuing political battles over whether pluralism should exist at all. As a result, the state has been stymied by an economic and political stalemate. This unresolved tension over pluralism can be seen in both the October 1993 storming of the Russian parliament and the subsequent success of extreme nationalist and communist political parties in the 1995 parliamentary elections. This Russian situation has serious repercussions. Since Russia is the most powerful state in the region, events in Russia will have a significant impact on the fate of its newly independent neighbors and, indirectly, on the rest of Europe as well.

Russia will be the first state we examine in this book. Since the Soviet model was imposed on the countries in the region, in addition to describing the contemporary Russian polity, the Russian chapter also describes the general features of that system. It provides the prism through which the region's post-1989 development can be examined.

WHY ANOTHER BOOK
ON CENTRAL AND EASTERN EUROPE?

With only minor modifications, all CEE states were forced to follow the Soviet model of development. It was not until 1989 that the Soviet Union changed its policy from one of control to what has been dubbed the "Frank Sinatra doctrine"[5] that allowed the Central and Eastern European states to go their own way. Thus, texts written before 1989 emphasized the similarities between the various states, not their differences. With each state today pursuing different policies, this approach is no longer useful.

Partially as a result of the rapid changes since 1989, most texts have focused on a specific aspect of change in the region, such as privatization, legal reform, and social transformation, rather than the polity as a whole. This book attempts to fill that void; it is the first comparative politics text that focuses on the polity as a whole. In addition, most comparative politics texts have been written by multiple authors, each of whom writes a specific country section. Although the authors may start from a common outline, their chapters often end up being organized differently, making it difficult to compare various aspects of the polities of the individual countries. In contrast, this text was written from a common outline by the same author.

The main goal of this book is to shed light on the profound changes occurring in Central and Eastern Europe following the demise of Soviet system. Governments of the region are faced with a situation unique in history. Never before has there been an attempt to restructure economic, political and social structures simultaneously. (It is worth remembering that Western states took decades to combine political pluralism with market economics and a civil society.) This experiment is made even more difficult by the lack of a model for CEE states to follow. Thus the revolutionary transition occurring in the region—an experiment in designing a polity—should be of special interest to students of international and comparative politics.

To help evaluate the outcome of the fascinating experiment to reshape the polities of Central and Eastern Europe, this book seeks to identify the key actors, institutions, and social-political forces which will affect the transition. Although the states of the ex-Soviet bloc have taken different paths, the ongoing transformation provides us powerful insights into the factors that affect political development as well as our own political system. For as Jacobs succinctly stated years ago:

> In learning about those who are different from ourselves is the opportunity to learn more about ourselves. The realization that others do things one way, while we do them other ways, serves to provide us with insights into our own behavior that are the mark of educated men and women, and gives us a more profound understanding of our institutions and values.[6]

WEB SITES

The CIA World Factbook
http://www.odci.gov/cia/publications/factbook/
Comprehensive information about each country's vital statistics, economy, government structure, and other features.

Department of State Background Notes
http://www.state.gov/www/background_notes/
Profiles of each country; directory of officials; and brief historical, economic, and governmental information.

Library of Congress Area Handbooks
http://lcweb2.loc.gov/frd/cs/
In-depth reports of countries in the region, including history, economics, politics, current events, and living conditions. Updated versions include graphs, charts, and maps.

Internet Law Library
http://law.house.gov/
Constitutions, treaties, and government publications about current topics. Maintained by the U.S. House of Representatives.

REES Web
http://www.ucis.pitt.edu/reesweb/
A comprehensive index of electronic resources on the Balkans, the Baltic states, the Caucusus, Central Asia, Central Europe, the CIS, Eastern Europe, the NIS, the Russian Federation, and the former Soviet Union. Maintained by the Center for Russian and East European Studies of the University of Pittsburgh.

Radio Free Europe
http://www.rferl.org/
News and current events.

Eurasia Research Center
http://eurasianews.com/erc/homepage.htm
News about and from Central and Eastern Europe.

ENDNOTES

1. These factors are measured not by constitutional guarantees but by whether the rights exist in practice. Examples include a free and independent media, open public discussion, freedom of assembly and demonstration, and freedom of political association.

2. Freedom House is a nonprofit, nongovernmental organization based in New York. Since its inception in the 1970s, the purpose of the annual *Comparative Survey of Freedom* has been to provide an annual evaluation of political rights and civil liberties everywhere in the world. The survey uses information and reports from over 175 nongovernmental and governmental organizations as well onsite investigation teams to complete a checklist that is used to determine the degree of freedom present in each country. For a detailed description of each checklist and the methodology used to compile it, see *Freedom in the World: The Annual Survey of Political Rights and Civil Liberties, 1996–1997* (New York: Transaction Publishers, 1997), pp. 572–578.

3. Examples include free and fair elections; elected officials having decision-making power; the existence of opposition parties; freedom from domination by the military; foreign powers, totalitarian parties, religious hierarchies, economic oligarchies, or other groups; and self-determination, self-government, autonomy, or participation for minority groups in the decision-making process.

4. Transparency International is an anticorruption nonprofit group that draws on surveys by Gallup International, the World Competitiveness Yearbook, the Political and Economic Risk Consultancy in Hong Kong, the DRI/McGraw Hill Global Risk Service, the Political Risk Services in Syracuse, New York, and data gathered from Internet sources to create a corruption perception index. Corruption is measured on a scale of 1–10, with the least corrupt states receiving the highest scores.

5. One of Sinatra's most popular songs was "I Did It My Way."

6. Jacobs et al., *Comparative Politics: An Introduction to the Politics of the United Kingdom, France, Germany and the Soviet Union* (Chatham, NJ: Chatham House Publishers, 1983), p. x.

1

RUSSIA

INTRODUCTION

Russia. Historically the name has invoked images of vastness, mysticism, grandeur, and power. As Winston Churchill once said: "Russia is a riddle wrapped in an enigma surrounded by a mystery." Since 1917, the word "Russia" has been synonymous with communism, authoritarianism, and state control over the economy.

With the demise of the Soviet Union in 1991, Russia again became a sovereign state.[1] However, the processes leading to the collapse of the Soviet Union have also created conditions that have put Russia in a continuing state of semirevolution. This makes it difficult to understand and interpret events because changes take place not in days but hours. The process of change is not over, and it is not likely to end in the near future. This situation makes it even more imperative to try to understand the economic, political, and social convulsions occurring in the world's largest state. The study of Russia is especially interesting and important because it was the epicenter from which recent global changes have emanated. Although the consequences of change were felt most intensively in Russia, repercussions have dramatically affected other members of the international community. In addition, because of its size, military power, nuclear arsenal, and numerous resources, Russia remains a global power.

As a result of its long history as an independent state, Russia is different from most other Central and Eastern Europe (CEE) states. Although other countries in the region can trace their heritage at least as far back as Russia's, their recent history has been one of domination and/or occupation by foreign powers. The legacy of 70 years of socialism also makes Russia different from the rest of the countries in the region. The Soviet political culture, in many ways a mirror image of Tsarist autocracy, was based on a strong,

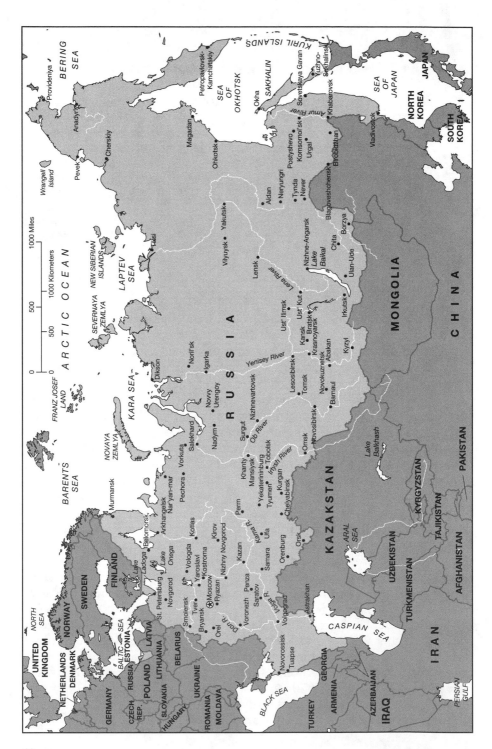

centralized administration that viewed any economic, political, or social initiative which did not come from the government as deeply suspicious and threatening.

As a result, the Communist Party of the Soviet Union (CPSU) was the last communist party in the CEE region to give up its monopoly of power. This legacy has produced a strong antidemocratic, anti-western coalition. As a result, Russia lags behind most other formerly socialist states in the implementation of economic and political reforms. Unlike citizens of other countries in the region, a whole generation lived under Soviet socialism.[2] Few people remember life before the revolution. This situation makes it more difficult to enact reforms. Consequently, Russians are some of the most dissatisfied with the postcommunist developments.

The process of a global power like Russia undergoing fundamental change is of great interest for students of political science and international relations. Through an examination of Russia, we can better understand the transformation occurring in other CEE states, how different types of institutional arrangements affect economic and political evolution, and how domestic politics and international politics interact.

NATIONAL DATA

Geography

Since Russia was the largest republic of the former Soviet Union, it should come as no surprise that it is the largest state in the world. It covers an area of 17,075,400 square kilometers, or 10.2 million square miles. This area is almost twice as large as that of the United States. It encompasses eleven time zones and stretches from the Baltic Sea to the Pacific Ocean. Russia's varied topography includes vast plains, many rivers, mountains, tundra, and thick forests.

Russia shares borders with fourteen different countries: Norway, Finland, Estonia, Latvia, Lithuania, Poland, Belorussia, Ukraine, Georgia, Azerbaijan, Kazakhstan, China, Mongolia, and North Korea. The capital, Moscow, lies in the European part of Russia between the Ural Mountains and the Baltic Sea. This long frontier, many unstable neighbors, a history of foreign invasions, and Russia's dependence on resources located in sparsely populated border areas foster an almost paranoia concerning security and territorial issues.

Resources

Historically an agrarian country, under the communists the Soviet Union was transformed at great cost into an industrial state. After World War II, it was the world's second largest industrial power behind the United States. Russia has abundant deposits of natural resources and is the world's largest producer of oil and natural gas.

In stark contrast to the success of industrialization, agriculture has been the country's Achilles heel. This situation in large part is a result of natural conditions, such as limited rainfall, poor soil, and Russia's location in the northern latitudes. These weaknesses were aggravated by a poor transportation infrastructure—30 percent of all crops spoiled before they reached the market—and the collectivization of agriculture under communist rule. Collectivization eliminated private property by forcing peasants to join large inefficient state farms in which they had little incentive to work.

As a result, even though 20 percent of the Soviet population was involved in agriculture—compared to four percent in the United States, food had to be imported. In an attempt to remedy this problem, private farms were legalized in 1992. However, only 120 of the 27,000 collective farms—comprising just 6 percent of Russia's farmland land—have actually been divided up and privatized by 1997. Notably, these farms and private plots account for half of Russia's meat production and a third of its dairy products.[3] Nevertheless, these sources cannot make up for the collapse of large-scale farming, which produced only 44 percent of its 1990 output in 1998.

Overall, the lack of investment capital, expertise, inflation, low government subsidies, limited property rights—farmland cannot be freely sold—

1928 COLLECTIVIZATION

In 1928, the communist leadership mistakenly foresaw a wheat shortage in the upcoming year. This prospect posed a serious threat to Stalin's first Five-Year Plan: if the cities lacked food, industrial growth would be stymied. As a result, the government began the forced collectivization of farmland, taking land from the peasants and consolidating it into large state farms. This turned out to be a disastrous decision, as it spurred a major peasant revolt which led to the mass destruction of crops and the slaughtering of farm animals. Collectivization also had a long-lasting effect on the agricultural sector because the lack of incentives led to great inefficiencies and a massive fall in output for the next several years. These shortages, paradoxically, hit the peasant farmers who were actually producing the food the hardest, since food from rural areas was confiscated and taken to the cities.

As a result, there was a massive famine in the major grain-growing areas during the winter of 1932–33. Stalin used the famine to terrorize rebellious peasants into submission. Despite the famine, the Soviet Union remained a net grain exporter, sending grain abroad while millions starved. The net result of collectivization was a death total of at least 10 million people, mostly in Ukraine and the North Caucasus and Lower Volga regions. The 1928 collectivization campaign is an example of Stalin's totalitarian rule of terror as well as of the economic problems inherent in a planned agricultural scheme.

and the difficulty of breaking from the collectivist mentality of the past have resulted in lower agricultural production than in the Soviet era.

People

In 1996, Russia's population was 147,500,000. Although less than half the total of the former Soviet Union, it still is the sixth largest country in the world. Of this population, more than 65 percent live in urban centers. There are nine cities with over 1 million inhabitants, with Moscow and St. Petersburg being the largest. Although the vast majority of the population lives in the European part of Russia between the Baltic Sea and the Ural Mountains, four of the nine largest cities lie east of the Urals. This is the result of the Soviet policy of developing the resources of Siberia and the Far East. However, the dearth of consumer goods and agricultural produce have made the people who live there resentful, fostering regionalism and separatism.

Before examining the current social situation in Russia, we first must understand the nature and extent of the communist social welfare system. In contrast to the Western industrial democracies, in the former Soviet Union economic, political, and social policies were inseparable and tightly controlled by the state. To lay the foundation for a future communist society in which workers would no longer be exploited, the state assumed control over the entire polity. This system was a combination of state paternalism and egalitarianism. For example, the 1977 Soviet Constitution guaranteed the right to work, the right to housing, the right to health care, and the right to education. The goal was to eliminate class differences and create a socially just society. State firms took an active role in providing social services to employees, providing cradle-to-grave coverage. As a result, there was virtually no unemployment in the Soviet Union or any other CEE states. Regardless of whether one worked in industry, agriculture, or directly in the state bureaucracy, all workers were covered by a full array of social programs. These included a free education, health care, child care, a subsidized apartment—which typically cost 3 to 5 percent of one's salary—and subsidized vacations. Therefore, although wages were low compared to the West, they were offset by deeply discounted social services and cheap consumer goods.

There were other benefits as well. One of the major accomplishments of the socialist regimes was a relatively equal distribution of income. This was the result of guaranteed employment and low wage differentiation. While crime, prostitution, drug abuse, unemployment, and poverty still existed, because of the extensive social system they were significantly less problematic than in the United States and most other industrialized democracies. In summary, Soviet-style socialism guaranteed most of the population a minimal level of economic security and freedom from the uncertainties of capitalism. A worker might have to stand in line for basic necessities but did not fear unemployment or skyrocketing prices. For example, although health care may have been provided in a corrupt and inefficient manner—small "gifts" were often given to physicians to ensure prompt treatment—at least they were affordable. In contrast, 40 million Americans lacked access to health care in 1997.

The transition from a state-controlled economy to a market economy has dramatically transformed the system. It has swept away decrepit economic and political structures but also brought the problems of capitalism—inflation, unemployment, and uncertainty. In addition, stark inequality has come to characterize societies raised on egalitarianism. In the area of health care, people today are frequently subject to long waits for treatments of rapidly worsening quality: "In some cases, patients at state hospitals have had to supply their own food, linens, bandages, and even basic medications." This situation is in stark contrast to private medical centers, which, while providing efficient and competent care, are prohibitively expensive.[4] Questions about the desirability of these developments are frequently at the center of political debates throughout the region.

There are numerous legacies of the communist system. Perhaps most significantly, it created a culture of dependency. People were not expected, or encouraged, to fend for themselves or pay more than a token fee for social services. This problem was magnified by the lack of direct taxes. As a result, people came to expect a certain level of "free" social services. The end of state control of the economy has significantly weakened the previous social system, bringing numerous problems to the fore. The first is a declining population. Because of a sharp rise in the cost of living, the decline of social benefits, housing shortages, and other social stresses that encourage high divorce, abortion, and suicide rates, the population is decreasing. These factors, coupled with a large number of women in the workforce and decreasing maternity benefits, have contributed to fewer people choosing to have children. This decline in births is compounded by a high infant and maternal mortality rate. In Moscow, where some of the best health care is available, only one in four births occurs without complications. Maternal mortality is five to ten times higher than in Western Europe. Social problems have also led to an increase in abortions. Since reliable contraception is difficult to obtain, abortion has become the primary means of birth control. As a result, Russia leads the world in abortions, with 225 abortions for every 100 births.[5]

Another related problem is a drastic decline in life expectancy. In 1985, the average life expectancy was 69 years, but by 1995 it had fallen to 64. The rate for males fell even further to 57 years, a figure below even that of Haiti. This situation is the result of increasing alcoholism, rampant chemical and radioactive pollution, contaminated drinking water, a surge in infectious diseases, a general decline in health care, and increasing violence. Although some of these problems were present in the Soviet era, the social convulsions of the last ten years and the weakening of state authority have greatly amplified them.[6] Between 1991 and 1996, the death rate increased 21 percent and the birth rate declined 23 percent.[7] In 1996, the number of deaths exceeded the number of live births by 60 percent. Together these factors caused the Russian population to decline by 500,000 people per year between 1992 and 1998.[8] This is unprecedented among industrialized societies in the absence of famine or war.

Another growing problem is the large-scale migration of youth from the countryside. Low-quality health care, lack of transportation, and inferior social services have left an aging population in the countryside. Since retirees comprise an increasing proportion of the population (20 percent vs. 12 percent in the United States), an increasing amount of resources will have to be devoted to an already inadequate rural health and social infrastructure. This need comes at a time when there will be fewer workers to support a growing number of pensioners. While not as politically active as their American counterparts, pensioners could become a powerful constituency in a country where there is widespread apathy and disgust with the political system.

Another manifestation of the changing polity is increasing political differences between generations. Most reformers are under 40, while people over 45 find the changes that have occurred since 1991 too difficult to live with. Too set in their ways to change but too young for retirement, these people are tired of watching younger people control the government and make millions in the private sector. As a result, they are opposed to change and sometimes look longingly to the past as a period of order and stability.

Ethnicity

Since the founding of the Soviet Union, many people outside the country incorrectly referred to all citizens of the Union of Soviet Socialist Republics as Russians. Within the USSR, however, Russians constituted only a plurality of the population. The USSR contained millions of non-Russians who, despite Soviet rule, retained their sense of national identity. They represent a wide variety of cultures, languages, distinctive traditions, and, in many cases, they harbor bitter memories of both Tsarist and Soviet repression.

The demise of the Soviet Union has made Russians the dominant nationality in the Russian Federation. Over 85 percent of the population is Russian. Overall, they constitute a majority in over half of the federal units. In addition, over 25 million Russians live outside the country. In Kazakhstan, Ukraine, Latvia, and Estonia, Russians number between 30 and 40 percent of the population. The condition of Russians abroad has been a foreign policy priority for Russia and a source of tension with its neighbors.

Non-Russian inhabitants of Russia can be divided into three groups: indigenous peoples who have their own ethnic territorial units, 12 percent of the population; indigenous peoples of the former republics of the USSR, 5 percent; and indigenous peoples who do not have ethnic territorial units in Russia or the former USSR, 1 percent.

Although there are still over 100 nationalities in Russia, most of them are small. Of the 21 non-Russian republics, only in Chechnya and North Ossetia (in the Caucasus Mountains), Tuva (on the Siberian border with Mongolia), and the Chuvash Republic (central Russia) does the local nationality have an outright majority of the population. In three other republics, Tatarstan, Kabardino-Balkaria (Caucasus), and the Kalmyk Republic (on the northern edge of the Caspian Sea), non-Russian groups have pluralities. The resurgence of regional autonomy and regional identity in postcommunist Russia has led to a resurrection of national languages. Most have given the local language "official" status, fueling an increase in non-Russian language books and newspapers. The ethnic make-up of the country had a large influence on the creation of the new Russian Constitution. In recognition of demands for greater freedom by various nationalities, the constitution gave them equal rights and local autonomy.

The breakup of the Soviet Union brought political freedom and economic instability, fueling a resurgent nationalism that has spread throughout much of Central and Eastern Europe. This trend has led to a growth of ethnic awareness among members of minority groups, creating sharper social and ethnic divisions as well as new political problems. As the civil war in Chechyna shows, the status of minorities will have a large effect on the development of the polity.

CHECHNYA

Russia was beset with both internal and external conflicts after the Soviet Union collapsed in 1991. Economically, it suffered from falling living standards; politically, separatist movements arose in several Russian republics. One of the most well-known of these movements took place in the southwestern region of Chechnya, which declared independence from the Russian Federation in 1991. While Yeltsin initially ignored the rebellion, afraid other regions would follow Chechnya's lead, in late 1994 he ordered the invasion of Chechnya.

After two years of bloody fighting, the Russian government offered Chechnya a compromise: if the region agreed to stay in the Russian Federation, it would be allowed greater autonomy. In March 1996, after over 30,000 civilian and military casualties, a ceasefire was signed between Yeltsin and acting Chechen president Zelimkhan Yanderbiyev.

Despite the ceasefire accord, fighting did not actually end until a peace agreement was signed in August 1996. As a result of the peace agreement, all Russian troops were withdrawn from Chechnya, and both sides agreed that the question of Chechnya's independence would not be decided until December 2001.

Growing societal frustration and increasing ethnic conflict has also fostered the creation of Russian nationalist groups. Today more than seventy-five ultranationalist/extremist groups promising to restore law and order through the reimposition of societal controls exist. These organizations can be divided into three main groups. The first want a return to Tsarism and submission to the authority of the Russian Orthodox church. The second group are anti-Semitic neocommunists who call for the overthrow of the current regime and the reestablishment, by force if necessary, of the Soviet Union. This group draws it support mostly from the old and poor. The third group can best be described as national fascists. By stressing that only a strong Russia will be respected by other states, these groups have been the most successful in involving young people in politics. Although divided by rampant egos, the existence of these groups shows the difficulty facing Russia in its attempt to create a civil society and democratic institutions. Thus they are helping to shape the debate about the future of the Russian polity.[9]

As a result, the classification of individuals by ethnicity, introduced in the Soviet Union under Stalin, remains a major factor in the development of the Russian polity today. A recent instance is the controversy surrounding the introduction of a new internal passport (identity document). Old passports had a line for the bearer's nationality. In an attempt to remove the de facto discrimination, this line was removed. Surprisingly, the strongest negative reaction came from minorities who feared assimilation. This example suggests Russia will have a difficult time creating the multinational state envisioned in the new constitution.

Class Divisions

Communist ideology required the Soviet leadership to claim that the Soviet Union was in the process of creating a "classless society." While claiming that the entire population were "toilers," the regime recognized the existence of two classes—the workers and peasants—and a stratum, the intelligentsia.

Although ideologically egalitarian, Soviet society was actually divided along educational, vocational, and political lines. It included the following: the ruling class, the "middle class," the intelligentsia, the urban working class, and the peasantry.[10] The ruling class, or *nomenklatura*, were all members of the CPSU. It included full-time party workers—*apparatchiki*, technocrats, economic mangers, and high-ranking members of the military and security forces.[11] Although workers made up the largest percentage of Party members, the elite was dominated by professionals and members of the intelligentsia.

This group was the most privileged part of the former elite. Membership in the governing elite provided various privileges—higher social status, better educational and job opportunities—thus preventing social mobility for others. More important, it was the only channel for social or political influence. Therefore, other groups were forced to accept the social and political norms established by the elite. In contrast, the salaries and other economic differences among the peasants, workers, and the intelligentsia were negligible. Thus, in reality there were only two major groups in society: members of the Party elite and everyone else.

The Soviet "middle class" included both Party members and non-Party members who served the regime and benefited from it. This group included managerial and technical personnel, accountants, clerks, and other "white collar" professions. In 1987, this group constituted approximately 26 percent of the population. This class overlapped with the intelligentsia, which in the broadest definition included teachers, doctors, artists, engineers, and scientists.

The urban working class was divided into three distinct substrata: highly skilled manual workers in special sectors of industry who made more money than members of the intelligentsia; semiskilled rank-and-file workers with some skills; and simple manual laborers.

The final group was the peasantry, or rural workers. The socialist regimes tried to eliminate the differences between the town and country, making peasants rural workers on collective or state farms. This class included machine operators, herders, milkmaids, and field hands. In 1987, this group comprised only 12 percent of the population, the smallest of the recognized social classes.

Significantly, there was a relatively high degree of social mobility in socialist societies. This mobility was the result of an expanding economy that needed a skilled workforce. However, it became greatly restricted in the 1980s, when declining economic growth rates and reduced educational opportunities favored the children of the *nomenklatura*. The collapse of the economic and political system in the late 1980s caused an upheaval in the class structure. This situation, coupled with economic changes, created new class divisions and exacerbated preexisting ones. Most significant is the enormous gap between the rich and poor. Because of the economic downturn, Russians have been forced to turn to the black economy to supplement their income.[12] Under the socialist regime, education and/or political connections were an important channel for upward mobility. Today, they are far less important than business acumen or the ability to react to economic changes. Under the old regime, for example, even though doctors were poorly paid, they were held in high esteem. Today, because they are employed almost exclusively by the state, their income and status is much less than that of an average entrepreneur.

Contemporary society can be divided into two groups, those who have benefited from reforms and those who have not. The winners comprise only about 7 percent of the population but control a majority of the wealth.[13] Members of this group include high-ranking government officials, former high-ranking members of the *nomenklatura*, industrialists, white-collar workers who work for international or multinational corporations, entrepreneurs, and employees of small private companies.

No Paycheck Means Apples Under the Bed

When Valeri Novikov and his wife, Galina, were youngsters and went to work at the "Ivanovo Order of Lenin Blended Yarn Mill, Named for Konstantin Frolov" (a local revolutionary hero), they were proud to belong to a flagship of the Soviet textile industry.

Today, after a year in which they were paid for only five months by a company struggling to survive, their attitudes are markedly less enthusiastic.

"The sooner I retire, the better," says Galina, a matronly woman who has stood at a loom each working day since she left school 28 years ago to begin her apprenticeship as a weaver.

And she is not alone. Nobody knows exactly how many Russian workers are owed back wages, but cash-strapped enterprises all over the country owe a total of $6.8 billion to their employees, according to government figures, and the problem is getting $500 million bigger every month.

If Galina's plight today is typical for Russia, so has her life been. When she first went to work, her future was secure in a Soviet sort of way, if hardly lavish. Marrying Valeri, a cheeky, quick-witted repairman she met on the factory floor, they started a family and moved into a single room in a dormitory-style building near the factory. By the time they had three children they were assigned a second room. Sixteen years after they made their application, they were allocated the sparsely furnished four-room apartment they live in today.

They weren't rich, but they managed. "We had enough for food, we had enough for clothes, and I could buy presents for the children," Galina recalls.

"Now we are down to just food," chimes in Valeri. And that, despite the fact that he and his wife have shown inventiveness and endurance in the face of great difficulties.

Month after Month: Not a Kopeck

Toward the end of last year, the Ivanovo Blended Mill Ltd. (it is now a joint stock company) began falling behind in paying wages.

"First they were a few days late, then a few weeks, and now they are several months behind," Galina says. "If we were paid regularly and on time, we would be OK. As it is . . . ." She shrugs.

As a skilled worker, Valeri takes home $113 a month. Galina earns $94, and their elder son, Misha, a driver at the mill, receives $47. These are below average but reasonably adequate wages by Russian standards.

"But those are our wages on paper, not in real life," Valeri points out.

In fact, Galina has not been paid since May, when she was given her February pay packet. Misha is in the same boat. Valeri was paid his July wages last week and told that his June pay had been "frozen." Precisely what that officially means was not explained.

What it means to the family's everyday life, though, is clear from a look inside their refrigerator. Although Galina insists they eat properly ("that is why we can't afford any new clothes"), the shelves are austere: a jar of preserved cabbage, a small enamel churn of milk, a single frankfurter, a pot of borscht, a plate of margarine, a lump of smoked pork fat, a saucepan of potatoes.

The freezing compartment, however, is stuffed full of nothing but chickens. Last April, Galina bought 21 day-old chicks, reared them in a cardboard box in the kitchen for a month, then took them to her sister in the country.

Her sister fed them over the summer as part of a deal whereby she would keep the hens. Galina ended up with 11 cocks, which will go into chicken soup for as long as she can make them last.

What more would she do if she had more money? "Buy meat," she replies.

In another deal with the farmhand sister, Galina and Valeri bought a calf recently; the sister will fatten it, and in the spring they will slaughter the animal and share the meat.

But that will be a feast. More everyday fare is considerably more basic—porridge, vegetable soup, fried potatoes, bread, and milk, with the occasional egg for variety. And much of what the family eats, they grow themselves on a small plot of land an hour's bicycle ride away.

The kitchen window sill is crammed with green tomatoes that will never ripen now, as autumn set in. Valeri and Galina's bedroom reeks of the onions and garlic that fill two sacks under the single bedside chair. Lyuba, their teenage daughter, has to clamber around a mountain of apples—it has been a good year for apples—to get into bed. Under the balcony outside the sitting room, Valeri has constructed a chamber where carrots will keep through the winter without freezing. A cousin has made room in his apartment for their potatoes.

"We know how to work with our hands, how to breed animals, how to grow things," says Valeri, a practical-minded sort of man. "If our land was closer we would have no problems—we could feed ourselves almost completely, and I could keep my family properly. I made a plow this year and used my two boys as horses. They can do all sorts of things, too."

A Family Secret

But even relative self-sufficiency and frugality do not see a family of five through four months without a kopeck in wages. How do they avoid starvation?

"That's a secret," says Galina with a guilty laugh. "I cannot tell you."

But eventually she does. Their eldest daughter, Natasha, who is married, has a job as a night watchwoman at a local kindergarten. Her husband does not like her to work alone at night, however, and earns enough himself to take care of his family. So Natasha's parents do her job, and Natasha hands them her $75 paycheck each month.

It is this moonlighting money that keeps them fed. But the price they pay is steep. It means that when Galina is on the late shift, as soon as she comes home at 10:15 at night, Valeri heads out for the kindergarten. There he puts in four or five hours while Galina sleeps, until she relieves him in the middle of the night.

When Valeri is on the late shift, it's the other way around. "We're working just about 24 hours a day," he says resignedly. "We don't see much of each other." And then, with a sly glance to Galina, "I didn't notice that my wife grew old."

And even then, the money they earn scarcely pays for the staple two loaves of bread and three liters of milk that Galina buys each morning. There is nothing left over for anything else. Lyuba is wearing the same clothes that her big sister wore 10 years ago; the last time Valeri and Galina bought anything for the house was in 1991, when grandpa, a World War II veteran, gave them his ration card to buy a sofa and two armchairs.

But Valeri and Galina aren't looking for work anywhere else, even if they are not being paid at the mill. Indeed, they even persuaded their son Misha to turn down a job he was offered at another plant. "His dad wanted to keep an eye on him, and the trouble is that if you move jobs you are more likely to be sacked if they start laying people off at your new place," Galena explains.

She herself is only two years away from a pension after 30 years' service. "Who would take me on now?" she asks rhetorically.

Street Stalls Not an Option

Galina doesn't feel able to go into the petty trading business, setting up a stall on the street, which is how many unpaid Russians make a living today.

"I can't even sell my apples, because I'd feel ashamed to stand on the pavement and sell things," Galina explains. "And anyway, I'm no good at mental arithmetic; I'd be cheated in no time."

Nor is Valeri attracted to commerce. "I'm a worker; that's not my kind of life, and I wouldn't be any good at it," he says. Nor is there much prospect of a job anywhere else in Ivanovo, one of the most depressed regions in Russia. "I don't know why I'm still at the mill really—maybe I don't know what else to do," he confesses. "These are difficult times, but I hope they will soon be over, and in the meantime all we can do is work.

"I like my job; it's interesting work, and I want to do it. I just don't like it when they trick me [over my wages]. Then I lose heart."

Source: Peter Ford, *Christian Science Monitor,* October 1, 1996.

The losers can be divided into two substrata that include the vast majority of the population. The first group, which has been most affected, includes laborers, workers, peasants, pensioners, invalids, students, and the unemployed. Since there was officially no unemployment under the old regime, there are few programs or institutions to deal with this problem. As a result, many people in these groups have become impoverished. In 1997, 70 percent of the population officially earned less than the average wage of $155 a month. Although this number does not include black, or unofficial market activity, many people can barely afford a diet of bread, cabbage, potatoes, eggs, and the occasional piece of cheese or sausage. Nonperishable goods, such as clothing and household appliances, are beyond their reach.[14]

The second group is comprised of the former privileged members of society—economic managers, government workers, the intelligentsia, professionals, and security service personnel. Since these groups were employed exclusively by the state, they have seen their standard of living drop dramatically as a result of the declining state role in society. For example, people trained as engineers for the chemical, manufacturing, and steel industries are no longer needed. As a result, 35 percent of the working population is on "short-time" work.[15] This group is one of the greatest threats to social stability.

As a group, women have suffered disproportionately from the transition to a market economy and the change in the political system. In the Soviet Union, 92 percent of women worked. Many became skilled workers and professionals. Today, they are the first to be laid off, constituting over 70 percent of the unemployed. Moreover, during the Soviet era, women's wages averaged 70 percent of men's. By 1995, that figure had dropped to 40 percent.[16] Since two-thirds of all marriages end in divorce and nearly all single-parent households are headed by women, this loss of jobs, compounded by an eroding public infrastructure, the closing of day-care centers, and a general reduction in social benefits, has caused women to suffer disproportionately from the change in regime.

Since pensioners are particularly dependent on the state, they have also suffered disproportionately. In 1997, the average pension was only 84 percent of the minimum subsistence level of $70. This has forced a large proportion of the older generation into poverty.[17] For society as a whole, average income levels in 1995 were only 50 percent of the 1990 level.

The effect of reforms can also be seen in increasing income differentiation. In 1996, the richest 10 percent of the population earned approximately thirteen times as much as the poorest 10 percent. This figure compares with 4.4 times in 1991.[18] In 1996, the average monthly wage was roughly two-thirds of the average wage in Hungary and Poland. Overall, annual GDP per person in 1996 was $4,480, or $373 per month.[19]

A significant feature of contemporary Russian society is the shrinking middle class. Since the communists forbade private ownership of the "means of production," the middle class was entirely dependent on either state redistributive mechanisms or the shadow economy. Even more than other socialist states, the Soviet Union had a large "middle class" as a result of the pervasive nature of the socialized economy.[20] With privatization, this group has been particularly affected. This class is more than a simple economic grouping. In the West the middle class not only influences government policy but also, since it forms the economic base, it plays a crucial stabilizing role in society. To date, Russian policies have limited the creation of this key economic stratum.

This situation has important implications for the political system. Increasing social problems—alcoholism, drug abuse, crime, and poverty—hinder democratic development. Disgust with the current political situation could cause people to look for political alternatives in the form of extremist parties, or support for an authoritarian regime which in the past provided predictability and—albeit at low levels—economic and social security. A 1995 poll showed that more than one-third of the population supported a return to communist rule.[21]

Economics

Like most other states in Central and Eastern Europe, prior to the 1917 Bolshevik Revolution, Russia was an agrarian state. In 1928, 80 percent of the population was agrarian. After the communists took power, they started to industrialize the country. In 1929, Stalin initiated the first in a series of Five-Year Plans, the cornerstone of centralized planning and the command economy. These plans created a comprehensive, detailed, and binding national economic blueprint that was based on governmental control over all sectors of the economy.

This blueprint included the nationalization of all industry, collectivization of agriculture, and an emphasis on heavy industrial—metallurgy, mining, and machine building—production. Light industry, such as consumer goods, was neglected. The goals of this program were to industrialize the country by compressing several centuries of economic development into a generation and to centralize power. After World War II, this model of development was forced on Soviet allies in the region. Although these plans made the Soviet Union the world's second largest industrial power, it left a dismal structural legacy—an inefficient and technologically obsolete industrial base with a dilapidated infrastructure. This model of industrialization also devastated the environment. Unlike market economies, where consumers have access to information and can retaliate against polluters through boycotts or legal action, Central and Eastern Europeans did not have the information or inclination to question the state.

One of the main reasons for the development of heavy industry was the desire to construct a modern technological base for the military. As a result, 40–60 percent of all industry in the USSR was defense related. Although military spending has been drastically cut, 11.4 percent of government expenditures in 1995 was still dedicated to defense spending, almost triple the figure for the United States.

Despite a horrendous human cost, the centrally planned economy worked well at first. In fifteen years, the Soviet Union went from being an economically backward state to a global power. However, this model of development later became a straightjacket. Without competition, industry grew inefficient, producing goods which society did not need or want. Consequently, it had to be heavily subsidized by the government. This situation can be seen clearly in the agricultural sector, which was one of the most inefficient in Europe. This legacy remains. Although 27 percent of the 1995 budget was allocated to agriculture, the harvest fell by 23 percent. In 1997, over 35 percent of the food consumed in Russia was imported.

Following the liberalization of the Soviet economy after the death of Stalin in 1953, Hungary and Poland diverged from the Soviet model. They allowed private, market-driven agricultural sectors and quasiprivate service sectors. As a result, their economies are considerably more advanced than

TURIN MEETS DETROIT—ON THE VOLGA

History is repeating itself in Nizhny Novgorod, 250 miles east of Moscow on the banks of the Volga river. Almost 70 years ago the Ford Motor Company showed the Russian government how to build a world-class car plant there. Cars, commercial vehicles and the odd missile-launcher have been rolling out of the gates of this "Gorky" plant ever since. In 1992 the plant was reorganised into a private enterprise known as GAZ, after the initials of the factory's Russian name, Gorkovy Avtomobilny Zavod. Now GAZ is seeking foreign help once again. Last month it set up a joint venture with Fiat to build another world-class car plant. This week General Motors said it might follow suit with another Russian car maker, Avtovaz.

Under communism the motor industry was starved of international expertise and market discipline. Since then it has been starved of investment, just like the rest of Russian industry. Its cars are lost somewhere in the Soviet 1970s—unsellable outside Russia, and sellable inside Russia thanks only to the 30% duty levied on competing imports, and to a huge dealer network. To escape from this time-warp, Nikolai Pugin, the president of GAZ, has signed a deal with Fiat to create a new joint-venture firm, Nizhegorod Motors, which will invest $850m in the new plant, producing 140,000 cars a year by 2003. Fiat and GAZ are each taking 40% of the new firm; the European Bank for Reconstruction and Development is taking the other 20%.

Progress is brisk. The lobby of Nizhny's one good hotel is filled with Italian voices. The Fiat-designated factory boss will be arriving soon from Turkey. And there is plenty of work to be done. Fiat and GAZ also want roughly 20 parts suppliers from Europe and America to set up factories in Russia, selling both to them and to the rest of the Russian car industry. The idea of integrating a main plant and suppliers was perfected by Fiat at its Melfi factory in southern Italy, opened four years ago. Melfi has a "supplier park" of 22 firms making everything from batteries and axles to seats and dashboards. The Russian scheme draws on that inspiration, though the incoming parts firms will be more scattered. They will be offered their pick of the region's idle defence-industry plants, which the government wants to convert to civilian use.

The Russian government has offered encouragement, promising tax breaks in exchange for high local content. But in the end it will be Mr. Pugin who determines whether the new firm prospers. Like any other enterprise in Russia, it will have to contend with inadequate infrastructure, the lack of a functioning legal system, a highly criminalised business environment and the attentions—rarely benign—of up to 90 government agencies. Fiat is betting that Mr. Pugin's back will be broad enough to shield the new plant from those extraneous pressures, and let it get on with the difficult enough business of making cars.

The Italians could scarcely have placed their bet more shrewdly. GAZ is commonly considered the best-run of Russian car makers, and Mr. Pugin one of Russia's best managers. He has made a good fist of limiting barter with suppliers, the acid test of any Russian boss. Barter quickly takes over any Russian firm where management is weak or where money is being siphoned off. At

GAZ it accounts for less than 40% of payments, perhaps half the motor-industry average. Mr. Pugin's plant is an oasis of order when compared with that of Avtovaz, the country's biggest car maker, in the Volga town of Togliatti. Last year 57 people were murdered in one three-month period in Togliatti; detachments of soldiers had to be brought in to keep criminal gangs away from the Avtovaz factory gate.

Prototype

The Fiat-GAZ joint venture ranks not merely as the biggest foreign investment in the Russian car industry, but as one of the biggest foreign investments in Russia of any kind. To date, no other car maker has risked a firm commitment to anything more than a modest assembly plant. General Motors has installed capacity for assembling up to 50,000 Chevrolet Blazer utility vehicles annually in Tatarstan. Kia Motors, a South Korean firm, has talked of assembling up to 80,000 small cars a year in Kaliningrad, though the financial difficulties of the parent Kia Group have overshadowed the project. Ford has a kit-assembly plant in Belarus, next to Russia.

Last year a total of 15,200 cars were produced in the country from imported kits—a drop in the ocean, when set against the million cars that were produced inside Russia's own factories. Last year Avtovaz alone produced more than 700,000 vehicles. GAZ ranked second with 250,000 vehicles, a mixture of "Volga" saloons and "Gazelle" light vans.

GM and Ford both have medium-sized projects in the planning stage and will be watching Fiat's progress. Ford will spend about $150m converting an engine factory near St. Petersburg to produce small cars and light vans. This week GM outlined its plans for an ambitious venture with Avtovaz in Togliatti. The first stage would involve an investment of $80m, to assemble 35,000 cars a year from imported kits. That might be followed by much bigger investment in a new factory producing 150,000 cars a year with substantial local content-a project similar in scale to the Fiat-GAZ joint venture. (Avtovaz's current Togliatti plant was designed 30 years ago by Fiat.)

The great lure for foreign car makers all too aware of the hazards of investing in Russia is the prospect of a market that has years of high-speed growth ahead of it. There are currently a mere 13m cars in private hands in Russia, which is a country of some 150 million people. Americans buy more cars than that in a single year. The average Russian car is almost ten years old, and is liable to be forced off the road by environmental controls.

And Russians are getting richer, at least in the cities. In Moscow or St. Petersburg it is not difficult to earn $4,000 a year, the income level at which car ownership typically becomes a passion in developing countries. Russian factories are already selling all the cars they can produce, and Mr. Pugin expects the market for cars to grow by 12–15% a year. Oleg Pavlov, an analyst with Brunswick Warburg, an investment bank, thinks the Russian fleet will expand to 18m by 2000.

If big joint ventures do prove the way forward for the Russian motor industry, it remains to be seen how much of the "old" industry they can carry with them. Mr. Pugin insists that the joint venture with Fiat will provide a model of technology and productivity from which the rest of GAZ can learn. But looking at the old GAZ plant—Henry Ford would doubtless recognise much of his firm's handiwork if he returned there today—it is hard to be optimistic. Russian factories require about 150 man-hours to make a car, ten times more than American or European plants, and three times more than those in developing countries. Russian costs are high, too, by developing-country standards.

The old factories may even become less efficient if the new joint ventures lure the youngest and best workers. That seems likely: the new ventures will offer western-style "compensation"—higher wages, but far more limited social benefits than in the traditional Russian factories. Younger and fitter workers will be tempted, while older ones will stay behind and cling to their welfare entitlements. But if that is a recipe for the death of the old production lines, it will at least be offset by the growth of new ones. And in a Russia that is nine-tenths industrial wasteland, that will count as a very happy ending indeed.

Source: *The Economist*, 7 March 1998: 65–66. © The Economist Newspaper Group, Inc. Reprint with permission. Further reproduction prohibited.

Russia's. While the latter is starting to catch up, its industry is still hopelessly run down.

Mass privatization has made Russians the legal owners of businesses for the first time in generations, reducing the state-sector share of the GDP from 95 percent in 1989 to 27 percent in 1997.[22] Forty million Russians now own shares in companies. However, the state still controls a majority of societal enterprises, such as power generation and telecommunications. Because only 25 percent of these enterprises are profitable, they are an enormous drain on the economy.

At the beginning of 1998, official unemployment was 10 percent, up from 8.8 in 1996. Interestingly, this is lower than in other states in the region. There are two main reasons for this anomaly. First, as a result of their collectivist upbringing, many workers are reluctant to leave their jobs, even when they have not been paid for months. Second, many of the officially unemployed earn money by working second jobs or engaging in small-scale retail trade in the black market. Other problems on the road to a market economy include the lack of a retail distribution system, an underdeveloped credit system, hostility towards the private sector, a complicated taxation system, a labyrinth bureaucracy, arbitrary exchange controls and customs regulations, the lack of legal protection for private property, and a growing government debt.

Many of these problems are interrelated, making them even more difficult to solve. For example, a growing debt has fueled unrest by delaying government wage and pension payments. The debt is partly the result of widespread tax evasion by individuals and businesses. A report issued by the Main Control Department of the Presidential Administration found only 16 percent of taxpayers paid on time and in full, while 50 percent have tax arrears and 34 percent do not pay taxes at all.[23] Avtovaz, the largest carmaker as well the largest debtor in Russia, owed over $500 million in taxes at the beginning of 1997.

This situation is partly the result of a tax system that is based on more than 5,500 documents—presidential orders, federal and local laws, decrees of the Finance Ministry and Tax Inspectorate—which collectively constitute Russia's tax code.[24] There are more than 200 taxes that can amount to 120 percent of profits. This makes it difficult for legitimate businesses to operate, stifles entrepreneurship, encourages tax evasion, and discourages foreign investment. The complexity of the tax system and its punitive rates have encouraged many firms and individuals to avoid tax registration, giving Russia a black economy equivalent to an astounding 40–50 percent of GDP. Large companies tend to regard paying tax as a matter of negotiation. In return for political favors, they kick in enough money to keep the government running. As a result, the government has been operating on tax revenues equivalent to about 10 percent of GDP, less than a third of the average level in Western Europe.[25] This has led to a vast accumulation of unpaid wages and has pushed half of Russia's economic transactions into barter, further starving the treasury of tax revenue.

Trade

Before 1990, most Soviet trade was with other socialist states. Largely in response to the Marshall Plan, the American policy to rebuild Europe, the Soviet Union created the Council for Mutual Economic Assistance (CMEA) in 1949. The goal of this organization was to facilitate and coordinate the economic development of the USSR's allies.[26] The CMEA was a barter and exchange system, with CEE states exporting low quality manufactures to the USSR and in return receiving subsidized raw materials—including oil and natural gas. Although this was a large drain on the Soviet economy, it gave the USSR enormous influence over their allies' economies.

Russia's subsequent economic collapse has brought a corresponding decrease in trade. For example, Russia's trade dropped 27 percent between 1991 and 1992. Although trade began to increase in 1993, it was mostly the result of increased exports of raw materials—45 percent of export revenue is from oil and gas. As a result, like other less developed states, Russia's exports are subject to global price fluctuations. This complicates economic planning and increases the power of international financial institutions. Germany is Russia's largest trading partner, followed by the United States, United Kingdom, Italy, and China. Not surprisingly, 26 percent of Russia's total trade in 1996 were with former Soviet republics such as Kazakhstan and the Ukraine.[27]

Although far richer in resources than other CEE states, Russia has received little foreign investment. While joint ventures employ 300,000 workers and account for 10 percent of Russian exports, political instability, a complex tax code, intrusive customs inspections, and protectionist policies have limited foreign investment. Between 1989 and 1996, Russia received a mere $13 billion in direct foreign investment. This figure compares to $31 billion in the rest of Central and Eastern Europe.[28] These figures show that Russia has yet to integrate itself into the world economy. Without more international investment and loans, Russia will be unable to service its foreign debts, ensuring years of poverty and economic stagnation.

Since the end of the Soviet Union in 1991, Russians have seen the economy contract 47 percent, living standards decrease, and their savings wiped out by inflation. Inflation, although down from 131 percent in 1995, was still over 21 percent in 1996.

The current business climate is also depressing. Small business formation remains stagnant, property rights are uncertain, an obstructionist bureaucracy remains in place, and organized crime dominated certain sectors of the economy. These conditions were reflected in the 60 percent decline in the stock market and a 300 percent devaluation of the ruble in 1998. The latter makes the import-dependent Russians even more impoverished because goods become more expensive as the ruble loses value. The government's ability to deal with the problems of the economic transformation will play a crucial role in determining the extent to which society will continue to support moves towards a market economy and democratic institutions.

POLITICAL HISTORY

Because of its size and location, we cannot understand the history of other Central and Eastern European states without knowing Russian history. As we shall see, the history of all the countries in the region are intricately intertwined with one another.

Before the Twentieth Century

The roots of the contemporary Russian political scene can be traced back to several key historical events. Among the most important were the rise of Moscovy, the creation of the Romanov dynasty, and the Bolshevik Revolution of 1917. These events can be seen as part of a recurring struggle between two diametrically opposed forces: one that advocated borrowing Western models and ideology to help Russia overcome its backwardness—a group that in the eighteenth century became known as the *Westernizers*—and one that believes the West is hopelessly corrupt and that Russia has a unique mission to develop the innate qualities of the Slavic soul and race—the *Slavophiles*. This identity crisis has fostered a unique process of political development whose legacy is reflected in the contemporary era.

Interestingly, Russia's early historical development did not even occur in what is today Russia. It was centered on Kiev, the capital of contemporary Ukraine. The Kieven Rus period of history was dominated by a series of competing independent principalities, with the Vladimir-Suzdal principality emerging as one of the most powerful. From this area, Moscovy—Moscow—emerged as the cradle of the Russian state. Moscovy took its religion, Eastern Orthodoxy, and its culture predominantly from Constantinople and the Byzantine Empire.

Between the twelfth and sixteenth centuries, Moscow's princes became the tribute collectors for the Tartars,[29] cooperating with them in the destruction of other Russian principalities. By the fourteenth century, Moscovy had become the dominant principality. The victory of Moscow's Prince Donskoi over the Tartars in 1380 shattered the myth of their invincibility, initiating a period of declining Tartar power. By 1552, Moscovy had not only annexed other ethnically Russian territories but had also seized Kazan, the capital of the Volga Tartars.

Although Moscovy was able to expand during this era by isolating Russia from Europe, the period of Tartar domination stunted Russia's economic and political development. Russians came to believe that a strong government was needed to protect the state from external threats. It is from this period that the term *tsar* came into use. The tsar (from Latin *caesar*) was the autocrat of Russia and accountable only to God in this Eastern equivalent of the divine right of kings.

During the reign of Ivan the Terrible (1547–1584), Russia was subjected to ruthless centralization. Even nobles lost their property rights to the state. Ivan abolished the privileges of the boyars, the hereditary nobility, replacing them with members of what came to be known as "service nobility." This latter group owed their positions and privileges to the tsar, resulting in a great increase in the power of tsar and the state. However, the state was greatly weakened after Ivan's death and the ensuing succession struggle, which led to a civil war that facilitated foreign incursions. This period is know as the Time of Troubles.

The creation of the Romanov dynasty in 1613 brought a return to centralized control. The Romanovs ruled Russia until 1917. This period was marked by the continuing struggle between Westernizers and Slavophiles. Under Peter the Great (1682–1725), Russia was opened to the West. Although he knew that the only way to rival the West was to imitate it, it is important to note that Peter wanted to copy only the West's technology, not their culture. On land annexed from the Swedes on the Neva River, Peter moved the capital from Moscow to St. Petersburg in 1709. This move had a twofold purpose. By gaining an outlet to the Baltic Sea, he could facilitate trade and other relations with the West. And since St. Petersburg was a new town, it would not be burdened by the medieval ideas that pervaded Moscow. Peter imposed Westernization on his subjects, making the nobles shave their prized beards—a symbol of masculinity and Orthodox piety in the old order.

Under the reign of Catherine the Great (1762–1796), the power of the state was lessened. A German princess by birth and anxious to increase her support among the Russian nobility, Catherine ended the hated Table of Ranks established by Peter the Great. This system of forced servitude had compelled the gentry to "earn" their position by serving the state. The gentry would become the intelligentsia of the eighteenth century, who in turn, ironically, would become the revolutionaries of the nineteenth century. Catherine also gave landlords the power to condemn their peasants (serfs) to forced labor without legal formalities. This action led to the strengthening of the institution of serfdom in Russia, causing a series of peasant revolts.

What made Catherine "Great," however, was her expansion of the Russian empire. Together with Prussia and Austria, Catherine partitioned Poland. To the south, two successful wars in 1768–1774 and 1787–1792 against the Ottoman Empire—contemporary Turkey—gave Russia most of the northern shore of the Black Sea. Russia also received the somewhat vague "right" to protect the Orthodox Christian population in the Ottoman Empire. Although Russia viewed itself as the defender of the Orthodox faith after the fall of the Byzantine Empire, this "right" was later used as a pretext for Russian intervention in Constantinople.

In contrast to Catherine, her successors Paul I (1796–1801) and Alexander I (1801–1825), believed in enlightened absolutism—that a powerful ruler was the only proper instrument of progress and well-being. As a result, they strengthened and centralized the state administration, again reducing the power of the nobility. Between the French Revolution and the Napoleonic Wars, Russia for the first time played a significant role in the politics of Europe. Its victory over Napoleon and its role in the Concert of Europe, a postwar alliance, made Russia one of the major continental powers and allowed it to extend its influence over Central and Eastern Europe.

Confusion over the accession of Nicholas I in 1825 and an influx of liberal ideas from Western Europe led to an attempted palace coup by a group of military officers, the Decembrists. They were supported by the progressive strata of society, including Alexander Pushkin and other poets and writers. However, the coup failed and the participants who were not executed were sent in chains to exile in Siberia as an example to others who might question the monarchy. This uprising led Nicholas to establish a police state, which in many ways was the precursor to the Soviet regime. The tsarist criminal code of 1845, for example, ranked crimes against the autocrat as the highest form of treason, and treason included "doubts" about the authority of the tsar.

The rigid autocracy of Nicholas I increased the influence of the Slavophiles. They argued that Russia's differences from the West were its major strength, and the opening of Russia to the West under Peter the Great had been a disastrous mistake. They believed faith in the church and the traditional Russian peasant community, the *mir*, were superior to the rationalism and individualism of the West. These beliefs form the core of contemporary Russian nationalism.

Russia's defeat in the Crimean War (1853–1855) marked the beginning of the end of the old regime. Russia had gained international importance through its large military, but this was no longer enough. The Industrial Revolution showed that power derived not only from a state's armed forces but, more important, from its economic and technological capabilities. The development of an advanced economy requires a free exchange of ideas and political participation by various groups, directly threatening the autocracy.

Realizing that Russia was falling behind the other major powers, Alexander II (1855–1881) reduced the power of the state by initiating a series of major reforms. The first was the Emancipation Edict of 1861. It ended serfdom in Russia, freeing more than 22 million serfs, who at the time comprised 38 percent of the population. Far from being a purely humanitarian gesture, the end of serfdom was intended to improve the military, increase agricultural productivity, and free a portion of the labor force for industrialization. Although the Emancipation Edict meant that serfs were no longer the property of the nobility, it did not grant them personal freedom as they were now bound to their village. Other decrees were designed to reform the military, establish local governments, and improve education. In a parallel to the dramatic economic reforms initiated by Mikhail Gorbachev in the 1980s, this Era of Great Reforms released powerful forces of change that split the political elite; some thought the reforms went too far while others thought they had not gone far enough.

However, the greatest threat to autocratic rule was not the peasants but the rapidly growing intelligentsia. Although most agreed on the need for reform, the intelligentsia was divided between those who wanted to reform the autocracy and those who wanted to destroy it. Since the peasants were the largest group in Russia, revolutionary groups such as Narodnaya Volya ("People's Will") went to the countryside to enlist the support of the peasants. However, the peasants did not respond to the radicals' calls for revolution. In fact, they turned many of the rebels over to the Tsarist secret police. Disillusionment in the countryside drove the revolutionaries to terrorism. In March 1881, they assassinated Alexander II. His successor, Alexander III (1881–1894), cruelly dealt with the remnants of this faction. He also suppressed groups that had advocated gradual, peaceful change. As a result, by 1885, both moderate and radical elements of the intelligentsia had been eliminated or discredited.

Although the regime was able to check the political pressure for change, new economic conditions fostered the creation of an increasingly impoverished industrial working class. To explain this situation, Russian revolutionaries turned to the "scientific" certainties of Marxism. Karl Marx was a German philosopher who believed economic relationships among the various parts of society determined the political relationships. His philosophy was based on the belief that history unfolds in a series of preordained stages, determined by the level of economic development. At each stage, there is conflict between those who own the means of production and those who do not. This conflict of opposites produces a resulting synthesis, a new stage of historical development, in which the differences between the haves and have nots decreases. Over time, this shrinking gap culminates in the creation of a perfect society—communism—devoid of conflict.

The last exploitative stage of historical development Marx called capitalism. In this stage, the industrial proletariat is exploited by the factory-owning bourgeoisie. Significantly, Russia had just entered this stage of economic development as Marx was developing his theories. However, according to Marx, Russia was not ripe for revolution. Since Russia was a largely agrarian state with only a small industrial proletariat, it first had to go through the capitalist stage of development. Passing through this stage would eliminate the last differences between classes as well as create the material basis for a communist society.

In spite of this obvious theoretical gap, Marxist ideas became increasingly popular in Russia as dissatisfaction with the regime increased. The Marxists were separated into two major groups: the revolutionaries, who like their predecessors wanted to use force to overthrow the regime; and moderates, who wanted a peaceful transition to socialism. The latter group was primarily influenced by Western European socialists, who argued that capitalism would gradually wither away. Russian revolutionaries, however, were a minority in society and were divided into numerous groups and parties, most of whom fought as much against each other as the regime. At the beginning of the twentieth century, Russia was in political turmoil, a result of the struggle between the forces of change and reaction.

The Twentieth Century

Vladimir Illich Ulyanov, more commonly know by his revolutionary pseudonym Lenin, developed a theory to reconcile Marxism with the conditions in Russia. The brother of a hanged member of the radical revolutionary group, Narodnaya Volya ("People's Will"), and son of an imperial bureaucrat, Lenin believed the process of historical evolution could be accelerated by skipping the capitalist stage of development. This would be accomplished through the creation of a revolutionary political party to "telescope," or escalate, the pace of change. Interestingly, the creation of a political party was something Marx had never suggested. Thus, Lenin significantly modified Marx's ideas. Lenin spelled out his beliefs in a 1902 pamphlet, *What Is to Be Done?*

In July 1903, the Second Congress of Russian Social Democratic Party, a Marxist party founded in 1898, convened in London. As a result of a struggle over who should control the editorial board of the RSDP's newspaper *Iskra* ("The Spark"), the party split. Lenin and his supporters formed the faction which he called *Bolshevik*, meaning "majority," even though the Bolsheviks were a minority in the RSDP. Lenin's opponents were dubbed *Mensheviks*, or "minority," even though they were actually the majority in the party.

Although control of the editorial board was the issue that facilitated the split of the RSDP, numerous other differences also divided the party. For example, Lenin and his supporters called for a revolutionary struggle under the leadership of a strictly organized hierarchical party. In contrast, the Mensheviks were social democrats who advocated economic development and working with all "progressive" parts of society to create the conditions for the gradual creation of a communist state. Less disciplined and united than the Bolsheviks, the Mensheviks adhered to the Marxist belief that the first revolution in Russia had to be bourgeois and democratic.

Interestingly, the first of three revolutions in Russia owed little to either the Bolsheviks or Mensheviks. Its immediate impetus was the defeat of Russia in the 1904 Russo-Japanese War, an outcome that caused a marked decrease in living standards. On January 9, 1905, a crowd of men, women, and children led by a priest carried a petition addressed to the tsar demanding a better government. When the marchers approached the Winter Palace, mounted troops panicked, killing scores. This massacre, known as "Bloody Sunday," united the people against the autocracy and undermined the power of the tsar. It also led to spontaneous urban and rural revolts.

In an attempt to channel political dissent and driven by panic, in 1904 Nicholas II established the first of four consultative representative assemblies or Dumas. However, their powers were very limited. For example, although Duma members could question ministers, they were not obliged to answer. The crown also retained all powers not specifically attributed to the legislature and the emperor had an absolute veto power. Although hailed initially as a measure to limit the autocracy, the weakness of the Dumas failed to lessen the pressure for change. As a result, between 1905 and 1917 Russia was convulsed by a continuing wave of strikes and demonstrations.

Initially, the outbreak of World War I fostered unity. With the largest army in Europe, Russians assumed the war would be quickly won. However, as casualties increased—Russia had the highest casualty rate—over 50 percent by 1917—and a military stalemate developed, discontent swelled. Military problems were furthered by a deteriorating economy, caused in large part by economic backwardness and bureaucratic ineptitude.

In March 1917, the Tsarist regime was overthrown by a spontaneous uprising. As in 1905, the Bolsheviks played no organized role in this event. Governmental power was split between a newly formed Provisional Government and the Petrograd Soviet of Workers and Soldiers deputies. The Provisional Government was headed by Alexander Kerensky and included members from most of the parties in the Duma. This broad coalition was unable to enact economic reforms and, at the insistence of its Western allies, continued the highly unpopular war effort.

In contrast, the Petrograd Soviet was created to represent the interests of the working class. It was led by the Menshevik Leon Trotsky, and its power increased as dissatisfaction with the provisional government increased. This body gradually came under Bolshevik control. In April 1917, Lenin returned to St. Petersburg from a Tsarist-imposed exile in Switzerland. He immediately called for a popular revolt against the Provisional Government. His simple slogan of "Bread, Peace, and Land" appealed to the masses. The Provisional Government, emphasizing their differences with the former autocratic regime, refused to arrest Lenin and other Bolsheviks. Linking themselves with the widespread desire for change, the tightly organized Bolsheviks took control of the Winter Palace on November 7, 1917. In 1918, the Russian Socialist Federated Soviet Republic was proclaimed. In 1922, other republics were included, and the Union of Soviet Socialist Republics (USSR) was formally established.

The success of the Bolsheviks was unexpected. However, it vindicated Lenin's belief that a well-organized party could change history. This was a significant development, because this deviation from Marxist theory would prove to be one of the key factors that led to the demise of the Soviet Union.

The new regime confronted numerous problems. Most significant were declining economic production and a civil war. To preserve power, Lenin initiated "War Communism" in 1918. This period was marked by an increase in the power of the central government and the banning of opposition movements. By 1921, Russia was again an autocracy.

Although Lenin believed in the inevitability of socialism, he was above all a pragmatist. In order to improve an economy devastated by the civil war, Lenin initiated the New Economic Policy (NEP) in 1921. The NEP was a relaxation of economic controls in an effort to restore production. Although the state retained ownership of industry, private retail trade was legalized. Peasants were also allowed to sell their crops on the open market. Lenin characterized this policy as "one step backward, two steps forward." With these stimuli, industry and agriculture quickly recovered. Although it was a temporary retreat from the creation of an equalitarian communist society, Lenin justified the NEP by noting that if the regime did not survive, a communist society could not be created.

Lenin's death in 1924 was followed by a brutal succession struggle between Trotsky and the former Bolshevik Commissar of Nationalities, Joseph Stalin. Stalin won this struggle through conspiracy, bribes, and the support of the Party bureaucracy. By 1927, he had made Leninism a state religion. This helped Stalin consolidate his power, for anyone who dared to criticize him was in effect also criticizing Lenin, the founding father of the new regime. As an illustration of his brutality, Stalin unleashed a devastating famine on the Ukraine. The purpose was to crush the peasantry, the group most opposed to the revolution. Between 1929 and 1934, approximately 15 million people were killed as a result of famine, execution, or deportation.

The famine was followed by the "Great Purges" (1934–1938). This campaign eliminated any opposition to Stalin, real or imagined. Cynically, in 1936 Stalin introduced a new constitution with lavish individual freedoms.

Vladimir Illich Lenin (1870–1924)

One of the foremost revolutionaries of the twentieth century, Lenin was largely responsible for Russia's 1917 revolution and the country's attempt to build a communist society.

His political career began in 1887, when he saw his brother hanged by the police for plotting to assassinate Czar Alexander III. From then on, Lenin turned into a radical revolutionary devoted to overthrowing the bourgeoisie class. His penchant for rebellion did not sit well though with the government and as a result he was forced to become an exile several times between the early 1890s and 1917. During these periods outside Russia, Lenin spent much time reading the classics of European revolutionary thought, especially the work of Karl Marx. In fact, Marx's writings influenced Lenin so much, that he quickly became a self-proclaimed Marxist. Soon he joined in with other exiled Marxists outside Russia and started to formulate his plans for the inevitable Russian Proletarian Revolution.

Lenin's visions of rebellion were finally realized in February 1917, when protests over the wartime food shortages led to a general strike in St. Petersburg that eventually turned bloody and led to the overthrow of the autocratic monarchy of Czar Nicholas II. A provisional government led mostly by the old liberal leaders of the Duma, many of whom were wealthy landowners or middle-class bourgeoisie, was established. The revolution in St. Petersburg quickly spread across the country.

This uprising took Lenin by surprise, forcing him to quickly make his way back to Russia. Arriving in St. Petersburg in peril, he quickly took control of the Bolshevik party. From this position, he argued for rebellion against the bourgeoisie provisional government and soon began planning a Bolshevik revolution. After a failed worker's uprising in July, he finally succeeded in convincing the party leadership to support the November Revolution that overthrew the provisional government.

After the November Revolution, Lenin was elected to the head of government as the chairman of the Council of People's Commissars. Almost immediately after gaining power, he was faced with a struggle to maintain control over the country. Lenin moved slowly towards the creation of a socialist state, not forcing the radical implementation of communist politics. Between 1918 and 1921, a brutal civil war raged between the Communist Red Army and white-Tsarist forces. After suffering three strokes, and before he was able to identify his successor, Lenin died in 1924. This led to political turmoil after his death.

However, they could only be exercised in accordance with the "interests of the workers and the purpose of strengthening of the socialist system," in other words, only if they strengthened Stalin's power. This provision was used to arrest and imprison anyone who might be considered disloyal. As a

---

JOSEPH STALIN (1874–1952)

Joseph Stalin was born Iosif Vissarionovich Dzugashvili in the then province of Georgia. While studying to become a priest, he began to read the writings of Karl Marx. In 1899, he left the seminary to become a revolutionary, working his way up through the Russian Social Democratic party. To evade arrest by the Tsarist secret police, he adopted the name Stalin, "man of steel." Following the death of Lenin in 1922, Stalin shared power with other party leaders. Using his position as General Secretary, by 1928 he gained control of the party and state.

Stalin used an iron fist to reform the USSR, killing millions to industrialize the country. One of Stalin's most notable policies was the "Great Purges." Beginning in 1934, Stalin began a series of arrests, show trials, and executions, ostensibly to rid the country of terrorist threats, but in reality to secure personal power. The purges came to a head in 1938 when Stalin initiated a purge of the Communist Party hierarchy. Of the 139 members of the Central Committee, 115 were killed. In total, almost half of the 2.3 million party members were executed or imprisoned. Military leaders and soldiers, industrial workers, writers, artists, even members of the general public were executed or imprisoned. In all, over 5 million were arrested, with only about 10 percent surviving.

Stalin turned the state apparatus into an instrument of his personal power, allowing him to dominate the polity until his death in 1953. Stalin's lust for power prevented not only the creation of the Marxist state envisioned by the revolution but also created an oppressive state apparatus that limited economic and political development, ultimately causing the destruction of the Soviet Union.

---

result, by 1939 a network of concentration camps, the GULAG, held over 10 million people, or 10 percent of the Soviet workforce.

In 1939, Stalin signed a nonaggression pact with Hitler. A secret protocol also split Poland between Germany and the Soviet Union, allowing Hitler to invade Poland without having to fear Soviet intervention. Interestingly, the secret protocol was denied by the Soviets until the Gorbachev era. Stalin thought this pact would satisfy Hitler's ambitions. He was wrong. In 1941, Germany invaded. The German attack and subsequent four years of World War II posed a grave threat to the existence of the USSR. Though poorly equipped, the Red Army emerged victorious. Noteworthy, Stalin used patriotic themes, not communist ones, to bolster support for the war effort. Although victory was achieved, the cost was high. Over 20 million civilians and 10 million Red Army troops were killed during the conflict. Soviet success in the war was due in no small part to foreign aid—in particular, the American Lend Lease program. However, this information was kept from the population. Stalin used the myth of Soviet invincibility to create the cult of the "Great Patriotic War," with his leadership a prominent feature of Russian victory. Immense sacrifices by the population were rewarded after the war by the reimposition of a strict discipline regime. Despite low living standards, Stalin continued to pour resources into the military and heavy industry sectors.

Since there was no formal succession procedure, as when Lenin died, Stalin's death in 1953 was followed by a power struggle, a period of collective leadership, and then the emergence of a single leader. Interestingly, this process was repeated in every succession. By 1955, Nikita Khrushchev had emerged as Stalin's successor. Under Khrushchev, the Soviet Union entered a new era. He denounced his former mentor and criticized the "cult of personality" that Stalin had created to strengthen his control over society. Khrushchev can be considered the grandfather of Gorbachev's post-1985 attempts to reform the Soviet polity. Without Khrushchev's rejection of Stalin's totalitarian system, Gorbachev's reforms would never have occurred.

Between 1956 and 1975, the USSR experienced a period of economic growth and development. However, revolts in Hungary (1956) and Czechoslovakia (1968) showed that states in the region were questioning the Soviet model. After 1975, growth rates rapidly declined. This situation was aggravated

---

NIKITA SERGEYEVICH KHRUSHCHEV (1894–1971)

Born in the Ukraine, Nikita Khrushchev joined both the Communist Party and the Red Army in 1918. He fought in the Civil War and quickly advanced in the Party hierarchy, becoming a member of Stalin's politburo.

When Stalin died in 1953, a power struggle broke out between KGB leader Lavrenty Beria, Prime Minister Georgy Malenkov, and Khrushchev, who had recently been appointed First Secretary of the Communist Party. First allying with Malenkov to get rid of Beria, Khrushchev, like Stalin, used his control of the party apparatus to force Malenkov's resignation in 1955.

During the Twentieth Party Congress in 1956, Khrushchev began the process of "de-Stalinization." He denounced Stalin's purges and reign of terror and accused him of responsibility for everything from the USSR's break with Yugoslavia in 1948 to the German invasion in the Second World War. Although involved in Stalin's purges, Khrushchev was able to cover up his own involvement while implicating his political opponents.

The last of true believers in communism, Khrushchev faced many problems during his time in power. He attempted to reform the agricultural sector, which had been devastated by Stalin. However, his "reforms" caused agricultural production to fall even further. Internationally, relations with the United States became more tense. Khrushchev's attempt to redress an arms gap with the United States led to the 1962 Cuban missile crisis. When the United States demanded that the USSR remove nuclear missiles it had recently installed in Cuba, Khrushchev was forced to give in. Because of this loss of face, as well as the de-Stalinization that alienated conservative party members, Khrushchev was ousted in 1964.

Leonid Brezhnev (1906–1982)

In October 1964, First Secretary of the CPSU Nikita Khrushchev was brought back from a holiday on the Black Sea and stripped of his office by the Politburo. His liberalizing and democratizing reforms, or what the official communiqué labeled "erratic leadership" and "hare-brain scheming," had alienated him from the rest of the ruling elite.

In contrast to his predecessor, Leonid Brezhnev, leader of the coup, emphasized stability. His domestic policy was called "developed socialism," a plan that focused on developing the economic framework for communism. This policy led to declining growth rates and stagnation. The end of his rule was accompanied by a nearly complete breakdown of the planned economy and agricultural sector, largely the result of the lack of incentives and motivation among the workers. Brezhnev's foreign policy agenda was much more successful than his domestic one because it was based on *détente*, or peaceful coexistence, with the Western states. This policy entailed a considerable thawing in the Cold War, signified by increasing cooperation between the United States and USSR on security concerns. Away from the West, Brezhnev was also successful in his efforts to spread Soviet influence through the developing world, establishing pro-Soviet regimes in Vietnam, Angola, Mozambique, and several other countries. Overall, Brezhnev's rule proved disastrous for the economy and the Soviet people, but his successes in foreign policy make him one of the most important Soviet leaders. His policy of *détente* remains the hallmark of his rule and was an important first step towards eventually ending the East-West conflict.

---

by the 1979 invasion of Afghanistan and an arms race with the United States. Together, these factors led to economic and political stagnation. Although reforms were desperately needed, they were consistently rejected by Party conservatives who saw them as a threat to their monopoly on power.

The death of longtime leader Leonid Brezhnev (1964–1992), initiated a period of instability. Within the next three years, two more leaders—Andropov and Chernenko—also died. The need to select conservative, aged leaders showed how ossified the Party had become. The old regime was in its death throes.

Since 1985

In 1985, a new generation took over the Soviet Union. Inexperienced and eighteen years younger than his predecessor, Mikhail Gorbachev became head of the Communist Party. His accession marked a turning point in Soviet history. Gorbachev was the first Soviet leader who had not been involved in the purges of the 1930s or the Great Patriotic War (World War II). Faced with

---

MIKHAIL SERGEYEVICH GORBACHEV (1931–)

Born in Privol'noye, in Southern Russia, Mikhail Gorbachev became General Secretary of the Communist Party in 1985 and President of the USSR in 1988. He tried to reform Soviet society between 1985 and 1991 by introducing *perestroika* (economic restructuring) and *glasnost* (political openness) and by transferring power from Moscow to individual republic legislatures. He was also responsible for many changes in the USSR's foreign policy: withdrawing troops from Afghanistan, normalizing relations with China, cooperating with the U.N. in the Gulf War, and signing agreements on arms control with the United States. Unlike his predecessors, Gorbachev did not intervene when CEE countries began to overthrow their communist governments.

As a result of this work, Gorbachev was awarded the Nobel Peace Prize in 1990. The next year, a coup was staged by hardline communists who resented Gorbachev's reforms and their own loss of power. Gorbachev returned to power within three days, but the coup attempt changed his policy. While maintaining the presidency, he resigned as General Secretary. He then reformed the military and KGB, replacing hardliners with reformers, and suspended Communist Party activities. At the same time, he granted independence to Estonia, Latvia, and Lithuania.

Gorbachev resigned his post as President when the USSR disbanded in December 1991. Since then, he has openly criticized the government for making economic reforms too quickly. His attempt to reenter politics failed when he received only .5 percent of the vote in the 1996 presidential election.

---

growing economic, political, and social stagnation, Gorbachev initiated a series of reforms to try to preserve the foundations of a disintegrating regime. Although he lacked the insight to see that the Soviet system could no longer survive, he was the first leader to realize that it could not continue as before. Economically, he launched *perestroika*, a series of reforms that would lessen the state's role in the economy. Politically, he encouraged freedom of speech and more openness in the press—*glasnost*. Instead of strengthening the regime, however, these reforms weakened it by unleashing long-suppressed hostility against the government.

As a result, between 1988 and 1989 a number of republics declared their independence from the Soviet Union. In June 1991, Boris Yeltsin, the former Communist Party chief of Moscow, was elected president in the first free presidential election in Russian history. In an attempt to prevent the breakup of the USSR, supporters of the old regime launched a coup against Gorbachev in August of 1991. The coup failed but hastened the end of the Soviet Union. On December 25, 1991, the Russian Republic declared itself independent and the Soviet Union was officially dissolved. One of the largest social experiments in history had come to an inglorious end.

BORIS NIKOLAYEVICH YELTSIN (1931–)

Born in Sverdlovsk (now Yekaterinburg), Boris Yeltsin worked his way up the Svedlovsk party hierarchy to become First Secretary. To shake up the entrenched Moscow Party Committee, he was made its First Secretary in 1985. After alienating conservatives in the party, he was stripped of his post two years later. Normally this would have been a career-ending move, but the more open political environment allowed him another chance. Yeltsin's popularity grew in the late 1980s when he criticized both the Party and General Secretary Gorbachev.

In 1991, Boris Yeltsin became Russia's first popularly elected president. Immediately, conflict broke out between him and conservative Party members. In an attempt to break governmental deadlock, in 1993 Yeltsin dissolved parliament and called for new elections and a new constitution. An armed revolt ensued, and hundreds of politicians and demonstrators occupied the parliament building in protest. The army was eventually brought in to stop the rebellion. The new elections gave Russia a new constitution, but economic hardships led to an electoral victory for Yeltsin's opponents.

Yeltsin's rule has been marked by frequent policy shifts and political maneuvers, a result of his declining health—he was hospitalized twice in 1995 and had a quintuple heart bypass operation in November 1996. In a sign of his declining authority and a lack of institutional and public support, in September 1998 he was forced to accept the Duma's candidate for Prime Minister after his first candidate was rejected. While his term of office does not end until 2000, Yeltsin's health problems, failure to create a political base of support, and refusal to break completely with the past suggest his influence will continue to decline.

In an attempt to implement economic and political reforms, Yeltsin disbanded parliament in September 1993. This body had been a haven for old communists opposed to change. His call for new elections and a new constitution led to an armed revolt that was put down by the army. At the end of a turbulent year, a bare majority of the eligible voters approved a new constitution. In simultaneous elections for a new Duma, dissatisfaction with economic reforms helped the ultranationalist and inappropriately named Liberal Democrats, led by Vladimir Zhirnovsky, win the largest number of votes.

In response to a declaration of independence by Chechnya and increasing domestic problems, Yeltsin decided to invade this Caucasus region in December 1994. The intervention, originally planned as a lightning strike to crush the separatists, turned into a protracted and bloody war. It cost thousands of lives, undermined political reform, showed the weakness of the Russia Army, and heavily damaged Russia's international prestige. A tenuous ceasefire was signed in August 1996.

In December 1995, Russia held its first fully constitutional parliamentary elections since the 1917 Bolshevik Revolution. In contrast to the 1993

ALEKSANDR LEBED

Aleksandr Lebed, a former two-star general, is one of Russia's most powerful men. During the 1996 presidential election, the previously unknown Lebed finished third. To help ensure his own victory, Yeltsin appointed Lebed as the new national security advisor and Security Council secretary a month before the runoff election. Soon after the election, though, Yeltsin, who feared Lebed could become a strong political adversary, fired him from this post. Since then, Lebed has been a powerful figure in Russian politics. To enhance his political visibility, he won the gubernatorial election in the Krasnoyarsk Province in May 1998. Part of his popularity arises from his outspoken style, penchant for reform, and realistic view of Russia. For example, in the September 6, 1994 *Financial Times* he was quoted as saying, "Most Russians don't care whether they are ruled by fascists or communists or even Martians as long as they can buy six kinds of sausage in the store and lots of cheap vodka." These blunt, candid quotes typify his outspoken style, making Lebed a leading candidate in the 2000 election. A June 1998 poll found 12 percent of respondents favored Lebed to be the next president. This was the second highest total of all potential candidates. Given his popularity today, even if he is not elected, Aleksandr Lebed will remain an influential figure in Russian politics in the near future.

elections, the biggest winner was the Communist Party. It won 21 percent of the vote, up 9 percent from 1993. Compared to the 1993 election, the biggest losers were the nationalists and the liberals.

In July 1996, Yeltsin was reelected president over Communist Party challenger Gennady Zyuganov. Yeltsin owed his victory to the support of retired General Alexander Lebed, who because of his emphasis on law and order won a surprising 15 percent of the vote in the first round of the election. After his strong showing, Yeltsin made Lebed Secretary of the Security Council, the national security decision-making body. With Lebed's electoral support, Yeltsin won the second round of the election with 53.8 percent of the vote. His victory was welcomed with a sense of relief, but not exaltation. The results showed that a deep chasm divides Russia. Of the 108 million registered voters, 34 million decided not to vote, 40 million voted for Yeltsin, 30 million voted for Zyuganov, and close to 4 million selected "against the two candidates."

Following his electoral success, Yeltsin appointed numerous reformers to the Council of Ministers. However, a scandal forced leading reformer and presidential Chief-of-Staff Anatoly Chubais to resign in 1997. In an effort to invigorate the reform process, in April 1998 Yeltsin dismissed Prime Minister Chernomyrdin. This action led to a confrontation with the Duma when Yeltsin threatened to dissolve it unless it approved his nominee, political novice Sergei Kiriyenko as Prime Minister. While it was eventually successful, the dismissal of Chernomyrdin removed Yeltsin's political buffer, making him directly accountable for the success and failure of government policy.

In August 1998, after a summer meltdown of the Russian economy that saw the stock market lose over 60 percent of its value since January, interest rates at over 150 percent, the ruble devalued by 85 percent, 500 percent inflation, the poorest harvest in 45 years, and shrinking foreign reserves, Yeltsin dismissed Kiriyenko. The decline of Yeltsin's authority became apparent when he was forced to drop his nominee for prime minister and select Foreign Minister Yevgeny Primakov, a candidate supported by the Duma, instead. Since then, Yeltsin has withdrawn from the political scene. Yeltsin's deputy chief-of-staff stated that Yeltsin, normally in the political limelight, would now leave the "day-to-day issues" to others. A lack of authority and health problems such as Yeltsin's second heart bypass operation in November 1996 have fostered uncertainty about his ability to serve his full four-year term. Even a healthy chief executive would be tested by the numerous problems—a deepening economic recession, budgetary problems, opposition control of the Duma—facing Russia today.

The continuing battles between the forces of reform and reaction show that the historical conflict between Westernizers and Slavophiles endures. Like Peter the Great, Yeltsin's greatest opponents are the forces of reaction. Interestingly, every period of radical reform in Russian/Soviet history has been followed by a period of reaction. As in all countries, the history of Russia has fostered unique attitudes and beliefs. The legacies of abolishing serfdom only a little over a hundred years ago, the devastation of the two world wars, and the isolation of the Cold War have had a dramatic impact on the Russian polity, which has always believed in its distinct uniqueness: perceiving itself as part of Europe, yet superior to it. The ramifications of a changed world have yet to be felt as Russia has not integrated itself into the international system. This can be seen in its lack of political stability, a continuing ten-year recession, and the lack of basic state services for the population.

Today a newly sovereign Russia is standing at a crossroads. Will it be able to realize its self-proclaimed goals of creating a market economy and pluralistic society based on the rule of law, or will historical legacies be too difficult to overcome?

INFORMING POLITICAL IDEAS

While everyone thinks about politics in a different way, most states have an ideology, a more or less coherent pattern of political thinking, which guides political development. Knowing a state's ideology helps us understand how the government is supposed to work, the individual's role in society, and what people can expect from the government. The articulation of interests;

the creation and implementation of laws; and the way people are socialized into political life are all directly affected by the prevailing ideology.

Political Culture (1927–1989)

The ideology that guided the development of the Soviet Union was Marxism-Leninism. In contrast to democratic ideology, its provisions included deference to state authority in economic, political, and social affairs. Like other ideologies, it creates a distorted image of reality.

Marxism-Leninism is based upon certain broad tenets and basic assumptions developed by Karl Marx (1818–1883) and Lenin. It endeavors to explain the entirety of human history in terms of "laws" based on historical materialism, economic determinism, the class struggle, and the dialectic. *Historical materialism* is history defined by economic exploitation, or who exploits whom. Marx believed in economic *determinism*—that history is driven by socioeconomic forces that are predetermined and cannot be avoided. In the first stage of history, defined as a primitive communist society, property was communal. In the next stage, the ancient period, classes—slave and owner—developed. This period of economic development, slavery, led to a class conflict between the slaves and the owners. In the next stage of history, the feudal period, the class conflict was now between the peasants and lords. Throughout this stage of history, society was agrarian. With the onset of industrialization, however, the class conflict moved to a contest between the owners of the means of production—the bourgeoisie—and the people who worked for them—the proletariat. This stage of development, called capitalism, was the result of the continued bourgeoisie concentration of wealth gained at the expense of an increasingly exploited proletariat. Inevitably, the proletariat would overthrow the exploiters, creating a socialist society. This revolution would be violent because the bourgeoisie would fight to keep their power and wealth.

The development of history was the result of the *dialectic,* or internal contradictions. The dialectic holds that opposites can never be reconciled or separated: war and peace, life and death, cannot be understood apart from each other. Marx called these terms the *thesis* and the *antithesis.* The clash of these opposites creates a new unity, or *synthesis.* Thus capitalism was doomed because it is the result of the clash of contradictory economic forces, the bourgeoisie and proletariat. This clash in turn forms a new synthesis, socialism.

During the socialist stage of history, the material conditions necessary for a communist society will be created, including a redistribution of wealth and workers' takeover of the means of production. This stage of history also eliminates the last societal contradictions and economic differences between the classes, creating a Communist society. Although the creation of a communist society will be a long and difficult struggle, its realization will mean the end of history. No longer will there be exploiters and exploited, but a classless society in which everyone is free to do what they want.

While Marx stressed the universality of his theory, he noted that every society must pass through all the stages of history. Since Western Europe was the most advanced economically, he predicted that the socialist revolutions would occur there first. This prediction presented Russian Marxists with a dilemma, because in 1917 Russia was still in the feudal stage of development. To remedy this ideological paradox, Lenin modified Marx's theory to apply to conditions in Russia. He believed that history could be "accelerated" to skip the capitalist stage of development. Thus a revolution could occur even in an underdeveloped country like Russia, in what Lenin called the "weak link" of the capitalist chain. For this revolution to occur, the workers had to be organized and their class consciousness enhanced. The vehicle for making this happen was the Bolshevik, later the Communist, Party. This tightly organized party of professional revolutionaries would lead the workers in their seizure of power, creating a "dictatorship of the proletariat."

Lenin's tenets were a significant departure from classic Marxism. First, Marx had stressed the necessity of going through the stages of history to create the necessary revolutionary conditions. Second, Marx had never discussed the creation of a political party, which, according to Lenin, was now necessary to ensure that Marx's inevitable revolution would occur.

This theory allowed Marxists to do three things: "correctly" explain the past, "correctly" explain the present, and "correctly" predict the future. This is what gave them their sense of certainty and conviction. Since Marxism-Leninism claimed to be "scientific" and inevitable, it gave Soviet leaders considerable latitude in their attempt to create a communist society. It is important to note that the Soviet Union never created the society Marx envisioned. According to its own ideologists, the Soviet Union was still in the "socialist" phase of development. However, Marx would never have recognized the Soviet Union as a socialist state. Although it had eliminated the bourgeoisie, they were replaced by a new class—the *nomenklatura*. Like the capitalists before them, this class used the state apparatus to control society. However, in contrast to the capitalists, they also enacted numerous programs that improved the living standards for the vast majority of the population.

The failure to make the Soviet Union the first communist state can be traced to three factors: an inability to incorporate new patterns of economic development into Marxist ideology (e.g., a market economy regulated by the state); distortions by Soviet leaders; and the problem of a doctrine of historical development that negates the importance of individuals. Significantly, a true communist society has yet to be created.

With the occupation of Central and Eastern Europe by the Red Army following World War II, the states in this region were "Sovietized." Although ideologically the Soviets were freeing formerly exploited peoples, in reality they were imposing their own model of development. This not only allowed the Soviet Communists to control these states, but also allowed them to rationalize their own system. Commonalities between the USSR and its allies included a monopoly on power; lack of political dissent; recognition of the leading role of the Communist Party and the unquestioned wisdom of the political leadership and its loyalty to Lenin's teachings; forced industrialization; collectivized agriculture; and the study of Marxism-Leninism in schools. Indeed, "the claim to possess 'truth' enabled communists to rationalize their use of repressive measures and their demands for great sacrifices from their subjects in the name of a happy future."[30]

In addition to conformity and allegiance to the state, Soviet political culture promoted the superiority of society and subordination of the individual to society. It also propagated the notion that the Soviet Union was superior to other countries and had the greatest experience in building a communist society. Finally, the official ideology stressed the advantages of state ownership and condemned the alleged evils of private gain and individual advantage.

Legitimizing Rationale

The Soviet-style socialist systems defined legitimacy much differently than their counterparts in the West. Western political scientists usually describe legitimacy in terms of the regime's acceptance by the majority of the population. Examples include free and fair elections and full access to the policy-making process. In contrast, in the Soviet political system legitimacy was the result of the CPSU's creation of first a socialist, and then a communist, society.[31] This new society would end the exploitation and alienation between different social groups and would be organized on the basis of the Marxian idea of "from each according to his abilities to each according to his needs." In the name of creating this utopia, the Communist Party did whatever was necessary to create support for this goal. As an illustration, anyone who was not helping to build a communist society was considered an "enemy of the people."

Little Traditions

The attempt to create a communist society in the Soviet Union had some unintended side effects whose legacies can be seen today. They include the belief that the state should solve societal problems, egalitarianism, and lack of societal norms.

The legacy of the communist-imposed mentality that individual self-reliance is "antisocial" has led to a commonly held belief that the state will solve societal problems. This conviction fosters dependency and lessens personal responsibility and initiative. The egalitarian mentality causes the vast majority of the public to think that income differentials are now too large. They believe social justice requires a "certain extent" of social equality. This view is at odds with the present government policy of introducing a market economy based on individual freedom and responsibility.

Perhaps the most important legacy of communism is a lack of societal norms. The communist regime made people feel vulnerable and dependent on the state. By imposing a large number of impractical and often illogical restrictions and limitations, the government created a system that would inevitably and routinely be breached. This served to blur the line between the permitted and the forbidden, the acceptable and the unacceptable. It also negatively affected the moral standards of society by stripping cheating, theft, and dishonesty of their moral repulsiveness. As a result, normally honest people would think nothing of stealing from the state.

This situation created a system in which anything was acceptable as long as the individual benefited. With such strong governmental control, people came to believe that only by putting their individual interests ahead of the government's could they improve their condition. Although this phenomenon went by different names in different states—in Russia it was called *na levo* ("to the left"), it was present in all Central and Eastern European states.[32] Its legacy can be seen today in lack of electoral participation and lack of faith in the government's ability to solve societal problems.

To differing degrees, all states in the region are confronted by a lack of underlying values among their citizenry. Good and bad are subject to individual interpretation. Given the changes in the system, values now need to be redefined and norms established. Unfortunately, this is likely to take at least a generation.

Other Traditions

Although communist ideology attempted to create a new "Soviet man," historical experiences played a large role in shaping the character and behavior of Russians. Some of the more recurring themes include autocracy, bureaucratism, political intrigue, anarchy, and nationalism/xenophobia.

One of the most enduring traits of the Russian political culture is a strong, centralized, autocratic political order. Throughout its history, Russia has been dominated by strong rulers whose main concern was increasing their power, which in turn increased the power of the state. Russian monarchs, for example, crowned themselves at their coronations to demonstrate their powers were derived from God and no one else. As a result, unlike other monarchies in Europe whose powers were gradually limited in the nineteenth and twentieth centuries, in Russia there were no checks on the power of the sovereign.

To ensure their power, the tsars established a strong bureaucracy. By creating a ruling class that owed their privileges to the tsar and not heredity, Russian monarchs centralized power. Thus there were no countervailing forces or institutions to check the growth of the power of the autocrat. As a result, although numerous legal codes have been promulgated throughout

Russian history, the tsars did not have to follow them. Therefore, intrigue and assassinations have been traditional Russian political tools. In contrast to the West, the idea of individual protection or restraints on government have no historical precedent in Russia. All citizens, for example, received an internal passport they had to carry until they died. It had three pages for photographs of the bearer at ages 16, 25, and 45. It contains not only the bearer's name, but date and place of birth, nationality, children, family status, military service, and place of residence. This passport was issued by the Ministry of Internal Affairs—the police—and failure to carry it was punishable by a fine or imprisonment. These legacies are a large obstacle to change today since Russia has no experience with political checks and balances.

One result of the historical tendency to centralize power has been a distrust of authority. This distrust can be seen in numerous revolts by both the nobility and peasants throughout Russian history. Russian historian Nicholas Berdyaev contended that Russians tend not to like the state, regarding it as something to be rebeled against or meekly accepted as conditions dictate.[33] Seemingly paradoxically, Russians also respect and value authority. Like Poland, Russia came under foreign domination when it did not have a strong leader. This attitude can best be summed up in the old peasant expression: "How can we live without our beloved Tsar?"

Another historical legacy is the lack of a tolerant political culture. This restricts the development of a civil society. Although free elections have been held, former Yeltsin advisor Sergei Stankevich has noted that "the key elements of democracy . . . the art of sensible compromise and shared interests . . . are still not very much in evidence in the Russian political landscape."[34]

These features point to perhaps the most vexing feature of the Russian political culture, the search for a national identity. As noted earlier, historically there has been a battle between the Westernizers and the Slavophiles over the development of the Russian polity. The Slavophiles wanted a theocracy administered by the tsar. They believed that secular, liberal forms of government copied from the West were not suitable for Russia because they would create a "spiritual bondage." This conflict was fought under both the tsars and the communists, and it can be seen again today. In its current form, it pits those who want to create a market economy and democratic institutions against those who advocate a "Russian" model of development. This latter tendency is so strong that at times it borders on xenophobia.

This conflict is partially the result of a deeply ingrained inferiority complex that has created a love-hate relationship with the West. This ambivalence can be seen historically in both the opposition to the reforms of Peter the Great and in the Marxist-Leninist paranoia over enemies (the West) who were always out to "get" them. More recently, the Federal Counter-Intelligence Service, one of the successors to the KGB, released a document in the spring of 1995 that accused U.S. think tanks, charities, and other organizations in Russia of spying for the CIA. It recommended increased counterintelligence surveillance, lessening Russian contacts with the West, and stiffer secrecy laws. According to Natalya Gevorkian, reporter for the *Moscow News,* "the KGB can change its name, but we can't change the people in it and they cannot switch their brains." Every time there is a crisis in Russia, she notes, documents like this get published: "It's an easy explanation, that the West is to blame for everything."[35] Nine years after the change in regime, the Tsarist/Marxist-Leninist fear of "enemies" lives on.

This search for an identity makes Russians different from other nationalities. They continue to search for their place in the world and to prove their worthiness and greatness. This tendency is reinforced today by the fact that Russians, no longer the dominant group in a multiethnic empire, have to find a new identity. Although political culture is not static and can be changed by experiences over time, various features can be highly durable. Thus the evolution of the contemporary polity will, at least in the short term, be limited and modified by the past.

Political Socialization

Since the goal of the Party was to fulfill historical destiny by creating a communist state, the Soviet polity did not leave political socialization—the training of citizens, political learning, and the perpetuation of certain political values, norms and attitudes—to chance. The CPSU used every possible method to maintain its control. Schools, social organizations, peer groups, and the media were used not only to indoctrinate the population and garner support for governmental policies, but also to help ensure that the Communist Party remained the "leading and guiding force" of society.

Education

Under the Soviet regime, the state assumed complete responsibility for education and closed all private schools. Education was seen as a strategic asset that not only created trained workers, but also provided a communist upbringing and a tool for indoctrinating children with communist values, thus strengthening the regime. The history of the Communist Party and Marxist-Leninist philosophy were required subjects.

The Soviet/Russian school system, like most others in Central and Eastern Europe, is based on the German educational system. The system is designed to give a basic education to all and advanced specialist training to a large part of the population. Until age fifteen, children attend a local primary school. Then they take a test that determines whether they will attend a basic technical secondary school (to learn a simple trade such as auto mechanics), a technical school, or a gymnasium (a college prep school). After completing technical school or gymnasium, students can take a test to enter either a university or a technicum, a technical university. However, depending on the institution and party status, "connections" could also get a less qualified student enrolled into a school of higher education. This system emphasized the memorization of theory and deemphasized the development of practical skills, such as accounting and computer literacy. Thus, while CEE states have a highly educated population, their entrepreneurial skills are significantly weaker than those of their Western counterparts.

While education was free and in theory accessible to all, in practice admission to higher education was limited to those who could compete effectively or whose families had political clout. Once students were accepted, their living expenses were paid for by the state; this gave the state another means of controlling student behavior and promoting conformity. In addition to not being entirely accessible, the Soviet higher education system, like most European higher education systems, is specialized and does not offer a liberal arts education. The general emphasis on scientific and technical training meant that certain subjects in the humanities and social sciences, such as history, economics, political science, were neglected or taught in a manner that conformed with Marxist-Leninist ideology.

Today, Russia is in the process of reforming its education system. It is introducing new textbooks not written from a Marxist perspective and has allowed private schools to reopen. As in the old system, all students are taught the same curriculum until the fifth grade. They then decide whether they want to focus on the subjects in humanities or natural sciences. Although students take courses in both areas, more emphasis is placed on the chosen curriculum. Russian students who plan to attend a technical school graduate in the ninth grade, while those who want to go to college take two additional years of school.

These reforms have been hampered by the lack of funding. In 1997, teachers from seventy of Russia's eighty-nine provinces went on strike to protest wage arrears and salaries that are only 63 percent on the average national wage.[36] The problems of the educational system have led to 1.5 million school-age children who neither study nor officially work. This educational limbo in turn has caused a sharp increase in the teenage crime rate, which accounted for 68 percent of all reported crimes in Moscow in 1996.[37]

Higher education is in even worse shape. Most universities have had their budgets cut drastically. The lack of money has lead to a sharp cutback in scholarships and grants for needy students. In addition, entrance requirements have been relaxed to accommodate students who can afford to pay tuition but lack the requisite test scores. Finally, since most faculty members receive their wages months late if at all, many have taken jobs outside academia.

Social and Peer Groups

Children as young as eight were forced to enroll in peer organizations—Young Octoberists—in which socialist values were taught. At age ten or eleven, children were enrolled in the Young Pioneers. In secondary school, the majority of the students joined the communist youth organization, the Komsomol. Although membership in these organizations was not mandatory, membership was a de facto prerequisite for many things—from a seaside vacation to attending a university. In addition, the only way to become a Party member was through the Komsomol.

There were also many social groups in the Soviet Union. Examples included sports clubs, women's groups, and so forth. However, they were neither voluntary or spontaneous, but rather institutional and controlled by the Party. Because of the boredom factor and a tendency to exercise excessive control, their value as socialization organs was limited. This can be seen in the quick downfall of the regime in spite of the fact that most people had been subject to lifelong ideological training.

Today peer organizations no longer exist, and because of budgetary reasons and a lack of interest, the number of social groups has dramatically decreased. While this trend can be seen in the context of a move towards a more pluralistic society, the demise of these groups has left a vacuum in society. Children no longer have role models, and the street and friends are the main factors in their socialization.

Mass Media

All sources of information—radio, television, movie studios, news agencies, printing plants—were under government control and published only official or pro-governmental information, including exhortatory articles and detailed production statistics. Items frequently seen in the West, such as human interest and political corruption stories, were usually omitted. The media's primary goal was to indoctrinate and mobilize the population, not to provide entertainment—as anyone who has every watched a Soviet movie can testify—or act as a check on the government.

The most important institution for controlling the press was the censor. Censors who could forbid the appearance of a an article or book existed almost as a state within the state. Censorship was imposed according to unwritten laws, and the censor's decisions could not be appealed. Although today the media are no longer censored or controlled by the state, they have yet to become truly independent.

BROADCAST MEDIA.   In the early 1990s, over 150 independent television and radio stations were opened. Within a few years, however, the cost of production, air time, electricity and other costs skyrocketed. This cost increase led to the concentration of ownership in a few holding companies. For example, Vladimir Gusinsky's Most bank group controls the Independent Television Network (NTV), Ekho Moskvy radio, and the daily newspaper *Segodnya*. It also partly owns several publications, including *Novaya Gazeta* and *Obshchaya*. Gusinsky and other media tycoons have become so powerful that they are consulted on almost every issue of national importance.[38]

Yuri Luzhkov (1936–)

Yuri Luzhkov, the current mayor of Moscow, is a serious contender to be the next Russian President. His short temper, sharp tongue, and obsession with mundane details have helped him to manage the Russian capital effectively amid all the distress of the post-Soviet era. Today, Moscow boasts the sole concentration of wealth within the country and receives two-thirds of foreign investment and four-fifths of all Russian capital. The city has average incomes over 200 percent higher than anywhere else in the country and, with only 6 percent of the total population, produces 13 percent of Russia's annual GDP. This success is largely a result of Luzhkov's push in 1992 to give Moscow an exemption from federal schemes to privatize state assets. As a result, the city has a share or partnership in over 200 firms and a stake in most property developments. Both through the city's commercial activities and through Sistoma, a holding company to which he is close, Luzhkov wields unparalleled influence over the capitol's business.

Luzhkov's efforts have given Moscow the most developed system of law and markets in Russia. His success in the capital has led to his increasing influence and power at the national level. He has used this base to start a Moscow-based television network that will doubtless boost his political image. Already his name is repeatedly mentioned for prime minister, and he is a serious contender for the presidency in 2000. A June 1998 poll found that 9 percent of Russians wanted Luzhkov to be the next president. Until then, though, Luzhkov is biding his time, using his mayoral position to enhance his national stature.

These information empires were assembled to compete for privatized state property and to attack political opponents. As an illustration, before the 1996 auction of shares in the state telecommunications firm, the media hurled charges of corruption, financial abuse, and theft against rival bidding groups. Television stations have become so important that Moscow mayor—and likely presidential candidate—Yuri Luzhkov created a countrywide network in 1997.

While it is the most serious limit to an independent government, the concentration of media is not the only limit. Because of its capacity to influence public opinion, the government still tries to influence the media. In 1995, Yeltsin dismissed Oleg Poptsov, head of Russian television and well known for his liberal views and political independence. Yeltsin accused Poptsov of giving the public too gloomy a picture of the situation and ignoring positive achievements. In general, "the presidential team has tried to tighten its grip on the media, especially on television."[39] Although the charges were later dropped, the Procurator General charged the popular political satire show *Kukly* with insulting the honor and dignity of government officials.[40]

PRINT MEDIA.   The end of the Soviet regime led to the creation of thousands of new publications. In mid-1995, the State Press Committee announced that 10,500 newspapers, most with print runs of less than 10,000, were published in Russia. However, the end of state subsidies led to dramatic increases in production and distribution. This situation led to a clash between Russia's free press and a market economy. Under the old system, the state monopoly, Soyuzpechat ("Union Press"), provided all the newsprint to newspapers and magazines and also maintained a USSR-wide production and distribution network. All prices were heavily subsidized, with subscribers paying only a fraction of the actual cost of the publication. Today the costs of publishing equal those of the West. In 1992 alone, there was a fortyfold price increase in the cost of newsprint.[41] But since the advertising market is small, only about 10 percent of the population can afford a daily newspaper subscription.[42] Although one would expect the number of papers to drastically decline as a result, there were still fourteen daily newspapers in Moscow and over 4,000 local papers in 1997. They survive through reduced government subsidies and money from owners who use them as partisan weapons in political battles. In a three-week period preceding the 1996 presidential elections, for example, none of *Pravda*'s fifty-six stories about Yeltsin was positive. Likewise, none of the sixteen stories about Zyuganov in *Izvestiya*, a pro-Yeltsin daily, had anything positive to say about Yeltsin's presidential rival.[43]

This problem is worsened by the lack of a libel law. Charges and countercharges cause the media to be viewed with suspicion, thus limiting the development of an independent press. A more serious problem is that bureaucrats increasingly contravene Russia's constitutional guarantees of press freedom. Examples include lease cancellations, denial of access to printing plants, arrests of reporters, and the denial of accreditation to journalists. Another impediment to a free press is a continuing state monopoly over distribution.

Because the press has been almost entirely taken over by financial groups, the independence of the media and ultimately freedom of speech—one of the few indisputable achievements of the post-Soviet regime—has been seriously deformed.[44] The irony of the situation is that because the media customarily attacks political opponents, there is a large degree of freedom of information. To get the complete picture, however, Russians must read at least half a dozen newspapers a day. Nonetheless, blatant attempts to restrict the media have failed, as shown in the clear failure of the government's campaign to mobilize support for the invasion of Chechnya in 1994. In summary, although Russia has a "freeish" press, it does not yet have a fair press. Since a free and objective press is a prerequisite for a democracy, this situation restricts political evolution.

To ensure the development of Soviet-style socialism, all Soviet client states had to adopt a similar system of political socialization and organization. Through direct party-to-party contacts, the Communist Party of the Soviet Union monitored the actions of local communist parties to ensure they followed the Soviet model. For all the effort put into molding the population, socialization had only a limited impact.

FORMAL GOVERNMENTAL INSTITUTIONS

The sudden end of seventy-five years of authoritarian government and the restoration of an independent Russia is both a tremendous opportunity and a enormous liability. The chance to create a new political system is an unusual occurrence. To build a new structure, however, the previous one must be dismantled. This would be a difficult process under ordinary circumstances, let alone one in which the economy is deteriorating and society is faced with rapid change. To chart the progress of the new regime, this section examines the previous Soviet governmental structures and compares them with their contemporary counterparts.

The Soviet System

Structurally, the government of the Soviet Union was similar to its Western counterparts. However, in contrast to Western governments, it had little power. It served mainly as the mechanism through which the Party controlled the polity.

Following the autocratic principles of "democratic centralism,"[45] the Party itself was organized on a hierarchical basis. At the apex of the party organization was the "political bureau" (*politburo*) of the Communist Party. It served as the collective leadership of the CPSU. Although its members were "elected" by a 400-person Central Committee, in reality the Committee merely ratified members selected by the Politburo. The most senior Party leaders were members of the Politburo. They included the General Secretary, the heads of the Moscow and Leningrad party organizations, the prime minister of the Russian Soviet Federated Socialist Republic (RSFSR), heads of the most populous or important of the fifteen constituent republics, and usually the foreign and defense ministers. Significantly, with the exception of the ministers and RSFSR prime minister, most Politburo members held no official government positions.

Another important Party body was the Secretariat. It served as the administrative arm of the Central Committee and was responsible for directing the party bureaucracy. This included the selection of Party members and supervising the implementation of Politburo decisions. The most important Soviet leaders were members of both the Politburo and the Secretariat. Membership in both bodies allowed them not only to create policy, but to oversee its implementation.

Since constitutionally the CPSU was the "leading and guiding force" of society, it was able to monitor and control the government bureaucracy at all levels, from the ministries in Moscow to rural villages. The Party thus maintained its supremacy over the government, making sure the state bureaucracy carried out Party policies. In addition to legal provisions, the Party was able to dominate the government through organizational means and its control over personnel appointments. At all administrative levels of the Soviet government, there was an interlocking relationship between Party and state agencies, in effect, a parallel administration. This allowed the Party not only to make policy but also, through its control of the state apparatus, control policy implementation. There were two important features of this structure. First, most government agencies had an equivalent party organization that supervised its government counterpart to ensure implementation of Party policies, for example, the Secretariat official in charge of agriculture supervised the Agriculture Minister. Second, in many cases local Party officials held positions in the government agencies they were supervising.

The CPSU also ensured control through its power to appoint all-important civilian and military leaders. Moreover, the *nomenklatura* list ensured that all people in positions of responsibility were politically loyal. In short, under the Soviet regime , the CPSU controlled the polity.

The Constitution

The first Soviet constitution was adopted in 1918. It was not drafted by jurists and was not based on any other constitution. Instead, it was based on the revolutionary struggle, claiming to have replaced "bourgeois democracy" with "proletarian democracy." The land, resources, and banking system were nationalized, and all means of production were placed under "workers' control."

A second Soviet constitution was adopted in 1924 as a result of the formation of the Union of Soviet Socialist Republics. Other constitutions were adopted in 1936 and 1977. Although the constitutions were adopted for different reasons, they shared many similarities. First, all constitutions were permeated with Marxist-Leninist ideology. Unlike democratic constitutions that are regarded as repositories for sacrosanct political principles, the Soviet Union adopted new constitutions when "substantial changes occurred in the relationship of class forces in the country."[46]

Second, Soviet constitutions bore little relationship to constitutionalism, for they did not effectively restrain the government. Unlike the U.S. Constitution, they did not limit the role of the government. Instead, provisions in the Soviet constitutions dealt mostly with vague social and economic rights, such as the right to housing, medical care, and education.

Third, also unlike Western constitutions, Soviet versions imposed obligations on its citizens. Article 62 of the 1977 Soviet constitution stated that "the citizens of the USSR are obliged to defend the interests of the Soviet state and to promote the strengthening of its might and authority." This provision was often used to prosecute dissidents who criticized the regime.

If the constitution meant so little in practice, why did Soviet leaders consider it so important to periodically revise it? The answer is that the constitution legitimized CPSU rule. Article 6 made the Communist Party "the leading and guiding force of society" and gave the regime the appearance of a conventional political order. It is important to note that the Soviet constitution was adopted almost verbatim by its allies in Central and Eastern Europe.

Even though the Soviet Union ceased to exist in 1991, Russia continued to be governed by the 1977 constitution. Because it did not fit the changed political environment—that is, Russian independence, free elections, and the introduction of economic reforms—the constitution was changed on average once a day between 1991 and 1993. Although most political forces realized a new constitutional order was needed, there was no consensus on what form it should take. The two most contentious issues were the division of power between the executive and the legislature and the relationship between the federal government and the republics.

In June 1993, President Yeltsin created a Constitutional Assembly to draft a new constitution. Unlike previous drafts written by the Constitutional Committee of the Supreme Soviet, this one created a mixed presidential-parliamentary system with the presidency as the locus of power. Although controversial, the new constitution was approved in a December 1993 referendum. After two years of political infighting over the actors, powers, and functions of the new political order, Russia had a new constitution. However, as a hint of future problems, it was approved by only 28 percent of all eligible voters, or 52 percent of the total votes cast.

The Constitution declares the Russian Federation a democratic federative state based on the rule of law. Similar to the American Declaration of Independence, it recognizes human rights and freedoms as inalienable and notes that the protection of these rights is the obligation of the state. Unlike other new CEE constitutions, and perhaps as a legacy of the previous regime, Article 7 notes that the Russian Federation protects "people's labor and health" and guarantees state support for "the family, mothers, fathers, children, invalids and elderly citizens."

In contrast to the parliamentary regimes of Bulgaria and Hungary, where power and control over the executive is vested in their respective parliaments, power in Russia is divided not only between the three branches of government, but also between the federal government and the various territorial entities. The constitution also provides for an independent judiciary to ensure the rule of law and the protection of civil rights. The supremacy of the Constitution has been strengthened by the introduction of a Constitutional Court. Its role is to ensure the constitutionality of all laws and executive acts. To prevent the instability of the past, the constitution is difficult to change.

Amendments require the support of two-thirds of all members of the Duma, three-fourths of the Federation Council, and two-thirds of the eighty-nine regions.

Although the Russian constitution is democratic, its low approval rating points to some problem areas. First, many people are unhappy with the sweeping powers granted to the president. The Russian presidency is the most powerful elected position in the world, dwarfing the powers of its counterparts in the United States or any other European state; the "power ministries" (defense, foreign affairs, intelligence and police) are directly under presidential control.

Another major area of contention is the relationship between the federal government and the republics. Included within the new constitution was the 1992 Federal Treaty, which defined the rights of the republics. This treaty has been criticized for ceding too much power to local authorities, thus threatening the stability of the federation. Constitutionally, the twenty-one republics have more power than American states. The central government has power to act only in areas of joint competence.[47] Examples include the protection of civil rights, foreign affairs, defense, and banking. Another problem is the failure to implement all the provisions of the constitution. According to Constitutional Court Justice Ernst Ametistov, more than forty constitutional clauses lack the enabling legislation to bring them into force.[48]

In spite of these shortcomings, the adoption of a new constitution was an important step toward creating democratic institutions and a law-based state. Unlike its Soviet predecessors, the new constitution cannot be changed by a simple executive order. More significantly, for the first time in Russian history there is a constitutional order which clearly defines and delineates the powers of each branch of government as well as the political process.

Regional and Local Government

Throughout most of its history, Russia has been a centralized state. Although it was officially a multiethnic empire under the Tsars, Slavs (Russians, Ukrainians, and Belorussians) dominated the government, leading Lenin to refer to Russia as the "prison-house of nations." Local self-government was not introduced until the latter part of the nineteenth century. Although it spread rapidly until the 1917 Revolution, local government became an agent of the central government after the communists took power. In effect, local government ceased to exist.

As post-Soviet Russia seeks to define its new identity and borders, the civil war that engulfed Chechnya has become symbolic of the problems Moscow faces in defining a new relationship between the center and the periphery.

Federalism

The Soviet Union was divided into union republics, autonomous republics, autonomous regions (oblasts), and national areas (okrugs). Although constitutionally the Soviet Union was a federal state in which territorial units had autonomy, in practice they had none. This was because Moscow did not give the republics independent taxing power and republican budgets were subordinated to the official state budget. Also, as a result of democratic centralism, the non-Russian republic Party organizations had to follow orders from Moscow, thus negating local control. The Soviet "division of powers" left few matters exclusively in the hands of the republics, allowing Moscow to dominate them. As an illustration, although Article 80 of the 1977 Constitution gave the republics the right to enter into foreign relations and participate in international organizations, this right was negated by Article 73, which gave the USSR the right to "establish the general order and coordination of the relations of union republics with foreign states and international organizations." In addition, since there was no constitutional court the republics had no right of judicial review in defense of their powers against encroachment by the central government. In summary, although the USSR had some of the features of a federal system, in reality it was a unitary state with power exercised by a central government controlled by the Communist Party.

The new constitution declares Russia a federal state. It is divided into twenty-one republics, fifty-five provinces, eleven autonomous districts, and two federal regions (Moscow and St. Petersburg). Each of the twenty-one republics has its own constitution and its own president, and the autonomous areas have charters and their own governors. Overall, the republics contain 16 percent of Russia's population. However, in most of them Russian speakers are a majority.

The republics have the most autonomy and can be roughly divided into four groups.[49] The first group consists of the ethnic trouble spots, regions with below average income in which Russians are a minority. Most of them (Chechnya, Ingushetia, Kabardino-Balkaria, Karachevo-Cherkassia, North Ossetia and Dagestan) are in the Caucasus. Tuva and Chuvashia are also included within this group.

The second group includes large resource rich republics in the north (Komi, Karelia, and Yakutia). They have above-average incomes and ethnic Russian majorities. Unlike the first group, many of whom want independence, these republics simply want more control over their natural resources.

The third group includes the republics along the Volga River (Bashkortostan, Kalmykia, Mari-El, Mordovia, Tatarstan, and Udmurtia). They have oil, and straddle the railways and pipelines that link Siberia with European Russia. They are also home to a majority of Russia's 18 million Muslims. These republics want more autonomy and control over their resources. The fourth group are republics (Adygeya, Altai, Buryatia, and Khakassia) that have a majority Russian population and few resources. Although they too want more autonomy, they are dependent on central government largess.

The territorial governments have gained more power as a result of the dissolution of the Soviet Union and the adoption of the new constitution. This can be seen in the creation of the Federation Council, the upper house of the parliament. It is comprised of two members from each of the eighty-nine administrative units. In this regard, Russian regional governments are more powerful than their German counterparts because the latter send representatives to the Bundesrat—the upper chamber of the German parliament, based on population.

The constitution spells out the division of power between the regional and other federal units. Federal jurisdiction includes areas such as finance and budget, state security, and defense. There is joint jurisdiction over such areas as guaranteeing human rights, natural resources, education, health, law enforcement, protection of minorities, and foreign economic relations. Like the American constitution which guarantees that all powers not specifically given to the federal government are reserved for the states, Article 73 declares that outside the "joint jurisdiction of the Russian Federation and the components of the Russian Federation, the components of the Russian Federation possess state power in its entirety."

As noted before, despite the fiction that the Soviet Union was a federal system, in reality power was centralized. Is this also the case today? So far, the answer is no. However, this is the result of chance, the instability of the contemporary Russian polity, and the ambiguity of the constitution rather than deliberate policy. These factors have led to many disputes between the federal government and the territorial units. One of the most significant is the federal structure itself. Some regions are based on ethnicity and some on geography. Since the ethnic ones have more power, it is only a matter of time before the geographical regions demand similar powers. Another area of tension is related to autonomy of individual regions. According to Article 72, the "establishment of general guidelines for the organization of the system of the bodies of state power and local self-government" falls under joint jurisdiction. However, the specifics of autonomy have yet to be defined. As an illustration, the constitutions of nineteen of Russia's twenty-one republics include provisions defining a degree of sovereignty that violates the Federal Constitution. In addition, the collapse of the ruble, cutoffs of federal funds, and shortages of staple goods have forced provincial leaders to act. They have enacted states of emergencies, ordered price controls, forbade currency transactions across their borders, and even threatened to print their own money, all of which violate the constitution.[50] Approximately one-third of the 16,000 regional laws examined by the Justice Ministry since 1995 were found to violate federal legislation.[51]

Although Moscow has tried to discipline the regions, it lacks the power to do so. As an illustration, in January 1997 the Russian Constitutional Court ruled a number of Udmurtia's laws regarding local governments were unconstitutional. In February and March, President Yeltsin signed decrees to implement this ruling. They were ignored. The governor of Udmurtia even prevented the local television station from televising Yeltsin's annual presidential message in which he criticized the governor by name.[52] In another example, the president of the Russian autonomous republic of Bashkortostan had himself reelected after refusing to put opposition candidates on the ballot.

Prior to 1996, regional leaders were appointed by the president. Since they served at his pleasure, they usually supported presidential policies. With incumbents losing twenty-six of the fifty-three regional elections held between August 1996 and April 1997, this situation has changed. The most frequent victors were independents not tied to any party.[53] Thus the leaders of Russia's administrative districts now owe their allegiance to the electorate rather than Moscow.

In an attempt to secure the support of the new governors and thus counter the Communist-dominated Duma, the Yeltsin administration has negotiated bilateral power-sharing agreements with the thirty-nine regional governments.[54] These agreements provide subsides, tax breaks, and most significantly, a large measure of autonomy. The 1998 fiscal and political crisis in Moscow has accelerated the trend toward decentralization of power. This has allowed many regional leaders to act as local tsars, not only flouting their citizens' rights, but also the constitution.

Local Government

In addition to the national areas, the Soviet Union was also divided administratively into territories (*krais*), regions (*oblasts*), counties (*raion*), and federal cities.

The oblasts and krais occupied a crucial place in the Soviet hierarchy. Although subordinate to the fifteen republic governments, they controlled the raions, towns, and villages within their territory. At each level, a council (soviet) was elected to head the local administration. The major functions of the soviets were to approve annual budgets and implement economic plans within their jurisdiction.

When the council was not in session, which was most of the time, an executive committee—*ispolkom*—was elected. It administered the local budget and was responsible for the fulfillment of the economic plan and law enforcement. Moreover, it contained the heads of the most important administrative agencies. Significantly, the executive committee was responsible not only to its soviet, but to the executive committee of the next highest soviet. In addition, the whole structure of local government was duplicated by a parallel party structure. This helped ensure Party control of governmental institutions.

The oblasts were responsible for ensuring the health, social security, education, finance, culture, road construction, trade, police, agriculture, and industry within their areas. Raions were responsible for local issues. These included housing, retail trade, public health, sewage, power, public transportation, education, social security, and cultural activities. Again, the departments charged with fulfilling these functions were responsible to their counterparts at the oblast level. Although responsible for these areas, local governments did not have the financial resources—they could not levy taxes—or the authority with which to fulfill them. City officials were often overruled by industrial enterprises whose managers answered not to local officials, but regional or even state ones. Even local Party officials were helpless in the face of directives from Moscow.

In summary, the Soviet administrative system was characterized by extreme centralization and a hierarchical system of county, municipal, and village councils that functioned more as agents of state control than as advocates of local interests. This bred apathy on the part of local officials, a legacy Russia is still struggling to overcome.

Today, in addition to the thirty-two territorial units, Russia has fifty-seven self-governing administrative districts. These include six krais, forty-nine oblasts, and two federal cities—Moscow and St. Petersburg. Before we examine the organization and powers of local governments, an important caveat must be made. When reading the rest of this section, bear in mind that what is described is by no means common in each of the districts. Rather, it is what the system of local government should resemble according to relevant presidential decrees and provisions of laws that in some cases have yet to be enacted. (For example, while self-government has been actively introduced in Yaroslavl oblast, it is non-existent in Mordovia.)

Organizationally, each administrative unit has its own directly elected soviet. Soviets have the power to elect committees and establish local administrative offices. Unlike Bulgaria, Hungary, and Poland, each soviet may organize its administration differently. For example, some have decided to create a mayoral position; others have contracted specialists. This person is the focal point of power. Although the soviet has the power to control the local administration, it rarely does.[55]

In general, local governments are responsible for providing public services and those delegated to them by central government. They include housing, local transportation, health care, education, maintaining public order, environmental protection, and local development. To support these activities, councils have the power to levy taxes. In theory, local governments in Russia have more administrative autonomy than their Bulgarian and Polish counterparts. However, it remains to be seen whether this will actually occur as there are several major impediments to independent policy making.

First, and most important, is the lack of a uniform law on local self-government. As a result, localities elect their executive bodies in different ways. For example, the Yaroslavl oblast has an elaborate system of self-government of its own design, while in the Ryzan oblast, only towns and villages, but not raions, have representative bodies. In the absence of elected bodies of self-government, the districts are governed by appointed bodies. These bodies can hardly be called self-governing since they remain part of the administrative hierarchy that has always existed.

A second obstacle to local autonomy is the lack of financial independence. Local taxes and shared tax revenues account for only a small fraction of local budgets. As an illustration, the city of Tver was allowed to keep only 5 percent of its personal income tax, while the rest was taken by the Tver oblast administration.[56] As a result, municipalities are dependent on subsidies from the federal government. On average, the central government provides more than 75 percent of local funding. In 1997, only 12 percent of the regions are self-sustaining and net contributors to the federal budget.[57] This situation greatly lessens the autonomy of the municipality.

Another problem involves the division of powers between the central and the local governments. Since there are administrators representing more than forty different federal agencies in each region, they constitute an almost parallel local government. Unfortunately, the new constitution does not address this issue. It merely declares that the federal and regional governments may share their responsibilities with the local units unless this contradicts the constitution or other federal laws. This leaves a lot of room for interpretation.

Control over local governments may also be exercised by "Representatives of the President" who are appointed by, and directly subordinate to, the President. Their function is to "monitor" local governments to ensure presidential decrees and federal laws are implemented. If not, he or she informs the Prosecutor's Office about the violations. The representatives are new positions and have a role similar to a French prefect. However, in contrast to France, Russian officials have no right to interfere with the operation of local government. Only courts may annul resolutions passed by local governments. The power of the representatives was significantly increased by a 1997 presidential decree. They are now responsible for supervising the personnel of regional branches of federal agencies and coordinating the activities of regional branches of all federal agencies. This expansion of federal power weakens the power of local politicians.

Another obstacle to the development of local self-government is the reluctance of regional governments to devolve authority to local governments. For example, the Republic of Udmurtia Soviet turned mayoralties and other elected offices into appointed positions and nationalized city property.[58] In many areas local governments have been abolished by arbitrary decisions taken by higher administrations. Although they are blatantly unconstitutional, since the central government does not have the resources to force compliance with existing laws, these actions continue. The Russian/ Soviet legacy of centralized government is thus a large obstacle to the development of self-government in Russia.

Nevertheless, the election of regional governors will accelerate the process of devolving authority to the regions. While this is probably a healthy development in what used to be one of the most centralized states in the world, the consolidation of power at the regional level could come at the expense of federal and local prerogatives. Seemingly contradictory, this process could make local governments even more dependent on Moscow. Although Russian administrative districts have more legal autonomy than in other CEE states, in reality, as in Bulgaria and Poland, there is very little local self-government.

The Legislature

Before looking at the role of the various organs of government under the old regime, we must first examine the overall structure of the regime. While formally separate bodies had various legislative, administrative, and judicial functions, in reality the CPSU controlled the political system. This was done by creating parallel Party bodies that, because of the constitutional provision that made the Communist Party the leading and guiding force of society, were superior to their governmental counterparts. Thus the Party used the government structure to implement Party policies.

The legislative branch in the Soviet Union was comprised of the Soviet of the Union and the Soviet of Nationalities. Together they formed the Supreme Soviet, constitutionally the "highest organ of state power." Although in the formal and legal sense this was true, as with all official government structures in the Soviet Union, this was not the case. The Soviet of the Union was based on population, while the Soviet of Nationalities was based on representation for various national territorial units. Members of the Supreme Soviet were part-time nonprofessional legislators "elected" to show that all of society was represented. Both chambers had equal powers and an equal number of deputies (750 in each). Joint sessions were held to elect the Presidium—executive council—and the Council of Ministers. Each chamber had identical commissions, committees, and held simultaneous sessions. As a model of governmental efficiency, it would be difficult to top the Supreme Soviet. It had only two one-week sessions a year and all its votes were unanimous.

These features notwithstanding, the Supreme Soviet had no power. The Central Committee of the CPSU met before sessions of the Supreme Soviet and the latter body merely rubber-stamped decisions made in the Central Committee. Thus, the Supreme Soviet, although effective in passing legislation, had no impact on it. In addition, rather than representing the broad spectrum of society, the majority of deputies—70 percent—were Party members bound by "democratic centralism" to support Party policies. While it had no power, the Supreme Soviet did fulfill certain functions. Like the constitution, it was a source of legitimacy for the regime. In addition, the

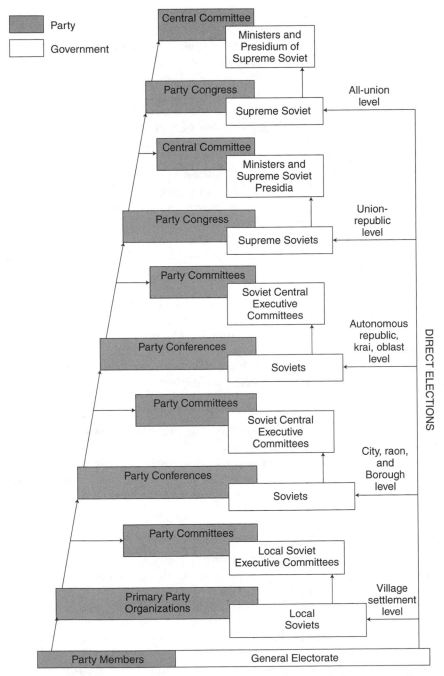

FIGURE 1.1   Overlap of the Communist Party Structure with Government Structure in the Soviet Union

participation of deputies in the work of the commissions provided opportunities for making Moscow officials aware of societal concerns.

The new constitution created a bicameral legislative structure. Designated the Federal Assembly, it consists of two chambers, the Federation Council and the Duma. Each body has specifically defined functions as well as shared responsibilities. The Duma consists of 450 deputies elected for four-year terms. The main powers of the Duma include approving the prime minister and the cabinet, initiating motions of confidence in the government, appointing the chairman of the national bank, and initiating impeachment procedures against the president.

The Federation Council was established to represent the provinces and ethnic republics. It is comprised of 178 members, two from each region. These officials are the governor and chairman of the regional legislature. Since each member's term is determined by regional legislation, members of the Federation Council, in contrast to the Duma, have no fixed term. Its powers include confirming border changes between members of the Russian Federation, confirming presidential declarations of martial law, deciding whether Russian military forces can be used outside Russia, appointing all high judicial officials, and scheduling presidential elections. To date, the Federation Council has been dilatory in performing its responsibilities because its members are so deeply enmeshed in provincial affairs that they lack the time to work in Moscow.

The Federation Council and Duma have joint responsibility for approving the federal budget and overseeing its implementation, overriding presidential vetoes, and ratifying international treaties. Both chambers can create committees and conduct hearings. In the Duma, committee chairmanships are handed out proportionally based on the number of seats held by each party. Overall, the structures and powers of the Russian parliament are closest to its Polish counterpart. However, because Russia is a federal state, the upper house has more power. For example, unlike the Polish Senate, the Federation Council participates in voting to override presidential vetoes.

The Electoral System

Under the old electoral system, the results of elections were known in advance. Even though it was officially a one-party state, the regime considered the legitimizing feature of elections so important that they developed a very elaborate electoral system.

Like the United States, the election of deputies to the Supreme Soviet was based on single-member districts. However, there was usually only one candidate in each district. Therefore, nomination was tantamount to being elected. Unlike the United States, candidates were selected not through a primary election, but by a unique process controlled by the Communist Party. After public discussions of the candidate's qualifications, the candidate was approved by acclamation. Since there were no competing candidates, the nominee would win the election with 99 percent of the vote. The actual voting process consisted of going to a polling station and dropping a preprinted ballot into a ballot box. This practice was rationalized by the explanation that it was a much more efficient system than its democratic counterparts. As a Soviet Communist Party member might say: "We think the possibility of making a wrong choice is reduced because we make the choice before the election."

The high voter turnout was the result of the Soviet practice of checking the voting roster on election day to see who had voted. If people did not vote, Party activists were dispatched to their apartment or work place to remind them of their civic duty. Refusal to vote was considered an unpatriotic act punishable by law. In addition, a person could vote in place of other family members. Despite their failure to give voters a choice between candidates or parties, the ritual of voting was maintained because it gave the regime the appearance of being democratic and having popular support.

The contemporary electoral system is a mixed proportional/plurality system that, like the Hungarian system, is based on the German model. It is designed to favor larger parties while still allowing smaller parties to gain representation. One-half of the seats—225—are elected by proportional representation. To fill any of the proportional seats, a party must receive at least 5 percent of the vote. For example, if the Beer Lovers' Party received 4 percent, it would receive none of the 225 proportional seats in the Duma. Only twelve members of any party may be from one territorial unit. The aim of this provision was to limit the proportion of deputies from Moscow and St. Petersburg. To register for an election, a party has to collect 200,000 signatures. This provision was included to ensure a party has widespread support. This laudable goal has been negated, however, since many parties have been able to "buy" enough signatures to register.

The other half of the Duma seats are filled by direct election in single-member districts. Candidates running in these districts must collect signatures from 1 percent of the voters in the district—approximately 5,000. While this provision was to ensure local interests were represented in the Duma, the lack of a second round runoff between the two top vote getters has allowed numerous extremists to gain seats.

This electoral system also causes numerous "wasted votes." This situation occurs when a party receives less than 5 percent of the vote. Since it did not overcome the electoral threshold, the party's votes are redistributed to parties that exceeded the threshold. This gives some parties influence far out of proportion to their electoral support. For example, although the communists won only 22 percent of the vote in the 1995 parliamentary elections, they ended up with 40 percent of the seats.[59]

To run for office, each candidate running in a single-member district must set up a special bank account to finance the campaign. The maximum a candidate can spend on their campaign is $120,000 dollars. In comparison, the average U.S. House of Representatives campaign costs over $400,000. The law also places strict limits on the amount a party or candidate can receive from various sources. Candidates can contribute only $12,000 to their own campaign, and a party can give only $18,000. The maximum a party can spend overall is $3 million dollars. Foreigners, local governments, state enterprises, military units, charity, and religious organizations are prohibited from making campaign contributions. However, since there are few mechanisms for monitoring party spending, these restrictions are frequently broken.

The Central Electoral Commission gives each party $18,000 for its campaign and all registered parties are given free and equal radio and television time. For elections to be valid, 25 percent of the eligible voters in an electoral district must cast ballots. These provisions notwithstanding, elections in Russia do not fulfill the democratic purposes for which they were intended— that is, governmental legitimacy, providing for meaningful citizen involvement in politics, and ensuring governmental accountability. As we will see, electoral outcomes mostly mirror informal political alignments.

The Executive

During the communist period, the highest executive and administrative state body was the Council of Ministers. Although it was appointed by the Supreme Soviet, ministers were selected in advance by the Party leadership. While the Council of Ministers was in theory similar to the cabinet in a parliamentary system, in reality it had few links with the Supreme Soviet. The main responsibilities of the Council were to carry out Party policies and oversee the running of the vast state bureaucracy. Most important, the Council was responsible for creating the central economic plan and ensuring it was implemented. As a result, it had the power to issue binding regulations and appoint the staff of ministries and state committees.

The Council was an extremely large body with over 100 members. It was headed by the Chairman of the Council of Ministers—that is, the prime minister, who was also a member of the Politburo. Members of the Council included the heads of numerous ministries, state committees, and other administrative agencies. Because of the Council's large size, however, the real decision-making power rested in its Presidium. Like the Presidium of the Supreme Soviet, this was a permanent body whose members held leading positions in the Party. Consequently, important policy-making decisions were made in the CPSU Politburo. When Prime Minister Tikhonov resigned in 1985, his letter of resignation was addressed to the General Secretary of the Communist Party, not to the Chairman of the Presidium of the Supreme Soviet, to whom the prime minister is constitutionally responsible.[60]

Although the new constitution created the position of prime minister and designated that person as head of government, the president is the focal point of power. While the prime minister is approved by the Duma, he or she is nominated by the President. In contrast to Bulgaria, Hungary, and Poland, the prime minister can only be removed from office after two votes of no confidence. Even if removed by a second vote of no confidence, the president can dismiss the prime minister rather than disbanding parliament and calling for new elections. The president also has the right to preside over sessions of the Council of Ministers. Thus, unlike other states in the region, the government is not independent of the presidency.

Like its Soviet counterpart, the Russian government is a large body.[61] Retaining the name Council of Ministers, the government is comprised of the prime minister, ministers, the chairs of various state committees, and the heads of various federal agencies. Members are jointly selected by the president and the prime minister.

There are three significant differences between the Russian government and its counterparts in other CEE states. First, the government is not responsible for creating state policy. Although it has the power to draft the federal budget, its main responsibility is to implement policy. Second, the president can fire any member of the government, or the entire government, at any time. As a result, the government is directly accountable to the president. Thus, the parliament has little control over the Council of Ministers. This is the result of two key factors. First, since the prime minister is appointed by the president, he or she does not need to have the support of the majority party or coalition in parliament. Second, the power ministers report directly to the president, not the parliament.

The Presidency

Uniquely, the Soviet regime had a collective head of state. The Presidium of the Supreme Soviet was "elected" by a joint session of the Supreme Soviet and consisted of a chairman, a first vice chairman, fifteen vice chairmen, and twenty-one other members. The Presidium performed many different functions and illustrates the fusion of legislative, executive, and quasijudicial power that typified the Soviet system.

While in theory it was accountable to the Supreme Soviet, in practice the Presidium exercised independent powers, functioning as the highest organ of state authority between sessions. This is because leading members of the Presidium were also leading members of the Communist Party. The Presidium merely legitimized laws drafted by the Politburo. For example, although Brezhnev was head of the Presidium, his power derived from his position as General Secretary of the CPSU. Thus the leader of the Communist Party was always a member of the Presidium. This gave the General Secretary a prestigious governmental position so that he could participate in purely state or diplomatic functions to which his title as General Secretary of the CPSU did not entitle him. Powers of the Presidium included issuing decrees with the force of law, amending the Constitution, appointing ambassadors, and proclaiming martial law. The Presidium's quasijudicial powers included granting pardons and "giving interpretations of the laws of the U.S.S.R." (Article 121). Meetings of the Presidium were not public and little is known about them.

In July 1991, Boris Yeltsin became the first popularly elected president in Russian history. However, his powers were largely dependent on the parliament because it could easily amend the Constitution. In November 1991, as a result of his overwhelming popularity after the August coup attempt against Gorbachev, the parliament granted Yeltsin special powers to conduct radical economic reforms. These reforms strained the relations between the executive and the legislature. When the parliament severely curtailed his powers in July 1993, Yeltsin ruled largely by presidential decrees. To overcome the parliamentary opposition, he convened a Constitutional Assembly and dissolved the parliament.

As a result of Yeltsin's influence in drafting a new constitution, the presidency was given significant powers. Unlike his CEE counterparts, the president has full control of the executive branch. He can initiate and veto legislation, dissolve the Duma, and hold new elections provided at least a year has passed since the last parliamentary election. In addition, the president has the constitutional power to issue decrees on any subject—without parliamentary approval—as long as they do not contradict existing law. Yeltsin has used this power to strengthen his control over the executive branch by creating a powerful presidential administration. Departments for economic analysis, finance, personnel, security, and foreign affairs have been established in the presidential apparatus. They were created to "provide the President with control over government policy."[62]

The president is also head of state and commander-in-chief of the armed forces. Shared powers include the ability to appoint all high judicial officials—with the consent of the Federation Council—and appointing the Head of the Central Bank—with the consent of the Duma. The president is elected for a four-year term and cannot hold office for more than two consecutive terms. To run for office, a presidential candidate must gather a million signatures. The Russian electoral system is modeled on the French two-ballot system. If no candidate wins an absolute majority in the first round, the top two vote getters meet in a second round three weeks later.

The power of the Russian presidency is demonstrated by the fact that while the Polish President—the next most powerful Central and Eastern European president—must have his executive orders countersigned by the prime minister, the Russian government is constitutionally bound to implement presidential decrees. These powers make for a strong presidency. There are, however, some checks on its power. First, the Duma has to ratify the appointment of the prime minister and other officials. However, if the Duma rejects three nominees, the president can dissolve it. Second, it can overturn a presidential decree by a two-thirds majority. In addition, the Duma can impeach the president and pass a vote of no confidence in the government. However, in contrast to Poland, the president has the right to ignore the first no confidence vote. If another is taken within three months and fails, the president can dissolve the parliament, forcing new elections. This provision makes the no confidence vote unattractive for the parliament. Thus the checks and balances between the Russian president and parliament are strongly tilted in favor of the former. This situation fosters instability as either the president or the parliamentary majority can dismiss cabinet ministers, creating a high turnover in ministers. Combined with the president's decree power, these factors make conflicts over legislation especially intense—causing political instability—as Yeltsin has often tried to impose policies that lacked legislative support.[63]

The Federation Council balances the military powers of the presidency through its power to decide whether the armed forces can be deployed outside the country. Inside Russia, the president can declare martial law only with its consent. For the first time in Russian history, there has been an attempt to define the responsibilities of both the executive and legislative branches. Not only does identifying these responsibilities make the governing process more transparent, it also acts as a check on the executive.

Although constitutionally the Russian president is the most powerful elected democratic president in the world, in practice the recent slow pace of economic and political reforms shows that in the absence of fully functioning political institutions, the president's powers are more theoretical than real.

The Judiciary

One of the basic characteristics of the Soviet legal system was that it was used an instrument of state policy. Unlike law in Western democracies, Soviet law was to serve state interests, not protect individuals. Like its Tsarist predecessors, the Soviet judiciary was more interested in social control than in pursuing truth and justice. Thus Soviet courts, law schools, judges, and legal professions were all parts of an integrated system under the scrutiny of the Communist Party. Examples included judges calling local Party officials before delivering a verdict—"telephone justice"—and surveillance of judges by the Ministry of Justice.

Russia took a major step in breaking from its past and creating a law-based state with the adoption of the new constitution. It provides for an independent judiciary, protection of civil rights, and constitutional oversight. Like most other European states, the legal system is based on civil law.[64] The new system also provides for jury trials and an "adversarial" legal system. Thus the new system is a combination of European and Anglo-American jurisprudence. Organizationally, justice is administered by the Constitutional Court, the Supreme Court, the Arbitration Court, regional courts, and "People's

Courts." Justices of the Constitutional, Supreme, and Arbitration Courts are appointed by the president and confirmed by the Federation Council. Lower court judges are directly appointed by the president. With the exception of Constitutional Court justices, all judges have unlimited tenure and cannot be removed from office unless they break the law.

The Constitutional Court is comprised of nineteen members who are selected for twelve-year terms. It is divided into two chambers, one with ten members and the other with nine. Both chambers can rule on any constitutional issue and have a rotating chairmanship.[65] As its name implies, the Court ensures that laws conform to the constitution. It has the power to challenge and overturn acts of the president, the government, the parliament, and Russia's twenty-one autonomous republics. Uniquely, the Constitutional Court must give its approval before any attempt to impeach the president can proceed. Similar to the U.S. Supreme Court, the Russian Constitutional Court has the power of judicial review. When created, it was hoped the Court would become one of the main guarantors of the supremacy of law in Russia. However, it has been reticent to challenge the authority of the executive. For example, the Court refused to rule on a Federation Council petition that declared Yeltsin's deployment of troops in Chechnya illegal because he failed to declare a state of emergency, which would have had to have been approved by the Council.[66]

The Constitutional Court is only one part of the reorganized judicial system. Two other courts, the Supreme Court and the Arbitration Court, also play important roles. The Supreme Court is the "highest judicial organ" and oversees criminal and civil law as well as all lower courts. The Arbitration Court rules on "economic" disputes between companies.

Although the structure is in place to create a law-based state, there are still serious problems to be overcome. First, like other governmental bodies, the judiciary suffers from a lack of funding. In 1996, courts received only 35 percent of their requested allocations. As a result, in St. Petersburg a majority of the district courts were forced to shut down.[67] This lack of funding is a major obstacle to dealing with an increasing criminal and civil caseload. This situation also limits the adoption of constitutionally mandated jury trials. These trials, which strengthen the rights of defendants, are more expensive and time consuming than traditional judge adjudicated trials. As a result, in 1996 jury trials existed in only nine of the country's eighty-nine regions.

As in other areas of the polity, one of the greatest impediments to change is the legacy of the past. Russian justice is still steeped in the Soviet tradition, where prosecutors ruled. "Our courts have always been part of a repressive system," says Sergei Parshin, a Moscow judge and legal scholar.[68] This legacy of the past has led to numerous legal irregularities. First, a rapidly increasing crime rate—the result of a lack of laws on organized crime and corruption and fundamental changes in the polity—has led to the initiation of extrajudicial measures to combat it.

Living in Lawlessness

In 1992 I made a television film about an extraordinary man: poet, mathematician, and dissident Alexander Esenin-Volpin, who drove the ruling order crazy simply by appealing to the law. Esenin had taken the trouble to read and study the Stalinist constitution, and he declared it beautiful. The problem was that no one used it—neither Stalin nor the people. Esenin decided to give it a try. Supported only by the law, he wrote a memorandum titled "How to Behave During Interrogations," which was used in the early 1960s by all dissidents who anticipated arrest. Never did I think that I would be using it thirty years later in the "new" Russia.

On December 5, 1965, Constitution Day, Alexander Esenin went out to Pushkin Square in the middle of Moscow with a poster that read: "Respect Your Own Constitution." Another proclaimed: "We Demand Glasnost in the Trial of Sinyavsky and Daniel." The posters merely called for obeying the Constitution. Esenin was arrested, not for the first time, but it was the first time that he was released on the same day. "You don't arrest people for carrying posters proclaiming 'Long Live May Day!' on May First," Esenin said, and that drove the system into a dead end.

No one before Esenin had thought to make the legal demand that the system obey its own laws. Vladimir Bukovsky, who was seeking a bloodless way to oppose the system, was delighted to use Esenin's concept, when he was arrested on the eve of a rally. I, too, accepted Esenin's idea as absolutely viable in all systems and countries, and I never failed, after meeting him, to ask everyone everywhere about the law.

To my great sorrow, the very first person with whom I had an opportunity to discuss the new laws of Russia, was Sergei Kovalev, a widely respected and beloved dissident and at that time Russia's first ombudsman, and he tried to evade the issue. My question was simple. I had entered the U.S. at the invitation of a university to lecture there and had stayed on after the failed coup of October 1993. A year later I learned that the Duma had passed a law replacing the former Soviet passports with Russian ones. The Russian Consulate General in New York refused to issue me a new passport, explaining that, according to the law, a new passport must be received at my permanent domicile—in Moscow. They then fined me $50, extended my passport, and told me that the passport was good for entering Russia.

My only question to Sergei Kovalev, who was in New York at that time, was: Where can I get a copy of the law on the new passports so that I can familiarize myself with it? My problem was that I was planning to go to Russia to see my dying mother and the American authorities were allowing me four weeks for the trip. I had heard rumors that it took two to three months to get a new passport. That was impossible for me, not only because of the four-week deadline but because my fourteen-year-old son would be home alone. Kovalev looked at me intently and said, "Come to Russia, we'll take care of your passport."

I was saddened. Naturally, I wanted the passport, but not through friendship or connections, as an exception, but according to the law. I asked friends at

major international human-rights organizations to request officially information on the law from Russia. They were all given the same evasive answer. The
law existed, but it was for domestic use and was applied individually, according to the specific circumstances.

I recalled how Esenin had ended up in America. He—the son of the Russian
peasant-poet Sergei Esenin—fought for the right of Soviet Jews to emigrate to
Israel. The day came when he was called to the KGB headquarters at Lubyanka
in Moscow and ordered to write a request to leave for Israel. Esenin tried to
explain that he personally did not wish to move to Israel, that he had been
fighting for the right of others to do so. "If you don't want to go to the Near
East, you'll go to the Far East," KGB officer snarled, a reference to Siberia. That
comment eventually turned into a joke. Esenin left, but for America.

And so, armed only with the passport of a nonexistent USSR, I landed at
Moscow's Sheremetyevo Airport in the fall of 1997. I was first in line at passport control. On seeing my passport, a sleepy young women woke up immediately and pushed a button under her counter, crying out almost joyfully for her
superior officer. I was told to step to the side because I was subject to "administrative detention" for "administrative violations." I knew where I was going
and knew what to expect, so I calmly moved aside. Her high heels clicking in
military rhythm through the gray corridor, the duty officer in a green army uniform came out, did not introduce herself, and demanded to see my passport.
She opened it, looked through it quickly, and said gleefully that I had to pay a
fine since my passport had expired.

"It was extended at the Russian Consulate, where I already paid," I said.

"I don't know what you paid to whom in America," the soldier said with
contempt. I learned later from her signature on the protocols that she was Lt.
L. I. Emets of military unit 9939. "You pay us here, and then you can go."

"How much?" I asked.

"$100," she quipped.

"I'm not going to pay a second time," I said firmly.

"Then, you won't get in."

I asked Lt. Emets to show me the law on which my detention was based and
which determined the amount of the fine.

"Not allowed," she said, with a smirk.

I asked her to call her superior. Citizens to the right and left of me meekly
determined the sums they had to pay, went off to a corner of the dimly lit airport, and paid. Soon I was the only one left in the corner where I had been told
to sit. About 15 young women, stocky and solid, dressed in the green border-
patrol uniforms, sat down opposite me, lit up cigarettes, and crossed their legs.

"What's she sitting there for?" one asked, nodding at me.

"Too cheap to pay!" another explained. "Wants to see the law."

"Hah! Let her sit, then!"

A sleepy-looking man in a different uniform, with a crumpled white shirt,
came over, looked at my passport, and said, "You have to pay."

"How much?" I asked.

"$100," Lt. Emets quickly prompted him.

"Or at least $73," he said, almost beseechingly, into my ear.

"What's that amount?" I asked, stifling a laugh.

"Minimum monthly wage times five, in dollars, at today's exchange rate," he said in a polished phrase.

"I see," I replied. "I'm willing to pay." I paused to note the gleam of triumph in the eyes of the smoking women in uniform. "On the condition that you show me the law."

"Believe me, it exists," the man said, intimately and seductively. "And it will indicate a much higher sum."

"I'm prepared to pay more, but it is my right to know what law I have violated," I said firmly, like a young Pioneer in opposition to senior comrades— like Esenin, Bukovsky, and Kovalev, who had dreamed of finding a form of bloodless resistance to the regime. The man in the crumpled shirt, with the shoulder boards of a branch of the military unknown to me, went off, having spoken a few words to the lieutenant.

Thus was the first hour of my dialogue with the authorities. In a friendly tone, I told the lieutenant that she would be facing a lot of trouble, not only because detaining me and demanding money from me were illegal but also because my luggage was surely getting lost because of her, and the people who were meeting me would call America, find out that I had taken the plane, and start a fuss. And, furthermore, I had an appointment at the Ministry of Foreign Affairs for the express purpose of getting my new passport, all in accordance with the law that passports had to be sought in one's place of residence, and that I would definitely inform them of the cause of my tardiness.

She very much hated me. She paged the people meeting me and soon my girlfriend appeared at the glass wall. She works in television and as soon as she learned what was causing the holdup, she said: "Pay them immediately and let's get out of here. You can't argue with them."

"No," I said and added that it wasn't the money, but the principle. She shook her head sadly at the sight of a person who had lost her mind and who hadn't learned a thing even in America. She went back to waiting. I had given her several telephone numbers to call if things dragged on. Since they weren't beating me, I didn't want to bother Kovalev.

"I insist that you call someone who can take decisions," I told the border-guard lieutenant.

"They're all in a meeting," she responded.

"All right then, you act. This can't go on forever," I said.

I don't know what prompted her to act, but she gave a few curt orders, and one of the smokers, a neat and bewildered female soldier, Corporal E. V. Kryazheva, started writing. I watched as Lt. Emets handed her the various "documents," inserting carbon paper; the corporal, apparently the only literate one in the group, crafted letters, checking with her superior.

I quote the texts in full here only because I had the rare opportunity, for a Russian citizen, to show them to someone at the Ministry of Foreign Affairs, who then explained that all of the documents were invalid.

The first was the protocol on an Administrative Violation, which gave the reasons for my detention: "a passport which had expired, which is a violation of crossing the border of the Russian Federation" and also of Art. 183.1 of the Code of Administrative Violations of the RSFSR. The second, the Resolution on Imposing an Administrative Penalty, read that commander of Army unit 9939 (with "acting commander" penciled in) Colonel V. V. Krysanov had acquainted himself with the case and determined that I had violated Art. 183.1 of the Code. "In accordance with Art. 30 of the Law of the Russian Federation on the State Border of the Russian Federation and Art. 261 of the Code of the RSFSR on Administrative Violations, I resolve to impose a fine in the sum of five times the minimum monthly wage. The execution of the resolution has been entrusted to Chief of the Sixth Section Kovalchuk"—with a copy for me. At the end, the document read: "This resolution can be appealed in court." Signed: "Commander Military Unit 9939 Major General Krysanov."

I wanted to laugh in their faces, even though things were very unpleasant.

"Sign the protocol," Corporal Kryazheva demanded. "Here—'signature of the violator.'"

"Never," I said with a smile.

Then write, 'refused to sign,' " Lt. Emets commanded.

The poor corporal scribe, accustomed to taking orders, added in my refusal. I am extremely grateful to her. Because now I have a document that shows how well I learned from the heroes of my television programs, for I had remembered from "How To Behave During Interrogations" not to sign protocols—ever.

As a favor to the corporal, I signed the notification of the proposed fine. When I was back in America, I let my son figure out the minimum monthly wage in Russia. He grabbed the calculator in disbelief, to recheck his mental calculations, when he came up with $13 and change. A fourteen-year old, he had made $15 an hour at his summer job. But that was all later.

For now, I was still in a gray corner, held in isolation, when a new character appeared—a small man in civilian dress, covered with beepers, pagers, and with a cell phone in hand. His eyes could barely open in the grip of his heavy hangover. "The consul on duty," the border guards explained. He opened my passport, shut it, and said to them—not me—"PWC," and turned to leave. Here I spoke loudly for the first time, so that my friend could hear over the glass partition that separated us, "Explain so that I can understand." "You are declared a Person Without Citizenship," the duty consul said. To which I responded: "And if I do not agree with you, since I consider myself a person with citizenship, where can I appeal, to argue with your opinion?"

"Wherever you want!" he said, carelessly waving his arm in the air. But he did not leave. "All right. Then tell me, on what basis, on what document, are you prepared to recognize my Russian citizenship?" (Besides with my dollars, I thought to myself.)

"Internal passport," he said, watching as I took out IDs from my purse—membership in the Cinematographers Union, my pass at the television station, my Dramatists Union card.

"All right, in thirty minutes I will show you my internal passport, and what then?" I asked.

"Yes!" the lieutenant demanded. "What do we do then?"

"Up to you," the duty consul barked and fled the battlefield.

The border guards sat all the while and smoked, as if they were paid to do so.

"What's his name?" I asked the lieutenant quietly and clearly.

"I don't know!" she exclaimed desperately. "He's simply the duty consul for us."

"I don't believe you," I said and shut my eyes in my dark corner. My friend had gone for my internal passport. I could hear the lieutenant and corporal put a kettle on and put out cups for tea. Lt. Emets then went on to work on a crossword puzzle. I'll never forget her loud voice calling out, "Ancient head covering, starts with M and ends in Y." The whole group guessed for quite a while, not getting it. Without raising my eyelids, I shouted even louder than she had: "Malakhay!" A terrible silence ensued. "It fits," the lieutenant whispered.

My internal passport was delivered. The unit was paralyzed, watching the lieutenant return my foreign passport, copies of the protocols, and the notice of a fine. She muttered something about my having to go through them again to leave the country. There was a real threat in her voice. "We'll discuss that then," I said and nodded agreeably. I left that strange corner where I had lost four hours of precious time.

Then came Russia. I needed to get to Ukraine. For that, I had to get something from the police—some kind of pass. The police precinct was guarded by a policeman with a submachine gun over his chest.

"Reason for travel?" he asked.

"My mother is dying."

"Telegram notarized by a doctor! Sent no more than two days ago."

"I don't have a telegram. They called me. I have a ticket reserved. I'll go without the pass," I said. He realized I wasn't kidding, and he told me to write down the number of an account into which I had to transfer an enormous sum of money and then to bring him a copy of the deposit slip. I did it all, waiting in an incredible line at the bank. Two hours later, he stuck a blue piece of paper into my passport stating that I was a Russian citizen.

The train started and a new nightmare began. Every three or four hours the train would stop and the door to my expensive compartment ($100!) would be opened by a special passkey from the outside, and a tall creep with a submachine gun would appear. "Documents!" he would shout, looking forward to some profit. "Citizen of where? Where are you headed? Reason for travel?" After three more hours, a group of big young men appeared—suddenly—like the first fellow, demanding to know in this case what I was carrying. Customs guards. And all the while, in the corridor behind them, people in civilian dress scurried around calling out, "Exchange, sell, buy marks, dollars, rubles, hryvnas."

And this was my route to Kherson, the city of my childhood. That was where the real hell started. There was hot water only two hours in the morning and two in the evening, and sometimes there was cold water all day. The stove didn't work, and it took me a while to find out from the building superintendent who could fix it. My mother was melting before my eyes, she needed morphine, and there was a law governing that, too.

I overcame all the obstacles, and a nurse, with a face I imagined was that of a drug addict, came to our house. My mother's friends cautioned me to look at the ampoule before the shot, to read what it said, and after the shot, to look at the syringe. They knew that the nurse often punctured the vein but did not inject the medication. I hated to do it, and I saw how angry it made the nurse, but I watched her closely. My mother stopped screaming in pain. And then she stopped breathing.

The law required a series of actions, and my friends and I took them, step-by-step—registering the death, getting the certificate, and on and on. Everyone told me I had better go to the cemetery in person to make arrangements.

An enormous woman was sunning herself on a bench. I explained that I wanted to bury my mother where my grandmother already was. "A coffin on top of another, that's eight hryvnas. Pay at the bank, bring me the receipt," she said. "All the rest you negotiate with the grave diggers."

They wanted 120 hyrvnas. I gave them half without a murmur, but when we arrived at the cemetery, there was no one near my grandmother's open grave. Helpless old men and women had accompanied my mother's coffin. The driver of the funeral van took a look and said, "Wait, I'll go find them." This was a well-rehearsed routine; the grave diggers were waiting around the first bend. He brought them back, and they demanded an additional amount. I merely nodded, and the coffin was lowered.

Then I had to deal with the privatized apartment. My mother had spent a lifetime waiting for a change for the better, from the end of the war when the Soviet army had freed her from a concentration camp in Germany. I believe she was one of the first to privatize her apartment, so that she could pass it on to her children. But the certificate of privatization was not to be found in any institution. Nor did I know where she had hidden her will. Her neighbors and friends knew that she had done everything in accordance with the law. An acquaintance, a former prosecutor, suggested I go to a special notary public office, the only one where they registered privatizations, and ask them—for a fee, of course—to reproduce the paperwork.

I had no time, no strength, and no desire to deal with this. Nor did I need the apartment. I've never been able to sell anything but my screenplays. And my mother's second husband, my son's beloved grandfather, was living in the apartment. What I needed to do was to make sure that he became the owner. I went to the housing authorities, where they first struck my mother off the residence list, leaving my stepfather as the only resident, which made the living space so large for one person that the fee he had to pay was greater than his pension. He panicked. A "nice man" appeared and told him that there was an organization that could help him by paying for the apartment. Of course, it would no longer be privatized (what had my mother paid for then?), and after his death it would again become state property.

I assured my stepfather that we would help out with the maintenance and that he should get the paperwork done. He became the "responsible apartment renter" and went off to the nearest notary, to have his will notarized, leaving the apartment to my son, his grandson. That's how I remember him: exhausted smile, will in hand, weary and proud that he had stood in all the necessary lines and had gotten all the paperwork done.

I arrived in New York in the evening. Until late that night, carefully choosing my words, I told my son how his grandmother had died, how we buried her, how his grandfather missed and loved him. "Let's think how we can bring him here," my son said. The next morning I was awakened by the telephone; it was the neighbor I had asked to keep an eye on my stepfather. I had given her my keys. She opened the door and found him on the floor. Dead. The autopsy showed that he had been killed. Someone he knew, because there were no signs of a struggle. "Quite possibly six months from now someone will show up with a deed of gift from him for the apartment," my former prosecutor acquaintance said bitterly. He added that murders for apartments had become quite common.

They died two weeks apart. My son and I had a memorial service for them in Manhattan. But my road back to New York had not been simple, either. My passport had been done for me not by the law, but out of friendship—by influential friends of friends. Quite cheaply—only $500. I no longer asked to see the law—I just wanted the passport. I had to hurry home from my mother's grave to my living son.

A friend, who works at Amnesty International and who was in Moscow for a conference, took me to Sheremetyevo Airport. No sooner did I show my passport than the customs officer smiled and said, "You're not going anywhere. Registration is closed."

"It closes 40 minutes before take off and it's only 55 before." He chuckled and said, "Then untie your luggage."

I had a cardboard box with old family photos, my son's drawings, and a few childhood books. He went through the yellowed letters of my grandmother with agonizing lethargy, then he nodded to a man waiting to one side, who came over and broke open my suitcase. He just cracked the whole lid. My friends were watching the whole thing. I was emotionless—I had been prepared for this meeting . . . my Homeland! But my friend from Amnesty lost her cool.

She stepped forward and shouted that she had come personally from London to make sure I got through the state border and that she was a witness of the authorities' violations of the rules. Without any particular show of emotion, the customs official indicated, with a nod, for the luggage wrecker to leave and then for me to go through.

There is a God. At the check-in, the uniformed woman told me that she could not accept a bag in that condition. I found twine in my pocket. I tied my suitcase up and turned it in.

I was the last to board the half-empty plane, and we took off. I am grateful to everyone who helped me. I now know from personal experience that almost all the stories about changes in Russia are lies. But I also know that the changes in Russia are enormous. I would not have survived if I had tried this in the old days. They would have broken my neck like a chicken's in that dark corner where I spent four hours mockingly solving their crossword puzzle and demanding that they show me the law. I know that the law exists. It is, as before, when Esenin read and studied the Constitution, beautiful. But, as usual in Russia, it does not work. No one reads it. But they will. I know for sure that, just as the dissidents taught the police and KGB a lesson during the trials of human-rights activists, the corporal scribe will remember me. For in her own hand she wrote down the position of a person in opposition to the authorities: "Does not consider herself a violator."

Source: Alexandra Sviridova, *East European Constitutional Review,* Winter 1998: 71–75.

Violent crime in the first part of 1995 was up 110 percent from 1994.[69] This included over eighty-four murders a day, twice as many as in the United States. A 1997 poll showed crime is the second most important public concern.[70] This is partly the result of Russia's headlong jump from a state-run economy to unrestrained capitalism. It has created a vicious environment where questionable business practices, corruption, and criminals go hand in hand. This situation is aggravated by a poorly paid, and consequently corrupt, police force. In 1996 alone, 21,000 police officers were fired for corruption, bribe taking, and ties with the mafia.[71]

To combat this situation, although the constitution stipulates that police cannot detain suspects for more than 48 hours without bringing formal charges, in 1994 Yeltsin signed a decree extending the period to 30 days. The decree also allowed the police to conduct searches without a warrant. Although this decree was finally struck down by the Constitutional Court in 1997, other decrees allow for arbitrary arrest and illegal search, seizure and detention. In addition, the right to a pretrial attorney is often overlooked, and although the constitution allows only judges to issue arrest warrants, prosecutors still have people arrested without a judge's permission. In criminal cases, over 90 percent of the defendants are convicted. This implies that either the police always get their man, or that trials are not fair. By April 1997, over 300,000 people were in prison awaiting trial—on average for ten months.[72] Overall, Russia has 694 prisoners per 100,000 inhabitants, the highest ratio in Europe.[73] While extreme times might call for extreme measures, there is a great risk that an attempt to establish order through unconstitutional means will destroy the foundations of the developing law-based state and open the way to arbitrary practices and human rights violations.

Another critical problem is corruption. Although judges are formally appointed by the president, they are often dependent on regional governors. Since judges depend on the goodwill of local politicians for perks that make up for mediocre salaries—middle-level judges earn less than half of what a secretary in a private company in Moscow earns—many judges follow their own interests by selling their verdicts to the highest bidder in commercial cases.[74] Under the communist regime, the sloppiness and servility of judges and lawyers did not matter much since they did what they were told. Now that the judiciary is independent, it must be professionalized to ensure it becomes nonpartisan and effective. As in most CEE states, the lack of experience with either constitutional democracy or an independent judiciary slows the development of a state based on the rule of law.

Perhaps the most significant problems facing the judiciary are the lack of judicial authority and a "tradition of disrespect for the law."[75] Since the law was used by the state to restrict rather than guarantee rights, most Russians follow the proverb that "wherever a court is, truth is absent." With over 50 percent of all court decisions routinely ignored, people often get entangled with organized crime to try to enforce contracts or to simply protect themselves. In summary, people have yet to see law as a means of protection.[76]

The danger for the future is that an entire generation is being raised that will turn not to official authorities, but rather to unofficial ones. These people are more likely to take the law into their own hands to pursue justice. In addition, until the state recognizes the rights of its citizens, democratic gains will be fragile at best. Between 1995 and 1997, the position of Human Rights Commissioner[77] was vacant after incumbent Sergei Kovalev was forced to resign for his outspoken criticism of the war in Chechnya. Firing a human rights advocate for opposing a war shows the concept of human rights is still developing in Russia.[78]

The Bureaucracy

In Western democracies, the focus of public and academic interest is usually on policy and ideology rather than on the bureaucracy. However, the bureaucracy is the arm of the government that ultimately has to deliver promises and interact with the public.

The Soviet administrative apparatus was probably the world's largest and most complex series of integrated bureaucratic structures. Since the state controlled all of society, all Soviet institutions were part of a single, giant bureaucracy. This gave the political leaders the opportunity to intervene in all spheres of life. Thus the common view that bureaucracies are neutral professional organizations, insulated from politics, was certainly not true in Central and Eastern Europe. Because of its sheer magnitude, the Soviet bureaucracy was distinguished by endless delays, evasive responses, arbitrariness, blind application of rules, and unresponsiveness. The servants of this system, the managers and bureaucrats, enjoyed job security. Many owed their positions to patronage rather than knowledge. This fostered poor performance and corruption.

These problems have grown worse since the end of communist rule. With the introduction of a market economy, many bureaucrats have combined public service with business activities. Since bureaucrats are now the virtually uncontrolled arbitrators of the distribution and control of state property, they have tremendous power. Combined with a lack of accountability and the breakdown of state structures, the scope for fraud, corruption and self-aggrandizement is broad.[79]

Some ministries are largely free of centralized control. For example, the Ministry for Nuclear Energy (Minatom) is not one of the "power ministries" that report directly to the president. Nor is it an economic ministry that reports to the prime minister. The ministry exists in administrative limbo, with no checks on its actions. This gives Minatom considerable freedom to sell nuclear technology, even if it conflicts with official government policy.[80]

In summary, the nonelected bureaucrat class still retains significant power in the Russian polity.

In an attempt to put an end to the situation in which the civil service becomes a source of personal enrichment, a law that forbade bureaucrats from working in the private sector was adopted in March 1991. This law did not have the intended effect since experienced bureaucrats simply quit their jobs to work in private businesses. Their replacements were "the ignorant, the inexperienced, and the dilettantes."[81] Yeltsin also enacted decrees that force cabinet ministers, parliamentary deputies, and other federal and regional officials to release income and property declarations as well as requiring companies to bid competitively for government contracts. To date, these measures have had little effect.[82]

Attempts to improve the civil service will continue to be ineffectual if high-ranking politicians continue to use the bureaucracy for their own personal interests. In spite of a law that forbids nepotism, Tatiana Dyachenko, President's Yeltsin's daughter, was made a presidential advisor in June 1997. This obvious violation of the law was explained away by a Kremlin statement that as a "category-A state official," the president is exempt from the law.[83]

A new recruitment procedure based on competitive examinations is desperately needed to bring stability and expertise into the public service. Unlike other states in the region, Russia has yet to introduce a law to professionalize the civil service. Since a large part of the economy is still controlled by the state, bureaucrats and politicians are reluctant to give up this important source of control and patronage, from which they profit handsomely in the existing unregulated environment.

Another obstacle to change is the lack of consensus on what role bureaucrats should play. In contrast with the West, where the power of bureaucrats is strictly limited, there are few limits in former socialist states. For example, in the United States someone who passes a driver's test and pays a fee cannot be denied a license. This is not the case in most of Central and Eastern Europe, where additional "fees" are often levied. Since bureaucrats have wide discretionary powers, they strongly resist reforms which threaten their power. Bureaucrats are also supported by people in the unreformed part of the economy—agriculture, oil and the defense industries—who know they cannot survive without state subsidies. Together they are a formidable obstacle to change. Ironically, because of a lack of alternatives, the very bureaucracy that ensured control in the old regime has now been given a central role in the process of creating a new polity. Thus, Russia today faces the worst of two worlds, a bureaucracy that is bloated and unwieldy, yet too weak and corrupt to enforce rules and regulations.

While these problems are present in all former socialist states, they are particularly acute in Russia because of a much longer period of bureaucratic control. They will remain until there is a change in societal attitudes, an unlikely event in the foreseeable future.

The Military

The role of the armed forces in society has always been an issue for every type of political system. The problem is how the state can utilize the military, with its indispensable professional knowledge and weaponry, to provide security for the state while at the same time preventing it from challenging the government.

The armed forces in the Soviet Union played a much larger role in the polity than their European or American counterparts. The Ministry of Defense was the largest governmental ministry and wielded enormous influence in military matters as well as overall public policy. The Soviet armed forces made the state a superpower, were a key agent of socialization, and helped preserve public order. As might be expected, Party-military relations followed an uneven course that depended on the degree to which the Party, or factions within it, had to rely on military support.

In order to ensure their control over the military, the Party used a variety of carrots and sticks. Perhaps most important was the requirement that all military officers had to become members of the Party. This requirement subjected them to Party discipline and control. A second tool of control was political indoctrination. This was part of the military training program and was conducted by the Party-controlled Main Political Administration (MPA). Officers not considered "reliable" were denied promotion or transferred to remote outposts. Another way to limit the power of the military was through the creation of other military units. In addition to the regular army, there were (and still are) sixteen other armed forces. As in the Soviet era, the largest today are the 250,000 interior ministry troops and the 200,000 border guards. These units were not and are not under control of the General Staff. Finally, the Party used secret police informers to infiltrate the ranks of the military.

These controls were supplemented with numerous incentives. The Soviet officer corps was a privileged class that had access to special stores, housing, and vacation resorts. Through these policies, the Party kept a tight rein on the military. However, at certain times, such as during a foreign policy crisis or a leadership struggle in the Party, the military was in a position to influence policy. Overall, even though the military was among the more powerful interest groups and disliked political controls, which were seen as an unwarranted intrusion on their professionalism, it was subordinated to Party control and was loyal to the regime.

The demise of Party control and changing domestic and international conditions have called into question the role and position of the military in the polity. The resolution of numerous short- and long-term problems will be key factors in determining what role the military will play in the developing system. Like other governmental institutions, the Russian military was greatly affected by the collapse of the economy and corresponding budget cuts. It has been forced to dig deeply into wartime stocks of food and fuel. In

July 1995, the Russian Defense Ministry said it did not have enough money to feed its troops. In some areas, food producers were refusing to deliver to army garrisons unable to pay for the food.[84] Training has been drastically curtailed, the air force in 1998 was able to conduct only 15 to 40 percent of its normal training flights. Less than 40 percent of the Ground Forces' eighty-one divisions are combat ready. Tanks and airplanes are falling into obsolescence and disrepair. More seriously, the central command of the Strategic Rocket Forces, which controls Russia's intercontinental ballistic missiles, had its power cut off because of overdue bills.[85] This incident caused many in the West to question the security of Russia's nuclear weapons.

Societal problems have also led to increasing draft evasion. Only 20 percent of military manpower needs are now met by the draft. In 1995, 250,000 men either dodged the draft, failed to report for reserve training, or neglected to register with their local military commissariat.[86] As a result, in contrast to the other CEE states, in 1995 Russia increased its length of service from eighteen to twenty-four months. A shortage of noncommissioned officers, men who would have sought military careers in the old days but are now drawn to higher-paying jobs in the private sector, means that even the 300,000 conscripts inducted each year receive little military training. The majority are used to sweep streets and help farmers at harvest time.

The officer corps has also been affected by societal problems. Because of persistent wage arrears, 29 percent of them live below the poverty line. This situation has led to an increasing suicide rate and widespread resignations. These problems have significantly weakened moral and combat readiness. The poor performance of the Russian army in Chechnya highlighted the leadership, manpower, and equipment problems facing the armed forces.

A more significant problem facing the armed forces is the development of civil-military relations. As noted, stability in Soviet civil-military relations was based on a generous funding of the military, a tradition of professionalism, and indoctrination and political control. These features have all crumbled since 1991. At the same time, new democratic institutions and instruments of control have yet to be firmly established. As a result, the military has had significant autonomy. Interestingly, although the military is impoverished, ill equipped, and ill disciplined, it still has the highest approval rating of any public institution.[87]

Noteworthy, civilian control of the military was not included in the new constitution. Thus parliament has no oversight over the military. Just as the absence of a stable legal framework has encouraged corruption and legal chaos in many areas of the economy, in the military sphere it has led to personalization and politicization of the armed forces. This has allowed Yeltsin to centralize and concentrate control of the military in the executive branch.

This situation has many negative ramifications. First, the failure to institutionalize civilian control has demoralized top military leaders. Political loyalty to the president rather than merit has become the primary criterion for holding high-ranking positions in the armed forces. This has led to regular purges of the Defense Ministry. In 1997 alone there were three different Defense Ministers. This situation has fostered corruption. Numerous high-ranking officers have been charged with using resources at their disposal—weapons, munitions, fuel—to line their own pockets. In May 1997, the Procurator-General announced eighteen generals were being investigated for corruption.[88] A decaying military that is losing its professionalism and suffers from low morale is susceptible to political intrigue. In a worst-case scenario, the military could collapse and/or break into armed groups which survive by selling nuclear or chemical weapons.

More significantly, Yeltsin has in effect handed his successors a ready-made instrument for authoritarian rule. By personalizing control, Yeltsin has allowed the military to become a possible instrument for extralegal rule.[89] In other words, the prospects for civil-military stability are highly scenario-dependent and unpredictable. Unless the military is more fully integrated into the reform process and a political consensus regarding their role is reached, Russian democratic development will be delayed and regional stability decreased.

THE ELITE

During the Soviet regime, the ruling class consisted exclusively of the leading members of the Communist Party. Although only 8 percent of the population were members of the CPSU, it had a monopoly on power. The Party was not bound by constitutional restrictions and could change the polity at will. Its power was enshrined in Article 6 of the Constitution, which recognized the CPSU as "the leading and guiding force of Soviet society, the nucleus of its political system and all state and public organizations." Party organizations were "elected" exclusively by party members, with lower-level organizations formally electing the next higher level. This electoral procedure was merely a formality, as the principle of democratic centralism ensured that lower-level party members were told whom to elect as their leaders.

At the state level, a party congress was "elected" by party members every five years. Largely symbolic, it met for only a few days. Leading members were "elected" to the most powerful party bodies: the Central Committee, its executive body the Politburo, and the Politburo's staff, the Secretariat. The leader of the Politburo, the General Secretary, was the most powerful person in the Soviet Union. As noted, members of the Party elite were the most privileged members of society. Although they did not own the means of production and resources as their counterparts in the West did, their positions gave them access to things unavailable to ordinary citizens. Examples included country homes, imported products, superior medical care, and opportunities to travel abroad. As a result of Gorbachev's general liberalization of society, these privileges became less important. This in turn weakened the power of the CPSU, culminating in the repeal of Article 6 in 1989.

Today, as in other democracies, various governmental and nongovernmental elites struggle for political power and influence. Governmental elites are those within the government who have a direct impact on policy, while nongovernmental elites are those who derive their power from other sources. Although the latter can have a large impact on policy, they are not directly associated with the government.

The Governmental Elite

The resurrection of the Russian state has led to the creation of numerous political parties. While usually this is a good indication that people are willing to get involved in politics, this is not the case in Russia. In contrast to the situation in most Western states, parties are generally based on personality rather than ideology. As a result, over forty-three parties and 8,000 candidates were on the ballot in the 1995 elections. Most parties are tiny and have platforms bordering on the absurd. As an illustration, the Sub-Tropical Russia Movement wants somehow to suspend the laws of nature, raising Russia's mean temperature to 77 degrees and lowering the boiling point of water to save energy.

While in the long term the struggle between various parties will strengthen society, there are numerous short-term drawbacks. First, many parties speak loudly for their own special interests, ignoring the larger picture. This greatly complicates the process of coalition building and compromise needed to create a societal consensus. Second, the plethora of parties strengthens growing societal divisions. Third, parties have become a vehicle for criminals to gain immunity from prosecution as members of parliament. In the 1995 electoral campaign, at least eighty candidates had served prison sentences for criminal convictions. Finally, limited ideological differences between the parties have caused them to recruit nationally known poets, singers, and actors as candidates. Since half of the Duma seats are elected from party lists, having a celebrity on the party list can improve the prospects of the whole list. The problem is these people have very little political experience.

These features all point to the relative unimportance of the Duma in Russia's strong presidential system. This can also be seen in the almost daily defections of members of parliament (MPs) from one party to another. Even cabinet members owe little allegiance to their party. Although Viktor Chernomyrdin's bloc, Our Home Is Russia, was created to be the pro-government party, several cabinet ministers chose to run as independents rather than staking their political futures on the bloc. This has created political instability as well as confusion among the electorate.

In contrast to the Western democracies, in which governmental elites share similar social and educational backgrounds, the governing elite in Russia varies depending on the party in power. The largest and most important parties are described here.

Russia's Democratic Choice (RDC)

Founded by former Prime Minister Yegor Gaidar, this was originally the wealthiest and most powerful party. It won the largest number of seats in the 1993 elections but fared badly in the 1995 elections. It supports radical economic reforms, civil rights, and a Western-oriented foreign policy. The party's support has drastically declined as a result of increasing resentment to the social costs of economic restructuring.

Forward, Russia!

A faction of Russia's Choice, this party was created as a result of disagreements between Gaidar and his former finance minister Boris Fedorov. Although Forward Russia supports reform, it also supports traditional social values—law and order—and is more populist than Russia's Choice.

Yabloko (Yavlinsky-Boldyrev-Lukin Bloc)

A takeoff on the Russian word for apple, this reformist party is led by Grigory Yavlinsky. In addition to economic reforms, this party advocates close links with former Soviet republics and wants to limit the powers of the presidency.

Although in the 1993 and 1995 parliamentary elections the combined vote of reformist parties topped 30 percent, personality clashes within and between parties have caused the reformist parties to fragment, greatly weakening them. The murder of a prominent reformer and the deteriorating economic situation led to the founding of an as-yet-unnamed center-right coalition. Its prominent members include Yegor Gaidar, Russia's first post-Communist prime minister; Anatoly Chubais, architect of Russia's mass privatization drive; and Boris Nemtsov, a former vice-prime minister who spearheaded the struggle against giant corporate monopolies. Despite the calls for unity that marked the party's founding conference, it remains to be seen whether the party can stay united. Nevertheless, it seems the reformers have finally realized that political unity is a prerequisite to power.[90]

Women of Russia

Led by Yekatrina Lakhova, Women of Russia is a pragmatic centrist party that supports women's rights, a strong social safety net, and moderate reforms. It was also strongly opposed to military intervention in Chechnya. In the 1993 elections, it received 8 percent of the vote, winning twenty-one seats in the Duma. In the 1995 election, however, the party won only three single member district seats because the party did clear the 5 percent threshold for proportional representation.

Overall, the proportion of women in politics has fallen drastically since the end of the Soviet era, when one-third of the seats in the Supreme Soviet were reserved for them. Women hold only 7.2 percent of the seats in the Duma. The Federation Council has one female member and there were only two women ministers in government in 1998.

Our Home is Russia (OHR)

Established in 1995 by Prime Minister Chernomyrdin, this center-right party of pragmatic reformers appeals to people who want "progress without shocks or revolutions, who are tired of disorder and lies, and who are proud of Russian statehood." Its supporters include members of the government, bureaucrats, big businessmen, industrial managers, and regional bosses—in other words, former middle-ranking members of the *nomenklatura*.

Communist Party of the Russian Federation (CPRF)

The successor to the CPSU, the CPRF is the only party that has a clear public identity and, by Russian standards, is coherent and united. Although it does not have the power it once did, the CPRF still has an extensive network and name recognition. Its half-million members, 20,000 regional and local branches, and 120 party newspapers constitute the only truly organized political party.

The CPRF calls for the "voluntary" re-creation of the Soviet Union and state control over the key sectors of the economy. The party's manifesto also calls for price controls; increases in the minimum wage, benefits, and pensions; "mercilessly" stamping out organized crime; and an end to the "pillaging of state and public property under the guise of privatization." With most of the country reeling from a collapse of traditional industries and the social welfare system, the communists have struck a chord in the electorate. The CPRF is strongest in the "red belt" of industrial cities around Moscow. The largest group of communist supporters are the poor and pensioners.

Agrarians (AP)

This party also has its roots in the old system. It is comprised of farmworkers and trade unionists from the old agro-industrial complex. The AP is against land privatization and supports agricultural subsidies.

Congress of Russian Communities (CRC)

Led by former Yeltsin advisor Yuri Skokov, this movement sprang to the forefront of Russian politics when retired General Alexander Lebed joined its leadership in 1995. A leading candidate in the 1996 presidential election, Lebed speaks in simple colloquial Russian with brutal clarity.[91] Its platform is based on patriotism, law, and order. The Congress believes foreign investors are stealing Russian resources and that the corrupt bureaucracy needs to be purged.

Liberal Democratic Party (LDP)

This inappropriately named party is led by the extreme nationalist Vladimir Zhirnovsky. The party's platform includes the retaking of Alaska, free vodka, and shooting criminals on sight. These policies appeal to chauvinistic feelings of disillusioned Russians, mostly blue-collar workers. Significantly, this party won the second largest number of seats in the 1995 elections.

The creation of parties shows the Russian society is becoming politically differentiated, with different demographic and economic groups supporting different parties. While a normal occurrence in the West, this is a radically new development in former socialist states. The Agrarians and Yabloko have more women supporters than men, while the LDP and Russia's Democratic Choice tend to attract a higher percentage of men. Women of Russia, RDC, and LDP attract younger people, while the Communists (the CPRF) and the Agrarians appeal to the older generation. The RDC and Yabloko attract the highly educated, while people with little education prefer the Agrarians, the LDP, and the Communists. In terms of geography, the reformist parties (RDC, Forward Russia!, Yabloko) draw the bulk of their support from Moscow and St. Petersburg; Yabloko, the Communists, and LDP do well in other big cities; Women of Russia and the Communists do well in small cities; and the Agrarians dominate the villages. Economically, the wealthy tend to support RDC and Yabloko, with the latter attracting some middle-class voters as well. The Communists, Agrarians, and LDP have the most support among the poorer segments of the society. Overall, Women of Russia has the most varied supporters; it attracts rich and poor, and people from both the cities and rural areas.[92] Interestingly, in contrast to

---

VLADIMIR ZHIRINOVSKY (1946–)

Vladimir Zhirinovsky, the leader of the grossly misnamed Liberal Democratic Party, is Russia's most visible ultranationalist leader. His views and goals include a military push to extend Russia's borders to the Indian Ocean, which would include the takeover of Pakistan, Turkey, Iran, Afghanistan, Kazakhstan and Kyrgyzstan, followed by the resettlement of Russians into these regions. He opposes free market reforms, has called for the reclamation of Alaska, has a vivid hatred of the United States, is blatantly anti-Semitic, and wants Russia cleansed of all alien religions. While these may sound like the rantings of a crazy man, to many Russians, Zhirinovsky represents Russia's future. Frighteningly, his party placed second in the 1995 parliamentary election. While his popularity has fallen recently, polls show that only 4 percent of Russians still think he should be president. Zhirinovsky remains a reminder of the potential backlash that continued reform failures could foster.

Western Europe, the electorate's attitudes toward new institutions and individual views of the past, not social backgrounds, have been the decisive factor in deciding elections to date.[93]

While the creation of political parties is a significant step towards the creation of a pluralist system in Russia, to date they have played only a minor political role. They are poorly developed, lack discipline, and are based more on personalities than on platforms. As with the rest of society, political parties are weak and divided and have little influence on the government.

1995 Parliamentary Elections

On December 17, 1995, Russia held its first fully constitutional parliamentary elections since the 1917 Bolshevik Revolution. The biggest winner was the Communist Party. It won 21 percent of the vote, up 9 percent from 1993. The second largest vote getter, also an antigovernment party, was the Liberal Democrat Party. Although the LDP received less then half of the votes it had won in 1993, its emergence as the second largest party gave the LDP political legitimacy it previously lacked.

The biggest losers were Our Home Is Russia and Yabloko. Despite the use of experts and consultants, economic and political pressure to convince

THE 1995 PARLIAMENTARY ELECTION AND THE COMMUNIST PARTY OF THE RUSSIAN FEDERATION

In the 1995 parliamentary elections, voters showed their dissatisfaction with nearly four years of failed reforms and falling living standards by making Gennady Zyuganov's Communist Party of the Russian Federation the most popular party in Russia. The voters' frustration with change can be seen by the fact that Grigory Yavlinsky's Yabloko Party, the most popular reformist party, ended up fourth behind the Communists and Zhirinovsky's nationalists. While the Communist victory did not signify a great threat to the evolving political system at the time, increasing economic uncertainty has seen the CPRF's popularity increase.

Strengthened by the 1995 victory and continuing failed reforms, Zyuganov placed second behind Yeltsin in the 1996 presidential election. Today his party makes up the only organized political force in the country and the biggest faction in the Duma. In September 1998, they demonstrated their strength by rejecting Yeltsin's candidate for prime minister, preventing the formation of a government to deal with the ongoing financial turmoil. With the ongoing economic, political, and social turmoil strengthening, the CPRF remains a powerful political force. If this turmoil continues, the party will be well placed to gain control of the presidency in 2000.

FIGURE 1.2   Duma Electoral Results—1993 and 1995

| | 1993 | | | | 1995 | | | |
Party	% of votes	party list seats	single mandate seats	total seats	% of votes	party list seats	single mandate seats	total seats
Russia's Democratic Choice (RDC)	15.5	40	56	96	*	0	9	9
Liberal Democratic Party (LDP)	22.9	59	11	70	11.2	50	1	51
Communist Party of the Russian Federation (CPRF)	12.4	32	33	65	22.3	99	58	157
Agrarian Party (AP)	8.0	21	26	47	*	0	20	20
Yabloko	7.9	20	13	33	6.9	31	14	45
Party of Russian Unity and Concord	6.8	18	9	27	*	0	2	2
Women of Russia	8.1	21	4	25	*	0	3	3
Democratic Party of Russia	6	14	7	21	—	—	—	—
Civic Union	*	0	18	18	—	—	—	—
Russian Movement for Democratic Reform	*	0	8	8	—	—	—	—
Our Home is Russia (OHR)	—	—	—	—	10.1	45	10	55
Power to the People	—	—	—	—	*	0	9	9
Congress of Russian Communities (CRC)	—	—	—	—	*	0	5	5
Independents	n/a	n/a	30	30	n/a	n/a	77	77

Note: Voter turnout: 1993—54.3%
                    1995—64.4%

*Received less than 5% of the vote needed for the party list seats.

Sources: Vera Tolz, "Russia's Parliamentary Elections: What Happened and Why," *RFE/RL Research Report*, 14 January 1994, Vol. 3 no. 2, and Robert Orttung, "Duma Elections Bolster Leftist Opposition," *Transition*, 23 February 1996, Vol. 2, no. 4.

the public to vote the "right way," and vast campaign expenditures, OHR won only 10 percent of the vote. This poor showing indicated the depth of discontent with the government. Yabloko, one of the leading reformist groups, was also repudiated by voters. Coming in fourth with 7 percent of the vote, it lost many of the seats it had won in 1993. Compared to the 1993 election, the biggest losers in 1995 were the nationalists and the liberals.

The election saw the creation of two main groups: the conservatives on the left and the reformists on the right.[94] Overall, the Communists now dominate the conservative camp because of the decline in support for ultra-nationalists. The latter's lack of success suggests that aggressive nationalism has a greater hold on the Russian elite than it does on the electorate.

The election also moved the reformers toward the left. They are now evenly split between Our Home is Russia and Yabloko. In the past, Russia's Democratic Choice dominated the reform camp. There are two main reasons for this outcome. First, as in the rest of Central and Eastern Europe, the lack of cooperation among the reformers split the reformist vote, lessening their overall success. Second, plummeting living standards, rising crime, and uncertainty about the future have combined to make the past look good. The Communist Party, drawing on its superior organizational skills, has taken advantage of this view.

A number of independent candidates also won seats. On average, four-teen candidates campaigned for each seat in the 225 single-mandate districts. This points to a larger issue, the lack of a stable electorate. Although each party has a stable core of supporters, a large part of the electorate consistently shifts political loyalties. This is the result of a couple of factors. First, people do not recognize the link between voting and their lives. Thus, supporters of one electoral bloc or candidate easily shift their allegiance. This situation, in which the public incessantly seeks a "spokesman" for its interests, facilitates the emergence of more and more candidates and parties.[95] This can be seen in the forty-three parties that contested the 1995 election. This condition fosters political instability and slows the development of a democratic polity.

In a hopeful sign, the electoral turnout has been increasing. There was a 64 percent turnout in the 1995 election, up from 54 percent in 1993. However, the increased turnout was likely the result of a popular backlash against the government, as a majority of votes went to antigovernment parties. Nevertheless, in the nine parliamentary and presidential elections between 1989 and 1996, turnout has remained reasonably high, averaging 70 percent. Thus it appears that free elections have become a part of Russian political life.

Significantly, as of June 1999 there have been no elections for the Federation Council. No compromise could be found between Yeltsin's desire to have appointed governors serve as members of the Council and a Duma bill that would have allowed only elected governors and chairs of the provincial legislatures to serve.[96]

While there are numerous political parties in Russia, for the most part they are ineffective. Most parties have not represented their constituents, and their future is uncertain. As an example, Vladimir Zhirnovsky's Liberal Democratic Party, a cross between a cult and political party, would collapse without Zhirnovsky. In contrast, the CPRF is the only countrywide party with a defined voter base and a well-articulated policy that might outlast a change in the party's leadership. However, even though it is the largest party in the Duma, its MPs frequently vote against the positions of the leadership.

Nongovernmental Elites

Prior to the start of Gorbachev's political reforms, the CPSU restricted or controlled all nongovernmental groups. Since 1989, nongovernmental elite groups have increased in size and influence, greatly affecting policy making and implementation. Most Russian and Western scholars believe the formal constitutional hierarchy is less important than the informal factions whose tentacles reach through and beyond the tiers of government. Their power has been increased by the fragmentation of political parties and the lack of state authority.

The nongovernmental elite is dominated by the "Big Seven" financial-industrial groups that control over half of Russia's economy. These conglomerates have banking, industrial, and media interests.[97] More important, these groups have powerful political allies. For example, former Deputy Security Council Secretary Boris Berezovsky, rumored to be the wealthiest man in Russia, has a direct entrée into the Kremlin via Valentin Yumashev, Yeltsin's chief-of-staff whom he used to employ and now "advises."[98] Berezovsky has become so influential that Yeltsin threatened to "drive him out of the country" if he did not stop trying to influence the government.[99]

As a result of close links between economic and political elites, the interests of the state are usually secondary to business interests. When individuals are both members of the government and represent a powerful interest group, distinctions among protectionism, lobbying, and corruption disappear. This can be seen in the appointment of Berezovsky, who has extensive holding in the oil and gas industries, to oversee the Chechnya settlement. It is no coincidence that the major oil pipeline from Azerbaijan to the Black Sea runs through Chechnya.[100] Without understanding the power and prestige of these groups, one cannot understand the contemporary Russian polity.

Why have government and business become so intertwined? First, because power is centralized in a presidential system, powerful business interests have tremendous lobbying advantages and almost hegemonic access to policy makers when compared to societal organizations and political parties. Second, Russia lacks a strong party system. In pluralist democracies, parties traditionally represent different societal interests. Even in the Duma, parties play virtually no role in articulating or representing them. Third is the lack of legal sanctions. There is a well-established system of bribe taking in the Duma in which business lobbies pay cash directly to MPs in return for their votes. These factors, combined with the traditional Russian acceptance of authority, have granted this new *nomenklatura* extensive power.

Ironically, the contemporary political environment mirrors the Soviet one, with political, economic, and judicial powers inextricably blurred. This situation has been a major obstacle to the development of a civil society, market economy, independent governmental institutions, and the rule of law.

BORIS BEREZOVSKY (1946–)

Boris Berezovsky demonstrates the deep link between business and the government inherent in post-Soviet Russia. Since the fall of communism, a group of seven business owners have created conglomerates that today control half of the country's economy. Berezovsky's fortune of approximately $3 billion is comprised of the car dealership Logovaz as well as stakes in banks, media, airlines, and one of Russia's largest oil firms, Sibneft. While he is not the richest member of the Big Seven, he is by far the most politically connected. He has served as deputy head of the Security Council and until 1999 advised President Yeltsin's chief of staff and Yeltsin's daughter and political confidant, Tatiana. This closeness to the president has left him in an influential position in the Russian government. His name has been linked to several important events, the most notable being the firing of Yeltsin's cabinet in March 1998 because the Chernomyrdin-led government did not support Berezovsky's business ventures. This event suggests that Berezovsky is an important figure with growing power in the Russian government. Even more important, though, it shows the degree of influence that informal government-business links play in Russian politics today.

While the August 1998 financial crash and the growing power of Prime Minister Yevgeny Primakov have weakened the tycoons, similar to U.S. "robber baron" capitalism of the nineteenth century, the oligarchs will continue to dominate the polity until popular revulsion leads to restrictions on their power.

Analogous conditions to those that led to the growth of the mafia in Sicily in the nineteenth century—the disintegration of the traditional political order, social turmoil, the weakening of state authority, and the decay of law enforcement—have caused a dramatic increase in the power of the Russian "mafia." Without any direct ties to their Sicilian counterparts, *mafioso* working with members of the old communist elite and corrupt officials have taken over much of the valuable property in Russia. Organized crime now controls an estimated 40 percent of the national economy and 80 percent of firms pay protection money.[101] This situation weakens the tax base and contributes to capital flight. The dramatic increase in organized crime in Russia is both a symptom and a cause of the country's chaotic transition to the post-Soviet era.[102]

This situation is made worse by the merging of organized crime and the state bodies. The President's Analytical Center for Socioeconomic Policy noted that corrupt officials are actually in the service of criminal formations or have become utterly dependent on criminals who use them to further their operations. This situation is different compared to Western Europe or the United States, where "organized crime controls only 'criminal' activities such as prostitution, drugs, and gambling. In our country, it controls all types of activity."[103] Thus the contemporary Russian polity is dominated by a very small elite who control property, social privileges, and political power. The rise of the mafia has several important implications, but most significantly, it inhibits the growth of democratic institutions. As Yeltsin noted: "The criminal world has openly challenged the state and launched into open competition with it."[104]

Another nongovernmental actor with a more limited role in the polity is the Orthodox church. Although 50 percent of Russians identify themselves as Orthodox Christians, only 4 percent regularly attend church. Thus, in contrast to Hungary and Poland, the Church as an institution has played only a minor political role. This is partially the result of the church having been under communist control for a longer period. In addition, Orthodoxy, unlike Catholicism, is a more mystical and personal religion that eschews politics. Recent events, however, suggest that the Church may play a larger role in the future. In 1997, the Church allied with nationalist groups to pass a new law restricting some religions. While still allowing religious freedom, the law created a two-tiered system of religious associations that favors established churches—Orthodoxy, Islam, Buddhism, Judaism and other "traditionally existing religions"—over new religious "groups." Examples of the latter include Baptists, Catholics, Methodists, and Pentecostals. These churches are denied tax exceptions and are prohibited from publishing, importing, or distributing religious literature. After fifteen years, they can apply for the status of a "religious organization," which would give them full legal rights.

Although this law was severely criticized in the West as a step away from the principles of equality under the law and freedom of conscience, its passage must also be examined from a Russian perspective. Since the history of the Orthodox church is inseparable from Russian culture, many Russians believe the future of Russia should include the return of millions of faithful taken away from the church by communist persecution. They do not think it is fair that the richer Western churches that never suffered this fate should have the same rights as the Orthodox ones that did. Although the Constitutional Court has yet to rule on the legality of this law, this controversy can be seen as part of Russia's broader, wounded sense of justice—fueled by the country's post-Soviet loss of standing and its identity crisis over rapid economic, political, and spiritual change.[105]

THE GENERAL PUBLIC

As elsewhere in Central and Eastern Europe, Russia's movement toward democracy was originally characterized by public euphoria and willingness to participate in the political process. However, the slow pace of change has fostered disillusionment with the new system. Public opinion polls show that a majority of the population view politicians as corrupt individuals who pursue only their own interests.[106]

People are tired of continuing political instability and declining standards of living. There is an increasing sense of despair in society and people have become pessimistic and tired of change. They want to lead a "normal life" with stability and order. The danger is they will not care if normality is achieved under a democracy or a return to an authoritarian regime. It is under these conditions that we examine the influence of the general public on the polity.

Political Recruitment

The primary way in which Russians can influence the political system is by joining political parties. However, since parties are weak, they do not actually provide a direct link between the people and the political system. This circumstance has made it difficult for parties to attract new members. In a December 1995 poll, only 6 percent of the respondents said they belonged to a political party.

Low participation in parties is the result of numerous factors. First, most people consider politics to be a dirty business and prefer not to soil themselves. Second, people have had little democratic experience. Schools do not teach the importance of participation or the connection between voting and policy. Therefore, people do not think their vote counts. Third, with so many political parties and so few political differences,[107] people are faced with a baffling array of choices that would confuse even a seasoned voter. Fourth, since parties were forbidden in the past, many people are reluctant to join them. Fifth, in an attempt to remain "above politics," Yeltsin and other political leaders have not encouraged the creation of political parties. Finally, many of the people in the forefront of change prefer to remain in the private sector, where their skills can lead to great personal profit. In other words, they see no advantage to being in a party.

This situation has important implications for the future development of the Russian polity. If political parties are unable to fulfill electoral platforms, not only will political apathy increase, but the legitimacy of the new democratic regime will be increasingly questioned. This in turn may foster calls for a return to an authoritarian regime.

Modes of Public Influence

The failure of traditional political parties to solve societal problems has fostered the creation of interest groups and civic organizations. In contrast to Hungary and Poland, however, these groups have had little political influence. While there are a record number of unemployed and underemployed, violations of labor laws, and millions of workers, including teachers, coal miners, and soldiers have not been paid—sometimes for more than a year—[108] there is little labor unrest. A one-day national strike in March 1997 could not even muster the support of 20 percent of union membership.[109] This is the result of the legacy of trade unions and worker-management relations, restrictive laws, and the lack of jobs.

Under the Soviet regime, trade unions were part of the state apparatus. As a result, they have no experience in standing up for their members' rights or in political lobbying. This can be seen in the relationship between workers and management. In contrast to unions in the West, there is little conflict between employees and employers because workers side with management in demanding budget money from the government. Thus the confrontation is between industrial managers and government officials, not workers and management. As a result, Mikhail Shmakov, the president of the Independent Trade Unions of Russia (FNPR), the largest labor federation in Russia notes: "the effectiveness of our trade union movement is not so high at the moment."[110]

Another limit on union activity are restrictive laws. Unions are wary of calling strikes because they are liable to pay material compensation to an enterprise for its losses if a court declares the strike illegal. Although informal groups of workers cannot be sued, even unofficial strikes are less common than in the West. Workers have nothing to gain by striking. If workers are not being paid because a factory has been shut down, striking accomplishes nothing. This situation is made worse by a large budget deficit that prevents the government from paying unemployment compensation.

These problems notwithstanding, trade unions could become more important in the future. In contrast to other pillars of the Soviet regime—the Communist Party had all its property confiscated and the state was dissolved—the FNPR has emerged as the largest property holder in Russia. It also controls the largest single nongovernmental sum of money, the national social security fund. In addition, declining living standards have fostered the creation of new independent trade unions. While they are relatively small and industry specific, their creation is nonetheless indicative of change.

Specific group interests are also starting to be articulated. An example is the rise of women's groups. Women have suffered disproportionately since the end of the USSR. In 1991, 5,300 women were murdered in the country. Since then, the numbers have soared. In 1993, 14,000 were killed by their husbands, lovers, or former partners—twenty times the equivalent figure in the United States and the highest in Central and Eastern Europe.[111] This situation led to the creation of the Women of Russia political party.

Since both of these groups have their roots in the Soviet era, a much more significant development is the rise of independent organizations. Starting from scratch after the change in regime, there are now more than 60,000 independent charities in Russia. While they have had little impact on federal policy, the need for their services has made them influential at the local level.[112] Nevertheless, there are obstacles to charities or other independent organizations playing a larger role in the polity. First, they lack the administrative skills necessary to grow. Second, and something to which many Western firms can attest, is a corrupt bureaucracy. As groups become more effective and involved with sensitive issues such as human rights or the environment, they are likely to fall afoul of the entrenched bureaucrats and criminal elements.

A final means by which the public could influence policy is by voting in national referendums. Although referendums are provided for in the Constitution, enabling legislation has not yet been written. This prevents the electorate from using this tool to affect policy.

In summary, although the general public now has the ability to directly influence the political system, society remains too fractured for independent organizations to collectively express grievances or change policy. In other words, the political void created by Russia's weak parties has yet to be filled by other organizations. This has limited the development of a civil society, a crucial element of a democratic polity. As a result, an oligarchy comprised of financial-industrial interests and criminal clans has been able to dominate the polity. Former Security Council Secretary Alexander Lebed noted that "ordinary Russians are now as far from the real levers of power as they were during Soviet Communist rule."[113]

This disempowerment has fostered societal apathy. A 1995 poll showed that 75 percent of people between 17 and 35 were "not at all or not very interested" in politics.[114] Most Russians do not think they have any influence in shaping the future of the country. As a result, they may be inclined to transfer authority to a leader who promises quick fixes.

POLICY MAKING AND IMPLEMENTATION

Prior to 1991, state policy-making bodies formally resembled their Western counterparts. Constitutionally, the Supreme Soviet was the highest organ of state authority and was responsible for passing laws, creating the state budget, electing the Presidium and the Council of Ministers, declaring war, and so forth. In practice, however, the Supreme Soviet had little power. It held only two or three short sessions each year and its deputies did not debate. Instead, they listened to speakers present policies already decided on by the CPSU leadership.

When the Supreme Soviet was not in session, authority was vested in the Presidium, whose chairman was also head of state. Although the Presidium had numerous constitutional prerogatives, its members played little role in actual policy making.

This model, which was forced on all other CEE states, was merely a facade for the real policy maker, the CPSU Politburo and its administrative body, the Secretariat. The departments of the Secretariat mirrored major government ministries and acted in effect as a parallel, but superior, government. As a result, the policy-making process took place behind closed doors and involved only a small number of people. To facilitate policy implementation, some high-ranking Party officials also held high-ranking positions in the state administration.

The end of the communist monopoly on power brought significant changes to the policy-making process. As the number of institutions and actors has increased, the policy-making process has become much more complicated. It is now the outcome of bargaining, compromise, or stalemate between various governmental and nongovernmental actors. In contrast to other states in the area, however, the number of actors is much smaller and nongovernment elites have much more influence.

The Formal Process

In discussing policy making, we have to differentiate between the formal and actual policy-making process. Constitutionally, there are three phases in policy formulation. First, after the government has officially commented on them, draft laws are submitted to the Duma. Thus, most bills are written by specialists in the ministry who will have jurisdiction over the enacted law.

After committee hearings, the Duma votes on the bill. If passed, the bill is forwarded to the Federation Council. The Council has fourteen days to vote on the proposed legislation. If they reject the bill, it is returned to the Duma. The Duma can overturn a Federation Council veto by a two-thirds vote.

After adoption by parliament, the draft legislation is submitted to the president for signing and promulgation. The president has fourteen days either to sign or to veto the legislation. If he vetoes the bill, the veto can only be overruled by a two-thirds majority of both houses.

The Constitutional Court is also involved in policy making through its power of constitutional review. On the application of the president, the government, or one-fifth of the members of the Duma or the Federation Council, the Court rules on the constitutionality of laws. In performing these functions, it has become involved in political disputes between the government and the president.

The Informal Process

While the formal policy-making process is relatively straightforward, policy making in Russia, in contrast to other Central and Eastern European states, has yet to become institutionalized. This can be seen in the lack of new legislation, numerous presidential decrees, and the influence of nongovernment elites.

The slow progress in enacting laws is the result of conflicts between the Duma and the Federation Council, conflicts within each body, and a large and unwieldy Council of Ministers. In an attempt to overcome the latter problem, in 1997 the number of ministries was halved and a number of agencies were disbanded or merged. In addition, a committee consisting of the prime minister and seven top ministers was established to coordinate the ministries.

Since the effect of these reforms has yet to be seen, most significant legislative initiatives continue to come from the president in the form of decrees. Since most of these decrees are prepared by the Executive Office of the President rather than the government, they often contradict basic state policies or violate the constitution. For example, when parliament overturned a presidential veto of the 1995 budget, Yeltsin ignored the constitution and refused to implement the decision.

Partially as a result of legislative and bureaucratic opposition and partially as a result of his autocratic decision-making style, Boris Yeltsin has created ad hoc bodies that create policy outside the formal bureaucratic structures.[115] Significantly, the president's administrative staff now numbers 40,000, several times larger than the staff of the Central Committee in the Soviet period.[116] In essence, this vast apparatus forms a parallel government that is not accountable to anyone but Yeltsin. The continued fragmentation of the Russian polity suggests that the use of decrees will continue to be the main policy-making mechanism.

This situation has numerous negative consequences. First, in contrast to laws passed through the normal legislative process, these decrees do not represent political consensus. Thus many important laws—such as the civil code, the land code, and legislation on political parties—remains incomplete. Interestingly, the power of the presidency has hindered the resolution of key policy issues.[117] Second, the combination of presidential decrees, the Constitution, the constitutions and charters of the federal units, and the uncoordinated laws by legislators of different levels produces legal entanglements and confusion. The resulting effect of legislative chaos is often arbitrary rule by local authorities. Finally, the failure to institutionalize policy making has given nongovernment actors, such as the financial-industrial groups, more power than governmental institutions.

Policy Making

The following case studies show how the interaction of formal and informal processes affects contemporary policy-making process.

Case Study: "Oil Production Legislation"

Acting on what Prime Minister Chernomyrdin described as a crucial piece of legislation, in June 1995 the Duma passed a law allowing Western oil companies to establish production-sharing agreements with Russian firms. The bill was then sent to the Federation Council for approval. In October, the bill was approved by a majority of the members present. However, because many deputies were in the provinces campaigning for December elections, a quorum was lacking and the bill was not passed. This example illustrates a major problem of the contemporary policy-making process, the lack of political discipline. Even though the bill had the support of the president, prime minister, oil minister, oil firms, and a majority of those who voted on it in both houses of parliament, it still failed to get enacted.[118]

Case Study: "Privatization"

Because foreign investors were reticent to invest in the Russian economy and the Duma opposed privatization, in 1995 a small group of presidential advisors devised what would later be called the "loans-for-shares" program. Enacted by a presidential decree, the goals of this program were to raise cash for the treasury and develop the private sector. In return for shares in large state companies, private banks extended loans to the government. However, the shares were sold at far below their market value. Banks that participated in the loans-for-shares program were also authorized to organize future auctions of the shares, giving them a decisive advantage over potential competitors.[119] This program thereby allowed a group of politically well-connected banks to gain control over a majority of the country's biggest oil and industrial companies for next to nothing.

This program, called by some "one of the most remarkable shell games in history,"[120] has allowed the financial-industrial groups to dominate the economic and political hierarchy and limit foreign and domestic competitors. This situation has numerous negative consequences. First, these groups have become so powerful that they have demanded a formal say in running the country via a "cooperation council" with the government. Second, the combination of old political elites and new economic elites has created an extralegal "shadow state" in which power is wielded by the nonelected. As many foreign companies have discovered, laws do not matter when they can be quickly be reinterpreted or rewritten. This weakens the rule of law, prevents much-needed economic reforms, and ensures a weak state government that will not threaten their interests. In summary, Russia's decision-making process is dominated by a narrow elite of corrupt governmental officials and private sector elites. This situation is very similar to that of the Soviet era, when policy making was dominated by secrecy and the power of shadowy figures occupying no clear governmental positions.

Policy Implementation

After a law or policy is adopted, it must be put into effect. Thus the success of the new policy depends largely on the actors involved in policy implementation. Under the communist regime, although they had no constitutional power, the CPSU Secretariat and individual members of the Politburo were responsible for ensuring that Party policy was implemented. After a policy was created, it was the duty of the governmental bureaucracy to implement it. This was ensured by Party oversight of government agencies at all levels.

This system has been fundamentally changed since 1991. In theory, policy is now implemented at both the state—central government—and local levels, free of political oversight. At the state level, ministries are responsible for policy implementation. They perform this function by issuing the necessary regulations, decrees, ordinances, and resolutions, which are enforced by either local branches of a ministry or local authorities.

While the administrative structure and responsibilities are defined, there are numerous impediments to policy implementation. The most significant is an ineffective bureaucracy. Since laws usually leave room for interpretation, the bureaucracy is an essential element in policy execution. As in other states in the region, bureaucratic inefficiency often delays policy implementation. For example, in May 1994, only 156 of 296 government resolutions were implemented.

Even presidential decrees are not executed. After a presidential decree is issued, federal ministries and local governments legally have two days to issue corresponding instructions.[121] This has not occurred. When asked to name the main weakness of the bureaucracy, a former presidential staffer noted the total absence of control and monitoring of the decisions. He stated that in the history of the Yeltsin presidency "you are unlikely to find a [presidential edict] fulfilled from beginning to end."[122] Interestingly, Lenin complained about the same thing in his time. In response, Yeltsin has strengthened his administrative staff and created new ad hoc administrative agencies to implement policy decisions. However, since these agencies often have overlapping administrative responsibilities, it is increasingly difficult to ensure their accountability.

In summary, the power and authority of the president's administrative staff continues to grow. This is the result of the new Constitution's concentrating power in the presidency and the failure of the Russian polity to evolve to the point where executive decisions are routinely implemented by the state bureaucracy.

In other states, policy implementation is also affected by nongovernmental groups. Under the old regime, however, society was either organized in mass organizations closely allied with the party or did not participate in public life. As a result, there was no tradition of representing independent interests or exerting influence on the government.

Today, new organizations are being created to try to influence policy. For example, nationalists forced Russia to take a pro-Serbian stance in the Kosovo conflict, weakening the effectiveness of U.N. mediation efforts. Nevertheless, while interest groups can help bring common people closer to the actual process of government, this is not yet the case in Russia. In summary, policy implementation in an unstable political environment is often a long and continuous struggle.

CONCLUSION

The Russian polity is still in a period of transition and the question of where it will end has yet to be resolved. Will Russia fulfill its stated goal of becoming a democratic, law-based state with a market economy, or will historical legacies and contemporary problems be too difficult to overcome? As we will see, the problems Russia faces are interrelated, making them difficult to solve.

Civil Society

Although there has been some movement towards the creation of groups and institutions that exist and act independently of the state, progress has been limited. Political participation by civic groups seems to have peaked in the countrywide anticommunist movement of the early 1990s. Since then, these groups have had little impact on state policy.

This situation is the result of numerous factors. First, the ability of independent groups to articulate and lobby on behalf of their interests has been impeded by the same factors that have retarded party development: limited structural changes in the economy, weakened representative institutions, and centralized political power in the executive.[123] Second is the absence of a middle class. In Western democracies, the middle class—because it has time and money—plays a key role in the founding and participating in civic organizations. Third, until political parties play a more substantial role in the polity, civic groups will not have agents to convert their interests into policy. Finally, societal apathy also limits the creation of a civil society. Accustomed to having the state dominate their lives, people are reticent to take the initiative. Having been told for seventy years that the Party would take care of everything, people are just starting to realize their fate is in their own hands. This is a necessary precondition for the emergence of a civic space between state institutions and individuals. This problem is closely related to the failure of dismantling old state institutions, which has precluded the creation of new, representative institutions. Without the latter there will be no individual liberties and no civil society.

One bright spot has been the emergence of a semi-independent media. During the war in Chechnya, the press defied the government's attempts to censor its coverage. However, the concentration of the press in the hands of few wealthy businessmen and court decisions that have substantially limited journalists' freedom to criticize public figures has limited the freedom of the press.

Going from the monopoly of communist party power to a system dominated by organized crime groups, narrow economic elites, and weak democratic institutions has greatly limited the development of a civil society. As a result, on a scale of 1 to 7, with 1 being the highest, Freedom House gives Russia a 4 in civil rights.

Democratic Institutions/Political Rights

Overwhelming participation in a series of parliamentary, presidential, and regional elections between 1993 and 1996 signaled an important turning point in Russia's slow transition to democracy. For the first time, actors committed themselves to a set of rules governing political competition before they knew what the results would be. Thus the institutionalization of elections for selecting government officials has at least in the near term negated alternative, nondemocratic models.[124]

Unfortunately there is no connection between voter turnout and the strength of Russia's political institutions. Seemingly contradictory, since constitutionally the government has more power than its CEE counterparts, in reality it is extraordinarily weak. It cannot perform even such basic duties as collecting taxes, enforcing contracts, protecting businesses and citizens from crime, or providing minimum social services. This is the result of the state having little coercive capability or legitimacy. A recent World Bank study found that the Russian people's trust in their government ranks last in the world.[125] To the extent the state functions at all, it primarily serves the interests of a small Moscow business elite. This situation greatly limits the state's ability to influence the development of the polity.

As a result of a constitution that has few checks and balances and gives the president power without accountability, Yeltsin has created a small, closed policy-making circle. Like Franklin Roosevelt, he plays members off against each other, preventing any one from becoming too powerful. This strategy can also be seen in Yeltsin's creation of numerous ad hoc bodies and his penchant not to sign laws passed by the parliament through invoking ridiculous technicalities. While this structure increases Yeltsin's personal control, it often causes a lack of coordination and generates confusion both domestically and abroad about the actual content of Russian policy. This situation weakens the ability of the government to implement policy and prevents parliamentary oversight and public scrutiny of decisions. Thus eight years after independence, Russia's fledgling democracy is characterized by weak governmental institutions.

Since the system is based on presidential control, when the president is not firmly in control—as in late 1996, when Yeltsin underwent heart surgery—nonelected officials gain broad discretionary authority. During this period, Yeltsin's chief of staff, Anatoly Chubais, created a new high-powered committee to prosecute large enterprises with major tax debts.[126] Although this action might have been necessary to further economic reform, using extra-constitutional bodies further weakens the legitimacy of political institutions. Thus contemporary political institutions reflect the power held by nonelected officials, not constitutional arrangements.

A related problem is failure of the postcommunist government to change traditional governmental practices. The Russian invasion of Chechnya in December 1994 showed the strength of the old decision-making model. The decision to invade was made by the president and a small group of aides in violation of the Constitution; members of parliament were not informed in advance, let alone consulted. This is a legacy of the communist regime in which state policies were created and implemented without societal input. An integral feature of any democratic system is a defined decision-making process.

ANATOLY CHUBAIS (1955–)

Anatoly Chubais, a 44–year-old St. Petersburg economist and the former First Deputy Prime Minister, is known as the leading advocate of free market reforms in Russia. Under his supervision, the government began the difficult task of selling off many of the formerly state-run enterprises to private investors. Chubais's success led to his appointment as Yeltsin's 1996 presidential campaign advisor, where he devised the strategy of allying with Lebed to take votes away from the Communist candidate, Gennady Zyuganov. After Yeltsin's reelection, Chubais was made chief of staff. Continuing his push for economic reforms and reducing the power of the business elites, Chubais made numerous powerful enemies, including the former deputy secretary of the Security Council, Boris Berezovsky.

Chubais was soon embroiled in scandal when a large book advance escalated into his forced resignation in 1997. However, his reputation as a reformer and his credibility with international bankers led to his selection as Russia's liason with the IMF in 1998. Chubais was also selected to turn the inefficient state-run utility, United Energy Systems, into a modern, partially private company. While having many enemies and being seen as too liberal and Western oriented for a top political post, Chubais nevertheless has significant influence as Russia's most prominent reformer.

While the authoritarian political institutions of the Soviet regime ensured control, the contemporary political institutions are fragmented, unaccountable, and incapable of repressing force and fraud. Seemingly paradoxically, this has created a situation in which people are even more vulnerable than they were under the old regime.[127] This situation has drastic consequences. For without democratic institutions, including a representative parliament and an independent judiciary, the state will not have the legitimacy to protect the rights of its citizens, fundamental features of a democratic regime. The contemporary Russia polity shows the difficulty of creating new institutions in chaotic setting. Freedom House gives Russia a 3 rating in the development of democratic institutions and political rights.

Market Economy

A further impediment to reform has been the lack of a systemic plan for a transition to a market economy. Like Bulgaria, Russia has adopted only incremental economic reforms.

Three features of Russia's emerging capitalism most affect the development of the polity.[128] First, capital is concentrated sectorally in extractive industries, trade and services, and banking. Second, capital is concentrated geographically, with an estimated 80 percent of Russia's assets located in Moscow. Third, capital is closely tied to the state. Through privatization and the loans-for-shares program, Russian banks are dependent on inside information and money from the state for profits.

Small businesses have been most affected by this situation. High taxes, inflation, the lack of property rights, the mafia, and the ability of large financial groups to control various markets have made it very difficult for small businesses to operate. The share of GDP produced by small businesses, after growing rapidly under Gorbachev, has steadily decreased. Consequently, this economic interest group—the foundation of most democracies—is weak and disorganized. On a scale of 1 to 4, with the latter being the highest,[129] the European Bank for Reconstruction and Development (EBRD) ranks the Russian economy as follows:

1. Privatization and restructuring of enterprises: 3
2. Competitiveness and openness of the market: 3
3. Ability of financial institutions to collect and channel savings to productive investments: 2.5
4. Extensiveness and effectiveness of legal rules on investment: 3

While Russia has made more progress reforming its economy than in creating a civil society and democratic institutions, its 2.87 average is the second lowest in our survey, only marginally better than Bulgaria's.

Rule of Law

As with the creation of a civil society, the rule of law has yet to take hold in Russia. The Russian legal system has been a weapon the powerful use to exploit the weak, not a system of enforceable rules that resolve conflict without violence and promote individual and societal cooperation. For example, the Federal Security Service, the successor to the KGB, still enjoys extrajudicial powers, including the right to search premises without a court order.

There are numerous reasons for this state of affairs. First, although the creation of new polity has led to the enactment of numerous new laws, communist-era judges have no training in applying them. Second, many of the newly drafted laws are ambiguous or inconsistent. Third, court rulings are often disregarded by executive branch officials. Another problem is the failure to enforce laws already enacted. For example, although Article 27.1 of the Constitution "guarantees the right to freedom of movement and to choose a place to stay and reside," Moscow Mayor Yuri Luzhkov introduced a residence permit (*propiska*). Even though the Constitutional Court struck down this law, the *propiska* requirement remains in effect.

This situation has led to a widespread consensus that the state has failed in its basic duty of enforcing the rule of law. The combination of a weak state and an ineffectual judicial system has produced a sense of anarchy in Russia, a frightening situation to a population accustomed to a powerful authoritarian state. Since the law does not regulate economic disputes or protect people, it is not respected. This state of affairs forces people to go outside official administrative and judicial channels to find redress; undermines public support for democracy and market reforms; and fosters moral decay, social discontent, and political alienation. Thus Russia receives a ranking of 2.27 (out of 10) from Transparency International, or 49th out of the fifty-two states ranked.

In summary, Russia has had some success in creating democratic institutions and a market economy but has yet to create a civil society based on the rule of law. Why does Russia lag behind other states in Central and Eastern Europe? Three factors stand out. First is the lack of change in the political culture. In contrast with other states in the region, there is no living memory of democracy or a market economy. Second is a political structure that concentrates power. This prevents the emergence of strong political parties and fosters confrontation instead of compromise. Finally, the sheer size of Russia slows its development; it is difficult to govern such a large and diverse area. While a federal system was created to disburse power, it limits the ability of Moscow to enact much-needed reforms. In summary, unlike other CEE states, Russia failed to bridge the gap between communism and capitalism by building strong democratic institutions and a market economy.

International Ramifications

In order to increase its security, ensure its hegemony, and counter the Western military alliance (NATO), the Soviet Union created the Warsaw Pact in 1955. The military equivalent of the CMEA, the Warsaw Pact allowed the Soviets to integrate the military capabilities of Bulgaria, Czechoslovakia, East Germany, Hungary, Poland, and Romania with their own.

The end of Soviet control over these states left Russia in a security vacuum. Former Russian rear areas, such as St. Petersburg, are now border zones. How this void is filled will be a crucial indicator of how the Russian polity will evolve. Unlike Bulgaria, Hungary, and Poland, there is a fundamental split in the Russian polity over whether Russia should cooperate with the West or whether it should follow its own traditional interests. As a result, Russian policy has vacillated between these extremes depending on the alignment of domestic political forces.

After Russia declared its independence in 1991, Yeltsin initially called for a common political and security system "from Vancouver to Vladivostok." Since then, although never completely renouncing cooperation with the West, Russia has attempted to reassert itself as a great power. This can be seen in Russian attempts to increase its influence in the "near abroad" (the former Soviet republics), which has led to the creation of a customs union among Russia, Belarus, and Kazakhstan, an attempt to create a collective security system with the former republics of the Soviet Union—the Commonwealth of Independent States (CIS)—and the signing of a union treaty with Belarus. The last agreement provides for common citizenship and the coordination of economic and security policies.

Because they require large financial subsidies, closer integration with former Soviet republics could slow down economic reforms in Russia. In addition, Russian involvement with these states is seen by many in both the West and the former Soviet republics as a manifestation of continuing Russian hegemonic aspirations. As a result, despite the signing of over 700 intergovernmental agreements and the creation of eighty supranational CIS organs, coordination of economic policies remains weak and political rifts continue to grow.[130]

Russia's desire to maintain its traditional sphere of influence can be seen in its strong opposition to NATO's plans for expansion into Central and Eastern Europe, a region Russia considers crucial to its security. Ominously, Russian spokespersons warn that NATO expansion could inaugurate a new Cold War in Europe. In contrast to the other states in the area, Russia has little foreign policy consensus. This suggests it will continue to fluctuate. Anyone who expected that a democratizing Russia would no longer challenge the West over fundamental questions of the international order has been sadly disappointed. Unlike other states in the region, Russia's foreign policy pronouncements suggest that it has not accepted the view that no country, regardless of its size and relative power, can exist independently from others in an increasingly interdependent world.

Summary

In the development of a civil society, democratic institutions, a market economy, and the rule of law, Russia lags behind Bulgaria, Hungary, and Poland.

The strength of big business, centralization of power, a large state apparatus, the lack of the rule of law and civic organizations, the weakness of political parties, and leaders who lack either the will or capacity to act have combined to create a situation in which the Russian state is dominated by the interests of the small, wealthy business elite. This dominance has limited the effect of political reforms and the development of a market economy. In other words, Russia has yet to overcome the legacies of its past.

Three factors could mitigate this situation. First, state leaders could turn against those who brought them to power and enact policies which benefit broader societal interests. Second, an external shock, such as a market meltdown or the return of inflation, could cause people to take to the streets as they did in 1991. Since the Russian state has limited legitimacy, it has little capacity to absorb even minor crises. Finally, as with the turn-of-the-century Progressive movement in the United States, Russians might elect the leaders of mass-based groups who are not beholden to big business and have the will to use the state to serve the interests of society.[131]

However, the key question remains: what is the likelihood that Russia will return to its autocratic past? The largest country in the world is gripped by chaos and decay. Small wars have erupted in border statelets and inflation, unemployment, wrenching economic changes have left a third of the population poor. Corruption, organized crime, and militant nationalists dominate the headlines. Government secrecy is returning and authorities disregard the law. There is no middle class, and churches and unions have little influence. Political parties are struggling to emerge and the country remains polarized between those who long for the past and those who reject their glorified view of the past. In other states, similar problems led to the creation of authoritarian regimes.

These problems notwithstanding, it is unlikely that Russia will find its future in the past. Too many fundamental changes have taken place. The whole decision-making process has been reorganized. The country is no longer run from Moscow, and for the first time in Russia's long history there are constitutionally guaranteed civil rights, a free press, and quasiconstitutional governance with an elected president and parliament. Freedom of speech and association are taken for granted.

Perhaps even more important for the future, people have begun to accept the free market—the right of individuals to acquire capital and own property—as permanent. Although privatization has rightly been criticized for transferring state assets to political insiders, it also allowed the new own-ers to implement the reforms necessary for the firms to compete internation-ally. As a result, private enterprise now comprises more than half of the economy and its share is growing. Russian society has become too complex, too open, too wealthy, and too decentralized for a return to the past.

This does not mean the polity will not be in a state of flux in the foresee-able future. Although Russia has changed since Churchill made his observa-tion that "There are still two kinds of politics in Russia—the kind you see and the kind you don't," this observation is still applicable today. On the surface, political life appears as it does in the West, with a variety of actors competing in the open for political power. To date, however, the real action is going on under the carpet, with only occasional bumps visible. Until ongoing issues are brought into the open, Russia will continue to lurch from crisis to crisis.

TIMELINE

1905

January 9   The "Bloody Sunday" massacre leads to countrywide revolts.

1906

To lessen growing dissatisfaction, the Tsar creates the Duma, a representative legislative body.

1914

Russia enters World War I.

1917

March   Spontaneous demonstrations in St. Petersburg force the abdica-tions of the tsar. A Provisional Government headed by Aleksander Kerensky is created.

November 7   The Bolshevik Party storms the Winter Palace and arrests the Pro-visional government.

December 29   The Treaty of Brest Litovsk with Germany ends Russian involve-ment in World War I.

1918

The Russian Socialist Federated Soviet Republic is created. "War Communism," a policy to eradicate capitalism and create the conditions for socialism, is enacted.

1921

Lenin initiates the New Economic Policy (NEP), relaxing War Communism.

1922

The Union of Soviet Socialist Republics (USSR) is created.

1924

Lenin dies and a power struggle ensues.

1927

Stalin consolidates power and initiates the first Five Year Plan.

1928

Collectivization begins. Between 1929 and 1934, approximately 15 million people die as a result of this program.

1934

Stalin initiates the "Great Purges." Millions are executed or sent to forced labor camps.

1939

August 23   The Molotov-Ribbentrop Pact, also known as the Nazi-Soviet Nonaggression Pact is signed. This agreement contains a secret protocol that split Central and Eastern Europe between Germany and the USSR.

1941

June   Germany invades the Soviet Union. The Soviet Union enters World War II on the side of the Allies.

1945

May 9   Victory over Germany ends the war on the Eastern Front.

1949

January   The Soviet Union establishes the Council for Mutual Economic Assisance (CMEA).

1953

March   Stalin dies and Nikita Khrushchev becomes the First Secretary of the Communist Party.

1955

May   The Warsaw Treaty Organization, also known as the Warsaw Pact, is created.

1956

November 4   To "protect socialism," the Soviet army invades Hungary.

1964

October   In a palace coup, Khrushchev is replaced as the First Secretary by Leonid Brezhnev.

1968

August 21   To "protect socialism," the Soviet army invades Czechoslovakia.

1979

December   USSR invades Afghanistan.

1982

November   Brezhnev dies, and Yuri Andropov, former head of the KGB, succeeds him as General Secretary.

1984

February   Andropov dies, and Konstantin Chernenko succeeds him as the General Secretary.

1985

March   Chernenko dies and Mikhail Gorbachev succeeds him as General Secretary. As a result of growing economic and political problems as well as social stagnation, Gorbachev initiates the policies of *glasnost* and *perestroika*.

1990

June   A Constitutional Commission is set up to draft a new constitution.

1991

August 19   An attempted coup to prevent the dissolution of the Soviet Union is suppressed.

September   Russia declares itself independent of the Soviet Union. Boris Yeltsin is elected president.

December 25   Gorbachev dissolves the USSR.

1993

September 21   Yeltsin dissolves parliament.

December 12   In the first free parliamentary elections since 1918, reformers win a majority. A new consitution is also approved by a small majority.

1994

January   Victor Chernomyrdin becomes prime minister.

November   After Chechnya declares its independence from Russia, Yeltsin orders an invasion of the country.

1995

December 17   The Communist Party of the Russian Federation (CPRF) wins the majority of seats in parliamentary elections.

1996

July 3   Yeltsin is reelected president.

November 5   Yeltsin undergoes open-heart surgery.

1997

May 27   NATO and Russia sign the Founding Act. This act upgrades political and military ties and clears the way for NATO expansion into Central and Eastern Europe.

December   A scandal forces leading reformer and presidential Chief-of-Staff Anatoly Chubais to resign.

1998

April   Chernomyrdin is dismissed as prime minister and is replaced by
Sergei Kiriyenko.

August   An economic crisis forces Yeltsin to fire Kiriyenko. He is replaced
by former secret police chief Yevgeny Primakov.

WEB SITES

Russian Constitution
http://www.uni-wuerzburg.de/law/rs_indx.hmtl
The 1977 and 1993 constitutions, as well as other political information.

Library of Congress Soviet Archives Exhibit
http://www.ncsa.uiuc.edu/SDG/Experimental/soviet.exhibit/entrance.html
Online exhibit offers a tour of the internal and external policies of the former
Soviet Union.

Soviet Studies Trails on the Internet
http://www2.uncg.edu/~lixlpurc/russian.html
A lengthy list of links to online resources for Slavic studies. Maintained by
the University of North Carolina, Greensboro.

Directory of Russian Periodicals Online
http://rs.informika.ru/
Links to various Russian periodicals, some in English.

St. Petersburg Times Online
http://www.sptimes.ru/index.htm
St. Petersburg's English-language newspaper.

Grandchildren of the Dazhdbog
http://metalab.unc.edu/sergei/Grandsons.html
Information about Russian traditions and culture, as well as politics and current events.

Friends and Partners
http://solar.rtd.utk.edu/friends/home.html
A website developed jointly by United States and Russian citizens to encourage
cross-cultural relationships. In addition to travel, business, culture, language,
and historical information, the site offers discussion groups and chat rooms.

WORKS CITED

"A Backbreaking Job." *The Economist* 25 July 1998: 34.
Belin, Laura. RFE/RL Political Analyst. Personal Interview. 23 July 1998.
Belin, Laura, and Robert Orttung. "Electing a Fragile Political Stability." *Transition*
7 Feb. 1997: 67–70.

Berdyaev, Nicholas. *The Russian Idea*. London: Geoffrey Bles, 1947.

Blank, Stephen. "Yeltsin Fosters a Military Threat to Democracy." *Transition* 9 Aug. 1996: 13.

Blocker, Joel. "Corruption Among State Officials in Eastern Europe." *RFE/RL Newsline* (13 June 1997): 2 pp. Online. Internet.

"Broken Code." *The Economist* 25 Oct. 1997: 81–82.

Bruszt, Laszlo. *Political Culture and Economic Orientations in Central and East Europe during the Transition to Democracy: 1990–1992*. Berlin: Wissenschaftszcentrum fur Sozialforschung, 1993.

Burger, Edward J. and Mark Field. *Health in Russia: Humanitarian and Foreign Policy Issues*. Washington: The Atlantic Council, 30 Nov. 1996.

Christensen, Paul. "Why Russia Lacks a Labor Movement." *Transitions* Dec. 1997: 44–51.

Downing, John. *Internationalizing Media Theory*. London: Sage Publications, 1996.

Duran, James. *Russia and Ukraine: Political and Economic Update*. Washington: The Atlantic Council, 1 Dec. 1995.

Economitcheskaya Gazeta 27 July 1991: 1+.

"Emerging Market Indicators." *Economist* 1 Nov. 1997: 97.

Fadin, Andrei. "In Russia, Private Doesn't Mean Independent." *Transitions* Oct. 1997: 90–92.

"Father and Daughters." *The Economist* 5 July 1997: 56.

"The Feministki Are Coming." *The Economist* 12 Aug. 1995: 44–45.

Ford, Peter. "Russian Unions Lack AFL Clout." *Christian Science Monitor* 20 Sept. 1996: 1+.

—. "Russia's Free Press Opts Not to Play Fair Before Elections." *Christian Science Monitor* 26 April 1996: 1+.

—. "Thug Capitalism Drives Up Crime in Russia, Testing New Freedoms." *Christian Science Monitor* 16 March 1995: 1+.

—. "KGB-Era Suspecions Lurk Within Russia's Refurbished Spy Agency." *Christian Science Monitor* 24 Jan. 1995: 4.

Fossato, Floriana, Stephanie Baker, and Laura Belin. "Yeltsin Pledges Fair Privatization." *RFE/RL Newsline* (17 Aug. 1997): 2 pp. Online. Internet.

Fossato, Floriana, and Anna Kachkaeva. "Russia to Have New Nationwide Television Network." *RFE/RL Newsline* (22 May 1997): 2 pp. Online. Internet.

Freedom in the World: The Annual Survey of Political Rights and Civil Liberties, 1996–1997. New York: Transaction Publishers, 1997.

Goldman, Minton, ed. *Commonwealth of Independent States and Central/Eastern Europe*. 3rd. ed. Guilford, Connecticut: Dushkin Publishing Group, 1992.

"Groping Ahead." *The Economist* 2 Sept. 1995: 42+.

Hesse, Joakim, ed. *Administrative Transformation in Central and Eastern Europe*. Oxford: Blackwell Publishers, 1993.

Hockstader, Lee. "Once upon a Ruble, Ah, Life Was Grand." *Washington Post* 12 Nov. 1995: A27+.

Holmes, Stephen. "When Less State Means Less Freedom." *Transitions* Sept. 1997: 66–74.

"How Many Other Chechnyas?" *The Economist* 14 Jan. 1995: 43–45.

Ingwerson, Marshall. "Moscow's Next Angst: Yeltsin Loses Power to Hinterlands." *Christian Science Monitor* 27 Nov. 1996: 1+.

—. "For Yeltsin's Top Aide, Can-Do Skills May Be the Ticket to Power in the Kremlin." *Christian Science Monitor* 1 Nov. 1996: 1+.

—. "Russia's Juries Give Police an O.J.-Style Rap." *Christian Science Monitor* 23 April 1996: 1+.

—. "Russian Tillers Still Struggle to Hoe a Row of Their Own." *Christian Science Monitor* 2 April 1996: 1+.

—. "Russia's Elections from A(pple) to Z(hirinovsky)." *Christian Science Monitor* 15 Dec. 1995: 7.

"Interview with Unnamed Russian Federation Security Council Staffer." *Komsomolskaya Pravda* 17 Feb. 1995. Trans. in *FBIS-SOV* 22 Feb. 1995: 18–20.

Jensen, Donald. "Patrimonialism in Post-Soviet Russia." *RFE/RL Newsline* (17 July 1997): 2 pp. Online. Internet.

"Lawless." *The Economist* 19 April 1997: 52–53.

Lipman, Marsha, and Lydmila Lateva. "Basic Information on Local Governments in the Russian Federation." *Local Governments in the CEE and CIS: 1994.* Budapest: Institute for Local Government and Public Service, 1994.

Liesman, Steve. "Surprise: The Economy in Russia Is Clawing Out of Deep Recession." *The Wall Street Journal* 28 Jan. 1998, western ed.: A1+.

—. "Coping Quietly: Despite Big Problems, Russia Remains Calm, Free of Much Protest." *The Wall Street Journal* 8 April 1997, western ed.: A1+.

"Mafia: Organized Crime in Russia." *Jane's Intelligence Review* Special Report #10, June 1996.

Mason, Dave, Antal Orkeny, and Svetlana Sidorenko-Stephenson. "Increasingly Fond Memories of a Grim Past." *Transitions* 21 March 1997: 15–19.

"The Master of Russia Returns." *The Economist* 8 March 1997: 55–56.

Mikhailovskaya, Inga. "Russian Voting Behavior as a Mirror of Social-Political Change." *East European Constitutional Review.* Spring/Summer 1996: 57–63.

Morvant, Penny. "War on Organized Crime and Corruption." *Transitions* 15 Feb. 1995: 32–36.

"New Russian Barometer." *The Economist* 2 March 1996: 48.

The OMRI Annual Survey of Eastern Europe and the Former Soviet Union: 1995. New York: M.E. Sharpe, 1996.

Orttung, Robert, and Scott Parish. "From Confrontation to Cooperation in Russia." *Transition* 13 Dec. 1996: 16–20.

Pestoff, Victor, ed. *Reforming Social Services in Central and Eastern Europe: An Eleven Nation Overview.* Krakow, Poland: The Krakow Academy of Economics and Friedrich Ebert Stiftung Foundation, 1995.

"On the Procedure for Realizing Decisions of the Security Council." *Moskovskiye Novosti* 19 July 1992: 4.

"Reorganizing the Security Council." *Kommersant* 3 March 1994: 1+.

Reshetar, John. *The Soviet Polity: Government and Politics in the USSR.* 3rd ed. New York: Harper and Row, 1989.

"Russia after Chechnya." *The Economist* 28 Jan. 1995: 21–23.

"The Russian Art of Survival." *The Economist* 3 Oct. 1998: 60–61.

"Russian Love in a Cold Climate." *The Economist* 15 Aug. 1998: 37–38.

"Russia's in-the-red Army. *The Economist* 2 Aug. 1997: 37–38.

"Russian Oil: Not a Gusher." *The Economist* 14 Oct. 1995: 78–79.

Schmemann, Serge. "Russia Drops Pledge of No First Use of Atom Arms." *New York Times* 4 Nov. 1993: A8.

"Special Report: Russian Electoral Survey." *OMRI Daily Report* (1 Dec. 1995): 10 pp. Online. Internet.

"Special Report: Russian Electoral Survey." *OMRI Daily Report* (28 Nov. 1995): 10 pp. Online. Internet.

Soberg Shugart, Matthew. "Executive-Legislative Relations in Post-Communist Europe." *Transitions* 13 Dec. 1996: 6–9.

Soviet Union. *Sovietskie konstitutsii sprovchnik.* Moscow: Gospolitizdat, 1963.

Stavrakis, Peter. "Russia's Malady: Asian Flu or Native Virus." *OMRI Daily Report* (15 Jan. 1998): 2 pp. Online. Internet.

Tolz, Vera. "The Moscow Crisis and the Future of Democracy in Russia." *RFE/RL Research Report* 22 Oct. 1993: 9.

Twigg, Judyth, L. "Russian Health Care in Critical Condition." *Transitions* Aug. 1997: 56–61.

"The Tycoons behind the Politicians." *Economist* 4 April 1998: 56–57.

Varoli, John. "Economic Reform Casts a Long Shadow in Russia." *Transitions* 21 March 1997: 6–10.

—. "There are More 'New Poor' than 'New Russians.'" *Transitions* 4 Oct. 1996: 6–11.

White, Stephan, Richard Rose, and Ian McAllister. *How Russia Votes.* London: Chatham House, 1997.

Williams, Daniel. "Death, Chess and Politics in Russia." *Washington Post* (13 Oct. 1998): 2 pp. Online Internet.

Zolotov, Andrei. "Why Russia Restricts Religions." Editorial. *Christian Science Monitor* 28 Oct. 1997: 18.

—. "Free-Wheeling Paper Falls to Free Market in Russia." *Christian Science Monitor* 26 May 1995: 4.

ENDNOTES

1. A note on the differences between Russia and the Soviet Union: Although theoretically the Russian Socialist Federated Soviet Republic was only one of the fifteen republics that comprised the Soviet Union, it was in fact the dominant one. Russian was the official language, Russians dominated the political hierarchy, and the Russian capital of Moscow was the capital of the Soviet Union. Therefore, the Russian state continued to exist even under the communists. However, to clearly delineate the difference between the Soviet Union and Russia, the term Soviet Union will be used for the years 1918–1991.

2. A note on terms: Although the Soviet Union was controlled by a communist party, it was not, contrary to popular opinion in the United States, a communist state. In fact, there has never been a communist state. As we will see, "communism" is a term that refers to a specific stage of economic development. According to Soviet political scientists, the Soviet Union was a socialist state building the foundations of a communist society. To avoid confusion, however, unless otherwise noted the terms *communist* and *socialist* are used interchangeably.

3. Marshall Ingwerson, "Russian Tillers Still Struggle to Hoe a Row of Their Own," *Christian Science Monitor,* April 2, 1996; *The Economist,* July 25, 1998.

4. Judyth L. Twigg, "Russian Health Care in Critical Condition," *Transitions,* August 1997, p. 57.

5. *OMRI Daily Report,* June 23, 1995.

6. *The Sacramento Bee,* November 19, 1995.

7. Interestingly, and with potentially significant future consequences, eight of the ten regions that registered population increases were non-Russian republics. *OMRI Daily Report,* February 3, 1997.

8. "Health in Russia: Humanitarian and Foreign Policy Issues," *Bulletin of the Atlantic Council,* no. 10, November 30, 1996.

9. *The Economist,* January 28, 1995, pp. 21–23.

10. This section is based on John Reshetar's discussion of classes in *The Soviet Polity: Government and Politics in the USSR,* 3rd ed. (New York: Harper and Row, 1989), 24–28.

11. As in the rest of the Soviet bloc, the elite perpetuated themselves by choosing reliable people who could be counted on to maintain the system. The *nomenklatura* was a list of thousands of government and party positions. This list was controlled by a special Party committee and appointment to one of these positions required CPSU approval. This tool was used by the Party to ensure loyalty.

12. John Varoli, "There Are More 'New Poor' than 'New Russians,'" *Transition,* October 4, 1996, p. 6.

13. Victor Pestoff, ed., *Reforming Social Services in Central and Eastern Europe: An Eleven Nation Overview* (Krakow, Poland: The Krakow Academy of Economics and Friedrich Ebert Stiftung Foundation, 1995), p. 252.

14. Varoli, "'New Poor,'" p. 9.

15. Rutland, pp. 12–18.

16. *The Economist,* August 12, 1995, p. 44.

17. Dave Mason, Antal Orkeny, and Svetlana Sidorenko-Stephenson, "Increasingly Fond Memories of a Grim Past," *Transitions,* March 21, 1997, p. 19.

18. Although income data must be treated with caution because of underreporting to avoid taxes, the figures show a growing income disparity. *OMRI Daily Digest,* January 15, 1997.

19. Calculated in purchasing power parity (PPP). PPP is defined as the number of units of a country's currency required to buy the same amount of goods and services in the domestic market as one dollar would buy in the United States. This is a more accurate measure of actual living standards than the traditional Gross Domestic Product (GDP) figure, which simply divides the GDP by the total population. Thus PPP will be the measure used throughout this book.

20. Mason et al., "Increasingly Fond Memories," p. 18.

21. "New Russian Barometer," Center for the Study of Public Policy, University of Strathclyde, 1995. Cited in *The Economist,* March 2, 1996, p. 48.

22. *The Wall Street Journal,* January 28, 1998.

23. *Segodnya,* February 5, 1997. Cited in *OMRI Daily Digest,* February 6, 1997.

24. John Varoli, "Economic Reform Casts a Long Shadow in Russia," *Transition,* March 21, 1997, p. 6.

25. *The Economist,* October 25, 1997, p. 81.

26. In addition to the Soviet Union, members included Bulgaria, Czechoslovakia, East Germany, Hungary, Poland, and Romania.

27. *OMRI Daily Digest,* March 4, 1997.

28. "Emerging Market Indicators," *The Economist,* November 1, 1997.

29. Also known as the Mongols, the Tartars were a tribe originally from Mongolia that overran much of Europe in the thirteenth century.

30. Reshetar, p. 88.

31. Although in the Soviet system "socialism" was a stage on the road to communism, in democracies "socialism" has a much different context. Socialists in the West are much less doctrinaire than communists. In the Soviet version of socialism, the state owned and controlled the economy. In contrast, socialists in pluralistic societies usually favor a mixed form of state and private ownership. These differences extended into the political sphere as well. Socialists respect basic civil liberties and do not suppress other parties; unlike communists, they participate in elections and leave office if they lose.

32. In Bulgaria it was called *vriske* (connections) and in Hungary *kiskapu* (finding a small open door in a larger closed one), and in Poland *koneksje* (connections).

33. Nicholas Berdyaev, *The Russian Idea* (London: Geoffrey Bles, 1947), pp. 142–144.

34. *New York Times,* November 4, 1993.

35. Peter Ford, "KGB-Era Suspecions Lurk within Russia's Refurbished Spy Agency," *The Christian Science Monitor,* January 24, 1995.

36. *OMRI Daily Digest,* January 14, 1997.

37. *OMRI Daily Digest,* March 10, 1997.

38. Floriana Fossato and Anna Kachkaeva, "Russia to Have New Nationwide Television Network," *RFE/RL Newsline,* May 22, 1997.

39. Constitutional Watch, *East European Constitutional Review,* Winter 1996, p. 24.

40. John Downing, *Internationalizing Media Theory,* London: Sage Publications, 1996, 144.

41. Ibid., p. 129.

42. *Christian Science Monitor,* May 26, 1995.

43. Peter Ford, "Russia's Free Press Opts Not to Play Fair before Elections," *Christian Science Monitor,* April 26, 1996.

44. Andrei Fadin, "In Russia, Private Doesn't Mean Independent," *Transitions,* October 1997, p. 90.

45. Democratic centralism was Lenin's policy of ensuring that various nationalist and other centrifugal forces inherent in Russia would not prevent the Communist Party from taking power. This policy had two key provisions: first, that the decisions of higher organs are absolutely binding on lower organs, and second, that Party members must combat "localism," the tendency to place regional or local issues ahead of state policy.

46. *Sovietskie konstitutsii sprovchnik* (Moscow: Gospolitizdat, 1963). Cited in Reshetar, *The Soviet Polity,* p. 175.

47. Joakim Hesse, ed., *Administrative Transformation in Central and Eastern Europe* (Oxford: Blackwell Publishers, 1993), p. 127.

48. Constitutional Watch, *East European Constitutional Review,* Winter 1998, p. 30.

49. *The Economist,* January 14, 1995.

50. Daniel Williams, "Death, Chess and Politics in Russia," *Washington Post,* October 13, 1998, p. A1.

51. Constitutional Watch, *East European Constitutional Review,* Winter 1998, p. 33.

52. Constitutional Watch, *East European Constitutional Review,* Winter 1997, p. 26.

53. *Wall Street Journal,* "Coping Quietly: Despite Big Problems, Russia Remains Calm, Free of Much Protest." April 8, 1997, p. A1.

54. Constitutional Watch, *East European Constitutional Review,* Winter 1998, p. 33.

55. Masha Lipman and Lydmila Lateva, "Basic Information on Local Governments in the Russian Federation," in *Local Governments in the CEE and CIS: 1994* (Budapest: Institute for Local Government and Public Service, 1994), p. 183.

56. Ibid., p. 185.

57. Varoli, "Economic Reform," p. 10.

58. Marshall Ingwerson, "Moscow's Next Angst: Yeltsin Loses Power to Hinterlands," *Christian Science Monitor,* November 27, 1996.

59. Laura Belin, RFE/RL Political Analyst. Personal interview. Prague, Czech Republic, July 23, 1998.

60. Reshetar, *The Soviet Polity,* pp. 192–193.

61. After "streamlining" in 1997, the government consisted of sixty-seven members: two first deputy prime ministers, six deputy prime ministers, twenty-three ministers, sixteen state committee chairpersons, and the heads of twenty federal agencies. *OMRI Daily Report,* March 27, 1997.

62. *RFE/RL News Briefs,* February 14–18, 1994, p. 3.

63. Matthew Soberg Shugart, "Executive-Legislative Relations in Post-Communist Europe," *Transition,* December 13, 1996, p. 6.

64. Like its counterparts in other Central and European states, the Russian legal system is quite different in form and substance from the legal system in the United States. Most European states are civil law states. This means their law and legal theory are based on the statutory law of the state. Since legislation is meant to provide exclusive coverage on any given topic, judges simply decide whether a law has been broken. In contrast, the American and British legal systems are based on common law. Common law allows for "judicial interpretation" (decisions not covered by specific legislation that fill in legislative gaps) and *stare decisis* (rule of precedence). These features make the legal system flexible but give American and British judges much more power than their continental counterparts.

65. *OMRI Daily Report,* February 20, 1995.

66. *The OMRI Annual Survey of East Europe and the Former Soviet Union: 1995* (New York: M.E. Sharpe, 1996), p. 218.

67. Constitutional Watch, *East European Constitutional Review,* Fall 1996, p. 24.

68. Cited in Marshall Ingwerson, "Russia's Juries Give Police an O.J.-Style Rap," *Christian Science Monitor,* April 23, 1996.

69. Peter Ford, "Thug Capitalism Drives Up Crime in Russia, Testing New Freedoms," *Christian Science Monitor,* March 16, 1995.

70. Vtisom, cited in *The Economist,* March 8, 1997.

71. *RFE/RL Newsline,* May 30, 1997.

72. *The Economist,* April 19, 1997, p. 53.

73. *OMRI Daily Digest,* March 4, 1997.

74. *The Economist,* September 2, 1995, pp. 46–48.

75. Vera Tolz, "The Moscow Crisis and the Future of Democracy in Russia," *RFE/RL Research Report* October 22, 1993, p. 9.

76. In February 1996, the Federal Security Service arrested Alexander Nikitin, a former nuclear submarine commander. Nikitin was accused of revealing state secrets in a report he wrote on nuclear waste for a Norwegian environmental group. He was held without bail for ten months, pending treason charges. Even when Nikitin was released from pre-trial detention, the charges against him were not dropped and he was forbidden from leaving St. Petersburg. Laura Belin and Robert Orttung, "Electing a Fragile Political Stability," *Transition,* February 7, 1997, p. 70.

77. The commissioner is responsible for overseeing state protection of individual rights and freedoms. This position is appointed and dismissed by the Duma by secret ballot.

78. Another illustration of the lack of respect for human rights can be seen in the roundup of minority ethnic groups in preparation for Moscow's 850 anniversary celebration. This included illegally evicting people from their apartments. *RFE/RL Newsline,* June 27, 1997.

79. Ukrainian Justice Minister Serhiy Holovaty, cited in Joel Blocker, "Corruption Among State Officials in Eastern Europe," *RFE/RL Newsline,* June 13, 1997.

80. *INTERFAX,* April 3, 1995. In *FBIS-SOV,* April 4, 1995; *ITAR-TASS,* June 19, 1995. In *FBIS-SOV,* June 30, 1995, p. 12.

81. *Economitcheskaya Gazeta,* July 27, 1991.

82. In 1997, only a few officials publicly released their income statements. Even among those who did, assets of family members were excluded and there was no punishment for those who failed to file.

83. Cited in *The Economist,* July 5, 1997, p. 56.

84. *OMRI Daily Report,* July 24, 1995.

85. *Associated Press,* September 23, 1995.

86. *RFE/RL Daily Report,* December 9, 1995.

87. The top three most trusted public institutions are the armed forces (48%), the Orthodox church (44%), and the security services (29%). *Mneniye* [Opinion], July 1997. Cited in *The Economist,* August 2, 1997.

88. *RFE/RL Newsline,* May 29, 1997.

89. Stephen Blank, "Yeltsin Fosters a Military Threat to Democracy," *Transition,* August 9, 1996, p. 13.

90. Fred Weir, "Unity Eludes Russian's Reformers," *Christian Science Monitor,* December 17, 1998, p. 6.

91. Marshall Ingwerson, "Russia's Elections from A(pple) to Z(hirinovsky)," *Christian Science Monitor,* December 15, 1995, p. 7.

92. Kiril Kholodkovski, *MEMO,* no. 10, 1995. Cited in *OMRI Special Report: Russian Electoral Survey,* no. 10, December 1, 1995.

93. Stephen White, Richard Rose, and Ian McAllister, *How Russia Votes* (London: Chatham House, 1997), p. 43.

94. In contrast to their usage in the West, the terms "left" and "right" have different connotations in Central and Eastern Europe. Leftist parties usually want to slow or halt change, while rightist parties favor reforms.

95. Inga Mikhailovskaya, "Russian Voting Behavior as a Mirror of Social-Political Change," *East European Constitutional Review,* Spring/Summer 1996, p. 61.

96. "Russia and Ukraine: Political and Economic Update," (Washington, DC: The Atlantic Council, December 1, 1995), p. 2.

97. For example, the "Uneximbank Group," headed by Vladimir Potanin, controls Uneximbak, MFK Renaissance Investment Group, Sidanco Oil Company, Norilsk Nickle Metal Company, Svyazinvest Telecoms, *Komsomolskaya Pravda, Russky Telgraf,* and *Investia.*

98. *The Economist,* April 4, 1998.

99. *RFE/RL Newsline,* April 16, 1998

100. Donald Jensen, "Patrimonialism in Post-Soviet Russia," *RFE/RL Newsline,* July 17, 1997.

101. "Mafia: Organized Crime in Russia," *Jane's Intelligence Review,* Special Report no. 10, June 1996.

102. In a briefing with journalists, Interior Minister Kulikov said there were over 9,000 criminal gangs with over 100,000 members operating in Russia. The number of reported crimes by organized groups increased 95 percent between 1992 and 1997. *RFE/RL Newsline,* June 16, 1997.

103. Cited in Penny Morvant, "War on Organized Crime and Corruption," *Transitions,* February 15, 1995, p. 33.

104. Cited in *OMRI Daily Digest,* March 6, 1997. In a particularly brazen act, Galina Starovoitova, one of Russia's most prominent women politicians and potential presidential candidate, was murdered outside her apartment in what most observers believed was a politically motivated killing. *AP,* November 22, 1998.

105. Andrei Zolotov, "Why Russia Restricts Religions," *Christian Science Monitor,* October 28, 1997, p. 18.

106. When asked whether politicians do their best, 70 percent of the population said no. This compares with 62 percent in Bulgaria, 67 percent in Hungary, and 43 percent in Poland. Laszlo Bruszt, *Political Culture and Economic Orientations in Central and East Europe during the Transition to Democracy: 1990–1992* (Berlin: Wissenschaftszentrum fur Sozialforschung, 1993), p. 91.

107. Forty-one percent of the respondents said there were no great differences between party platforms. "Special Report: Russian Electoral Survey," *OMRI,* November 28, 1995.

108. A 1998 survey found only 18 percent of wages were paid on time and 57 percent of the workers were not paid at all. ISM Research Centre, cited in *The Economist,* October 3, 1998. As a result of these problems, employees at many enterprises receive wages in kind. For example, workers at a factory producing women's underwear in Vladivostok have been receiving bras in lieu of wages. Short on cash, the factory has handed out seven to nine bras a month to both male and female employees. *OMRI Daily Digest,* January 21, 1997.

109. In 1996, approximately 17 million workers in 96,000 companies and organizations were not being paid. Back wages total $9 billion. Steve Liesman, "Coping Quietly: Despite Big Problems, Russia Remains Calm, Free of Much Protest," *Wall Street Journal,* April 8, 1997, p. A1.

110. Peter Ford, "Russian Unions Lack AFL Clout," *Christian Science Monitor,* September 20, 1996. See also Paul Christensen, "Why Russia Lacks a Labor Movement," *Transitions,* December 1997, pp. 44–51.

111. *The Economist,* August 12, 1995, p. 44.

112. *The Economist,* August 15, 1998, p. 37.

113. *OMRI Daily Digest,* January 6, 1997.

114. *The Washington Post,* November 12, 1995, p. A27.

115. "Reorganizing the Security Council," *Kommersant,* March 3, 1994.

116. *RFE/RL News Briefs,* November 2, 1994, p. 1.

117. Robert Orttung and Scott Parish, "From Confrontation to Cooperation in Russia," *Transition,* December 13, 1996, p. 18.

118. *The Economist,* October 14, 1995, pp. 78–79.

119. Floriana Fossato, Stephanie Baker, Laura Belin, "Yeltsin Pledges Fair Privatization," *OMRI Daily Report,* August 17, 1997.

120. Peter Stavrakis, "Russia's Malady: Asian Flu or Native Virus," *OMRI Daily Report,* January 15, 1998.

121. "On the Procedure for Realizing Decisions of the Security Council," *Moskovskiye Novosti,* July 19, 1992, p. 4.

122. "Interview with unnamed Russian Federation Security Council staffer," *Komsomolskaya Pravda,* February 17–20, 1995. In *FBIS-SOV,* February 22, 1995, pp. 18–20.

123. *Freedom in the World: The Annual Survey of Political Rights and Civil Liberties, 1996– 1997.* New York: Transaction Publishers, 1997, p. 22.

124. *Freedom in the World,* 18.

125. Cited in Alexei Izyumov, "Rebuilding Authority in Russia," *Christian Science Monitor,* December 11, 1998, p. 19.

126. Marshall Ingwerson, "For Yeltsin's Top Aide, Can-Do Skills May Be the Ticket to Power in the Kremlin," *Christian Science Monitor,* November 1, 1996.

127. Stephen Holmes, "When Less State Means Less Freedom," *Transitions,* September 1997, p. 68.

128. Freedom House, p. 19.

129. Most advanced industrial economies qualify for the 4* rating.

130. *OMRI Daily Digest,* March 28, 1997.

131. *Freedom in the World,* p. 24.

2

BULGARIA

INTRODUCTION

This chapter examines the Republic of Bulgaria, one of the least known states in Central and Eastern Europe. Although recognized for its beautiful scenery, rose oil, wine, and yogurt, Bulgaria rarely makes the headlines of the world press. Therefore, its political development has been of little interest to the rest of the world. A small Balkan country, it was part of the Ottoman Empire for 500 years. After liberation in 1878, Bulgaria enjoyed a sixty-year period of independence before it was incorporated in the Soviet bloc after World War II. Like Hungary, its 1989 shift to democracy came in a peaceful, communist-led transition that had little in common with the Solidarity-led electoral revolution in Poland or the attempted coup in Russia.

As a result of Bulgaria's almost slavish alliance with the former Soviet Union, it has most of the latter's economic, political, and social problems. Often referred to as the sixteenth Soviet Republic, it never opposed its "Big Brother." Even though other socialist states enacted limited economic reforms and periodically revolted against communist rule, Bulgaria remained politically loyal and economically dependent on the former Soviet Union.

Although there was a societal consensus on the need for reforms immediately following the downfall of the old regime, this political and economic legacy has made it difficult to create a civil society, democratic institutions, and a market economy based on the rule of law. Bulgaria has been plagued by governmental instability. This is the result of an extremely polarized polity. The first free elections, held in 1990, were won by the Bulgarian Socialist Party—the former communist party. Their victory provoked general discontent and they were soon forced to hand over power to a politically neutral, technocratic government. The victory of the democratic forces in the second election in 1991 did not end the political stalemate. After

only nine months in power, it was forced to cede power to another techno-cratic government that also failed to enact political and economic reforms. As a result, December 1994 elections gave the BSP a majority in the National Assembly, ending five years of weak coalition governments. Popular revulsion to increasing economic problems led to early elections in 1997. These elections swept the BSP from power and gave the United Democratic Forces a majority in the parliament.

Because of this succession of revolving door governments—eight between 1989 and 1997—and lack of political courage, Bulgaria has only recently begun to enact major economic reforms. As a result, Bulgarian economic performance is among the worst in the region, a situation that has greatly exacerbated social tensions. Domestic problems have been aggravated by international events. The United Nations' economic embargoes against Iraq and Yugoslavia, two formerly important trading partners, cost the Bulgarian economy billions of dollars. As a result of these economic and political problems, Bulgarians' enthusiasm for change has dramatically less-ened. The percentage of people optimistic about the future, which used to be one of the highest in the region, has dramatically declined. According to a 1995 Gallup poll, 91 percent of the population is dissatisfied with the coun-try's development since 1989.

Like Russia, Bulgaria has not achieved a quick transition from a one-party communist regime to a pluralist democracy. Interestingly, although Bulgaria has constitutional safeguards such as a restrictive German-type electoral law, the lack of a political center has fostered political instability. This instability has been a key reason that Bulgaria has lagged both economi-cally and politically behind most other former socialist states. Inflation in Bulgaria was over 300 percent in 1996, ten times the average rate of other states in the region.

Unlike Hungary and Poland, Bulgaria has not yet been able to over-come geographical and historical legacies, such as authoritarian regimes and political and economic backwardness. Therefore an examination of the Bulgarian polity will help provide answers to the important question of why states sharing common economic and political backgrounds for forty-five years have had such different experiences in their economic and political transformations. As with any country, these answers will only be found by exploring historical, contemporary, domestic, and international factors that have influenced the development of the Bulgarian polity.

NATIONAL DATA

Geography

The Republic of Bulgaria is located on the Black Sea on the eastern part of the Balkan Peninsula. It occupies the crossroads of important trade routes between Europe and the Middle East and shares borders with Serbia, Macedonia, Greece, Turkey, and Romania. The capital, Sofia, is located in a mountainous basin near the western border of the country. Bulgaria has a total area of 42,823 square miles, approximately the size of Tennessee.

Contemporary Bulgaria includes portions of historic Macedonia. This has caused tensions with Macedonia as Bulgarians considers all Slavic-speaking Macedonians to be ethnic Bulgarians. As a result, while Bulgaria was the first state to recognize Macedonia as a sovereign state in 1992, the two neighbors have not signed a single official document since then. This situation is the result of two reasons: first, Sofia is afraid that if it recog-nizes a separate Macedonian language, it will open the door for claims a Macedonian minority exists in the southwestern region of Bulgaria, known as Pirin Macedonia. Second, the symbolic value of language is very important for states in the region. In contrast to Western states, where citizenship is largely centered around state institutions, citizenship for most Central and Eastern European states is centered around language and ethnicity.[1] Most of the conflicts in this region have their roots in this difference.

Resources

Bulgaria has traditionally been an agrarian country. The Danubian Plain and the southeastern portion of the country are covered with fertile soil ideal for agriculture. However, as a result of forced industrialization after World War II, some parts of the country are now heavily polluted.

Because of its location in the middle of the Balkan Mountains, Bulgaria has large deposits of stone—marble, limestone, granite, sandstone, and clay—that are used in the building industry. Overall, however, Bulgaria is not well endowed with natural resources. It has some deposits of coal, but they are of low quality. There are small amounts of oil and natural gas, but they lie at considerable depth. This lack of indigenous resources not only hindered industrial development, but also made Bulgaria very dependent on imports from the Soviet Union.

Its location in the Balkan Range has given Bulgaria an abundance of mineral springs. There are more than 600 mineral springs spread throughout the country. The medical qualities of the water as well as their beautiful natural setting have potential tourism value.

People

In 1996, Bulgaria had a population of 8,385,000, 67 percent of whom live in urban areas. This is the lowest percentage among the states in this book. As a result of social and economic changes after 1945, notably the introduction of free medical care and improved working conditions, Bulgaria's death and infant mortality rates dropped significantly. This caused a rapid increase in the population and urbanization between 1945 and 1980.

Since the change in regime, a continuing economic recession—with its corresponding decrease in living standards, increasing unemployment, and a deteriorating health care system—have caused the birth rate to decline and the mortality rate to increase.[2] Between 1990 and 1996, the birth rate dropped from 12.1 to 8.6 per thousand and is now one of the lowest in the world. Since the last census in 1985, the Bulgarian population has declined by 5 percent, or over 420,000 people.

These conditions have fostered large-scale migration. Between 1990 and 1996, over 500,000 mostly young people left the country. This situation has numerous negative repercussions. First, it is causing a "brain drain" because most emigrants are highly educated specialists desperately needed in Bulgaria. Second, although it currently has no direct effect, in the next ten to fifteen years this situation will pose a major problem. When the current working-age group begins to retire, there will be fewer workers to support them. In 1995, 21 percent of the population was already over age 60, up from 18 percent in 1985. This problem is shared by most other European states.

Ethnicity

The Bulgars, a tribe related to the Huns, crossed the Danube from the north in A.D. 679 and subjugated the Slavic population in what is now contemporary Bulgaria. Over time, they adopted Slavic customs and language, creating a unique Bulgarian nationality.

Although the Bulgarians consider Bulgaria to be a homogenous state, ethnic and religious minorities made up over 15 percent of the population in 1996. Ethnic Turks and gypsies—Roma—are the two largest minority groups. The Pomaks, who make up the third largest minority group, are ethnic Bulgarians who converted to Islam during the period of Ottoman rule. Overall, Bulgaria's population includes approximately 822,000 Turks, 313,000 gypsies, and 275,000 Pomaks.[3]

As in the rest of the region, a legacy of repression combined with newly acquired political freedom and economic instability have fueled a resurgent nationalism. There has been a growth of ethnic awareness among members of minority groups, creating sharper social and ethnic divisions as well as new political problems. Bulgaria has not been immune to this trend. The presence of minority groups has played a role in the polarization of society as political parties seek to exploit this situation. A 1994 U.S. State Department Human Rights report noted that xenophobia, nationalism, and antiethnic attitudes among the population were on the increase. Significantly, Bulgaria is one of five states that refused to sign the Convention for the Protection of National Minorities of the Council of Europe. However, the Constitution protects the right of any citizen whose mother tongue is not Bulgarian to study and use his or her own language. A look at the main minority groups offers a glimpse into the situation facing Bulgaria today.

ETHNIC TURKS.   Although the origin of Bulgaria's Turkish population is disputed, ethnic Turkish Bulgarian citizens consider themselves Turks. They live chiefly in the northeastern and southwestern parts of the country, constituting a majority of the population in these areas.

Since liberation from Ottoman Turkish control in 1877, the ethnic Turks who remained in Bulgaria have been seen as a potential "fifth column." In general, the Bulgarian perception of Turks is negative. They have typically been portrayed as devious and untrustworthy, the traditional enemy. This image has been formed by collective memory, education, and the media and is perpetuated in literature, schoolbooks, works of art, and folklore. As a result, various governments have periodically used the Turks as scapegoats. For example, because of increasing pressure to enact reforms, between 1984 and 1989 the government decided to deflect popular attention

THE BULGARIZATION CAMPAIGN

"Bulgarization" was Communist Party leader Todor Zhivkov's answer to slowing economic growth and growing pressure for political liberalization in the 1980s. In 1984, Zhivkov launched an ethnic nationalization campaign against the Turkish minority that outlawed the use of the Turkish language in public and forced them to take Slavic names. This policy was intensified when government historians "discovered" the Turks were actually Bulgarians who had lost their sense of national consciousness during earlier centuries of Turkish rule. The implementation of this campaign involved the deployment of troops and a number of casualties. The campaign reached its peak in 1989, when over 350,000 Turks were forced to emigrate to Turkey. The timing of this final act is important because it shows Zhivkov's use of nationalism to increase the legitimacy of his own rule. Even after the Bulgarization policies were reversed and the Bulgarian Turks civil rights restored in late 1989, tension between the Turkish and Bulgarian population remains. This can be seen as the creation of the Turkish-dominated Movement for Rights and Freedom Party.

by launching a program that forced ethnic Turks to adopt Slavic names (Bulgarization).

Interestingly, this xenophobic policy, which was similar to Romanian campaigns against their ethnic Hungarians, is completely alien to the Marxist ideology that socialist states professed to follow.[4] The process culminated when the government actually changed names on tombstones. This program caused 350,000 ethnic Turks to flee to Turkey, although approximately half returned after the fall of the communist regime.

Since 1989, ethnic Turks have been allowed to study Turkish in school and observe Islamic holidays. Although they are constitutionally equal, like the black population in the United States before the civil rights movement ethnic Turks are discriminated against. As a result, the majority live in tightly knit ethnic communities and work in agricultural production. Partially because of a collapse of agricultural exports, ethnic Turks suffer from an 80 percent unemployment rate. Recently, the government has tried to alleviate the consequences of ethnic discrimination perpetuated by the former communist regime. In 1998, a government ordinance allowed the payment of pensions to Bulgarian citizens currently living in Turkey.

ROMA (GYPSIES).   Half of Bulgaria's Roma are Muslims and the other half are Christians. To the average Bulgarian, the Roma constitute a homogeneous group; in reality, there are several subgroups with different cultures and political programs. During the early years of socialism, the state allowed the Roma to develop their own culture. This policy was changed in the 1950s when the authorities tried to discourage Romany identity by integrating them into the Bulgarian Slavic community. These efforts were largely unsuccessful.

Today the Roma community faces large-scale malnutrition, crime, disease, and lack of formal education. These problems have been accented by a deteriorating economic situation in which gypsies are usually the first to be fired and last to be hired. This has resulted in a 50 percent unemployment rate among the Roma; not coincidentally, a disproportionate number—33 percent—of crimes are committed by them.

Despite religious affinities with both Slavs and Turks, the Roma are considered an alien group. As in other Central and Eastern European states, gypsies are frequent targets of discrimination and police brutality.

POMAKS.   Pomaks are Bulgarian Slavs whose ancestors converted to Islam between the seventeenth and nineteenth centuries. Thus they constitute a religious rather than an ethnic minority. Pomaks speak Bulgarian and live in the mountainous central part of the country. These Bulgarian Muslims typically work in agriculture and tend to live separately from neighboring Christians. There have been several campaigns to assimilate them into the Christian Slav population, the most vicious occurring between 1971 and 1973. The Pomaks' isolation, coupled with the decline of government subsidies for local industry and tobacco, has caused a dramatic decline in their standard of living. This situation has fostered political cooperation between the Pomaks and the ethnic Turks.

As a result of the upheaval that followed the demise of the communist regime, differences between Slavic Christian Bulgarians and other ethnic/religious groups have become even more pronounced. This conflict has significantly strengthened group identities.

Class Divisions

Although Marxist ideology said that social and economic classes would cease to exist in a socialist state, this did not occur. As in Russia, before 1989 Bulgarian society could generally be divided into five strata: the ruling elite, the "middle class," the intelligentsia, the urban working class, and the peasantry. Membership in the latter classes depended on education, vocation and/or ethnicity while membership in the ruling elite was solely the result of Communist Party membership.

Since 1989, political criteria no longer determine one's status in society as class structures have undergone a transition along economic lines. Decreasing state control over the economy has created three classes: the new rich, a lower middle class, and the poor.

The new rich includes ex–Communist Party *nomenklatura,* who used the confusion surrounding economic and political changes to take control of businesses and industries that were formerly state monopolies. Also included within this category are entrepreneurs. These groups control most of the privatized economy, even though they constitute a very small portion of the population. Although not as stratified as in Russia or the United States, but nevertheless a major change from the past, the wealthiest 10 percent of the population receive over 25 percent of the national income.[5]

Under the old regime, the middle class consisted of the formerly privileged group of economic managers, civil servants, intelligentsia, and military officers. As a result of previous educational policies, many people were trained as engineers for the chemical, manufacturing, and steel industries, skills that are no longer needed because the industrial, military, and scientific centers of the country have been the hardest hit by economic changes. The end of government subsidies and preferential treatment for these sectors has caused numerous plant closings and has reduced work for those that remain open. Consequently, highly skilled or educated people often work as taxi drivers, salesmen, or manual workers—occupations that ensure a better income.[6] As in Russia, the demise of the middle class has greatly hindered the development of a civil society.

Worsening economic conditions have also created a large impoverished class. Comprising approximately 70 percent of the population, it includes common laborers, pensioners, the unemployed, invalids, minorities, and young workers. Between 1990 and 1996, this group's living standards decreased by over 300 percent. Pensioners have especially suffered. The average pension is only 28.6 percent of the average income.[7] Interestingly, in contrast to Russia, women in Bulgaria have benefitted from the change in regime. A 1995 United Nations–sponsored report ranked Bulgaria twentieth among 116 surveyed countries in "women's opportunity for participation in political and economic decision-making." This ranking is due to the relatively large share of educated women holding administrative and managerial positions.[8]

To lessen social unrest, successive governments have kept price controls on staple commodities. However, this has not prevented the prices of most goods from escalating beyond the reach of most of the population. Between 1989 and 1996, prices rose over 2500 percent. In 1996 alone, the cost of living tripled. Prices of bread and cheese—the most basic staple in Bulgaria—nearly doubled between June and August. At one point, bread prices rose daily and some stores refused to stock products because their value might decline before they were sold. Consequently, Bulgarian families were reported to be spending over 50 percent of their income on food.[9]

This situation has caused a drastic decrease in the standard of living for most people. According to the World Bank, 90 percent of the Bulgarian population lived below the poverty-line income of $4 per day in 1997,[10] compared to 38 percent in 1989.[11] Between 1991 and 1995, Bulgaria slipped from 33rd to 65th on the U.N.'s Human Development index. Reminiscent of the Great Depression, for a short period in 1997 soup kitchens were established in Sofia.

In summary, society has become even more stratified than it was under the old regime. In the short term, three to five years, this situation will continue. The effects can be seen in increasing crime rates,[12] emigration, and a lack of societal consensus for reforms.

Economics

Traditionally an agrarian country, Bulgaria was industrialized after World War II through a series of Five Year Plans. The goal was to develop a Soviet-style centrally planned industrial economy. As a result, machine building, ferrous and nonferrous metallurgy, textile manufacturing, and agricultural processing became the pillars of the economy, with almost 40 percent of the workforce employed in these sectors. However, in contrast to the Soviet Union, Bulgaria and Hungary lacked the natural resources necessary for the development of heavy industry. Despite a favorable climate and good soils, the agricultural sector remained distinctly underdeveloped under the socialist regime.

While the socialist industrialization policy helped develop the Bulgarian economy, it left the same dismal legacy that faces all former socialist states. Some areas of the country suffered more from this policy than others. The concentration of industry in the northwestern part of the country, the Montana region, has caused this area to have the highest unemployment rate. Today the goal of the Bulgarian polity is to create a "mixed" economic system, private property and free enterprise combined with substantial state involvement. A key facet of this system is the development of a "social market economy" to maintain the extensive and expensive, but popular, social welfare system of the old regime. A key obstacle to economic reform has been the question of how to preserve a role for the state while simultaneously encouraging free enterprise. As a result, the economy is a mixture of decrepit state industry and underdeveloped private enterprise.

Because of the political costs of imposing unpopular economic reforms, few have been attempted. As a result, the economy has been devastated by high inflation and declining output. In 1996 alone, inflation was over 310 percent and the economy contracted 10.6 percent. The extent and severity of the economic situation can be better understood when compared with the Great Depression of the 1930s, when the GDP of the United States declined 25 percent. Between 1990 and 1997, Bulgaria's GDP declined over 45 percent.

Privatization, considered by many as a panacea for Bulgaria's economic ills, is proceeding slowly. Although a 1991 Privatization Law provided the legal framework for the transition of state companies to private ownership, many large and unprofitable companies have yet to be privatized. In contrast to other states in the region, Bulgaria did not initiate a mass privatization program until 1997. Fearing increased unemployment, the government has been reticent to close loss-making state-owned companies. With the end of central planning, there are approximately 3,500 state enterprises over which the state has little control but is financially responsible for. Since almost 50 percent of industrial enterprises lose money, the financial drain is enormous. This situation is worsened by the fact most firms lack the money to service their debts.

This situation has brought the banking system to the point of collapse. Two-thirds of the banks are insolvent. Bank failures have led to the devaluation of the currency, the lev. In the second half of 1996, the lev lost more than 600 percent of its value. Although international financial organizations made loans conditional on closing these companies, the government has failed to act. Of the sixty-four state-owned companies the government promised to close in 1996, only five were actually closed.

Another obstacle to privatization is its cost. Economic development since 1946 has put the state in the position of paying compensation to the heirs of the land that was nationalized and is now used by factories, schools, and so forth. Because of a huge budget deficit, the government has been reluctant to take on this responsibility.

Lack of societal consensus has also limited privatization. Trade union leaders have criticized this process, calling it a sellout to the West. Many people fear that a new entrepreneurial class will be created at the expense of thousands who will become unemployed. These fears are fueled by an increase in the unemployment rate from less than 1 percent in 1989 to 13.4 percent in 1997. Although this figure is probably exaggerated—a large portion of people "officially" unemployed work illegally in the private sector—it is indicative of the overall economic situation. Nevertheless this is a major change from the previous regime as everyone was guaranteed a job. Unemployment is projected to increase to over 18 percent as privatization increases.

However, the most important impediment to economic reforms has been political. For example, in 1995 the new BSP government, overriding a presidential veto, amended the Land Restitution Act. The amendments stipulated that any land for sale must first be offered to the government, which has three months to buy the land at a fixed, nonnegotiable price. In addition, any Bulgarian company with foreign capital is forbidden from owning land. Although these amendments were subsequently overruled by the Constitutional Court, this illustration shows how political battles have prevented crucial economic reforms.

Although there are some hopeful signs—for example, between 1992 and 1997 the private sector's share of GDP rose from 15 to 46 percent and now employs 42 percent of the workforce[13]—overall the economy is in bad shape. However, there are some mitigating factors. Unusual in the region, more than 80 percent of the population own their own homes. In addition, half of the population cultivate some land and an estimated 25 percent of economic activity is in the black, or nontaxed economy. Therefore, although the average pension is not enough to heat an apartment in Sofia, few starve or freeze.[14]

Trade

The emphasis on industry under the socialist regime was reinforced by Bulgaria's membership in the Council for Mutual Economic Assistance. In 1990, CMEA purchased 80 percent of Bulgaria's exports and provided 76 percent of its imports. In contrast, only 30 to 35 percent of Poland's trade was with other CMEA states. Thus, the collapse of CMEA and the switch to world market prices affected Bulgaria more than any other CMEA member. The end of subsidized Russian oil caused energy shortages. Gas and electricity became prohibitively expensive, fueling inflation. In addition, without the Soviet market, low-quality Bulgarian industrial goods could no longer be sold. This led to the closure of numerous factories, bringing unemployment to Bulgaria for the first time and fostering popular discontent.

Bulgaria's trade links with the Soviet Union had been forged at the expense of trade with the West. Prior to the demise of the USSR, only 11 percent of Bulgarian trade was with the West. Bulgaria has tried to diversify its trading partners, but progress has been slow. Although it signed a trade agreement with the European Union (EU), its ratification was delayed on technical grounds. In addition, Bulgaria's most competitive exports—agricultural products, steel, and textiles—are restricted by the EU. Nevertheless, by 1996, 39 percent of all Bulgarian trade was with EU countries.

Since the vacuum created by the collapse of the CMEA has not been filled by the West, Bulgaria has attempted to compensate by turning to its former partners. After falling 60 percent in 1991, imports from former CMEA countries began to increase. By 1996, trade with Russia accounted for approximately 19 percent of Bulgaria's total imports and exports.[15] As a result, Russia has again become Bulgaria's largest trading partner. Regionally, Bulgaria has increased trade with Greece and Turkey. It was a founding member of the Black Sea Economic Cooperation Region, a group that promotes trade and economic cooperation between states in the area. The importance of its neighbors can be noted by the fact that in 1994, 28.5 percent of Bulgaria's exports went to other Balkan states.[16]

Although Bulgaria has diversified its trading partners, the United Nation's sanctions against Yugoslavia and Iraq had severe repercussions for the economy. As a result of sanctions, Iraq defaulted on its $2 billion debt to Bulgaria. U.N. sanctions against Yugoslavia removed Bulgaria from its position as the main land route between Western Europe and the Middle East. Between 1991 and 1993 it was estimated that Bulgaria lost over $1.8 billion in transit fees alone.

Because of the delay in implementing reforms, political instability, a six-year debt moratorium, and proximity to the wars in former Yugoslavia, Bulgaria has received little financial help from Western governments or international institutions. In contrast to the $8.5 billion Hungary received in foreign investment between 1990 and 1996, Bulgaria received only $716 million.[17] Repayment of its large debt—$11.9 billion in 1996—and the revival of the economy has been greatly limited by the lack of foreign assistance.

The year 1996 was particularly disastrous for the economy. The lev collapsed, prices soared, real wages plummeted, and poverty increased. The Bulgarian economy has been "trapped" in a cyclical pattern unique in Central and Eastern Europe. With its large foreign debt and low attractiveness to foreign investors, Bulgaria has not been able to pay for imports and service its debts. And since postcommunist governments have not seriously pursued reforms, international lenders are reticent to extend loans. This causes periodic "runs"—a weakening of the lev as everyone runs away from it and buys dollars—whenever Bulgarian foreign currency reserves become low and it appears no new credit is coming into the country.[18]

Ten years after the fall of communism, Bulgaria is paying the price for economic procrastination. It has yet to complete agrarian reforms, privatize most state-owned enterprises, or enact structural reforms. As a result, in 1998 Bulgaria's average monthly income was $350 ($4,190 per year), the lowest of the states in our study.

Realizing the severity of the economic situation, the new ODF government has started down the path of economic reform. It has lifted price controls, rescheduled part of the external debt, and created a currency board. The latter requires that each lev in circulation be fully backed by foreign currency, precious metals, or foreign securities. This brought about much-needed financial discipline—immediately reducing inflation from 670 percent in 1997 to 9 percent in 1998 and fostering economic growth of 4 percent in 1998 by preventing the Bulgarian National Bank from lending to the government or providing credit for troubled banks and industries. Although incomes are growing faster than inflation for the first time since 1990 and Bulgaria received more foreign direct investment in 1997 than in the preceding seven years, it is still too early to judge the effectiveness of reforms. However, they are the most far-reaching changes enacted since 1989.

POLITICAL HISTORY

Since its founding in the seventh century, Bulgaria has had a history dominated by periods of independence interspersed with periods of foreign domination.

Before the Twentieth Century

The three main periods of foreign influence were by the Byzantine Empire (1018–1185), the Ottoman Empire, (1396–1879), and the Soviet Union (1945–1989). Several contemporary problems can be traced back to these experiences.

They include a distrust of Turkey, a historical claim to Macedonia, and a suspicion of foreign influence.

The Bulgarians are descendants of Slavic tribes who settled on the Balkan peninsula in the fifth century. In the early part of the seventh century, the Slavs living south of the Danube were conquered and organized into a political unit by the Bulgars, a Turkic people from the Volga region of contemporary Russia. In 680, Byzantine emperor Constantine IV led an army against the Bulgars, but he was defeated. In 681, Byzantium recognized Bulgar control of the region between the Balkans and the Danube. This date is considered to be the founding of the Bulgarian state.

The first rulers, Asparukh (r. 680–701) and Tervel (r. 701–718), began a long series of wars against the Byzantine Empire. Instead of consolidating the state, succeeding rulers were drawn into an attempt to conquer Constantinople. During the reign of Khan Krum (808–814), the Bulgars achieved their first real victories against Byzantium. Under Krum's successors, Bulgaria enjoyed an extended period of peace with Byzantium and expanded its control over what is today Macedonia and Serbia.

In 865, Boris I (r. 852–889) made Eastern Orthodoxy the state religion. He negotiated with both the Pope in Rome and the Patriarch at Constantinople, but chose Orthodoxy because of its assurance that the Bulgarian church would be free of outside interference. This choice meant that Bulgarian culture would thereafter carry the stamp of Byzantine civilization. During Boris's reign, disciples of Cyril and Methodius introduced the Cyrillic alphabet.[19] Bulgaria's conversion also had a political dimension since it contributed both to the growth of central authority and to the melding of Bulgars and Slavs into a unified Bulgarian people.

The reign of Simeon I (r. 893–927) marked the high point of the first Bulgarian state. Simeon encouraged the building of palaces and churches and the translation of Greek books into Slavonic. He was also a gifted military leader. His campaigns extended Bulgaria's borders, but they ultimately weakened the state in an attempt to take Constantinople. In 1018, Bulgaria lost its independence. For more than a century and a half, it remained under Byzantine rule.

In 1185, two brothers led a revolt against a Byzantium that had been greatly weakened by constant warfare. Their success forced Byzantium to recognize Bulgarian independence. This marked the beginning of the Second Bulgarian state. The Second Bulgarian state reached its apex during the reign of Czar Ivan Asen II (r. 1218–1241). During this period, the first Bulgarian coinage appeared and the head of the Bulgarian church received the title of Patriarch—Pope. However, Asen's successors were unable to preserve the state. Bulgaria was beset both by Mongol attacks from the north and internal peasant revolts. The combination of external and internal strife led to the end of Bulgarian independence in 1396, when Czar Ivan Shishman was defeated by the Ottoman Turks.

The next five centuries—from 1396 to 1879—are engraved in Bulgarian consciousness as the era of the "Turkish yoke." During this time, traditionally seen as a period of darkness and suffering, Bulgaria lost both its national and ecclesiastical independence. Bulgarians were also forced to submit to many humiliating restrictions. For example, the "blood tax" took a periodic levy of male children for conversion to Islam and service in either the army or the Ottoman government administration. In reality, however, the true picture was not as bleak as Bulgarian history books suggest. In the first centuries of the Empire's existence, it was a well-organized state that included Bulgaria in a *Pax Ottomanica*—a marked contrast to the preceding centuries of strife and war. Moreover, the Ottoman Empire had a political system that provided for local autonomy. It divided its people not according to nationality but religion. Under this system, called the millet, the Bulgarians were under the jurisdiction of the Eastern Orthodox Patriarchate, thus helping to preserve their national and religious identity. It was only when the Ottoman Empire began to decline and the power of local officials increased in the seventeenth century that Bulgarians found Ottoman rule unbearable. Significantly, religious tolerance under the Ottomans compares favorably to widespread persecution of religious minorities under the Hapsburg and Russian empires.

The Ottoman Empire's recognition of Greece's independence in 1830 and the granting of autonomy to Serbia and Romania fostered a revolutionary movement in Bulgaria. Bulgarians organized secret committees in preparation for a general uprising. Vasil Levsky, the greatest hero of the revolutionary movement, was captured and hanged in Sofia in 1873. Against the background of a wider Balkan crisis, Bulgarian revolutionary committees laid plans for a nationwide uprising in April 1876. The uprising began prematurely and was violently suppressed by the Turks. Atrocities committed against the civilian population, including the massacre of up to 30,000 civilians, intensified the desire for independence.

1877–1945

In 1877, a war broke out between Russia and the Ottoman Empire. The Russian army marched through Bulgaria, liberating the country. On March 3, 1878, hostilities between Russia and the Ottoman Empire were ended by the Treaty of San Stefano, which created a large independent Bulgaria stretching from the Danube to the Aegean Sea and from the Vardar and Morava river valleys to the Black Sea. However, the creation of a large Bulgarian state was seen as the embodiment of a Russian attempt to dominate the Balkans. This was unacceptable to Austria and Britain, who demanded a revision of the treaty. A few months later, at the Congress of Berlin, a new treaty created a much smaller Bulgarian principality, autonomous but under the sovereignty of the Ottoman Administration in the territory between the Danube and the

Balkan mountains. To the south, the treaty created the autonomous province of Eastern Rumelia—contemporary southern Bulgaria, subject to the sultan but led by a Christian governor. Macedonia, long associated with Bulgaria, was returned to Ottoman control.

This sequence of events had two important ramifications. First, it created a strong emotional tie with Russia as Bulgaria's liberator. Second, the dismemberment of the country after the Congress of Berlin left Bulgaria disappointed and determined to regain the territory delineated by the Treaty of San Stefano. The desire to incorporate Macedonia within Bulgaria shaped Bulgarian foreign policy until 1940. This has been Bulgaria's main *irrendeta* and the repeated failures to acquire it have led to bitterness, frustration, and an inferiority complex in the body politic.[20] For ideological reasons, the "Macedonian question" lost political vitality during communist rule. However, the ongoing language dispute has fostered concerns in neighboring states regarding Bulgaria's intentions towards the newly independent Republic of Macedonia.

As Great Britain and Austria expected, Russia exerted a strong influence on Bulgaria. This was partially the result of Bulgaria's lack of an indigenous political structure when it became independent. With Russian assistance, a constituent assembly of the country's notables wrote a constitution. The constitutional debate was dominated by the question of how the state should be governed. Conservatives believed the educated or administratively experienced elite should dominate politics and run the state in a patriarchal manner. In contrast, liberals believed in full political equality. At first, the liberal view prevailed. The resulting constitution, known as the Turnovo Constitution,[21] established a constitutional monarchy and a parliamentary government. It also guaranteed basic civil rights, established universal male suffrage, and prohibited class distinctions. When enacted, it was one of the most progressive constitutions in Europe.[22]

The Russians influenced the developing Bulgarian polity by ensuring that their candidate, Alexander Battenberg, was put on the throne. However, because of differences over Bulgaria's goal of annexing Macedonia and Thrace (contemporary northern Greece), relations with Russia deteriorated. In 1886, Russian-trained Bulgarian army officers deposed Alexander. This act led to an anti-Russian backlash. In 1887, a Catholic German prince, Ferdinand of Saxe-Coburg-Gotha, was put on the Bulgarian throne. This was the beginning of a Bulgarian-German connection, one that would see Bulgaria becoming a Germany ally in both world wars. After a brief flirtation with liberalism, Prince Ferdinand and his son Boris III strengthened their own power by cooperating with the conservatives. After 1923 the constitution was frequently disregarded, in 1934 it was suspended.

In foreign policy, the unresolved Macedonia issue continued to eclipse all others. This led Bulgaria to sign a series of secret treaties with Serbia and

Greece against Turkey. The First Balkan War (1912) resulted in a quick victory for the allies. However, they could not agree on the distribution of newly captured Turkish territories. The Second Balkan War (1913) found Bulgaria fighting alone against both its former allies as well as Turkey and Romania. Bulgaria was defeated, losing the territory it had gained the year before.

During World War I, the Central Powers promised Bulgaria more Macedonian territory than the Entente. As a result, Bulgaria was the only Balkan state to join the Central Powers. Bulgaria's defeat and the corresponding harsh peace treaty imposed on it made Bulgarians even more determined to regain what they consider historic Bulgarian territory. Postwar parliamentary elections in 1919 gave a majority in the National Assembly to the Agrarian party. Its leader, Alexander Stambolisky, who had strongly opposed the war, became prime minister. He immediately initiated drastic economic reforms. Most significantly, he broke up large urban and rural landholdings. His goal was to lessen the power of the "harmful" classes of society—lawyers, bankers, and merchants—and raise the living standards of landless and poor peasants. This policy led to almost open class warfare. In foreign affairs, Stambolisky's attempt at reconciliation with Bulgaria's neighbors and his downplaying of the Macedonian issue provoked nationalist discontent. These policies led to his assassination in a 1923 military coup. The Communist Party led a revolt against the new regime, but the coup was poorly timed and many of its members were executed or imprisoned.

The interwar period brought to the fore several problems whose legacies can also be seen today. Since King Ferdinand did not respect the constitution, he frequently changed ministers. Thus the rule of law was not incorporated into the polity. This helped foster an extremely fragmented political system. Favoritism, nepotism, partisan behavior, assassinations, coercion of public officials, and various other types of "persuasion" were the normal order of business. Although there were numerous political parties, they were dominated by individual rather than ideological competition. In general, Bulgarian society during this period was traumatized by national, political, and economic problems. Unemployment was high, and frequent coup d'etats caused political instability. Politicians used the system for their personal benefit rather than to create a stable polity. Because Bulgaria lacked a large educated middle class, a crucial base for political parties, the vacuum was filled by charismatic leaders and powerful institutions: the monarchy, authoritarian governments, and the military. Thus in the 1930s, Bulgaria was again on the road to an authoritarian regime. Using Italian fascism as their model, a 1934 coup abolished political parties and dissolved the National Assembly. With the transfer of its powers to the king, Boris III dominated the polity.

In a continuing effort to regain Macedonia, in March 1941 Bulgaria joined Germany, Italy, and Japan in the Tripartite Pact. Bulgaria declared war on Britain and the United States, but because of the historic pro-Russian sentiment of many of its people, refused to declare war on the Soviet Union. Bulgarian troops served chiefly on garrison duty in Greece and Yugoslavia. Unlike Hungary, Bulgaria resisted Nazi pressure to enforce anti-Jewish policies. Although laws were passed for restriction and deportation of the 50,000 Bulgarian Jews, they were never enforced.

In summary, the historical legacy of 500 years of Ottoman rule, the Macedonian question, and historical ties with Russia and Germany dominated Bulgarian policy in this period.

1945–1989

On September 5, 1944, the Soviet Union declared war on Bulgaria. Although the Red Army entered the country unopposed, it stopped outside Sofia. This allowed partisan groups under the leadership of the Fatherland Front—established and controlled by the communists, to overthrew the government on September 9. The new government immediately signed an armistice with the Soviet Union. An "Allied Control Commission" dominated by the Soviets was established. This led to a political struggle between the communists and democratic forces. Benefiting from infighting between anti-communist groups, the Fatherland Front won the most votes in the 1945 legislative elections.

The Bulgarian Communist Party (BCP), in cooperation with one faction of the Bulgarian Agrarian National Union (BANU), quickly consolidated power. "People's Courts" sentenced 2,730 royal advisors, ministers, MPs, senior statesmen, and military officers to death and exiled thousands to concentration camps. With the opposition out of the way, the BCP-BANU alliance won a series of electoral victories, including a plebiscite abolishing the monarchy. In 1947, the name of the state was changed to the People's Republic of Bulgaria. Georgi Dimitrov, a prominent Bulgarian communist and head of the Comintern,[23] returned from Moscow to serve as both BCP head and prime minister until his death in 1949.

From 1950 to 1954, Vulko Chervenkov, known as Bulgaria's "little Stalin," was head of Party and state. After Soviet First Secretary Khrushchev's "Secret Speech" in 1956, he was replaced by Todor Zhivkov. Zhivkov dominated the Bulgarian political scene for the next thirty-five years.

With the establishment of the communist regime, Bulgaria adopted new constitutions in 1947 and 1971. Both were modeled on their Soviet counterparts, providing the legal framework for building a socialist political and economic system. The various articles were based on the principles of Marxism-Leninism: democratic centralism, socialist internationalism (the support of other socialist states), and the fusion between the Party and the state apparatus. As an illustration, the 1971 constitution created the State Council, whose members included Zhivkov and leading members of the BCP.

GIORGI DIMITROV (1883–1949)

Giorgi Dimitrov, the first communist leader of Bulgaria, began the Sovietization of the country. Born into a working-class Protestant family in 1882, Dimitrov rose in the labor movement of Sofia and soon became a leader in the growing pre–World War I Communist Party. Gaining the attention of Moscow, he served as a delegate to the Comintern but was deported from Bulgaria in 1923. Ten years later, he was captured by Nazis and only released after the intervention of the USSR. Moving to Moscow, Dimitrov became a Soviet citizen and from 1935 to 1943 served as Secretary General of the Communist International (Comintern).

Still a Soviet citizen in 1945, Dimitrov returned to Bulgaria to head the Fatherland Front. Eventually he became chairman and General Secretary of the ruling party's Central Committee. His most significant achievement was the 1947 Dimitrov Constitution, which was used until 1971. Closely patterned on Stalin's 1936 constitution, it liquidated private business and abolished all religions. By the time he died in 1949, Dimitrov had established a close link between Bulgaria and the Soviet Union that would characterize Bulgaria's relations with the Soviet Union until 1989.

Although the parliament continued to exist, the Council had the power to issue decrees with the force of law. In other words, laws could be made without legislative approval. Perhaps most significantly, the constitutions legalized the role of the Communist Party as the leading and guiding force of society. To a greater degree than in other Central and Eastern European states, Bulgaria adopted Soviet economic, political, and social structures. All human, industrial, and agricultural resources were controlled by the state, which in turn channeled them into building a socialist society.

Although it started from a low economic level and was poorly endowed with natural resources, Bulgaria achieved dynamic growth until the mid-1970s. This was the result of successful incorporation of Soviet economic techniques, including the nationalization of industry, collectivization of agriculture, and economic Five Year Plans. The alignment of the Bulgarian economy with that of the USSR established the pattern of development for the next forty-five years. Sovietization was so completely embraced by Bulgaria's communists that not only were the economic and political structures modeled on the Soviet Union, but the military even adopted the Soviet uniform and command organization. As a result of its close ties with the USSR, Bulgaria was the only Warsaw Pact country that bordered a Western state and did not have Soviet troops stationed in it.

The relatively successful economic performance in the first three decades under communist rule deflected serious criticism of the government

---

TODOR ZHIVKOV (1911–1998)

Todor Zhivkov, the head of Bulgaria from 1954–1989, was the country's most significant leader in the post–World War II era. Following Khrushchev's accession and his purge of Stalinists in the Soviet Union, the Russian leader turned his attention to Stalin's puppets in Central and Eastern Europe. Bulgarian Communist Party General Secretary Vulko Chevenkov, who was responsible for collectivization and purges in the country, was one of the first to be removed in 1954. In his place, Khrushchev put Zhivkov in power.

Following closely the Soviet model of development, Bulgaria became known informally as the "Sixteenth" Soviet Republic. Bulgaria was the Soviets' most loyal ally, even sending troops to support the 1968 invasion of Czechoslovakia. The states were so close that Zhivkov often described the Soviet Union as the lungs and Bulgaria as the blood of a single body.

This dependent relationship with the Soviet Union was to lead to Zhivkov's demise. In the 1980s, the new Soviet leader, Mikhail Gorbachev, introduced the policies of *perestroika* and *glasnost*. This complete change in ideology was anathema to the older, hard-line Zhivkov, and he constantly tried to limit their influence in Bulgaria. However, increasing social unrest in the late 1980s, as well as his attempts to violently repress protesters and democratic movements, showed that Zhivkov's time was up. By the end of November 1989, the Soviet leadership decided that he no longer represented the "enlightened interests" of the Soviet Union. He was forced to to resign his position as General Secretary and President. Zhivkov's resignation ended forty-five years of rule and paved the way for Bulgaria's first democratically elected government since 1947. Never apologizing for his politics and defiant to the end, Zhivkov died in August 1998.

---

and prevented economic or political reform movements from gaining strength. However, declining living standards, economic problems, and direct and implicit criticism from the new Soviet government of Mikhail Gorbachev set the stage for change within the BCP. While the regime tried to forestall change by playing the nationalist card—the infamous "Bulgarization Campaign"—and a massive increase in imports—dramatically increasing its foreign debt—these policies only delayed the inevitable.

Since 1989

Demonstrations during the summer and early fall of 1989, combined with the accelerating pace of change elsewhere in Central and Eastern Europe and a growing political-economic crisis within Bulgaria, led to calls for round-table talks similar to those held in Hungary and Poland. However, in contrast to those states, because the Bulgarian opposition was weak and could have easily been silenced by the powerful security forces, the focal point for change came from within the Party. Thus the BCP remained the only significant political actor. It was a split in the party's ranks that caused Zhivkov's resignation on November 10, 1989.

Since then, the Bulgarian polity has been characterized by social fragmentation. This effect can be seen in the existence of numerous political parties. Previously allied with the Communist Party, the BANU asserted its independence in 1989. Along with sixteen new parties, one faction of the BANU formed an electoral alliance with the Union of Democratic Forces (UDF) to oppose the Bulgarian Socialist Party—formerly the BCP—in the first free elections since 1946.

In contrast to other former CEE states, the BSP won the first election. Their success was the result of numerous factors that still affect the polity. First, in contrast to Hungary and Poland, there was no legacy of organized opposition to the communists. After the communists consolidated power in 1946, they launched a mass campaign that neutralized their political opponents. On a per capita basis, more Bulgarians were killed than in any other Soviet bloc state. Thus only the BSP had an established and well-organized party structure. In addition, because of Russia's role in liberating Bulgaria from the Ottoman Empire, Soviet domination was not viewed as negatively as in other states. The UDF also made the tactical mistake of attacking the former communists. Since Bulgarians are a fundamentally conservative people who eschew radical change, this was not a wise policy.

The BSP victory led to several months of political stalemate, delaying the selection of a new president. The impasse was resolved by the negotiated withdrawal of the BSP and BANU candidates in favor of the UDF leader, Zhelyu Zhelev. Early in August, a BSP government was formed under former Communist Minister of Foreign Economic Relations, and reputed architect of Zhivkov's removal, Andrei Lukanov. As a result of continuing political unrest, he relinquished power in December 1990 to Dimitar Popov, a political independent.

A second general election in October 1991 gave the UDF a narrow victory. The first noncommunist government since World War II was formed under the leadership of UDF leader Philip Dimitrov. A year later, however, the UDF government fell when its tacit ally, the Turkish-dominated Movement for Rights and Freedom (MRF), concluding that they would have more influence with a BSP government, withdrew its parliamentary support.

After three months of negotiations, another independent government, this time under Professor Lyuben Berov, was put into power. It was formed using the mandate assigned to the smallest parliamentary group—the MRF—after the two major political forces in parliament—the UDF and BSP—were unable to form a government. Berov declared that he would implement the program of the UDF, but because of internal infighting and a desire to see their own leader as prime minister, they refused to support him. As a result, the cabinet won support from the BSP, the MRF, and UDF defectors. This gave the Socialists de facto control over the government. Frustrated at the lack of political progress, the Berov government resigned in September 1994. Continuing political chaos could be seen in the number of parties (48) that competed for seats in the December 1994 parliamentary elections. These elections and local elections in 1995 gave the BSP control of both the National Assembly and a majority (195 of 225) of municipalities. Only the three largest cities of Sofia, Plovdiv, and Varna remained in the hands of the opposition.

However, the BSP squandered its power by failing to address key problems that plagued the country. With the economy in shambles, the currency collapsing, rampant inflation, the prospect of food and energy shortages, and large-scale corruption that played a role in the assassination of former prime minister Andrei Lukanov, voters took revenge on the BSP government by electing UDF candidate Peter Stoyanov in November 1996 presidential elections. Although the presidency is largely a ceremonial position and the BSP still controlled the National Assembly, Stoyanov's election was a catalyst for change.

Blamed for the poor BSP showing and facing mounting criticism for his failure to reform the economy, Socialist Prime Minister Zhan Videnov was forced to resign. Sensing an opportunity, opposition groups began large-scale—50,000 to 100,000 people—daily demonstrations in an effort to force early elections. Faced with a mounting political and economic crisis, the BSP agreed to elections in April 1997, nineteen months ahead of schedule.

The newly renamed and united opposition party, the United Democratic Forces (ODF in Bulgarian), won a majority of seats in the new parliament. The ODF promised to reform the economy and cracked down on rampant corruption. Led by Ivan Kostev, the ODF initiated crucial economic reforms, finally putting Bulgaria on the road to economic and political stability.

In contrast to Hungary and Poland, change has come very slowly to Bulgaria. The incompetence of the UDF and the power of the former *nomenklatura* combined to limit economic and political reforms. As a result, the most progress has come under pressure from international organizations. For example, Anne MacGuire, the International Monetary Fund (IMF) liaison, has used her position to foster both economic and political reforms. This has given Kostev the political cover to enact necessary, but politically unpopular economic reforms.[24]

Stephen Sofianski (1951–)

Born on November 7, 1951, in Sofia, Sofianski is today the mayor of Sofia. A 1973 economics graduate of the University for National and World Economy in Sofia, he began his political career as an economist in the Ministry of Communications and Information, later moving to the National Center for Creation and Development of a United System for Public Information until 1980. Sofianski later became involved in politics, serving as the chair of the Democracy Party in 1991, which later joined the Union of Democratic Forces (UDF). In the UDF, Sofianski quickly took a leading role, becoming deputy chair of the coalition from 1993 to 1996, and later a member of the National Coordination Council. He was elected a member of parliament from Russe in 1994 and was selected as the deputy chair of the Budget Committee.

Frustrated with the BSP parliamentary majority, Sofianski was elected major of Sofia in 1995. Quickly tackling Sofia's problems, Sofianski gained a national reputation as a hard worker and problem solver. After the resignation of the BSP government in 1997, he was selected as an interim prime minister. Today, still the mayor of Sofia, Sofianski is considered a future presidential or prime minister candidate.

INFORMING POLITICAL IDEAS

Political Culture

Although the official political culture was similar throughout the Soviet Bloc, historical experiences fostered a unique set of Bulgarian subcultures. They include two somewhat contradictory tendencies. On one hand, Bulgarians suspect other states' intentions—especially those of the great powers—distrust government, have little respect for the law, and are suspicious of too much economic and political freedom. On the other hand, they have historically tolerated foreign rule and continue to look to the state to solve societal problems.

Bulgaria has spent nearly half of its history under foreign domination. It has also frequently either been allied with, or assigned to, the sphere of influence of a powerful state. Consequently, Bulgarians often see themselves as pawns of the great powers. In this "conspiracy theory," Bulgarians believe the great powers scheme to keep them weak. Even though international conditions have dramatically changed, this belief is still widespread. Bulgarians were very suspicious, for instance, of the 1989 U.S.–USSR summit in Malta. Many believed that Europe was again being divided and Bulgaria was once again being put under Russia influence.

Another legacy of foreign domination is distrust of governmental institutions. As a result of extended periods of foreign control, the government was often used as a tool of foreign oppression. Even during the periods of Bulgarian independence, usually because of political infighting, governments were unable to solve social problems. As a result, Bulgaria has never experienced a period of both political pluralism and stable economic growth that would help legitimize the government. This led to a large gap between the rulers and the ruled. As a result, Bulgarians generally loathe the state and its officials. Unable and unwilling to challenge the state openly, people learned to react covertly. For example, taxes were, and are, considered an evil. As a result, there is large-scale tax evasion. Although the private sector produces almost 50 percent of GDP, it pays only 35 percent of the taxes.[25] The historical distrust of the state and the legacy of Ottoman rule have fostered a destructive sense of individualism in which society is much less important than taking care of oneself.

Under the communist regime, the only means of overtly expressing dissatisfaction was to ridicule state officials. The police were especially hated. Today, largely as the result of numerous corruption cases, the police are still despised, fueling the historical suspicion of the state and its officials. This is a major obstacle to Bulgarian political development, as respect for governmental institutions is a prerequisite for democratic development.

Other communist legacies include the lack of societal norms and the rule of law. The communist regime made people feel vulnerable and dependent on the state. Since laws were used to restrict rather than guarantee citizen's rights, many Bulgarians view the law as something to be flouted rather than followed. Also, since laws could quickly change, Bulgarians view events and act accordingly, through a very short-time horizon. Thus they tend toward immediate consumption and living life for the moment. This limits long-term development. By imposing a large number of impractical and often illogical restrictions and limitations, they were inevitably and routinely breached. For example, since it took at least three months and numerous visits to city hall to get a building permit, people often built illegal buildings. In other words, the system rewarded people who violated the law and penalized those who followed it. This situation blurred the line between the permitted and the forbidden, the acceptable and the unacceptable. It also negatively affected the moral standards of society by stripping cheating, theft, and dishonesty of their moral repulsiveness. As a result, normally honest people would think nothing of either stealing from the state or cheating the authorities.[26] In order for a democratic system to flourish, certain values have to be relearned and norms created.[27]

Little Traditions

Paradoxically, although Bulgarians generally distrust both foreign control and a powerful government, they have usually accepted foreign domination and look to the state to solve societal problems. Five hundred years of foreign domination have made Bulgarians politically apathetic. They view politics as something distant, outside their control. As a result, in contrast to Hungarians and Poles they tend to be much more politically lethargic. This can be seen in their lack of open resistance to invaders or authoritarian governments. Unlike other Balkan states, Bulgarian liberation from Turkish rule was a result of the Russian-Turkish War, not an indigenous liberation movement. In the postwar period, Bulgaria was the only CEE state that did not revolt against its communist regime or Soviet influence. This emphasis on survival can also be seen in the conformist tendency of Bulgarians. In 1944, for instance, there were only 20,000 Communist Party members. Three years later, there were over 500,000.

Bulgaria's history has made society very conservative, almost fearful of change. This can be seen in Zhivkov's ouster by palace coup rather than a mass movement that got rid of communist leaders in the rest of the region, and in the victory of the former communists in the first parliamentary elections. These tendencies can be partially explained by the lack of a civil society under the communists. All social and cultural organizations, even the Red Cross, were under Party control. This "historic" apathy has carried into the contemporary era through a continuing lack of political involvement. It can also be seen daily in the desire of people to not get involved with anything that does not directly affect them. It is not uncommon for thieves to break in or steal a car in broad daylight, with no one bothering to call the police.

Another communist legacy is the belief that people should depend on the state to solve their problems. This was the result of government propaganda that stressed that individualism was "antisocial." This paternalism has also contributed to the lack of political involvement. Interestingly, this suggests that it is easier for governments to force society to follow a given policy, such as socialism, than to force people to accept responsibility for their actions.

Although the state followed a de facto "three-keys" policy to avoid unrest,[28] the official policy fostered an egalitarian mentality whose ramifications can be seen today. Over 90 percent of the public believe that income differentials are now large and that social justice requires a "certain extent" of social equality.[29] Continuing battles over land privatization show the depth of this belief. However, Western democratic experience suggests that until people believe they can control their own destiny—of which property ownership is a key component—political progress will be stymied.

Another important element of Bulgarian political culture is the view that democracy equals instability. In spite of the widespread Bulgarian belief that the struggle for democracy has been a central and recurring theme of Bulgarian history, this has not been the case. Historically, "democracy" has been a very abstract term. Today people equate democracy with freedom of speech, higher standards of living, and, most important, with how well the government works. Since government has been largely ineffective, democracy is also seen as ineffective.

Although Bulgaria adopted one of the most liberal constitutions in Europe, between its enactment in 1879 and World War I, only 40–50 percent of the population bothered to vote. While the electoral turnout improved immediately after World War I—up to 84 percent in the 1919 elections—it soon declined.[30] Thus the attempt to transplant a Western political system into Bulgaria after World War I failed because of a weak middle class, socioeconomic backwardness, and political immaturity.[31] Interestingly, this pattern of significant involvement after a national crisis, followed by dramatically decreasing involvement shortly thereafter, is being repeated today. The high voter turnout of 84 percent in the first parliamentary elections of 1990 decreased to 74 percent in 1994 and 59 percent in 1997. Historically, this pattern of limited involvement weakened the legitimacy of the regime, fostering political instability and several coup d'etats. An example was King Boris III's declaration of personal rule in 1934.

In contrast, the periods during which Bulgaria has been under an authoritarian regime are viewed as times of economic and social stability. Many people believe only an authoritarian regime will provide the necessary stability for social and economic restructuring. This can be seen in an April 1993 public opinion poll, in which 49 percent of the respondents supported a "restriction of democracy" in order to restore order in the country.[32] These values and beliefs show that there are serious obstacles to democratic political development in Bulgaria.

Another element of Bulgarian political culture is the lack of political tolerance and the use violence against adversaries. Bulgaria's history is filled with bloody acts of political violence, including numerous assassinations in the 1920s and the bloodiest communist purges in Central and Eastern Europe. Although current times are not as violent, the lack of political tolerance can still be seen today. When the UDF came to power, it passed a law that purged former communists from the military, educational, and cultural institutions. This law was one of the most vindictive in the region. In addition, Bulgaria was the first CEE state to prosecute former communists. The use of "law" for political retribution weakens the legitimacy of the regime and contributes to the polarization of society.

In summary, there is no firm base for economic and political change. This is the result of a somewhat intolerant political culture, a severely divided and polarized society, a conservative populace, and the lack of an agreed-upon foundation on which to reconstruct the polity.[33] Thus, the political culture presents numerous obstacles to change in the contemporary period.

Political Socialization

Like other Socialist states, the Bulgarian polity did not leave socialization to chance. The Communist Party used every possible method to create and maintain support for the regime.

Education

As with most states in the region, Bulgaria has a well-educated population. The average Bulgarian has completed ten years of school. However, as in other social spheres, the change in regime has decimated the educational system. The end of centralized educational control and drastic funding cuts have greatly affected the educational system. With an average monthly salary of $50 dollars, many teachers have found other jobs. Even when they get paid, they receive their salaries three to four months late. The lack of money has also prevented the purchase of new ideologically neutral textbooks and forced 1,600 schools to close. These factors have led to a dramatic increase in dropout and illiteracy rates. Between 1985 and 1995, the number of dropouts increased 500 percent.[34] With cuts in state funding, many institutions of higher education have been forced to introduce tuition. As a result, for many students money has replaced intellect as the primary entrance requirement, resulting in a decrease in academic standards.

The lack of new educational laws and continuing legal ambiguity has limited the creation of new schools. Since most were established without official approval, the state does not recognize their degrees. Even in schools recognized by the government, such as the new American University located in Blagoevgrad, American accreditation is not accepted by the government. Students are forced to pass a separate Bulgarian state examination.

Social and Peer Groups

The downfall of the communist regime and accompanying economic problems have caused culture and education to be neglected. Social and peer organizations have almost ceased to exist. The few that remain are usually attached to a political party or government body. In addition, traditionally highly valued—and thus heavily subsidized—groups are now bereft of government funding. Many *chitalista*—unique Bulgarian public cultural and educational centers—have either closed or become private clubs. The closing of these hearths of the Bulgarian nation is considered by some to be one of the most devastating results of the political and economic crisis.

Mass Media

The change in regime brought major changes to this former tool of political socialization. Although the state still controls distribution, the press has been freed, leading to a proliferation of newspapers. Unfortunately, economic realities have forced a number to close. In 1992, there were 920 newspapers with a total circulation of over 1098.6 million. By 1995, these numbers had dropped to 880 and 615 million.[35] Most newspapers are now affiliated with political parties or big businesses. As a result, the print media is again controlled by a small elite. Since most newspapers have become mouthpieces for their owners, they lack objectivity. When combined with libel law that recognizes "moral harm" and courts that consistently support the state,[36] the media have helped fuel political and societal divisions.

In the broadcasting sphere, political change has brought openness and journalistic freedom, though not as complete as with the printed press. While over sixty private radio and three private television stations have been licensed, there is still significant governmental influence. When clashes between demonstrators and police in January 1997 left several hundred people injured, the state-controlled Bulgarian National Radio and Television (BNRT), though not ignoring events, issued only sporadic information. According to some journalists, even this information was heavily censored.[37]

The desire of politicians to maintain some control over the media can be seen in that fact that it took seven years before Bulgaria's first postcommunist law on the electronic media was enacted. The 1996 law created the National Radio and Television Council (NRTC), which oversees media operations and elects the heads of state radio and television. Since the council is selected by the Parliamentary Committee for Radio and Television, overseeing the state media is left to the majority political party. While this would not necessarily be a problem, in a country like Bulgaria where the firing of state television bosses has coincided with government changes, the tendency to exert the greatest possible influence over the electronic media is clearly discernible.[38]

Numerous examples show the lack of media independence. In the 1995 local elections, the media displayed an obvious pro-BSP bias. In addition, journalists suspected of sympathizing with the opposition are often harassed. Seven reporters from Bulgarian National Radio who signed a protest against political pressure and censorship were fired. Since the BSP controlled the parliamentary committee in charge of the media, repeated efforts by the opposition to initiate a parliamentary review of the actions of the NRTC were thwarted.[39]

Significantly, the Constitutional Court declared the statute that gave the National Assembly control over the NRTC unconstitutional. The BSP then used its majority to try to transfer some of the Assembly's powers to the parliamentary Committee for Radio and Television. This attempt was also ruled unconstitutional when the Court declared that a parliamentary committee cannot make decisions on behalf of the parliament. The fights within and about the state media, as well as the legal quarrels regarding its control, show that the media are considered a political weapon rather than a guardian of the people's liberties.[40]

The ability of the media to transmit democratic values is of great significance since most Bulgarians trust it more than they do the official state institutions.[41] Although channels for future political socialization exist, no "institution" has filled the vacuum left by the end of the communist regime. This raises the question of how new political ideas will be communicated. The desire of politicians from across the political spectrum to control the media in order to further their political agendas greatly slows democratic development and the creation of a civil society. Nevertheless, the rise of an independent new media, which can be seen in live radio broadcasts during the January 1997 protests, shows the state is no longer able to limit or control information.

FORMAL GOVERNMENTAL INSTITUTIONS

The Constitution

Although in 1989 there was widespread agreement that the old constitution needed to be changed, the enactment of a new one was very controversial. This was the result of partisan political battles rather than disagreement over specific provisions. Not only were there the expected struggles between the UDF and the BSP, but also disagreement within the UDF itself. To ensure the adoption of a new constitution, a large group of UDF deputies cooperated with the BSP, leading to the creation of the "Group of 39." These UDF members refused to sign a constitution they viewed as undemocratic and "communist." In addition to refusing to sign the Constitution, the UDF dissidents led street demonstrations against its ratification. However, since the BSP and its allies had a two-thirds majority in the Grand National Assembly–Constituent Assembly, the Constitution was adopted in 1991.

The first of the new CEE European constitutions, the Bulgarian Constitution was an attempt to formally break with the communist past. It draws its inspiration, as well as various provisions, from numerous Western European constitutions. The Constitution's basic principles include respect for national and international law and individual rights. It also provides "for a pluralistic society, whose citizens enjoy equal rights and the freedoms normally associated with democracy."[42] However, an article that stipulates that no political party may be formed on the basis of ethnicity is controversial and is seen by some domestic and international observers as limiting the rights of the large Turkish minority.

The conflict surrounding the adoption of the new constitution had two significant effects on the development of the polity. The failure of the UDF to unite was the first in a series of events that allowed the BSP to dominate the political scene until 1997. Second, and more significantly, the lack of a national consensus ensured that the Constitution, instead of unifying the population and providing a source of governmental legitimacy, would be a source of continuing political division.

The Constitution makes the National Assembly the focal point of government by vesting it with legislative power and control over the executive. The prime minister and other ministers form the Council of Ministers, the principle organ of executive power. However, unlike most other parliamentary regimes, here the parliament is not "supreme." Both the president and council of ministers have distinct constitutional powers. For example, although the government has the power to appoint ambassadors, it cannot exercise this power without a presidential decree. Thus the system can be characterized as one of "mutually dependent competency."[43] This system was designed to prevent power from being concentrated, as in the old regime.

The Constitution also provides for an independent judiciary to ensure the rule of law and the protection of civil rights. The supremacy of the Constitution has been strengthened by the introduction of a Constitutional Court. Its role is to ensure the constitutionality of all laws and executive acts. The Constitution may be amended by either a specially convened Grand National Assembly—comprised of 400 specially elected representatives—or a two-thirds vote of the National Assembly.

Although the Bulgarian Constitution is democratic, as in Hungary and Poland, the vague division of powers between the president and the parliament, and between the president and the government, has been a source of tension. As an illustration, since the defense minister is responsible to the prime minister, and the chief of the General Staff to the president, the military chain of command is not clear.

Regional and Local Government

In the socialist era, local self-government did not exist. All local governmental bodies were directly subordinated to the central government. The new Constitution divides the state into ten regions, which are in turn divided into 255 self-governing administrative municipalities with directly elected governments. Regions are headed by a governor appointed by the prime minister. They are responsible for implementing laws and preserving public peace. To support these activities, governors have regional administrative offices. Each region is divided into numerous municipalities. The Constitution created a local separation of power by establishing municipal councils and mayors. The councils are policy-making bodies. While they have control over the local economy, environmental issues, construction programs, and social security, the majority of their budget is spent on health care, education, and cultural activities.[44] In order to support these programs, councils have the power to levy taxes.

Executive power within the municipalities is vested in the mayor. However, the council can annul the mayor's decisions. The mayor can challenge the council's decisions by using her suspensive veto power. If the council reaffirms its decision, the mayor can appeal to the courts.

Although municipalities legally have administrative autonomy, there are numerous obstacles to independent policy-making. The first is the division of power between the regional/central authorities and the municipalities. Not only is the mayor the executive officer of the local council and thus accountable to the local electorate, she must implement state policies. This accounts for at least 20 percent of the mayor's time and greatly lessens local autonomy.[45] For example, in education, local inspectors play a key role in enforcing ministerial regulations. Therefore, in numerous policy areas the local government is reduced to acting as an arm of the state. Second, police and fire forces are controlled by the state, not the municipality. As a result, police will not provide security for a public event unless they are paid extra because this is not part of their responsibilities. The lack of control over the police prevents mayors from cracking down on crime, something most people view as one of the greatest threats to society.

Another obstacle to local autonomy is the power of the regional governor to annul acts of the municipalities. The governor can also use a suspensive veto to prevent the implementation of any local law until a court rules on its legality. While this does not happen often, governors often interfere on important matters, such as the restructuring of the local economy.

Finally, since a large portion of each municipality's property is actually state property, the local government cannot levy taxes on it. As a result, over 50 percent of the local government's budget comes from the central government. Thus, although the municipalities inherited a large number of social organizations—schools, hospitals, cultural institutions—and are responsible for them, they have not been given either the authority or the money to run them.

A related problem is that the central government's budget—that is, the amount of money available for local governments—is determined annually. This greatly limits the ability of local governments to engage in long-range planning. In addition, the percentage of the state budget that goes to the municipalities—22 percent in 1993—is annually redistributed. Thus lobbying by one city limits the funds available to another. This system favors the municipalities whose government is run by the same party that controls the central government. As a result, autonomous local government can hardly be said to exist.[46]

There are also local obstacles to policy making. One of the most significant is the power struggle between the municipal council and the mayor. Although the council is legally the supreme organ of local power, the law on local government does not define the rights and responsibilities of mayors.

As a result, deputy mayors and the directors of municipal services can be appointed by the council despite the opposition of the mayor. The mayor does not have the power to remove these "appointees." Institutional conflict is the inevitable result. This situation is worsened by the local electoral system. Although the mayor is elected by a plurality, the council is elected on the basis of proportional representation. While the goal of this electoral system, along with the constitutional separation of power at the local level, was to decentralize power, this diffusion of authority makes policy making difficult.

A 1995 law gave the councils even more power. After six months, councils can now remove mayors from office with a two-thirds vote. Although it was always possible to legally remove a mayor, the new law makes it even easier. Since the law does not define the criteria for removal, it is likely that the law will force mayors to serve council interests rather than constituent interests. This situation allows councils to get involved in areas outside of its competence, often with significant policy ramifications. When the council micromanages the local administration, it slows down the process of government. More significantly, it also opens up numerous possibilities for graft, corruption, and nepotism. As an illustration, the city council in one city held up the consideration of new laws until their personal property was restituted. Acts such as this increase public apathy and lessen governmental legitimacy.

Another important obstacle to local government is the lingering belief that the state will take care of society. Until 1991, there was no history of local self-government in Bulgaria. In other words, people had never been forced to work together at the local level. Overcoming this legacy will be crucial for the development of the polity. For until people become involved in areas that directly affect them, democratic progress will be stifled.

The Legislature

The center of governmental power in Bulgaria is the National Assembly. Unlike its Polish or Russian counterparts, it is a unicameral body. Its 240 members are elected by universal suffrage for a four-year term. The chair of the Assembly is selected by the majority party, with deputy chairpersons selected from each party represented in the parliament. The representatives form parliamentary groups—factions—based on party affiliation. Factions must have a minimum of ten members to be recognized as an official group. This status gives them office space, administrative support, television time in elections, and a time quota during parliamentary debates.

The National Assembly has numerous standing commissions, called committees,[47] and can form ad hoc ones. Membership is determined on a proportional basis that reflects the overall composition of parliament. Each committee has a chairperson and up to two deputies. Both the chairperson and committee members are determined on the basis of their party's parliamentary representation. Therefore, in contrast to the United States, members of opposition parties chair committees. Committees have the authority to hire experts and technical specialists to support their work. Also in contrast to the United States, Bulgarian MPs can serve on only two standing committees, and these committees have little power. For example, their structure and meeting times can be changed at will.

The Assembly has two primary mandates: controlling the executive and creating legislation. Other legislative functions include levying taxes, declaring war, ratifying international treaties, and scheduling presidential elections. These functions are fulfilled through a variety of formal and informal methods.

Although the parliament is the locus of power in the Bulgarian polity, there are some constitutional limits on its power, the most important of which is the power of the presidency.

The Electoral System

As in other socialist states, during the communist era the results of elections were known prior to election day. The old electoral system consisted of going to a polling station and dropping a preprinted ballot with one name on it into the ballot box.

Today, members of parliament are elected from a national party list. Parties must clear a 4 percent threshold to gain representation. This requirement limits the number of parties in parliament and prevents the extreme fragmentation common in pre-1993 Poland or contemporary Italy. However, this proportional electoral system drastically increases the influence of parties. In contrast to the United States, individual representatives have little political influence in Bulgaria. Candidates are selected and approved by each party's hierarchy; thus their reelection depends on the approval of the party. As a result, constituency service and the elector-representative bond is almost nonexistent. Thus, local interests have very little impact on the legislative process. This situation has provoked calls for change. However, since the parliament would have to approve any electoral changes, it is unlikely to introduce a system that will lessen the chances of its current members being reelected.[49]

Organizationally, Bulgaria is divided into thirty-one electoral constituencies. Each administrative unit, or okrag, is one constituency, with the exception of the Plovdiv okrag, which is split into two constituencies, and the Sofia okrag, which is divided into three. Depending on the population of the okrag, the constituencies send between four and thirteen deputies to the National Assembly. This system was established in an attempt to foster minority representation.

All parties registered with the Central Electoral Commission get state funding. The actual amount is based on the number of candidates in the election and their success in the last election. If a party exceeded the 4 percent threshold in the last election, it receives a grant from the state. In the 1994 elections, the state gave parties $500 per candidate. If a party did not surpass the electoral threshold, it is eligible for an interest free state loan. Parties that won parliamentary representation in the most recent election have an advantage because they receive free radio and television time. Although the state provides a majority of a party's funds, parties also raise money through membership fees and donations. Therefore, large parties have a decided advantage over their smaller counterparts. This can be a significant problem in local elections, since wealthy parties can purchase all local advertising, in essence limiting other party's ability to publicize their platform.

Although democratic, the proportional electoral system has fostered political instability. Under a proportional system, people are forced to vote for an entire party list. Because it gives parties so much power, this system amplifies the already deep political divide. Party headquarters, rather than governmental institutions, dictate policy. Thus the institutions of government represent party interests rather than societal interests. Although there are numerous stable governments elected by proportional electoral systems, out of the eight governments since 1990, none has completed its full four-year term.

The Presidency

The establishment of the presidency was a source of great controversy. Its introduction was influenced by the temporary interests of the political parties in 1990. Although the Constitution gave it only limited powers, the first president, Zhelyu Zhelev, managed to increase its power and influence. As a result, what the president's actual role should be has become a key political question.

The president is elected by universal suffrage for a five-year term and can be reelected only once. To run for office, he or she must be nominated by either a political party or by gathering 5,000 signatures. The president is meant to be a neutral figure above politics, responsible for ensuring the stability of both the government and the state. The formal powers of the president are derived from his or her status as head of state, which are mostly ceremonial. They include nominating the prime minister and representing the state internationally. The president can also issue decrees, but any of consequence must be countersigned by the prime minister. In contrast to the Hungarian president, the Bulgarian president does not have the right to initiate legislation.[50]

The Bulgarian president does not have the sweeping power of the French president, who can dissolve the National Assembly at almost any time. Nor does he have the power of his Polish counterpart to convene and preside over meetings of the cabinet. This is because the prime minister "heads, coordinates and bears responsibility for the overall policy of the government."[51] The only formal responsibilities which give the president more than symbolic authority are his position as commander-in-chief of the armed forces, the right to delay legislation passed by the parliament, the right to submit legislation to the Constitutional Court for review, and the power to schedule elections.

Nevertheless, the Bulgarian presidency differs markedly from the mostly ceremonial presidencies in Hungary, Germany, and Italy. It derives significant informal power from being the only directly elected governmental office. The president's national constituency allows him to claim that he is the embodiment of the unity of the state. Thus the informal powers of the Bulgarian president have become more important than the formal ones.[52] They include lobbying and drawing attention to issues through an address to the National Assembly or society at large. As an illustration of this informal power, the withdrawal of MRF support for the UDF government in 1992 was largely the result of a presidential address in which Zhelev sharply criticized the government. Therefore, although the Bulgarian president has fewer powers than his Polish and Russian counterparts, they are significantly stronger than those given to the head of state in a pure parliamentary system such as Hungary.

In summary, the Bulgarian presidency is a hybrid between a presidential republic, in which presidents are elected by popular vote and endowed with broad powers, and parliamentary republics, in which the presidency is elected by the parliament and has mostly a ceremonial role. The president's independence from other branches of the government has greatly aided the peaceful transition of the polity. The restrained performance of Zhelev made the presidency a neutral political arbitrator, which in turn has a calming effect on the political process. Although people are tired of political intrigue and declining living standards, they still have confidence in the presidency. A 1995 poll of the governmental institutions found that it ranked second highest in public support.[53] This support increases governmental legitimacy and social stability.

The Executive

As in other parliamentary regimes, elections do not directly determine who will become prime minister in Bulgaria. To be elected prime minister, a nominee, usually the head of the largest party, must have the support of a majority in parliament. To date, however, majority coalitions in the National Assembly have tended to fragment quickly, causing frequent governmental changes. For example, the first noncommunist government came to power in 1991 as a result of a de facto coalition between the UDF and MRF. This cooperation turned out to be short-lived because the MRF, dissatisfied with governmental policies, withdrew its support. The government was then forced to resign after being unable to secure a vote of confidence. Unlike in Germany and Hungary, the Bulgarian parliament does not have to choose a new government before removing the previous one.[48] After a government falls, the president asks the second largest parliamentary group to try to form a government. If this group fails, the mandate goes to the third largest, and so forth. If no party is able to form a government, the president can call a new election. The Cabinet, also called the Council of Ministers, is selected by the prime minister but must be approved by the parliament in a majority vote. Constitutionally, the cabinet "directs and executes" the domestic and foreign policy of the state. Although responsible to the National Assembly, unusual in parliamentary systems, the government is also separate from it. Thus, members of the Council of Ministers cannot also be members of the parliament.[54] Since the prime minister is selected by the National Assembly, the prime minister is directly responsible to the Parliament, not the electorate.

The National Assembly controls the Council of Ministers through both formal and informal means. Formally, since it has the sole prerogative of approving the state budget by refusing to accept the budget or requiring its modification, the assembly can directly influence governmental policies. It can also pass a vote of no confidence. A call for a vote of no confidence must be supported by one-fifth of all members of the National Assembly. It must then be approved by a majority of all members. If the government is defeated, the prime minister must tender his resignation. This fusion of legislative and executive power, a fundamental characteristic of parliamentary regimes, has fostered governmental instability since 1989. Expediency has been sacrificed to political infighting and long-term policy has been ignored. This has fostered institutional instability. This situation is analogous to that existing in France during the Fourth Republic, which led to the strong executive of the contemporary Fifth Republic. On the positive side, the frequent governmental changes have occurred in an orderly and democratic way. Thus, technically the new political system works well. Most Bulgarians, however, do not share this view. Informal parliamentary means of controlling the government include "question hour" and the creation of ad hoc commissions. Every Friday, any MP is free to ask ministers about their policies. This brings attention to government policies or the lack of them. Ad hoc commissions have wide investigative powers, including inquiries into the actions of the cabinet or individual ministers.

The Judiciary

During the communist era, the rule of law was subordinate to the ideological demands of the party. All judges were members of the Communist Party and were instructed to base their decisions on the interests of the "working class" and the BCP. Judges administered "justice" for offenses such as "fleeing the republic" and "behavior damaging to the state." This resulted in numerous political prisoners and biased legal judgments. Therefore, as in other CEE states, the reform of the judiciary is an important task facing the Bulgarian polity.

The Constitution guarantees the independence of the judiciary, whose primary role is to "safeguard the rights and legitimate interests of all citizens, legal entities, and the state." In the performance of their functions, "all judges, court assessors, prosecutors and investigating magistrates shall be subservient only to the law." Judges themselves do not reflect the society they serve. The majority are either recent law school graduates or are at the end of their careers. The middle-aged members of the judiciary have left to work in the private sector. This helps foster the impression that the judicial system is comprised of political appointees and is corrupt. Organizationally, there is a Constitutional Court, Supreme Court, Supreme Court of Cassation, Supreme Administrative Court, appeals courts, military courts, and district courts.

Each court has very different responsibilities. The Supreme Court is legally separate from the rest of the judicial system and ensures equal application of the law by all courts. The thirty-six-member Supreme Administrative Court rules on the legality of acts of the Council of Ministers and the seventy-two-member Supreme Court of Cassation hears civil and criminal appeals. The "presidents" (Chief Justices) of these two courts are elected by the Supreme Judicial Council for seven-year terms.

The Constitutional Court is the most important feature of the new judicial order. Its twelve members are selected for one nine-year term. One-third are selected by the National Assembly, one-third by the president, and one-third by a joint meeting of the justices of the Supreme Court and the Supreme Administrative Court. As its name implies, the Court ensures laws conform with the Constitution. It has the power to challenge the legality of political parties; overturn acts of the president, government, parliament, and municipalities; and veto Bulgarian participation in international organizations. Like the U.S. Supreme Court, the Bulgarian Constitutional Court has the power of judicial review and is considered one of the main guarantors of the supremacy of law in Bulgaria.

In contrast to the United States, where the principle of the rule of law is well established, the Bulgarian Constitutional Court has had to continually assert itself against onslaughts by the parliamentary majority. Twice in 1995, the BSP displayed its defiance of the Court by simply readopting laws declared unconstitutional. On both occasions, the Court struck them down again. This led the Cabinet of Ministers to order the Constitutional Court to move to another building. Although the Court voided this decision, the message from the Cabinet was clear.

The Court has also reversed politically unpopular decisions. As an illustration, the Court ruled that following a change in government, the

Chairman of the National Assembly would have to step down, even though she has a four-year term of office. After a political outcry, the court reversed itself. This reversal led many people to question the Court's neutrality. Like the Supreme Court in the United States, the Bulgarian Constitutional Court ensures the constitutionality of legislation and acts as the highest court of appeals. Another similarity with the United States is in the highest legal authority—a non-judicial body, the Supreme Judicial Council (SJC). While Americans usually associate constitutional review with supreme legal authority, in actuality, the Justice Department has supreme legal authority as it ensures laws are enforced. The SJC, a twenty-five-member body, is an integral part of Bulgaria's constitutional scheme to guarantee judicial independence. It has the power to appoint, promote, demote, reassign, or dismiss the justices, prosecutors, and investigating magistrates. Significantly, members of the Constitutional Court are not under the jurisdiction of the SJC.

Members of the Council are elected for five-year terms. Eleven members are appointed by the Supreme Court and eleven by the National Assembly. Its three ex officio members are the chairperson of the Supreme Court, the chairperson of the Supreme Administrative Court, and the chief prosecutor. This selection process allows the National Assembly to exercise political influence over the election of judges. It can also cause friction between the judiciary and the executive. As an illustration, after high-ranking governmental officials made critical remarks about the judicial system, the SJC accused the cabinet of "inadmissible interference in the affairs of the judiciary." The National Assembly responded by passing a bill that stipulated that members of the Judicial Supreme Council had to be judges with five years of experience. While the cabinet claimed that this act would ensure the efficiency and quality of the judiciary, political observers agreed its goal was to remove the chief prosecutor and Supreme Court chairperson, both vehement anticommunists.[55] Although overturned by the Constitutional Court, this law was an obvious attempt to limit the independence of the judiciary.

The judiciary's past role as guarantor of communist power makes it suspect in the eyes of the public. Although envisioned as the major defender of civil rights and the rule of law, the judiciary has become involved in political battles, seriously lessening its effectiveness, and more importantly, calling into doubt its role as a neutral arbitrator. A related problem is the belief of many that by using the judiciary to resolve conflicts rather than trying to establish a societal consensus, the polity is weakened as legal conflict replaces political cooperation.[56]

In spite of these problems, the judiciary is beginning to play an important role in the polity. In 1996 the Constitutional Court disqualified the Socialist Party's presidential candidate Georgi Pirinski. The Court ruled that Pirinski, born in the United States to a Bulgarian father and an American mother, was not a Bulgarian citizen by birth and therefore ineligible to be

---

GEORGI PIRINSKI (1948–)

Born to an American mother and Bulgarian father in New York, Pirinski returned to Bulgaria in 1952. A graduate of the Economy of Foreign Trade department at the Sofia University for National and World Economy, Pirinski began his political career working as an economist in the "International Organizations" department of the Ministry of Foreign Trade from 1974–76. He remained in this department throughout the rest of his bureaucratic career, serving as Deputy Minister of Trade from 1980 to 1990.

In 1990, Pirinski moved out of the bureaucracy into mainstream politics, becoming a member of the BSP Supreme Council in 1990. An important figure in the BSP since its creation, he served three terms as an MP. As a relative political newcomer because he was not associated with the old Communist party, Pirinski was selected as the BSP presidential candidate in the October 1996 elections. Although public opinion polls showed him to be the most popular politician in Bulgaria, his candidacy was rejected by the Constitutional Court on the basis of not being a Bulgarian citizen by birth. Despite his forced withdrawal, Pirinski still remains active in politics. After the fall of Zhan Videnov's government, he was selected as deputy chair of the BSP and remains an important political figure.

---

president. This was a very controversial ruling since Pirinski was the most popular politician in Bulgaria and his party controlled the parliament.

The Bureaucracy

The socialist system of state control created a powerful caste, the bureaucracy. In contrast to bureaucrats in democratic regimes, bureaucrats in socialist states had tremendous power. Because the state controlled almost everything aspect of society and there was no recourse other than another part of the state apparatus, bureaucrats had numerous opportunities to extort bribes. Without an explanation or reason, applications were routinely denied or "new" rules introduced.

In spite of political changes, bureaucrats continue to maintain a large degree of influence. This is the result of a couple of factors. First, the continued state control over a large part of the economy still provides opportunities for bureaucrats to enrich themselves. Poor wages and working conditions make government officials susceptible to corruption. In 1995, 1,500 police officers were dismissed for abuse of office or corruption.[57] The extent of this problem can be seen in a 1997 policy that for the first time gave the army the power to help collect customs dues. In March alone, the army took in as much as had been collected in all of 1996. Second, frequent ministerial changes makes middle- and lower-ranking officials even more powerful because they are the only ones familiar with various bureaucratic procedures. Finally, officials retain too much power and bureaucratic procedures lack transparency.

A 1994 public opinion showed that 47 percent of the respondents believed that bureaucrats would only do their jobs well if they were offered bribes.[58] Since people's perceptions of government are often the result of interactions with government officials, arrogant and corrupt bureaucrats contribute to the general public's distrust of the government. This in turn weakens the government's authority and ability to act.

The Military

In contrast to the Soviet Union, the armed forces in CEE states were much more politicized and much less professional. Consequently, they had limited political influence. In Bulgaria, Hungary, and Poland, they had no separate political role and were completely controlled by the Party. In addition to their usual role in national defense, the armed forces were used as an indoctrination tool. With the change in regime, the armed forces in these states were quickly depoliticized. Party organizations and the political structures overseeing their activities were abolished.

The role of the military in the contemporary polity is still evolving. It faces many of the same problems that affect society at large. According to a 1995 government briefing paper, "the grave economic and cultural crises experienced by the country have had an adverse effect on the Bulgarian military." The report identifies the major problems facing the military as a lack of combat readiness; a discrepancy between the existing legal framework that governs the military and reality; severe financial and logistical shortages; and an exodus of officers who have seen their formerly privileged status ended with a decline in living standards.[59] According to the briefing paper, these problems have severely undermined the ability of the armed forces to guarantee the territorial integrity and the sovereignty of the country. As an illustration, the commander of the Air Force noted 30 percent of military aircraft and 46 percent of the helicopters were beyond repair.[60]

Immediately following the regime change, there was overwhelming support for cutting the armed forces. However, as a result of the wars of Yugoslav succession, there is a growing sentiment that strength of the armed forces should be increased. A March 1994 opinion poll showed that 65 percent of Bulgarians wanted the military budget increased, even though this would mean cuts in other areas.[61]

In spite of numerous problems, the armed forces have the highest public support of any governmental institution—over 70 percent in the same poll. Unusual in Bulgaria's history, the military has managed to keep aloof from political infighting. In contrast with Russia, where the army has been deeply involved in the political process, the Bulgarian military has aided in the overall democratization of society by remaining neutral.

However, if national interests were threatened—for example, if Macedonia became unstable—or if the government suffers from a lack of popular support, the armed forces may play a more influential role in the future. Already there have been calls for the army to end the growing crime wave. Notably, with the exception of abolishing communist political structures, the military is the only state body that has not undergone significant change. Although it is legally forbidden from "solving interior political problems" and is under strict civilian control, the military has a history of political involvement.

Significantly, the armed forces are the only organization with the structure that would allow them to play a more "active" political role. Although middle-ranking officers realize they could not run a modern economy, some higher-ranking officers believe the armed forces have a duty to preserve society.

THE ELITE

Under the old regime, the Communist Party both created and implemented policy through an interlocking directorate of party and state leadership. Thus the elite was comprised mostly of high-ranking party members who dominated the polity. Although the workers made up 44 percent of its members, the Party elite was dominated by professionals and members of the intelligentsia.

With the change in regime, monolithic party control ended. Today, as in other CEE states, various governmental and nongovernmental elites struggle for political power and influence. While in the long run this conflict will strengthen society, it has numerous short-term drawbacks. Various constituencies advocate their own special interests, ignoring societal interests. In contrast to established democracies, there is no check on these interests, allowing them to dominate the polity. This greatly complicates the process of coalition building and compromise needed to create a national consensus.

The Governmental Elite

In contrast to Western democracies, in which governmental elites share similar social and educational backgrounds, today's governing elite varies according to the party in power. This is a new development, since under the previous regime the *nomenklatura* list ensured that the party elite had similar backgrounds and experience.

Even before the communist takeover, political parties were marginal actors in the Bulgarian polity. Although present in the legislature, they had little influence since the executive and bureaucracy dominated politics. In addition, as in Germany during the Weimar Republic, the party system in Bulgaria was extremely fragmented. This legacy continues today as fifty-seven parties competed for seats in the 1997 elections. This situation has made it difficult to form stable parliamentary majorities, thus reinforcing the power of the bureaucracy and nonstate groups. The largest and most important parties are described here.

The Bulgarian Socialist Party (BSP)

As in the other states in the region, the Socialist Party, formerly the Communist Party, has had a significant impact on the development of the polity. The BSP won the first free elections in 1990 and, after a four-year hiatus, returned to power in 1994. This is the result of two factors: the historical lack of a well-organized opposition such as Solidarity in Poland; and its image as the party of "responsible, conservative change" that would lead Bulgaria in its peaceful democratic transition. The emphasis on continuity and peaceful change proved very appealing, especially in light of the violent events in neighboring Romania and Yugoslavia.

Although the top positions in the BSP have been held by the *nomen-klatura* from the previous regime, people from a variety of professions— lawyers, engineers, economists, doctors, teachers, journalists—have been included on the party's electoral lists. This notwithstanding, the party draws most of its support from pensioners, industrial workers, older intellectuals, the middle aged, and people in rural areas. Overall, 40 percent of the BSP membership is over 55 years old. In general, these people are conservative and leery of change.[62] Since these groups provide a disproportionate number of the unemployed, they are the most disillusioned with economic reforms. The broad appeal of the BSP can be seen in the fact it has over 300,000 members and is the largest party.

In contrast to its counterparts in Hungary and Poland, the BSP remains deeply divided between those who want to create a West European social democratic party and those who want a more Marxist-oriented party with closer ties to its communist past. This situation is the result of numerous factors. First, the BCP was closer to the Communist Party of the Soviet Union than any other CEE communist party. Second, party members had much less access to the West than their CEE counterparts and thus did not see that the Soviet model of development no longer worked. Third, the conservative nature of the population makes it difficult for the older generation to renounce the ideology they were raised under and believed in.[63] Even today, the BSP leadership continues to use thoroughly discredited terms such as democratic centralism.

The split between the factions could be seen in the composition of the BSP government following their 1994 electoral victory. It was a compromise between the party's older and younger generations, or as Stefan Prodev, the editor-in-chief of the BSP's daily newspaper *Duma*, put it, a compromise between "the red cell phones and the red grandmothers."[64] The early resignation of the BSP government—after some BSP MPs voted against their own government to force new elections—and their defeat in the 1996 presidential and 1997 parliamentary elections showed the split had become a chasm. Its previous success not withstanding, the BSP will remain in the political wilderness until it either splits into its natural divisions or finds a common unifying theme. Although it remains the largest party, its declining popularity can be seen in its loss of 42,000 members 1997.[65]

Euroleft

Founded in 1994 by former BSP Deputy Prime Minister Alexander Tomov, this party is supported by former BSP supporters who left the party because of their opposition to its neocommunist policies. Their goal is to create a European style social democratic party. This program appeals to the young and educated. Although the Euroleft narrowly failed to cross the four percent electoral barrier in 1994, swollen by BSP defectors, it won fourteen seats in the 1997 election.

The Union of Democratic Forces/United Democratic Forces (UDF/ODF)

Formed by former dissidents, the Union of Democratic Forces (UDF) is an anticommunist coalition created from thirteen parties and groups in 1989. According to its first leader, former President Zhelyu Zhelev, the UDF was to be a temporary alliance against the Bulgarian Communist Party. Its diverse membership included the Social Democratic Party, the Green Party, the Bulgarian Agricultural Union (BANU)–Nikola Petkov, the Democratic Party, the Radical Democratic Party, and the Eco-Glasnost National Movement. Although the UDF has been viewed as the party of change, the lack of a parliamentary majority limited its ability to enact reforms. The typical UDF supporter is young, urban, and well educated.

While the main unifying principle of the UDF was the desire to prevent the communists from returning to power, the lack of ideological affinity greatly weakened the coalition. Unlike the Solidarity movement in Poland or the Democratic Forum in Hungary, whose members had a common ideology, the UDF was simply an electoral coalition. This situation fostered a split within the coalition between those who focused on the past and consequently refused to work with the BSP and those who realized compromise is necessary to create a new political system. As a result, the UDF underwent a series of divisions and realignments. This internal crisis cost the coalition much of its initial postcommunist support. In the 1994 parliamentary elections, the UDF had its worst showing since its founding.

Following the disastrous electoral showing, the UDF elected Ivan Kostev as their new leader. Realizing the UDF would never regain power without fundamental structural changes, Kostev created a grassroots organization—

Ivan Kostov (1949–)

An economist with a doctorate in mathematics, Kostov became a professor at the Technical University of Sofia in 1982. His first experience in politics came as a member of the Council of Economic Experts of the Union of Democratic Forces (UDF) in 1990. This experience led to his selection as Minister of Finance in the cabinets of Dimitar Popov and Filip Dimitrov from 1990 to 1992. Chosen as a UDF MP, Kostov was named to chair the Parliamentary Committee on Economic Policy. After the UDF electoral defeat in 1994, he was selected as chairman of the UDF. Realizing that to gain power the UDF would have to become more united, he created a new executive council, turning the coalition into a unified party (the United Democratic Forces). These organizational efforts helped the UDF win a majority in the 1997 elections. As leader of the party, Kostov became prime minister after the election. His time in office has been marked by wide-ranging economic and political reforms.

---

thus removing some obstructionist party leaders—and transformed the UDF from a coalition to a party, the United Democratic Forces (ODF in Bulgarian). This change helped the ODF win April 1997 parliamentary elections.

Alliance for National Salvation (ANS)

Founded in 1997, this group is comprised of several small centrist parties, including liberals, environmentalists, and monarchists. Although members have more differences than similarities, the creation of this group is significant. Like the PU and BBB, its electoral success suggests the public is ready for change.

The People's Union (PU)

This party was created through an alliance between the Bulgarian National Agricultural Union (BANU) and the Democratic Party. The latter party was a member of the UDF but left because it believed it was losing its identity within the coalition. The PU won 6.5 percent of the vote in the 1994 election, making it the third largest party in the National Assembly.

Although the alliance includes several experienced political leaders, the urban-rural partnership is problematic. The party platform supports economic and political reforms, a smaller state sector, and subsidies for business and agriculture. Because of their different backgrounds, the PU not only draws support from pensioners but also has the highest number of supporters with a university education. In 1997, the PU ran joint candidates with the ODF.

The Movement for Rights and Freedoms (MRF)

The Movement for Rights and Freedoms (MRF) is not easy to define in terms of the communist/anticommunist division that has characterized the Bulgarian polity. Although its official program is "to defend the rights and freedoms of different ethnic communities," its predominantly Turkish leadership and constituency cause it to be viewed as the party of ethnic Turks. As a result, the MRF has often been accused of promoting Turkey's political interests. This has fostered ethnic xenophobia and nationalism which extends to the highest government offices. In 1995, BSP Education Minister Ilcho Dimitrov said the MRF was "anti-constitutional and its policies harm national interests."[66]

The MRF draws the majority of its support from the predominantly Turkish regions around Shuman and Razgrad in the north-west part of the country and Haskovo in the southwest. Initially part of the UDF, its political importance was not acknowledged until after the 1990 elections when it won independent representation in the National Assembly. Using its new found influence, it helped empower, and later bring down, the first UDF government. Its mandate was used to form the "technocratic" Berov government that was in power 1992–94. Like the UDF, political infighting cost the MRF support in the 1994 elections. Their de facto alliance in the Berov government with the BSP—the successor party to the BCP that had forced 350,000 ethnic Turks to migrate in the 1980s—split the party.

This policy split the ethnic Turkish vote in the 1994 elections, reducing their parliamentary representation. Although officially part of the ANS in the 1997 elections, many members split from the leadership and ran as members of the ODF.

The Bulgarian Business Bloc (BBB)

One of two new parties—the other was the PU—to gain representation in the 1994 elections was a business party headed by George Ganchev. An eccentric former emigré, Ganchev leads an anti-establishment party whose platform is anything but coherent. Generally, the party is in favor of free market economic reforms. Its core supporters are young, well-educated, urban voters, small businessmen, and middle class voters who have traditionally voted for the UDF. Seemingly contradictory, after the 1994 elections, the BBB supported the BSP in parliamentary voting. This caused a split in the party, with three of ten MPs leaving the Bloc. Abandoning its de facto alliance with the BSP, the BBB won twelve seats in the 1997 elections.

Recent Elections

Against a backdrop of economic, political, and social instability, in 1994 Bulgaria held its third general election since 1989. Taking 44 percent of the vote, the BSP won an outright majority of seats (125 out of 240) in the National Assembly. The UDF won 24 percent of the vote and sixty-nine seats, the newly formed People's Union 6.5 percent and eighteen seats, and the MDF 5.4 percent and fifteen seats. This electoral outcome was analogous with those of other recent elections in the region. In the mid-1990s in Hungary, Poland, and Russia, the former communist parties either regained control of the government or made significant electoral gains.

This was the first time since 1991 a single party controlled the parliament. Although this majority could have presaged dramatic changes, living standards and social conditions grew worse under the BSP. Internal splits in the party encouraged the three major opposition groups to agree on a common candidate for the 1996 presidential election. To this end, a U.S.-style primary was held. Peter Stoyanov, a lawyer from Sofia, soundly defeated the incumbent president, Zhelyu Zhelev. During the November election, Stoyanov defeated the BSP candidate Ivan Marazov with 59.7 percent of the vote. Significantly, Stoyanov won a majority of the vote in small towns and villages, traditional BSP strongholds. Perhaps the most interesting feature of the presidential election was the 22 percent of the vote garnered by BBB head Georges Ganchev in the first round. His support, coupled with a relatively low voting turnout (61.5 percent), suggested people are growing tired of the bipolar model of politics that has dominated the polity.

The 1997 parliamentary election campaign was marked by a substantial restructuring of the major parties and coalitions. A united opposition (ODF) won 52 percent of the vote, giving it 137 seats. The BSP saw their percentage of the vote decline from 43 to 22 percent, reducing their number of seats from 125 to 58. The ANS won 7.6 percent of the vote and nineteen seats, the BBB 4.9 percent and twelve seats, and the newly formed Euroleft won 5.5 percent and fourteen seats.

In summary, five parties surpassed the electoral threshold and the winning coalition holds an absolute majority in the National Assembly. The success of the centrist Euroleft party and Alliance for National Salvation and the unprecedented attempt by the new ODF government to get all deputies to consider the passage of a joint declaration outlining the country's policy priorities[67] suggests the political system is undergoing a fundamental change. However, although new parties are being created, they lack the natural constituencies of their Western counterparts. Until the economy is developed and parties become linked to economic or social classes, the parties will continue to reflect the polarization of society.

FIGURE 2.1 National Assembly Electoral Results—1991, 1994 and 1997

	% of votes in			total seats* in		
Party	1991	1994	1997	1991	1994	1997
Union of Democratic Forces (UDF)	34.4	24.2	52.3	110	69	137
Bulgarian Socialist Party (BSP)	33.1	43.5	22.1	106	125	58
Movement for Rights and Freedoms (MRF)	7.5	5.4	7.6	24	15	19
People's Union	—	6.5	—	—	18	—
Bulgarian Business Bloc (BBB)	—	4.7	4.9	—	13	12
Euroleft	—	—	5.5	—	—	14

Note: Voter turnout: 1991—80%
1994—75%
1997—59%

*The threshold needed to gain seats in the National Assembly is 4%.

Sources: Evgenii Dainov, "Bulgaria: Politics after the 1991 Elections," *RFE/RL Research Report*, 10 January 1992, vol. 1, no. 2, and Sofia Khorizont Radio Network, 27 December 1994, cited in *FBIS-EEU*, 28 December 1994. "Bulgaria: Hope at Last," *The Economist*, 26 April 1997, 48–49.

Summary

Ten years after the end of the communist regime, political consensus is only beginning to emerge. As in Poland and Russia, the Bulgarian opposition had one common goal—the ousting of communists. However, unlike those states, the Bulgarian opposition split even before this goal was achieved. This split was one of the major reasons for the narrow victory of the anticommunist coalition in the October 1991 parliamentary elections. Only a year after it came to power, the UDF split again, bringing down its own government. The fragmentation of the UDF is not an accidental phenomenon, but rather a Bulgarian political tradition. In the 1920s, there were eleven factions of the Bulgarian Agricultural National Union (BANU). This greatly limited the effectiveness of their government between 1920 and 1923. In 1994, there were still ten different BANUs. Each had a similar program but a different ambitious leader. To date, politicians have been more interested in promoting their own narrow interests, to the detriment of the system as a whole.[68] Thus, in contrast to Hungary and Poland, the construction of political parties continues.

In addition, unlike in the United States, the parties represented in the National Assembly have occupied very different parts of the political spectrum. With centrist parties only starting to win electoral support, policymaking has often been hostage to ideological clashes and emotional debates. Besides splitting the electorate, this situation fosters intolerance, extremism, and if the past is a guide, violence.

Nongovernmental Elites

Until 1989, the BCP prohibited nongovernmental groups not controlled by the Party. The ouster of Zhivkov brought a host of new and revived groups into the political arena. The most influential are business groups, entrepreneurs, criminal syndicates, and the church.

The business groups can be roughly divided into two groups: new entrepreneurs and members of the old *nomenklatura*. Their differing interests can be seen in their political allegiances. The entrepreneurs, with few links to the past, support sweeping economic reform. This makes them natural allies of the ODF and the BBB. In contrast, because they dominate large sectors of the economy, shadowy groups tied to the old regime that endorse a continued state role in the economy support the BSP. The latter group has been the locus of power in Bulgaria. Since the state is ineffective, battles within this group have been the key determinants in the evolution of the polity.

The influence of the latter groups is partly a result of their access to "red money." This is money that before and during the confusion of regime change was deposited in foreign bank accounts. Former Communist Party head Todor Zhivkov said $2 billion was sent abroad in 1990 alone.[69] This money was then "laundered" by former members of the *nomenklatura*, who brought it back into Bulgaria. They used it to create new companies or, through their connections with other former *nomenklatura* in the bureaucracy, buy state companies at a fraction of their cost. Since usually only one enterprise controlled an entire part of the economy, buying a former state company gave these new entrepreneurs a natural monopoly. Members of the BSP also placed supporters in key positions in state banks and industries who—under the guise of reform—diverted resources into the new businesses.

An example is the Multigroup company. Closely tied to former communist prime minister Andrei Lukanov, this giant holding company is involved in many sectors of the economy and is considered to be one of the most powerful entities in Bulgaria.[70] In 1994 Multigroup's economic turnover was over $1 billion dollars, approximately 10 percent of the entire Bulgarian GDP. As in Russia, the Multigroup company is a typical example of how the old *nomenklatura* transformed their political power into economic power and continue to control the country from behind the scenes. Interestingly, in a country where annual per capita GDP is less than $4,200, five of the twenty cabinet members in the 1995 BSP government cabinet were millionaires. The economic clout of these companies has led to massive corruption and fosters the perception politicians are simply tools of big business, promoting their interests at the expense of the rest of society. It also makes people cynical about the effects of change, as they see the same people who previously held power once again dominating society. Thus the power of these groups limits change and the creation of new elites.

Another group linked with the previous regime is the "mafia," a term is loosely used to denote various criminal syndicates. One of the most powerful groups is the "Wrestlers." After the downfall of the old regime, former athletes were hired as bodyguards for some of the new businessmen. After a while, they removed their former employers and today comprise a substantial part of Bulgaria's underworld.[71] They have increased their power by allying themselves with former figures in the state security apparatus to create auto-theft rings, racketeering groups, and powerful protection rackets that the state has been powerless to stop. Operating under the guise of insurance companies, of which there were over 100 in 1997, these groups have dominated the polity. Battles among them have been the main factor behind a dramatic increase in crime. Between 1990 and 1994, the crime rate increased 350 percent.

This situation has been aggravated by a politicized judiciary, the lack of structural economic reforms, a weak and demoralized police force, corrupt state officials, and a legislative vacuum. As a result, criminal organizations have become more powerful than the government. BSP Interior Minister Nachev noted that " organized crime is gathering strength. It may well get out of state control and turn into a 'parallel society.'"[72] Recognizing the seriousness of this problem, after only three months in office, the new ODF government passed laws that criminalized racketeering, established more stringent requirements for insurance companies (e.g., barring them from commercial activities such as providing security services), and increased the power of the police. The government also published a list of "credit millionaires," individuals who received billions of leva from various state banks and never repaid the money. Anyone on this list was also banned from parliament. The list included Ilia Pavlov, CEO of Multigroup and personal advisor to Ahmed Dogan, the leader of the MRF.[73] While it is too early to judge the impact of these measures, they are a crucial step in separating the economic and political structures which have dominated the polity since 1989. Significantly, in 1998 the Multigroup Company publicly announced it would no longer fund political parties.

In contrast to Poland, where the Catholic church has historically played an active role in politics, the Bulgarian Orthodox church did not. Since Orthodoxy is much more closely linked to the state than Catholicism, as in Russia the church was not independent of the regime. Its leaders collaborated with the authorities and the church did not actively oppose the government. While there are a large number of church members in Hungary and Poland, only 26 percent of Bulgarians define themselves as "believers."

As a result of this legacy, today the church is divided between those who collaborated with the communists and those who did not. This cleavage extends to the position of patriarch or Pope. Bulgaria currently has two patriarchs, neither of whom recognizes the other. Since Patriarch Maksim was appointed by the former communist regime, some church leaders consider him illegitimate. In 1992, the UDF supported the election of Patriarch Pimen. With the fall of the UDF government, Pimen's election was not recognized by the Directorate of Religious Affairs. In 1997, the Supreme Administrative Court voided the claim of Patriarch Maksim. This interchurch feud has divided the religious community and undermined the authority of the church.

To fill a perceived ideological and social void, the number of religious sects and communities has mushroomed. Concerns about the legitimacy of some sects and their activities have emerged, especially in light of their generous funding from abroad. Apprehension regarding their possible foreign influence is augmented by the fact their followers are mainly young people.

The Bulgarian Orthodox church also suffers from a lack of funding. In contrast to Hungary, Poland, and Russia, the government has yet to return expropriated property to the church. These factors suggest the Orthodox church will continue to have limited influence.

THE GENERAL PUBLIC

As a result of a legacy of political indoctrination, economic hardship, and widespread corruption, there is a lack of political involvement among Bulgarians. Only dramatic events (e.g., an increase in inflation to over 300 percent in 1996) have mobilized the population.

Why is this the case? Most people consider politics to be a dirty business and do not want to soil themselves. This is partly the result of the candidate selection process. Because the proportional electoral system selects members of parliament on the basis of their party's percentage of the total vote, party lists must be assembled. At the state level, they are compiled at the party's headquarters. A member's rank on this list is the result of bargaining within the party as well as the influence of the party's major outside supporters. Generally, top positions are reserved for party notables, followed by representatives of factions and interest groups. This system is mirrored at the local level and prevents those who do not want to be affiliated with a party from running for office. Consequently, elections often bring opportunists into office, reinforcing the negative image of politics and politicians. This contributes to inefficient policy formulation and implementation which in turn increases public apathy. Reinforcing each other, these two processes hinder democratic development.

In contrast to Western democracies and other CEE states, Bulgaria lacks large numbers of nongovernmental elites. Unlike Hungary and Poland, antigovernment groups did not exist in Bulgaria under the communist regime. Thus only recently have nongovernmental groups begun to play a role in the polity.[74]

Modes of Influence

A history of government repression, contemporary public apathy, and a bipolar political divide have all limited the public's political influence. Nevertheless, some organizations have had a role in influencing policy.

Under the old regime, every worker had to belong to a union. Since the union was under the control of the state, collective bargaining, the right to strike, and the free election of union officials were unknown. As a result, although it has a membership of over 3 million, the communist era Confederation of Independent Trade Unions in Bulgaria (CITUB) does not have much influence. In contrast, the Podkrepa Labor Federation has played a role in the polity. Formed after Zhivkov's ouster in 1989, at its peak Podkrepa had approximately 450,000 members. Its supporters control crucial industries such as mining, oil, and steel. In 1990, it which played a key role in bringing down the first socialist government by launching a general strike.

In addition to using demonstrations and strikes to influence policy making, the unions have also been involved in direct political battles with the government. In May 1992, Podkrepa, in an unprecedented alliance with CITUB, called for the resignation of Prime Minister Dimitrov's cabinet. This demand was accompanied by relentless criticism of the government's economic performance. Although the unions failed to bring down the government, the Minister of Industry was subsequently forced to resign. He was replaced by Rumen Bikov, a staunch Podkrepa supporter.[75]

The potential power of the trade unions can be seen through their inclusion in the National Council for Tripartite Cooperation. Established to coordinate economic and social policies, this government-sponsored group is comprised of representatives from employers, trade unions, and employees. Consent of the unions has been instrumental in implementing government initiatives. Threats by union leaders to leave the Council, usually accompanied by warnings of a strike, have caused the government to change its policy. Overall, however, the lack of cooperation between unions and decreasing living standards have caused their membership and influence to decrease.

Quasipolitical groups, those with a political agenda outside the political mainstream, also exist. As a result of people's dissatisfaction with traditional parties, extremist ones have formed. For example, in 1993 there was a considerable increase in the number of supporters of the Monarchist Party, the Internal Macedonian Revolutionary Organization (IMRO), and neofascist skinheads.[76] As with other extremist parties, they offer simple solutions to complex problems. Though they have had little impact, they clearly indicate discontent with the current state of affairs.

The general public has also gained some political influence with the regime change. In addition to voting for political parties, as in Hungary and Poland the population can voice its opinion through national referendums. However, the effectiveness of this tool is limited as referendums can only be called on matters within the responsibility of the National Assembly; they cannot overturn judicial decisions. A national referendum can be proposed by the president, the government, or one-quarter of the MPs. However, the National Assembly has the final decision on whether to hold a referendum. This greatly limits the ability of the electorate to affect policy with this tool. Thus to date there have been no national referendums.

Local referendums are much more common. They can be called by a mayor, one quarter of the municipal councilors, or one-quarter of the voters. Although they cannot change the municipal budget or local taxes, any other issue may be brought before the voters. For example, one town used a referendum to determine whether the streets should be cleaned by the people who live there or by the local government.

As a result of numerous societal problems, there are a growing number of nongovernmental groups, such as the National Public Council for Fighting Crime or the Bulgarian Committee for Free and Fair Elections and Civil Rights. Although groups like this are the foundation of a civil society, they have little influence. This is the result of a general lack of understanding about what a civil society means; what it requires (i.e., popular participation); hostility from the government, which sees these groups as agents of foreign interests; and the lack of funding and effective organizational structures. Although varying in degree, these problems are similar to those faced by civil activists throughout the region.

> Seven years after the end of the all-providing communist state, the concepts of self-help groups, individual initiative, civil rights, the rule of law, and a 'third sector' of nongovernmental or nonprofit organizations have yet to be accepted either by the government authorities or the populace.[77]

The lack of progress in the creation of a civil society in Bulgaria has been reflected in its continuing economic and political crises. However, the role of students and ordinary citizens in bringing down the BSP government in 1997 suggests this situation might be changing.

POLICY MAKING AND IMPLEMENTATION

Prior to 1989, state policy-making bodies resembled their Western counterparts organizationally. However, in practice they played quite different roles. Constitutionally, the most important body was the National Assembly. All of its 400 members were also members of the Bulgarian Communist Party or the allied Bulgarian Agricultural Union (BANU). The Assembly was the "embodiment" of the country's precommunist parliamentary tradition of vesting supreme authority in the National Assembly. However, as in other socialist states, the parliament was merely a rubber stamp for the real policy makers, the Politburo and the Secretariat of the BCP. As a result, it held only a few short sessions each year and its deputies did not debate. In between sessions of the Assembly, supreme power was vested in the State Council— the Durzhaven Suviet. This non-elected body was usually headed by the general secretary of the Communist Party. While governmental authority legally resided in the thirty-four-member Council of Ministers, this group was only responsible for executing policy. What power this body did have was the result of the fact that ministers simultaneously held senior posts in BCP.

The end of the communist monopoly on power brought significant changes to the policy-making process. The new constitution vested the National Assembly with supreme legislative power, greatly expanding the number of individuals and groups involved in the policy-making process. However, in practice the Bulgarian decision-making process remains dominated by a small elite that is ideologically split. Thus, policy making is dominated by partisan struggles. This legacy from the 1920s has hindered policy formulation by diverting attention from policy issues to inter- and intraparty squabbles.

There are four phases in policy formation. In the first phase, draft legislation is submitted to the chairperson of the National Assembly either by an individual deputy, the cabinet, a standing parliamentary committee, or a parliamentary group. Individual legislative initiatives occur more often in Bulgaria than in Hungary, Poland, or Russia. Of the 642 bills and draft resolutions introduced to parliament between 1991 and 1993, 67 percent came from individual MPs, 30 percent from government bodies, and only 3 percent from political parties.[78]

After the BSP victory in 1994, the cabinet became the chief initiator of legislative initiatives. This has fostered better coordination between the policy-making and policy-implementing bodies.[79] This trend is likely to continue as the ODF Cabinet also has a strong parliamentary majority.

Within three days of submission, the chairperson must send the bill to the appropriate standing committee for discussion. This procedure is different from Poland, where bills are not sent to committees until after they have their respective first—introduction to the full parliament—and second readings. Thus, the Bulgarian procedure is similar to that of the U.S. Congress. Once a bill is introduced into committee, forty-eight hours must elapse before it can be "discussed" in order to give MPs time to study it.

After deliberation, the committee returns the bill, with recommendations, to the Assembly for its first reading. Recommendations include adoption of the bill, suggested modifications, or rejection. As in Poland, if the initiator of the bill disagrees with the recommendations of the committee, she can withdraw the bill from the committee. However, after the first reading, the bill can only be withdrawn with the consent of the National Assembly. During the first reading, the text of the bill is voted on as a whole. If changes are made, the bill is returned to committee.

At this point, committees can become a serious hinderance to the legislative process. Since there are no procedural rules to limit their deliberations, there is no mechanism for breaking a committee deadlock. Therefore, returning the bill to the full chamber for a second reading can take some time. Once the draft legislation is read out of committee, it is discussed and voted on in two additional parliamentary readings. However, if a bill sponsored by the majority party in parliament leaves the committee after its first reading, party discipline ensures it usually becomes law. If the bill is passed, it is sent to the president for promulgation: if the president vetoes the bill, it is returned to the National Assembly. However, as in Hungary and Poland, the president's veto only delays another parliamentary vote on the bill. After fifteen days, the veto can be overridden by a simple majority of all MPs. In contrast, it takes a two-thirds majority in the United States to override a presidential veto. The president or forty-eight MPs can ask the Constitutional Court to rule on the constitutionality of any law.

Policy-Making Influences

While the formal aspects of policy making are straightforward, they are only part of the process. As in any system, there are numerous governmental and nongovernmental actors which influence policy formation.

Perhaps the most important factor influencing policy making is the absence or presence of a governmental majority in the National Assembly. From 1991 to 1994, this condition was absent and legislation was held hostage to shifting political alliances. For example, between January and June 1994, only two laws were passed. Opposition parties can also directly influence the policy-making process. They can submit draft legislation and, through the committees, amend government bills. They can also use the floor of the National Assembly as a forum to criticize the government.

The lack of societal consensus and the resulting political polarization have allowed poorly written bills to become law. Between 1991 and 1994, bills that became laws were often the result of compromise between diametrically opposed parties. As a result, many were incomplete and/or vague. Therefore, the passage of legislation depends either on one party with a stable majority or cooperation between parliamentary parties. The lack of a parliamentary majority greatly hindered the enactment of economic and political reforms. After the 1994 parliamentary elections gave the BSP an outright majority in the National Assembly, it passed sixty-nine decrees and eighteen bills in the first 100 days of its tenure. This situation also meant more legislation was written by specialists, greatly improving the legislation's form and content. The passage of 145 laws and 122 administrative decisions in the first year of the ODF government suggests this trend will continue.

Nongovernmental actors also influence policy formulation. During the 1994–96 socialist government, an "Expert Legislative Council" staffed by

BSP-appointed "experts" was in charge of drafting bills,[80] greatly limiting the ability of the opposition to influence legislation. One of the first acts of the new ODF government was to abolish this body. Finally, depending on the prevailing policy-making process, lobbyists and interest groups can influence draft legislation before it is approved by the cabinet. These groups can get MPs to offer an amendment to a bill during its first reading.

Case Study: The Land Tenure Act

In 1991, the Grand National Assembly passed the Land Restitution Act. Its goal was to return expropriated land to its original owners. Seven years later, only 38 percent of this land has been returned. What accounts for this situation?

Between 1991 and 1994, the act was amended several times, with the government of the day adding provisions that accommodated the interests of its supporters. The net effect was to slow the return of land. To stop this process altogether, the BSP drastically amended the law in 1995. New provisions give titles to those who had obtained them under the communist regime. In effect, land distributed under the communists would not be returned to its original owners. The law also forced owners who wanted to sell their land to first offer it to the local government. Before the parliamentary vote, members of the opposition walked out of the National Assembly. President Zhelev vetoed these amendments, calling them constitutional violations of individual civil rights. After the National Assembly overrode the president's veto, forty-eight members of the UDF asked the Constitutional Court to review the new law. The Court ruled that the new law violated the Constitution and voided it. Other obstacles include the destruction of land deeds, which made it difficult for original owners to support their claims, and the resistance from farmers to the Liquidation Committees, which were set up to dispose of collective farm assets. As this example demonstrates, policy making in Bulgaria has been a hostage of partisan political interests.

In addition to partisan battles, policy making is controlled, as in the communist era, by a small elite. While the Communist Party apparat has been replaced by the state bureaucracy, the continuing lack of a civil society and the desire of the state to keep control over the policy process means limits public involvement in the policy process.

Case Study: Media Law

Since the change in regime, the party in power has used its influence to dominate the broadcast media. This was facilitated by the government's control over state employees who not only produce programs but also grant licenses to private stations. After taking power in 1997, the ODF government introduced a bill that would change the licensing law. Currently, one agency grants both licenses and operating concessions. The new law would have split this authority between two separate agencies. Partially as a result of less than explicit government intentions, the bill's introduction was immediately criticized.[81] The media opposed the bill because it would make getting a license and concession more difficult. There would now be two steps rather than one, increasing possible government interference and the risk of censorship. Denouncing what they considered to be the ODF's attempt to limit the media, the BSP joined broadcasting interests in opposing the bill. They also appealed to the Council of Europe to examine the law. After numerous parliamentary and public debates and a Council of Europe recommendation that the bill be changed, the government backed down and agreed to merely streamline the existing process. This example shows how both domestic and international factors can influence policy making.

Policy Implementation

Although the Council of Ministers is technically responsible for policy implementation, in reality this power has been delegated to other government bodies. At the highest level, ministries are responsible for issuing the necessary regulations, decrees, ordinances, and so forth to ensure laws are implemented. Actual policy implementation is left to state agencies and local governments.

Even though these responsibilities are fairly well defined, the ability to actually implement policy is often restricted. This is the result of three factors. First, incomplete or vague legislation makes it difficult for the ministries to interpret the intent of a law. Second, the frequent changes of high ministerial officials impede policy implementation. A third problem is an inefficient bureaucracy. The first two problems are the result of a new group of inexperienced legislators and a very divided society. These impediments often make actual policy implementation a long and continuous struggle. These problems can be seen in various governments' attempts to privatize the economy. Mass privatization, ostensibly begun in 1991, still remains in its initial stage, registration of participants. Although a Privatization Agency was established to implement privatization policies, as a result of the problems just noted, the agency has had very little success. Its chairperson blamed the parliament and the bureaucracy for "virtually impeding the process" of privatization.[82]

Policy implementation is also affected by nongovernmental groups, including interest groups, unions, and political parties. Green Patrols, for example, monitor the implementation of ecological regulations. In addition to ensuring that governmental policy is enforced, they bring average citizens closer to the actual process of government, helping to counter apathy. Overall, however, interest groups have little influence. For example, after the adoption of a value-added tax (VAT), newspapers and radio stations refused to pay it as they considered it detrimental to the future of an independent media. A four-day general strike by newspapers and radio stations was not successful in changing the law since the National Assembly and the Council of Ministers refused to exempt the media from the tax.

Finally, because of the atmosphere of economic, political, and social crisis that has dominated the Bulgarian polity since 1989, political parties play a significant role in policy implementation. They have mobilized their supporters to either support or actively block various policies of the government in power. In 1992, the BSP encouraged its local supporters to resist the implementation of the UDF government's policy of abolishing collective farms. This resistance greatly slowed the process of decollectivization. Another example is the reaction to a bill that for the first time allowed Turkish to be taught in school, although not in the core curriculum. The MRF viewed this policy as discriminatory; they wanted Turkish included in the core curriculum. The day the policy went into effect, the MRF organized school boycotts. As a result, implementation of this policy was postponed.[83]

In spite of opportunities to influence the polity, the average Bulgarian tends to accept the implementation of policies rather passively unless directly affected. The general lack of interest, as well as a limited ability to directly influence policy, largely limits public participation in the process of governance.

CONCLUSION

The end of the communist regime in 1989 fostered widespread euphoria. For most people it was the first time in their lives they enjoyed the freedom to form political associations, vote in democratic elections, and start their own businesses free from the autocratic rule of the state. The past seemed a distant, bad memory. This euphoria was short-lived. As a result of numerous problems, such as a weak economy, powerful nonstate institutions, and a very divided society, Bulgaria has had only limited success in transforming its polity.

Civil Society

Although there has been some movement toward the creation of groups and institutions that exist and act independently of the state, progress has been limited. Of the four transition goals, this area has seen the least movement. This situation is the result of numerous factors. First is the conservative nature of society. Five hundred years of Turkish occupation taught people not to get involved in politics, a mentality that was reinforced by the communist regime. As in Russia, the Bulgarian state completely dominated society. It encouraged people to rely on the state to solve problems and punished those who did not. In other words, it removed the incentive to take risks. In addition, with constantly increasing living standards during the communist period and the ownership of private property—with the exception of small plots—forbidden, people had little reason to form groups to protect their interests. This conservative mentality can be seen in the former communists' victory in the first free elections in 1989 and 1994.

This legacy is still present. It can be seen in the determination of the central government to limit the power of local governments, preventing them from tackling problems they are better equipped to deal with. Prior to the 1997 elections, relations between the state and civil society were often conflictual. During the Videnov government, NGOs were heavily taxed, their activities restricted, and they were attacked in the state press. These policies limit the creation of nonstate organizations and citizens' political involvement. Another problem is a lack of information about the outside world. Since Bulgarians have been subjects rather than citizens, they lack the knowledge of the role nonstate actors play in democratic regimes.[85] Thus while NGOs have been growing rapidly, there were over 4,000 in 1998, it will take some time before they play a significant role in the polity.

Another problem is restrictions on the media. Correspondents have been arrested and charged with libel for reporting on corruption. In 1996, the director-general of the state-run Bulgarian National Television was dismissed by the National Assembly after being accused of "disrespect for political forces." Overall, Freedom House gives Bulgaria a ranking of 3 in civil rights.

Democratic Institutions/Political Rights

The creation of democratic institutions and political rights has been Bulgaria's most significant accomplishment to date. The country has a well-functioning political system with free and fair elections, civilian control of the military, and peaceful transitions of power. Nevertheless there are still numerous problems associated with the development of democratic bodies. First is the lack of institutional mechanisms to limit the power of the state. The party that controls the parliament has used its position to weaken other parts of the government not under its control. For example, in August 1995, the Council of Ministers evicted the Constitutional Court from its offices. Although this decision was later voided, the president of the Court noted the government had "declared war on the Constitutional Court."[86]

Another problem is the lack of cooperation among the various branches of government and the failure to devolve power to regional and local governments. Too often, because of political and personal reasons, the executive, legislative, and judicial branches do not work together. Through conflicts with the other institutions, each attempts to increase its own power. This greatly weakens the power and legitimacy of the state. According to a former presidential chief-of-staff, this situation has created a duopoly of power in which government institutions function but are irrelevant. Thus, they cannot address the myriad of problems facing society, allowing other groups to gain control over the polity.[87]

Like Russia and to a lesser extent Poland, Bulgaria suffers from the lack of a clear separation of power between the executive and legislative branches of government. Since both president and the National Assembly are popularly elected, they both see themselves as guardians of the public trust. This situation puts a strain on the policy-making process. In the fall of 1998, President Stoyanov vetoed a series of ODF laws, forcing the Constitutional Court to play the role of final arbiter. The vetoes marked a new stage in the relationship between the president and the parliament. New mechanisms for addressing these disagreements need to be introduced to foster cooperation between the two institutions. As President Zhelev noted "even Jesus Christ would be unable to make things better in Bulgaria if he were president under the present Bulgarian Constitution."[88]

Vague constitutional descriptions have also fostered political instability. In January 1997, this situation led to a minor constitutional crisis. Socialist Prime Minister Videnov resigned, and, although Article 99 states the president is required to "appoint the Prime Minister–designate nominated by the party holding the highest number of seats in the National Assembly to form a government," there is no time limit for the nomination. President Zhelev used this ambiguity to delay the designation of a new prime minister, forcing the BSP to call an early election. Many observers criticized his behavior as a dereliction of duty. Actions like this weaken the legitimacy of government institutions.

While these problems are serious, Bulgaria has created a functioning, constitutional system. In contrast to the last democratic period, ministers have not been assassinated and most people accept the legitimacy of state institutions. As a result, Freedom House gives Bulgaria a ranking of 2 in the development of democratic institutions and political rights.

Market Economy

The still-developing civil society and limited power of Bulgaria's democratic institutions have greatly slowed the development of a market economy. Most significantly, they have prevented the enactment of structural economic reforms. Even Bulgarians who have taken advantage of the changed conditions to start their own businesses have had to overcome many legal and illegal obstacles. These include inconsistent government policies, lack of laws and regulations, severe taxation, and racketeering by both corrupt state officials and criminal groups. This has largely been the result of the legacy of state control over society and the country's domination by powerful nonstate groups. In 1998, for the first time, a poll showed a majority of Bulgarians (74%) prefer private ownership over state ownership of the economy. The same poll also showed 62 percent of the respondents must learn to take care of themselves rather than relying on the state.[89] The delay in economic reforms has drastically increased criminal activity, allowing corruption and racketeering to flourish. According to the National Police Director, this problem is compounded by a poorly paid police force and a judicial system unable to break the influence of criminal groups.[90]

In 1999, Bulgaria trailed far behind most other CEE states. Bulgaria's decline in output has been greater, inflation higher, and the extent of privatization and restructuring less than in Hungary or Poland. The EBRD ranks the Bulgarian economy as follows:

1. Privatization and restructuring of enterprises: 2.8
2. Competitiveness and openness of the market: 3
3. Ability of financial institutions to collect and channel savings to productive investments: 2.5
4. Extensiveness and effectiveness of legal rules on investment: 3

Overall, Bulgaria's success in creating a market economy ranks lowest of the states in our study, with only a 2.8 average out of 4. This situation has significant consequences in other areas, most specifically in creating a law-based polity.

Rule of Law

As in Russia, the rule of law has yet to take hold in Bulgaria. During the communist era, the law was used to restrict freedom, not guarantee it. This situation has continued even after the change in regime. The party that controlled the governmental institutions used the law to weaken their opposition.

For example, while Hungary, Poland, and Russia have all declared political amnesties for former communist officials in an attempt to unify society, Bulgaria has not. The first UDF government passed a law barring former high-ranking communists from higher academic and government posts. In response, one of the first acts of the new BSP government was to repeal this law. The UDF government then reinstated it. The extreme polarization of society has been a key factor in preventing the emergence of a law-based regime.

This condition has numerous negative consequences. Perhaps most significantly, it has fostered the use of ethnicity as a political weapon. Traditional Balkan xenophobia has expressed itself in the adoption of a law banning ethnically based political parties. When the MRF managed to bypass the ban by declaring itself the party of all minorities, it provoked wide protest. In an era of economic hardship, nationalists may use legal manifestations of ethnicity as a tool to further their own xenophobic agenda. Although violent attacks against minorities like those in Bosnia have not yet occurred, without adequate legal protection, ethnic divisions may yet provoke strife.

Another problem restricting the creation of law based regime is the power and mentality of the state apparatus. In an attempt to crack down on illegality acquired wealth, in 1997 police started stopping expensive cars. If the owners were not able to prove they had gotten the money to buy the car legally, the cars were impounded. While generally applauded by the public, this policy makes law a tool of the state, not a guarantee of individual freedom as in other democratic states.

An inevitable consequence of this situation is that people do not trust the law. The Shopes—Bulgarians who live in a region close to Sofia—have a saying that reflects the prevailing view of the law: "The law is a gate in a field which must be gotten around." This belief undermines public support for democracy and market reforms and fosters political apathy. Although a lack of data prevents Bulgaria from being ranked by Transparency International, it would rank only marginally higher than Russia.

Like Russia, Bulgaria has much more success in creating democratic institutions and a market economy than in creating a civil society based on the rule of law. Interestingly, although change occurred faster in Bulgaria than in Hungary, Poland, or Russia—in 1988, few Bulgarians thought that within a year they would be voting for a democratically elected parliament— it has since lagged behind these states. What accounts for seeming contradiction? While political battles have certainly played a role, Bulgarian intellectuals often blame the country's problems on a mentality hostile to the development of a civil society. The historical power of the Orthodox church and Bulgaria's location at the crossroads of several different cultures are often used as explanations.[91] However, this explanation fails to explain why societies with similar cultures and histories—Georgia, Macedonia—have been able to stabilize their economies.

A more plausible explanation is the lack of political consensus. In contrast to other states in the region, Bulgaria lacked both a reformist communist elite, and an organized opposition. As a result, post-1989 changes have been led either by a diverse and divided democratic coalition or by the former elite, who have substituted economic control for political control. This had led to a fragmented and very polarized polity. Instead of contesting ideas, politicians in Bulgaria have been content to battle over who initiated a policy, rather than its merit. This has led to some "interesting" results. As an illustration, although the UDF is in favor of joining NATO, when NATO requested overflight rights to supply troops in Macedonia, the UDF opposed the request simply because the BSP supported it. This type of vindictive mentality pervades society. Both the UDF and BSP have failed to work toward overcoming this deep societal division. Rather than starting a dialogue, they continue to blame the country's problems on each other.

The effects of this situation can be seen in many areas. Institutionally, governments have lacked the longevity and resolve to reform the legal system or implement the unpopular economic policies needed to improve the economy. While many of these problems are the result of a transitional period, the key question is whether these problems are merely "teething pains" or indicative of much deeper difficulties. Regardless, the principal goals of the 1989 revolution—the creation of a fundamentally new polity—has yet to be fully realized.

International Ramifications

The demise of CMEA and the Warsaw Pact left Bulgaria in a political, economic, and security vacuum. Thus an important question is how to fill this vacuum. In terms of security, without the protective umbrella and security guarantees of the Soviet Union, Bulgaria is worried the wars of Yugoslav succession could spread to include Macedonia and perhaps even Bulgaria itself.

The demise of the Soviet Union has made traditional adversaries Turkey and Greece the most powerful states in the region, fostering a feeling of insecurity in Bulgaria. However, this has not prevented Bulgaria from expanding economic and political ties with them. Greece is one of the biggest investors in Bulgaria and its third largest trading partner. Relations with Turkey are also good. Since President Stoyanov publically apologized for Bulgaria's behavior to its ethnic Turks under communism, agreements on everything from the abolition of customs tariffs to the cementing of links between the two armies' general staffs has been signed. Although some Bulgarians complain about Turkish interference in Bulgarian domestic affairs, bilateral relations continue to improve.[92]

While generally stable, relations with Bulgaria's western neighbor Macedonia are overshadowed by Sofia's refusal to recognize the existence of a Macedonian language, insisting it is a Bulgarian dialect. As a result of this standoff and Macedonia's insistence that official documents be in both the "Macedonian and Bulgarian" languages, numerous bilateral treaties and agreements remain unsigned.[93]

Since 1989, Bulgaria has reoriented its foreign policy towards the West. Economically, the top priorities of government are to integrate Bulgaria's economy with the European Union's, revitalize foreign economic ties with Bulgaria's traditional partners, and diversify its trading partners. To further these ends, Bulgaria has been actively participating in various regional forums. They include the Central European Free Trade Area (CEFTA), the Black Sea Economic Cooperation Council, and the EU. Although Bulgaria formally applied for EU membership in 1995, it was not included in the list of former socialist countries that have been invited to start integration talks with the EU.

While most people agree on the economic aspect of Bulgarian foreign policy, other aspects have been hostage to domestic political battles. Although previous governments actively supported participation in both the Organization for Security and Cooperation in Europe (OSCE) and NATO's "Partnership for Peace," a program that links NATO members and Central and Eastern European states, the socialist government elected in 1994 announced its intention to slow efforts to join NATO. The political aspect of this decision can be seen in the fact that the day after President Zhelev stated that it is "very important that Bulgaria declares clearly and categorically its urgent request for membership in NATO," Prime Minister Videnov stated that "Bulgaria was in no hurry to apply for NATO membership."[94]

To attract financial support and foreign investment, Bulgaria has to continue its image as an "oasis of stability." Thus the goal of Bulgarian foreign policy is to create the conditions for economic, political, and social development that will foster its inclusion into European and international economic and security structures without alienating its traditional allies and trading partners—namely, Russia. This will be a difficult feat.

Perhaps more than domestic factors, international factors will play a key role in the development of the Bulgarian polity. For example, the NATO bombing of Kosovo and the reimposition of sanctions on Yugoslavia will cost Bulgaria millions in lost transit fees and sever its most direct trade route to the European Union. As Foreign Minister Mihailova stated: "Kosovo cannot be considered a purely internal affair of Yugoslavia . . . as events there can lead to problems in other countries."[95] In addition to security issues, international factors will likely have a significant affect on other areas. Since the overriding goal of Bulgarian foreign policy is to join the European Union, this situation makes it very susceptible to EU requests to reform the bureaucracy, enact new laws, and so forth. In summary, international events will have a large impact on Bulgaria's developing polity.

Summary

Like the situation it faced after its liberation from five hundred years of Ottoman rule, Bulgaria had to reconstruct its polity in 1989. Unlike 1878, however, the Bulgarian polity is fundamentally split between those who want to build on the achievements of the socialist experience and those who want to rebuild the polity. Both views have prevailed since the end of the communist regime, and their struggle has wasted precious time.

It is not an understatement to say the Bulgarian polity is in a period of transition. The key question is: Where will the transition lead? Will Bulgaria be able to fulfill its goal of becoming a democratic, market-oriented, law-based state, or will historical legacies and contemporary problems be too difficult to overcome? Optimistically, Bulgaria has made significant progress since 1989. Small businesses are growing, democracy is generally accepted, and perhaps most significantly, for the first time in its modern history Bulgaria has managed to stay out of a Balkan war.

On the other hand, Bulgaria has numerous, serious problems. The polity is polarized, personalities are more important than policies, living standards are dropping, and political apathy is increasing. Although these features are present to some degree in Hungary and Poland, they are more pronounced in Bulgaria. Seemingly contradictory, when compared with these other states, Bulgaria's voter turnout and optimism are among the highest in the region.[96] This is largely because the average Bulgarian expects less than his Hungarian, Polish, or Russian counterpart, since Bulgaria started from a much lower social and economic level. Though it cannot claim the political stability of Hungary or the economic prosperity of Poland, Bulgaria has not experienced violent societal clashes as in Romania, or an attempted coup as in Russia. To many observers, the ability of Bulgaria to keep civil peace despite economic hardships, the war in neighboring former Yugoslavia, and the pettiness of politicians is nothing short of miraculous.

As we have seen, there are many obstacles which slow the creation of a new polity. However, demonstrations in 1997, the largest since the end of the old regime, suggest the situation has gotten so bad that reforms can no longer be avoided. Interestingly, for the first time change is being pushed from below, by the people. Without their active involvement, the situation would probably have continued as before. Perhaps this event was the genesis in the development of a new polity. Another hopeful sign were the 1996 and 1997 presidential and parliamentary elections. For the first time, the major opposition parties fielded a common slate of candidates and ran on a clear political and economic platform. While contradictory evidence exists as well, there seems to be consensus for change.[97]

The developments of the winter of 1996–1997 proved that while the country is still prone to political crises, its democratic framework is surprisingly stable, capable of absorbing mass protests and facilitating political compromise. Since the ODF gained power in 1997, Bulgaria has made dramatic progress. Economic and political stability has allowed people to start planning for the future rather than living day by day as before. In addition, crime is down and people are generally optimistic about the future. While the gap between rich and poor is increasing and people are still anxious, they finally seem to have realized there is no future in the past.

TIMELINE

1944
September 5   The Soviet Union declares war on Bulgaria.
September 9   The Soviet Army enters the country unopposed after a coup by the communist-dominated "Fatherland Front."

1945
The Fatherland Front wins a majority of votes in parliamentary elections. The Bulgarian Communist Party (BCP) allies with a faction of the Bulgarian Agrarian National Union (BANU). The BCP-BANU alliance proceeds to consolidate power.

1946

September 15   Following a national referendum, the monarchy is abolished.

November   Georgi Dimitrov, First Secretary of the BCP, becomes chairman of
              the Council of Ministers. Dimitrov serves as head of both the BCP
              and the Council of Ministers until his death in 1949.

1947

December   A Soviet-style constitution is ratified and the country is renamed
              Bulgarian People's Republic.

1949

January   Bulgaria joins the Council for Mutual Economic Assistance
              (CMEA).

July   Vulko Chervenko replaces Dimitrov as head of the BCP. Chervenko
              becomes known as "Little Stalin" through his purges of the BCP.

1950

Collectivization of agriculture begins.

1954

March   With the death of Stalin, Chervenko's control is weakened. As a
              result, Todor Zhivkov becomes the First Secretary of the BCP. He
              rules for the next thirty-five years.

1965

The suppression of an attempted army coup helps Zhivkov
consolidate power.

1981

To lessen economic hardships, the New Economic Model (NEM)
is introduced. However, the program brings only temporary
economic improvement.
Bulgaria celebrates its thirteen-hundred-year anniversary as a
country.

1984

Using the Turkish minority as a scapegoat for growing economic
problems, Zhivkov initiates a program to assimilate ethnic Turkish-
Bulgarians. This program, which includes changing names on
tombstones, causes thousands of Turks to immigrate to Turkey.

1987

July   To deflect growing demands for change, Zhivkov allows the
              formation of non-Party environmental and human rights groups.

1989

Second Turkish assimilation program begins. The international
community condemns Bulgaria.

November 10   Zhivkov is forced to resign as General Secretary of the BCP and is
              replaced by Petur Mladenov, the Minister of Foreign Affairs.

1990

February 3	Andrei Lukanov is elected prime minister by the BCP-dominated National Assembly.
April 3	Mladenov is elected president by the National Assembly. The BCP changes its name to the Bulgarian Socialist Party (BSP).
June 10	In the first free parliamentary elections in forty-five years, the BSP retains control.
August 1	Zhelyu Zhelev, leader of the Union of Democratic Forces (UDF), is elected president by the National Assembly after Mladinov resigns.
November 29	The Lukanov government resigns following an agreement to form a multiparty government under nonpartisan Prime Minister Dimitur Popov.

1991

July 12	The National Assembly ratifies a new constitution.
October 13	In the first free parliamentary elections, the UDF wins a narrow victory over the BSP. Filip Dimitrov, chairman of the UDF, becomes prime minister.

1992

January 19	In the first national presidential election, Zhelev is reelected president.
October 28	Disagreements between Dimitrov and President Zhelev force the Dimitrov government, after a vote of no confidence, to resign.
December 30	After the UDF and BSP fail to form a new government, the MRF nominates nonpartisan professor Lyben Berov for prime minister. He obtains parliamentary approval to form a new government.

1993

June	Disagreements between the UDF and the president reach a breaking point, resulting in demonstrations calling for the resignation of the president.

1994

January	Former BCP leader Zhivkov is sentenced to seven years in prison for embezzlement of government funds.
June	After the Berov government survives the no-confidence vote, the UDF members boycott National Assembly sessions.
September 8	The Berov government resigns after criticism of its privatization program.
October 12	Unable to form a new government, President Zhelev dissolves the National Assembly and calls elections for December. After a landslide victory, BSP leader Zhan Videnov becomes prime minister.

1995

March	The National Assembly abolishes a law, adopted by the UDF Government in 1992, which barred former communists from senior governmental positions.

1996

November 3   Helped by a deteriorating economy, UDF presidential candidate
             Petar Stoyanov defeats Ivan Marazov of the BSP.
December   Prime minister Zhan Videnov resigns.

1997

January   Mass demonstrations call for the overthrow of the government.
April 19   Parliamentary elections result in the victory of the ODF, gaining
             more than 50 percent of the votes.
July   To reduce inflation and instill fiscal discipline, a currency board is
             established.

1998

October   The National Assembly enacts a law which prevents former state-
             security officials and former high-ranking Communist Party leaders
             from occupying positions in the state apparatus for five years.
             BSR appeals to the Constitutional Court.

WEB SITES

Bulgarian Constitution
http://www.uni-wuerzburg.de/law/bu__indx.html
The 1991 Bulgarian Constitution and other political information.

Government of the Republic of Bulgaria
http://www.bulgaria.govrn.bg/
The Bulgarian government's website. Includes links to the websites of the
president, the prime minister, the national assembly, and various ministries
and government agencies.

Bulgaria-Related Electronic Resources
http://www.b-info.com/places/Bulgaria/list.shtml
List of web sites about Bulgaria, created and maintained by Arizona State
University.

Bulgarian Universe
http://www.cs.columbia.edu/~radev/u/db/bg/
Directory of web sites about Bulgaria maintained by Columbia University.

A Reader's Guide to Bulgaria
http://www.b-info.com/places/Bulgaria/ref/index.html
Historical and current information compiled by the School of Area Studies,
Foreign Service Institute, U.S. Department of State.

Wonderland Bulgaria
http://www.omda.bg/
A commercial site which offers information about the country, peoples, culture, and current events.

Internet Resources on Bulgaria
http://www.ssees.ac.uk/bulgaria.htm
Excellent list of links, mainly government/politics. Maintained by University of London School of Slavonic and East European Studies.

WORKS CITED

24 Chasa 24 Feb. 1995: 1.

Avramov, Ognyan. Legal Advisor to the President of the Republic of Bulgaria for National Security. Personal interview. 19 July 1995.

Balabanova, Hristina. "The Legal Situation of the Office of the Mayor." *Pravna Misul* 2 (1992): 16.

"BBSS Gallup Poll." *24 Chassa* 24 Feb. 1995: 3.

Bell, John. "Post-Communist Bulgaria." *Current History* Dec. 1990: 417–423.

Bliznashki, Georgi. Personal interview. 5 July 1995.

—. "The Model of Parliamentary Rule in Bulgaria." *Konstitutsionno Pravo* 1 (1994): 3–14.

—. "Functions of the Presidency." *Pravna Misul* 3 (1992): 3–10.

Brook, Robin. "Movin' On Up: Bulgaria's Transition from the Ghetto to the Suburbs," *Center for East European and Slavic Studies Newsletter* University of California-Berkeley (Spring 1999): 3–7, 17.

Brown, J. F. *Bulgaria under Communist Rule.* New York: Praeger, 1970.

Bulgaria. National Statistical Institute. *Statistical Reference Book of the Republic of Bulgaria.* Sofia: 1994.

Bulgarian Economic Outlook Apr. 30–6 May 1993: 8.

Bulgarian Economic Outlook 5–11 Nov. 1993: 8.

Chin, Jill. "Political Attitudes in Bulgaria." *RFE/RL Research Report* 30 Apr. 1993: 39–41.

Christy, Tatiana. "Poor Prospects Cause Brain Drain." *Transition* 29 Nov. 1996: 40–42.

Dimitrov, Philip. "Freeing the Soul from Communism." *Wall Street Journal* 23 Mar. 1992, national ed.: A10.

Donkov, Rumen. "Rationalized Parliamentarism and Political Instability in Bulgaria." *Pravna Misul* 2 (1993): 74–75.

Engelbrekt, Kjell. "Bulgaria: Balkan Oasis of Stability Facing Drought?" RFE/RL *Research Report* 7 Jan. 1994: 106–110.

—. "Bulgaria's Cabinet Shake-up: a Lasting Compromise?" *RFE/RL Research Report* 10 July 1992: 3–4.

—. "Bulgaria's Communist Legacy: Settling Old Scores." *RFE/RL Research Report* 10 July 1992: 6–10.

"The 1995 Bulgarian Human Development Report." *Bulgarian Telegraph Agency* 28 April 1995.

Georgiev, Ivo. "Indecisive Socialist Party Stumbles into Crisis." *Transition* 27 Dec. 1996: 26–27.

Gomez, Victor. "News of Note Across the Region." *Transition* 9 Aug. 1996: 2.

Jowitt, Kenneth ."The Leninist Legacy." *Eastern Europe in the 1990's.* Ed. Ivo Banac. Ithaca, N.Y.: Cornell UP, 1991.

Kettle, Steve. "Trying to Move Mountains." *Transition* 27 Dec. 1996: 29–31, 64.

Koinova, Maria. "The Voice of Demonstrators: Interview with Yasen Boyadzhiev." *Transition* 7 March 1997: 14–15.

Kontinent 23 March 1994: 6.

Kontinent 18 March 1994: 6.

Koritarov, Georgi. RFE/RL Political Analyst. Personal interview. 28 July 1998.

Krause, Stefan. "Bulgaria's Controversial Electronic-Media Law." *Transition* 18 Oct. 1996: 32–34.

—. "Socialists at the Helm." *Transition* 29 March 1995: 33–38.

Masava, Eliana. Mayor of Blagoevgrad. Personal interview. 11 July 1995.

Milanov, Zhivko. "The Constitutional Court: Hopes and Problems." *Pravna Misul* 2 (1993): 83.

Mitev, Peter. "The Post-Totalitarian Development: Protodemocracy or Protoauthoritarian Regime? Alternative Variants for Bulgaria." *Political Research* 4 (1994).

Morris, Stephen J. "The New Face of Bulgaria." *Wall Street Journal* 18 June 1997, eastern ed.: A22.

Naidenov, Valeri. "Who Is Afraid of Referendum?" *24 Chassa* 17 March 1993: 8.

Nivat, Anne. "Media Watch." *Transitions* Aug. 1997: 86.

"PA Approves Program till 1997." *168 Hours Bulgarian Business News* 2 Jan. 1994: 15.

Perry, Duncan M. "Bulgaria: A New Constitution and Free Elections." *RFE/RL Research Report* 2 Jan. 1993: 78–82.

Petkova, Silvia. "Environmental Activists Start Proceedings against Hilton Project." *The Sofia Echo* 24–30 July, 1998: 3.

Petrov, Svetoslav. RFE/RL Sofia Bureau Chief. Personal interview. 28 July 1998.

Popov, Ilian. Secretary of the Blagoevgrad City Council. Personal interview. 10 July 1995.

"Real Purchasing Power Halves 1990 to 1994." *168 Bulgarian Business News* 9 Jan. 1995: 8.

Spasov, Basil *The President of the Republic.* Sofia: St. Kiril and Methodius UP, 1992.

Spasov, Boris. *Learning about the Constitution.* Sofia: Government Publishing House, 1990.

"Those South-Eastern Laggards." *The Economist* 19 Oct. 1996: 54–55.

Todorov, A. "Political Cultures in Modern Bulgaria." *Political Research* 3 (1993).

Tracey, Roman. RFE/RL Bulgarian Programming Director. Personal Interview. 22 July 1998.

Trud 15 July 1996: 1.

Tzvetkov, Plamen S. "The Politics of Transition in Bulgaria: Back to the Future?" *Problems of Communism* May-June 1992: 34–43.

Vatchkov, Vesselin. "Divided by a Mutual Tongue." *Transitions* Sept. 1997: 76–81.

Wyzan, Michael. "Why is Bulgaria a Land of Failed Reforms?" *Transitions* Sept. 1997: 86–89.

—. "Renewed Economic Crisis May End Foot-Dragging on Reforms." *Transitions* 23 Aug. 1996: 40–44.

ENDNOTES

1. Vesselin Vatchkov, "Divided by a Mutual Tongue," *Transitions*, September 1997, p. 79.

2. Hospitals have become so impoverished that patients have to buy or bring in their own bandages, gauze, and antibiotics. *Bulgarian Telegraph Agency* (hereafter BTA), January 9, 1997.

3. *Statistical Reference Book of the Republic of Bulgaria* (Sofia: National Statistical Institute, 1994), p. 29; *RFE/RL Research Report,* March 19, 1993, p. 35.

4. Marx said nationalism was simply a policy the bourgeoisie used to exploit differences among the workers, preventing them from overthrowing the capitalist system.

5. Nikolai Genov, "The 1995 Bulgarian Human Development Report," cited in *BTA,* April 28, 1995.

6. For example, since private practice is very restricted Bulgarian doctors are one of the most economically disadvantaged groups. With an average salary of $40 per month for doctors in 1996, there has been a wave of corruption scandals involving doctors who refuse to operate on patients unless they are given bribes. Tatiana Christy, "Poor Prospects Cause Brain Drain," *Transition,* November 29, 1996, p. 40.

7. *BTA,* November 27, 1996.

8. Cited in *Freedom in the World,* p. 170.

9. *Trud,* July 15, 1996. Cited in Michael Wyzan, "Renewed Economic Crisis May End Foot-Dragging on Reforms," *Transition,* August 23, 1996, p. 40.

10. *Wall Street Journal,* June 18, 1997, p. A22.

11. "Real Purchasing Power Halves 1990 to 1994," *168 BBN,* January 9, 1995.

12. In the 1980s, there were an average of 50,000 crimes a year. In 1994, there were over 223,000. In addition, while 50 percent were solved in the last decade, only 20 percent were solved in 1994. Genov.

13. "Transition Report," *EBRD* 14.

14. *The Economist,* October 19, 1996.

15. Stefan Krause, "Socialists at the Helm," *Transition,* March 29, 1995, p. 35.

16. *BTA,* May 30, 1995.

17. *BTA,* November 28, 1996.

18. "Renewed Economic Crisis," p. 40.

19. The brothers Cyril and Methodius were Byzantine monks who were selected by Constantinople to create a new alphabet for the kingdom of Moravia—the contemporary Czech Republic—to counteract the influence of Rome. A religious backlash led to the expulsion of their students, three of whom found refuge in Bulgaria. Their spreading of the "Cyrillic alphabet" to other Slavic countries is a source of great national pride for Bulgarians. The modern Russian, Ukrainian, Belorussian, Serbian, and Macedonian alphabets are all cyrillic based.

20. J. F. Brown, *Bulgaria under Communist Rule* (New York: Praeger, 1970), pp. 226–269.

21. Named after Veliko Turnovo, the city where it was written.

22. See John Bell, "Post-Communist Bulgaria," *Current History,* December 1990, p. 417 and Boris Spasov, *Learning about the Constitution* (Sofia, 1992), p. 107.

23. The Comintern, or Communist International, was established in 1919 to unify the world's Communist parties in their battle against capitalism. However, in reality it was a tool of the Soviet Union to control other Communist parties. The Comintern required abject loyalty of its members to directives issued from its headquarters in Moscow. It was dissolved in 1944.

24. Robin Brooks, "Movin' on Up: Bulgaria's Transition from the Ghetto of Europe to the Suburbs," *Center for Slavic and East European Studies Newsletter,* Spring 1999, p. 7.

25. *BTA,* January 5, 1995.

26. Philip Dimitrov, "Freeing the Soul from Communism," *Wall Street Journal,* March 23, 1992.

27. Ken Jowitt has noted how Leninism left its imprint on the collective psyche, generating behavior patterns that even if only in a residual way, continue to affect public perceptions and actions. See Kenneth Jowitt, "The Leninist Legacy," in Ivo Banac, ed., *Eastern Europe in the 1990's* (Ithaca, NY: Cornell University Press, 1991).

28. Even though private property was to be abolished in a communist society, the government allowed people to own apartments, summer cottages, and cars. As a result, Bulgaria had the highest percentage of home ownership in Central and Eastern Europe—85 percent.

29. Public opinion poll conducted by *Trud* and the Sofia Open Society Fund, reported in *Bulgarian Economic Outlook*, November 5–11, 1993, p. 8.

30. A. Todorov, "Political Cultures in Modern Bulgaria," *Political Research*, no. 3, 1993, p. 8.

31. Plamen S. Tzvetkov, The Politics of Transition in Bulgaria: Back to the Future?" *Problems of Communism*, May-June 1992, p. 37.

32. *Bulgarian Economic Outlook*, April 30–May 6, 1993, p. 8.

33. Peter Mitev, "The Post-Totalitarian Development: Protodemocracy or Protoauthoritarian Regime? Alternative Variants for Bulgaria," *Political Research* 4, 1994.

34. BTA, July 18, 1997.

35. *Bulgarian Statistics Yearly* (Sofia: Bulgarian Statistical Institute, 1994).

36. Yovka Atanassova, a journalist in Stara Zagora, was brought to trial five times between January and June 1997. Her alleged crime was writing articles about former secret police informers who now hold political office or run security services. According to one defendant, an article caused him "moral harm." *Transitions*, August 1997, p. 86.

37. Maria Koinova, "The Voice of Demonstrators: Interview with Yasen Boyadzhiev," *Transition*, March 7, 1997, p. 14.

38. Stefan Krause, "Bulgaria's Controversial Electronic-Media Law," *Transition*, October 18, 1996, p. 33.

39. Constitutional Watch, *East European Constitutional Review*, Winter 1996, p. 5.

40. *The OMRI Annual Survey of Eastern Europe and the Former Soviet Union: 1995* (New York: M.E. Sharpe, 1996), p. 157.

41. A 1994 poll showed that radio, television, and the press are trusted more than the Parliament, the government, the judiciary, or the trade unions. *24 Chasa*, February 24, 1995.

42. Duncan M. Perry, "Bulgaria: A New Constitution and Free Elections," *RFE/RL Research Report*, January 3, 1992, p. 78.

43. Ognyan Avramov, Legal Advisor to the President of the Republic for National Security. Personal interview. Sofia, Bulgaria, July 19, 1995.

44. Ilian Popov, Secretary of the Blagoevgrad City Council. Personal interview. Blagoevgrad, Bulgaria, July 10, 1995.

45. Eliana Masava, Mayor of Blagoevgrad. Personal interview. Blagoevgrad, Bulgaria, July 11, 1995.

46. Hristina Balabanova, "The Legal Situation of the Office of the Mayor," *Pravna Misul* 2, 1992, p. 16.

47. Fourteen in 1996, the actual number of committees varies with each government.

48. Called a "constructive vote of no confidence," this provision fosters political stability.

49. Valeri Naidenov, "Who Is Afraid of a Referendum?" *24 Chassa*, March 17, 1993, p. 8.

50. Boris Spasov, *The President of the Republic* (Sofia: St. Kiril and Methodius University Press, 1992), pp. 95–97.

51. Article 108(2) of the *Bulgarian Constitution*.

52. Georgi Bliznashki, "Functions of the Presidency," *Pravana Misul*, March 1992, p. 3.

53. "BBSS Gallup Poll," cited in *24 Chassa*, February 24, 1995.

54. I am indebted to Professor Georgi Bliznashki for noting this very significant distinction. Personal interview, Sofia, Bulgaria, July 5, 1995.

55. Kjell Englebrekt, "Bulgaria: Island of Stability Facing Drought?" *RFE/RL Research Report,* January 7, 1994, p. 106.

56. Professor Zhivko Milanov, "The Constitutional Court: Hopes and Problems," *Pravna Misul,* no. 2, 1993, p. 83.

57. *BTA,* November 7, 1996. According to BSP Interior Minister Dobrev, "criminal gangs have more agents in the Interior Ministry than we have among them." *OMRI Daily Report,* December 17, 1996.

58. *Kontinent,* March 18, 1994, p. 6.

59. "Bulgarian Army White Paper," cited in *BTA,* March 22, 1995.

60. *RFE/RL News Briefs,* January 31–February 4, 1994.

61. *Kontinent,* March 23, 1994, p. 6.

62. Stefan Krause, "Socialists at the Helm," *Transitions,* March 29, 1995, p. 38.

63. Georgi Koritarov, Radio Free Europe political analyst. Personal interview. Sofia, Bulgaria, July 28, 1998.

64. Cited in Ivo Georgiev, "Indecisive Socialist Party Stumbles into Crisis," *Transition,* December 27, 1996, 27.

65. *RFE/RL Newsline,* April 25, 1998.

66. *OMRI Daily Report,* January 27, 1995.

67. Constitutional Watch, *East European Constitutional Review,* Spring/Summer, 1997, p. 7.

68. Kjell Engelbrekt, "Bulgaria's Communist Legacy: Settling Old Scores," *RFE/RL Research Report,* July 10, 1992, p. 6.

69. *OMRI Daily Digest,* December 13, 1996.

70. As an illustration, in 1996 Prime Minister Videnov ordered the state natural gas supplier, Bulgargas, to sell half its shares in a joint venture with Russia to private companies. Multigroup bought the majority.

71. Victor Gomez, "News of Note across the Region," *Transition,* August 9, 1996, p. 2.

72. *BTA,* May 6, 1995.

73. "Constitutional Watch," *East European Constitutional Review,* Winter 1998, p. 8.

74. In July 1998, several environmental NGOs organized protests at the construction site of a new Hilton Hotel in Sofia. *The Sofia Echo,* July 24–30, 1998, p. 3.

75. Kjell Engelbrekt, "Bulgaria's Cabinet Shake-up: a Lasting Compromise?" *RFE/RL Research Report* 28, July 10, 1992, pp. 3–4.

76. Kjell Engelbrekt, "Bulgaria: Balkan Oasis of Stability Facing Drought?" *RFE/RL Research Report,* January 7, 1994, p. 106.

77. Steve Kettle, "Trying to Move Mountains," *Transition,* December 27, 1996, p. 29.

78. The large percentage of individual initiatives is a result of the proportional electoral system which has yet to create a clear delineation of power between individual deputies and parliamentary groups. This is rather unique; in most other parliamentary democracies, bills are usually introduced by parliamentary groups. This prevents the submission of bills on similar issues by MPs from the same party, helping to ensure party discipline. See Rumen Donkov, "Rationalized Parliamentarism and Political Instability in Bulgaria," *Pravna Misal* 2, 1993, pp. 74–75.

79. Georgi Bliznashki, "The Model of Parliamentary Rule in Bulgaria," *Konstitucionno Pravo* 1, 1994, p. 3.

80. Constitutional Watch, *East European Constitutional Review,* Spring/Summer 1997, p. 7.

81. Roman Tracey, RFE/RL Bulgarian Programming Director. Personal interview, July 22, 1998, Prague, Czech Republic.

82. "PA Approves Program till 1997," *168 Hours BBN,* January 2, 1994, p. 15.

83. Duncan M. Perry, "Bulgaria: A New Constitution and Free Elections," *RFE/RL Research Report,* January 2, 1993, p. 78.

84. Brooks, "Movin' On Up," p. 6.

85. Svetoslav Petrov, RFE/RL Bureau Chief. Personal interview. Sofia, Bulgaria, July 28, 1998.

86. Cited in *OMRI Daily Digest*, Part II, August 4, 1995.

87. Avramov interview.

88. *BTA*, September 4, 1996.

89. *Embassy of Bulgaria*, Press Release, June 26, 1998.

90. *OMRI Daily Report*, February 9, 1995.

91. Michael Wyzan, "Why Is Bulgaria a Land of Failed Reforms?" *Transitions*, September 1997, p. 89.

92. During the run-up to local elections, the Bulgarian government sent a note to Turkey complaining that Turkish diplomat's behavior went "beyond normal activity." *BTA*, November 18, 1995.

93. *The OMRI Annual Survey of Eastern Europe and the Former Soviet Union: 1995*, p. 155.

94. *OMRI Daily Report*, April 19, 1995.

95. Cited in *RFE/RL Newsline*, March 31, 1998.

96. Jill Chin, "Political Attitudes in Bulgaria," *RFE/RL Research Report*, April 30, 1993, p. 39.

97. After a long debate in which BSP members walked off the National Assembly floor in protest, in 1997 the government passed a law entitled "Access to Former State Security Record's Act." While supporters argued it would close a chapter in history, opponents said it violated civil rights provisions of the constitution and opened the possibility the files could be used for political blackmail.

3

HUNGARY

Introduction

The Republic of Hungary has traditionally been in the forefront of change in Central and Eastern Europe. Under the socialist regime, Hungary was the first to introduce economic and political reforms. After 1989, it continued to lead the region. Politically, it has achieved a quick and peaceful transition from a one-party regime to a multiparty democracy. As a result of constitutional safeguards, such as a restrictive German-style electoral law, Hungary has not been plagued by governmental changes or a parliamentary stalemate, as in Bulgaria and pre-1993 Poland. Political stability has been a key factor in Hungary's economic success, characterized by moderate inflation, a growing economy, and high levels of foreign investment.

Hungary has overcome numerous geographical and historical problems to become a stable and prosperous state. Therefore, an examination of its polity should help provide answers to the central question of how a state that has historically been economically backward, dominated by authoritarian regimes, and racked by deep social divisions and political and economic backwardness has become a political, economic, and social model for the rest of Central and Eastern Europe.

NATIONAL DATA

Geography

Hungary is situated in the Carpathian basin at the geographical center of Europe. It shares borders with Slovakia, the Ukraine, Romania, Serbia, Croatia, Slovenia, and Austria. The capital, Budapest, lies near its northern border with Slovakia. In addition to being the seat of government, Budapest

dominates the economic and cultural life of Hungary. Twenty percent of the total population and 70 percent of university graduates live there. Hungary has an area of approximately 35,900 square miles or 92,100 square kilometers, which is slightly smaller than the state of Indiana.

Resources

Hungary has historically been an agrarian country. Approximately 70 percent of its land is covered with fertile soil ideal for agriculture. Major crops include wheat, maize, vegetables, grapes, fruit, and wine. Its nonagricultural resources include small amounts of bauxite, coal, uranium, natural gas, and oil. This lack of resources not only hindered industrialization, but also made Hungary dependent on imports from the Soviet Union.

Hungary is a popular tourist destination. Budapest is one of the five most visited cities in the world, and the country is rich in hot springs and lakes. Lake Balaton, located in the south central part of the country, is the largest warm-water lake in Europe. In 1996, the country earned over $2.1 billion—more than 4 percent of its GDP—from tourism.

People

In 1996, Hungary had a population of 10,245,000 people. The population density is 110 people per square kilometer. Although over 60 percent of the population lived in rural areas in 1949, the creation of an industrial economy caused a dramatic population shift. Today 65 percent of Hungarians live in urban areas.

While industrialization facilitated population growth, it also fostered changes that have led to a decreasing population. As in Bulgaria, Poland, and Russia, the movement of people to the cities left a predominantly elderly population in the rural areas, drastically reducing the number of women of childbearing age there. In urban areas, housing shortages and other social problems have led to high divorce and abortion rates. The result is fewer couples choosing to have children. This is not a new phenomenon; the population has been in decline since 1981. However, cuts in maternity benefits and social spending have accelerated this trend. This situation has caused the population to grow older. Over 20 percent of Hungarians are pensioners. In contrast to the United States, however, they are not organized and thus have little political influence.

Since a declining population limits future economic growth, the government has tried to encourage reproduction by offering incentives such as financial aid and house building grants to families with children. However, cuts in social spending have negated these efforts and have had a dramatic impact on children. Since 1989, the number of children below the poverty line has increased from 1 to 8 percent of the population. As in other states in the region, the societal upheaval surrounding economic and political changes has encouraged women to become more politically involved. In the 1994 elections, the number of women in the parliament doubled.[1]

Other social problems include the second highest per capita number of heart attacks in the world, the highest suicide rate in Europe, and the highest cancer rate in the world. This situation is partially the result of too much smoking and drinking, too little exercise, and large meat consumption. Since Hungary had the highest standard of living in the region, its people could afford to eat more meat. This in turn led to increasing health problems. As a result, Hungary's death rate is higher than Cambodia's.

Hungary's high suicide rate, 39 people per 100,000 in 1995, has declined only slightly with the regime change. Prior to 1989, sociologists explained the high rate as linked to the ability of Hungarians to travel: according to this theory, Hungarians saw how people in the West lived and when, for political reasons, they could not emulate this standard of living, decided to take their own lives. This explanation is not supported by evidence; the rate for Poles, who could also travel, was only 13.9 per 100,000.[2] A better explanation lies in Hungary's high rates of divorce and alcoholism. These factors contribute to depression, leading to suicide. Hungary currently has 1.8 million alcoholics, about a sixth of the population.[3]

Under the socialist regime, Hungary had the highest per capita social expenditures in Central and Eastern Europe, with 27 percent of the budget dedicated to social spending. After regaining control of the country after the 1956 revolution, the Communist Party in effect bought off the population to lessen political pressure for change. As in the other states in the region, this policy created a culture of dependency and entitlement. Because of pressure from trade unions and government efforts to involve various groups in the decision-making process—"interest coordination"—Hungary was slow to enact major economic reforms such as privatizing industry and reforming the health care and pension systems. By 1995, however, the rampant social spending and a ballooning budget deficit forced the government to enact the Stabilization Program, which encouraged exports and slashed social spending.[4] Although this policy caused real wages to fall by 10 percent—the largest drop in forty years—the harsh austerity measures resulted in large reductions in the trade and budget deficits.[5]

Ethnicity

Hungarians are of Finno-Ugric origin and have lived in the Danube Basin for more than a thousand years. Hungary is one of the most ethnically homogeneous states in the world. The Magyars—what Hungarians call themselves—are the dominant ethnic group and comprise more than 98 percent of the population. This is in large part the result of historical efforts to maintain ethnic homogeneity. Hungary's isolated position in the midst of a sea of Slavs and Germans has led it to pursue policies to limit the potentially subversive presence of minority groups. However, this has often led to minority persecution or expulsion. While the Hungarian nationalities policy officially followed the lead of the Soviet Union during the communist regime, with declarations of international solidarity and equality for all ethnic groups, in reality Hungarians continued to foster a homogeneous nation-state.

Border changes and population transfers after World War I left a large number of Magyars—approximately 5 million—outside the borders of Hungary. The two largest concentrations of ethnic Hungarians are in the Transylvanian part of Romania (1.8 million) and Slovakia (600,000). Their importance can be noted in the Constitution: "The Republic of Hungary bears responsibility for the fate of Hungarians living beyond the borders and promotes their contacts with Hungary." A separate agency, the Office for Hungarians in the Neighboring Countries, was established in 1992 to facilitate these goals.

As a result of discrimination against Magyars in neighboring states—usually a reaction to Magyar discrimination against minorities prior to 1919—Hungary has adopted a liberal policy toward its own minorities in hopes of serving as an example for neighboring countries where ethnic Hungarians live. Recognized minority groups—national and ethnic minorities that have lived in Hungary for at least 100 years and have their own language and culture—are legally entitled to equal opportunity and cultural autonomy. These rights were expanded by the 1993 Act on the Rights of

National and Ethnic Minorities, which legalized both individual and collective rights of minority groups as well as self-government and representation. The activism of Hungary's minorities can be seen in the 1994 local elections, when minorities elected their own local councils in 605 areas of the country.

The most significant minority groups are Germans, Slovaks, Croats, and Poles. Most speak Hungarian as well as their own languages. In contrast to other states in the region, most minorities live interspersed throughout the population. Two of Hungary's largest minority groups do not have minority status. The 150,000 Jews are recognized as a "religious community" and are accepted by most of society. They constitute the third largest Jewish community in Europe—the two larger ones are in Russia and France.

In contrast, the gypsy community of 400,000 to 600,000 lives separately from most of the population. Gypsies have little education and few skills; as a result, they were the first to suffer from economic and political changes. Despite the creation of a National Gypsy Autonomous Government and government policies to foster economic improvement and political representation for gypsies—such as funding for minority-language schools and institutes fostering minority cultures and traditions—this group is frequently discriminated against by employers and educators, relegating it to a marginal position in society.

Class Divisions

As in the rest of the region, Hungarian society under the communist regime was divided along educational, vocational, and political lines. However, membership in the Communist Party was by far the most important factor because it provided certain privileges—higher social status, better educational and job opportunities, and so forth. In contrast, the salaries and economic differences among the peasants, workers, and the intelligentsia were negligible. Thus in reality there were only two major groups in society: members of the party elite and the rest of the people.

In contrast to Bulgaria and the Soviet Union, as a result of economic liberalization following the introduction of economic reforms in 1966, by the late 1970s political criteria were no longer the sole indication of social position. Class divisions came to reflect economic stratification, the result of different technical and educational backgrounds. Three classes emerged: the affluent (communist party industrialists and some entrepreneurs); a middle class (economic managers, civil servants, intelligentsia, and military officers); and the poor (workers, pensioners, and the unemployed). Overall, Hungarian society was much more diversified than its Bulgarian or Russian counterparts.

Economic reforms have caused society to become much more stratified as some groups have benefited more than others. These include "red technocrats"—former communist-era heads of industry; small entrepreneurs from the old regime who had the business skills to take advantage of new economic opportunities; white-collar workers (bankers, employees of multinational corporations); and employees of small private enterprises, which pay higher wages than state factories. Comprising approximately 5 percent of the population, these groups control over 60 percent of the wealth. The largest of these groups is the red technocrats. In 1993, 81 percent of the private sector mangers had been employed by the party or state in senior economic positions.[6] Thus the key variables to success today are business acumen, the ability to react to economic changes, and, to a lesser extent, political connections. Under the old regime, it was political connections first and education second.

As in other CEE states, the majority of the population has not benefited from economic reforms. Since most people worked in the state sector or the shadow economy, the collapse of both of these areas has propelled them into a lower economic strata. This group includes blue-collar workers, pensioners, women, peasants, and the unemployed.

Even members of the previously privileged classes have suffered from recent changes. Bureaucrats and professionals (doctors, teachers) saw their living standards decrease 15 percent between 1989 and 1995. While the unofficial economy mitigates this situation, insecurity, uncertainty, and fear of the future have limited the political involvement of this crucial group. In addition, the dissatisfaction with economic reforms can be seen in the electoral success of parties which promise to limit their effects.

However, in spite of the growing gulf between classes, the collapse of the system in the late 1980s did not cause a societal upheaval. This is the result of relatively high Hungarian living standards. In contrast with the other states in this survey, Hungary has a much smaller portion—3 percent—of the population in poverty. In Bulgaria and Russia, over 30 percent of the population live in poverty. Even in fellow reformer Poland, over 10 percent of the population lives below the poverty line.[7] In addition, in contrast to Bulgaria, Poland, and Russia, even though economic data show there is little movement between classes, as in the United States, people still believe it is possible.

Economics

Traditionally an agrarian country, Hungary was also industrialized along the Soviet model after World War II. To improve underdeveloped districts, socialist economic policy clustered industries in certain areas. The legacies of this policy are concentrated areas of unemployment and industrial pollution. For example, in the northeastern counties of Szabores and Szatmar, unemployment in 1996 was approximately 30 percent, compared with a national average of 11 percent. In contrast, the Keckemete area in the center of the country is an entrepreneurial enclave. It has the highest GDP and three times as many cars per capita as Budapest. Since the soil in this area is very poor, the socialists never collectivized the farms in this region. As a result, private enterprise flourished.

Before 1989, the economy was divided into state, cooperative, and private sectors. However, the majority of the land and most industrial enterprises were owned by the state. Thus the majority of the GDP was generated by the state sector. In 1980, approximately 80 percent of GDP was generated by the state sector, 15 percent by the cooperative sector, and 5 percent by the private sector.

In contrast to Bulgaria and Russia, Hungary has made dramatic progress in privatizing the economy. Unique to the region, immediately after the change in regime Hungarian managers took control of their firms. This "spontaneous privatization" quickly put 60 percent of the economy in private hands. Legal changes have also aided privatization. While Russia has yet to pass a law allowing for the private ownership of land, Hungary has returned nationalized property to its precommunist owners or compensated them monetarily. This policy greatly facilitated the development of the private sector. In 1995, the state started selling off large stakes in such strategic sectors as gas, electricity, banking, and telecommunications, leaving only the most dilapidated industries under governmental control. Although supporting those industries has been a significant drain on the state budget, the government would rather subsidize them than increase unemployment.

Another factor that fostered the development of a market economy was Hungary's early enactment of economic reforms. In 1966 a new system of economic management, the New Economic Mechanism (NEM) was introduced. This policy lessened state control in some sectors of the economy and introduced market reforms. So did the creation of worker economic units (WEUs) in the early 1980s. Workers were allowed to organize and work after hours for themselves in state factories as long as they filled their state quotas. By 1989, the WEUs controlled 60 percent of the service industry and 30 to 40 percent of agriculture. Many of these groups later became private companies.

These policies and reforms have greatly aided Hungary's transition to a market economy. By 1997, the state sector produced only 15 percent of the national income while the private sector accounted for 75 percent and multinationals 10 percent. Over 50 percent of the workforce today works in the private sector. As a result, Hungary is economically better off than Bulgaria, Poland, or Russia. With the exception of the Czech Republic and Slovenia, Hungary has a higher per capita income—$6,410 in 1996—than any other Central or Eastern European state.

Trade

In addition to improving economic efficiency, the NEM also allowed companies to develop markets outside the CMEA. Thus, when the regime changed,

Hungary was already well on its way to reorienting its trade to the West. In December 1991, it concluded an association agreement with the European Union that reduces trade barriers over a ten-year period. By 1992, the EU was Hungary's most important trade partner. In 1995, the EU accounted for 64.7 percent of total exports and provided 62 percent of Hungary's imports.[8] Hungary's four largest trading partners are Germany, Russia, Austria, and Italy. Hungary has also attempted to increase its presence in former CMEA states. In addition to increasing trade with Russia, Hungary signed free trade agreements with other members of the Visegrad group—Poland, the Czech Republic, and Slovakia. Partially because of previous links with the West, Hungary has been able to reorient its foreign economic relations more successfully than Bulgaria, Poland, or Russia.

A more lasting legacy of the past is Hungary's large foreign debt. Until recently, it had the largest per capita debt ($3,100) in the former socialist block. Until the debt is paid off, valuable capital cannot be invested domestically. In contrast to Poland, whose debt was owed to international organizations, the Hungarian debt is owed to private banks, which are much more reluctant to write it off. To maintain its credit rating, Hungary has been forced to adopt market policies that have in turn led to unusual economic openness. As a result, Budapest has become a regional center for trade and investment. In addition to hosting thirty-nine of the fifty largest multinational companies, Hungary ranks first in foreign investment in the former Soviet bloc. Of the $46 billion in direct investment in the region between 1989 and 1997, Hungary received $14 billion. Poland was second with $9 billion.[9] This situation shows the strong links between the international system and domestic policies.

While foreign investment has aided the growth of the economy, it also makes Hungary dependent on foreign capital. Many people think foreign money wields too much power and that government policy is tailored to international interests. As an illustration, privatization chief Ferenc Bartha was removed in January 1995 because he supported an unpopular deal to sell half of a state-owned hotel chain to an American investor.

Paradoxically, Hungary's early implementation of reforms at first made it complacent. In contrast to fellow reformer Poland, Hungarians thought their more open economy would allow them to implement economic reforms gradually. In addition, until recently Hungarians compared themselves to the rest of the states in the region, not to the West. This gave them a false sense of security, slowing reforms. Overall, in contrast to most other CEE states, the Hungarian economy has performed well. Although GDP fell by more than 20 percent between 1989 and 1993, the economy has grown 2 percent annually since then. While inflation remains high (18 percent in 1997) and unemployment remains stubbornly above 10 percent, a market economy is well entrenched and is accepted by most people.

POLITICAL HISTORY

Hungarian history has been dominated by two somewhat paradoxical goals: preserving the Magyar culture and integrating the country with the Western world. These aspirations have fostered a unique course of political development whose legacy is reflected in the contemporary polity. Like other countries of Central and Eastern Europe, Hungary has a history of class, religious, and ethnic conflicts which have often been inflamed by the actions of larger, more powerful neighbors.

Before the Twentieth Century

Approximately two thousand years ago, the territory of contemporary Hungary was included in the Roman provinces of Pannonia and Dacia. In 896, this territory—occupied by scattered settlements of Slavs—was conquered by the Magyars, a tribe from what is today central Russia, led by Prince Árpád. Significantly, their language is not from the Indo-European family of languages but is Finno-Ugric in origin. Their uniqueness encouraged the Magyars to develop an organized political structure in order to protect themselves from the surrounding Slav and German tribes.

In 970, Árpád's great-grandson Géza began to organize the various Magyar tribes into a united state. After he died, the process continued under his son Istvan I. To consolidate power, Istvan asked Pope Sylvester II to recognize him as king of Hungary. The pope agreed, and on Christmas Day in the year 1000, Istvan was crowned Stephen I. With Stephen's crowning and the acceptance of Catholicism as the state religion, Hungary entered the European community. As a result, Hungarians came to view themselves as the eastern outpost of West European culture.

Stephen's consolidation of power dramatically changed some political and cultural aspects of Hungarian society. Previously organized by clans, society was reorganized under Stephen on the basis of class and land ownership. Two classes emerged, the freemen nobles and the unlanded. Nobles were either paternal descendants of Magyars who had originally migrated into the Carpathian basin or people who had received a title from the king. As free citizens, they were the only people who could hold office or present grievances to the king. Free of obligation, the only duty of this class was military service. The unlanded, the vast majority of the population with no political voice, were slaves, freed slaves, women, immigrants, or nobles stripped of their privileges. The king had direct control of the unlanded, thus preventing the nobles from increasing their power. The king's power was enhanced by his control of two-thirds of the land. Although stable, this system retarded the introduction of private property, thus preserving a feudal system long after it had been abandoned by other states. Administratively, the kingdom was divided into a system of counties, each governed by an "ispans," a royal official appointed by the king.

Hungary's geographic position in the center of Europe placed it in a precarious position. Recurring invasions provided an impetus for reorganizing society to preserve the state. In the thirteenth century, the king began making land grants to nobles in order to ensure their loyalty. Thus, royal lands were transformed into individual estates, creating a landed oligarchy of magnates whose wealth and power far surpassed that of the more numerous "lesser nobles." Although the latter group had the same rights and responsibilities as other nobles, the magnates controlled the majority of the country and were powerful enough to question the authority of the king.

This division of society ultimately led the lesser nobles to rebel. In 1222, they forced King Andrew II to sign the "Golden Bull." Similar to the Magna Carta in England, this document limited the king's power, declared all lesser nobles legally equal to the magnates, and gave them the right to resist the king's illegal acts. The lesser nobles also won the right to present Andrew with grievances, a practice that led to a regular assembly of nobles. This assembly evolved into a formal parliamentary assembly (the Diet). Thus the protection of political rights was a key feature of Hungarian political development.

Hungary prospered under Mattias Hunyadi (r. 1458–1490), becoming a center of Renaissance culture. His death in 1490 weakened Hungary, dramatically affecting its political development for the next 500 years. With Hunyadi's death, the Diet gained political power. In an attempt to weaken the power of the crown, in 1514 the Diet passed an act known as the Tripartitum. This act was the basis of Hungarian law until the 1848 revolution. It split power between the sovereign and nobility. While the nobles pledged their allegiance to the crown, they elected the king. As in Poland, an elected monarchy greatly weakened central authority, leading to Hungary's defeat by the Ottoman Turks at the Battle of Mohacs in 1526. Central and eastern Hungary were occupied, and Transylvania became an Ottoman principality. Taking advantage of Hungarian weakness, the Austrian Hapsburg empire incorporated the northern and western parts of the country into their empire. Although Hapsburg control allowed these areas to escape Ottoman control, the centralizing tendencies of the empire challenged established Hungarian traditions. The Hapsburgs refused to recognize the principle that the consent of the Hungarian aristocracy was needed for either taxation or legislation and also resettled Hungarian lands with other nationalities to weaken the power of the magnates. However, in contrast to the Austrian-occupied part of Poland, continued resistance allowed the Hungarians to maintain a degree of autonomy in the empire. As a result, Hungarian lands remained in the possession of the Hungarian aristocracy, not the Hapsburg emperor.

In 1699, the Hapsburgs drove a weakened Ottoman army out of Hungary. This was a mixed blessing, for now Hungary came completely under Hapsburg control. The Hapsburgs ruled autocratically, stifling economic and political development. This situation fostered the development of Hungarian nationalism, eventually leading to the revolution of 1848.

In the religious sphere, under the Muslim Ottoman Turks, the eastern part of the Hungarian territory (Transylvania) had developed a tradition of religious freedom, allowing the growth of both the Protestant and the Catholic churches. Austrian Catholic discrimination against non-Catholics caused an insurrection in Transylvania between 1703 and 1711. Led by Francis Rakoczi, the insurgents demanded religious and political autonomy. Although unsuccessful, the call for autonomy was widely supported through Hungarian territory.

To appease the Hungarians and increase the stability of the empire, Charles VI signed the Pragmatic Sanction in 1720. While declaring the Empire indivisible, it gave the Hungarians a special status. It allowed them to maintain their feudal Diet and the rights of their landed class. It also preserved the *comitat*, a unique autonomous local government composed of elected members of the gentry.[10] While this settlement maintained the positions of both the gentry and the magnates in society, it continued to retard economic modernization. As a result, Hungary remained an agrarian country until the end of the nineteenth century.

The Hungarian nobility struggled with the Hapsburg emperor for political control. Their goals, however, were complementary; both the nobles and the emperor worked to preserve the established order. During the reign of Maria Theresa (1740–1780), special schools were established to attract members of the Hungarian magnate class to Vienna. These people became Germanized and lost their Hungarian national identity; sometimes they even forgot their knowledge of Hungarian.

The rise of nationalism in the nineteenth century led to the politicization of the lesser nobles. This group, which in contrast to the magnates was predominantly Magyar, became the repository of nationalism. They could see how impoverished Hungary was compared to the rest of Europe, causing a conflict in their relationships with both the magnates and the Hapsburgs in Vienna. A reform movement led by Count Szechenyi in the early 1800s revived Hungarian national pride by promoting economic and social reforms as well as the use of the Hungarian language.

This movement quickly turned into an anti-Hapsburg campaign. Led by Lazlo Kossuth, it echoed the democratic and liberal nationalist movements springing up all over Europe. Kossuth argued only political and economic separation from Austria would improve Hungary's plight. He called for a parliamentary democracy, industrialization, and the abolition of feudal privileges and serfdom. Noteworthy, Kossuth was a Magyar chauvinist whose rhetoric provoked strong resentment among Hungary's minority groups.

In March 1848, a rebellion erupted in Vienna. The Hungarians took advantage of this situation in the Hapsburg capital to declare the creation of an independent Hungarian republic. Under the leadership of the gentry, the regime lasted for four months before the Hapsburgs, with Russian military aid, regained control of the country.

Although the uprising was ruthlessly crushed, it facilitated an increase of Hungarian influence in the empire. The defeat of Hapsburg forces by France and Italy in 1859 and Prussia and Italy in 1866 forced Emperor Franz Joseph to consider Hungarian demands for self-determination. Led by Ferec Deak, Hungary expanded its special position in the Hapsburg empire through *Ausgleich*, more commonly known as the Compromise of 1867. This arrangement created a dual monarchy with jointly conducted foreign, military, and financial affairs. However, each country retained its own separate government. The struggle, which had been initiated by the gentry in defense of their privileges against both the Hapsburgs and the Hungarian magnates, culminated in the recognition of a separate Hungarian state.

The Compromise of 1867 fostered economic growth by forcing the landed aristocracy to pay attention to a now autonomous national economy. Most of the economic growth was in the agrarian sector, since Hungarian markets and capital were both tied to Austrian industry. With increased economic activity, German and Jewish bourgeoisie classes began to emerge. Although they played a major role in Hungarian industrial and financial development, they were prevented from playing a commensurate role in political life because the landed elite refused to give up its social and political status.

Thus Hungary entered the twentieth century with firmly entrenched economic, political, and social structures. Economically, the magnates dominated. Politically, the magnates directed relations with Vienna while the gentry dominated local politics. The peasants, workers, and bourgeoisie were excluded from power, both economically and politically. This class structure prevented the emergence of a strong middle class, isolating Hungary from the democratization process occurring throughout the rest of Europe.

Democratization was also hindered by Hungarian discrimination against ethnic minorities. The 1868 Nationalities Law defined Hungary as a single nation comprised of different nationalities whose members enjoyed equal rights in all areas except language. However, this law was frequently ignored since local governments and schools were Magyarized. Consequently, the Romanian, Slovak, German, Ruthenian, Croat, and Serbian communities were treated as second-class citizens after Hungarians and Austrians.

The Twentieth Century

The defeat of the Hapsburg empire in World War I led to its disintegration and to the end of the ossified Hungarian political structure. On November 16, 1918, a bourgeois-led revolution declared Hungary a republic. Various political parties formed a provisional National Council to govern the country. However, the democratic forces, led by Mihaly Karolyi, could not gather enough support to form a new government. This was the result of two factors. First, both the magnates—who were afraid of losing their privileges— and the working class—which was influenced by the new socialist regime in Russia—were opposed to the new regime. The second factor was a note from the victorious Entente powers that delineated postwar boundaries unacceptable to all Hungarians. This boundary dispute allowed the communists led by Bela Kun to seize control in March 1919. They proclaimed the establishment of a Hungarian socialist republic, the first communist government in Central Europe. It lasted four months before being toppled by anticommunist forces supported by Czech and Romanian troops.

Because of its alliance with the Central Powers in World War I, Hungary was treated harshly by the victorious Entente. The 1920 Treaty of Trianon took away three quarters of prewar Hungarian territory and two-thirds of its population. Large Hungarian minorities outside the state fostered an irredentist foreign policy whose legacy can still be seen in the contemporary concern for Hungarian minorities in neighboring states.

In 1920, Hungary stood at a political crossroads. Penniless refugees from former Hungarian lands poured into Hungary, burdening an already war-devastated economy and fueling unemployment and inflation. Politically, the first parliament elected after the Czech and Romanian intervention created a constitutional monarchy. However, the election of a king was postponed until after civil disorder had subsided. Admiral Miklos Horthy, the former commander-in-chief of the Austro-Hungarian navy, was elected regent. He was empowered to appoint Hungary's prime minister, veto legislation, dissolve the parliament, and command the armed forces. Horthy appointed Istvan Bethlen as prime minister. Bethlen dominated the government between 1921 and 1931. Although he stabilized the economy and improved relations with heretofore hostile neighbors, "Hungary had yet to arrive in the 20th century either socially or politically."[11] The Great Depression caused an economic collapse, and by 1933 unemployment had reached 36 percent.

As in Germany, economic problems fostered support for Fascist parties. In the June 1939 elections, the Arrow Cross Party, Hungary's equivalent of Germany's Nazi Party, won the second-largest number of votes. This shift to the right, combined with an irredentist foreign policy to regain traditionally Hungarian lands,[12] led Hungary to ally with Germany in World War II. When it became clear Germany was going to lose the war, Horthy tried to withdraw from the alliance. Hitler had him replaced by the leader of the Arrow Cross, Ferenc Szalasi. Although it had avoided fighting on its territory, after 1944 Hungary became a battlefield. By the time the Red Army occupied Budapest in 1945, over one-half of Hungary's economy had been destroyed.

The end of the Fascist regime led to the creation of a democratic republic. In the 1945 elections, the Smallholders' Party, an alliance of peasants and small landholders, won 57 percent of the vote. However, as a result of Soviet occupation, the Smallholders were forced to form a coalition with the Social Democrats, the Communists, and the National Peasant Party. The leader of the communists, Matyas Rakosi, then employed "salami tactics"—first discrediting and then removing political opponents bit by bit from positions of power—to weaken the multiparty government. In this way, a minuscule communist party lacking popular support was able to gain political control.

In 1948, the Communist Party merged with the Social Democrats to form the Hungarian Workers' Party (HSWP). In 1949, the Hungarian People's Republic was proclaimed and all other parties were abolished. The government nationalized land and industry, neutralizing all who opposed them. Hungary had now become part of the Soviet bloc. As in other Soviet states, the HSWP consolidated power through purges, trials and internal exile. Cardinal Mindszenty, the head of the Roman Catholic Church and leading opponent of the communists, was arrested and sentenced to life imprisonment. As in Bulgaria, Hungary's attempt to regain territory lost in World War I played a key role in the loss of its postwar sovereignty.

The death of Stalin in 1953 fostered the creation of a moderate government led by Imre Nagy. He initiated the "New Course," a policy to liberalize the economy. Agricultural collectives were dissolved and resources were reallocated to light industry and private enterprises. Although successful, Nagy was forced to resign because of a conflict between the Stalinists and the reformers in the party. His ouster brought the return of centralized economic

---

MATYAS RAKOSI (1892–1971)

Although Matyas Rakosi began his involvement in the Hungarian Communist Party in the early 1920s, he became one of its most infamous members in the 1940s with the help of the Soviet leader, Josef Stalin. Called "Little Stalin" for his blind obedience to the Soviet dictator, Rakosi is responsible for a reign of terror and the purges that eliminated political leaders and enemies, imagined or real. Hundreds of people, including future leader Janos Kadar, were tortured, arrested, and imprisoned or executed. Although he took power with the slogan of "Land, bread, liberty!" none of these occurred under Rakosi's rule. Land and agriculture were collectivized, living standards decreased, and no political dissent was tolerated. Rakosi dominated the Hungarian polity until the early 1950s. When his mentor Stalin died, Rakosi's authority and power died as well. Rakosi was soon replaced by Imre Nagy after the new leader of the USSR, Nikita Khrushchev, started a de-Stalinization campaign.

control. Popular disillusionment with the failures of the Soviet economic model and riots in Poland led to mass demonstrations in Budapest. As a result of popular pressure, Nagy was brought back to power. Failing to harness the popular revolt and miscalculating Soviet tolerance for deviation in Central and Eastern Europe, Nagy called for the creation of a democratic regime and the withdrawal of Hungary from the Soviet-dominated Warsaw Pact security alliance. The Soviet Union did not tolerate this challenge to its control. On November 10, 1956, the Soviet Army invaded Hungary and removed Nagy from power. Between 3,000 and 7,000 people were killed in the invasion and another 200,000 were exiled or fled the country.

The Soviets installed Janos Kadar as leader of the HSWP. Kadar purged both Nagy's supporters and remaining Stalinists. Over the next five years, approximately 200 people were executed; 25,000 were imprisoned; and another 120,000 fired from their jobs. The revolution of 1956 sent a clear warning that communist control was in danger. This threat led Kadar to introduce the NEM in 1966. This program, known in the West as "Goulash Communism," lessened state control of the economy. Decision making was moved from central ministries to industrial groups, and individual enterprises and managers were forced to rely on market mechanisms. As in Poland, state control in Hungary was much less pervasive when compared with Bulgaria and Russia.

Imre Nagy (1896–1958)

Once a professor of agricultural science and member of the Hungarian Academy of Science, Imre Nagy is regarded as a tragic figure in Hungarian history. A member of the Communist Party who took refuge in the Soviet Union during World War II, he returned to Hungary with Soviet troops in 1944. In 1946, Nagy openly criticized Stalin's protégé and Hungary Communist leader Matays Rakosi for his "left-wing deviationist" policies, which included collectivization and cutting the living standards of the Hungarians. As a result of his criticism, Nagy was branded "right wing," forced to confess to "opportunism," and removed from the party leadership.

The death of Josef Stalin in March 1953 led to the downfall of Rakosi and Nagy's resurrection. Nagy released people imprisoned by Rakosi and abandoned forced industrialization and collectivization. He also pledged to restore a multiparty political system and international neutrality. In 1956, the Soviets, perceiving this as an ideological challenge and threat to their control over the region, invaded Hungary and replaced Nagy with Janos Kadar. Riots ensued and Nagy was taken to Romania where he was tortured and eventually executed in 1958. Imre Nagy is seen as a Hungarian martyr for resisting Soviet rule and is often cited as a catalyst of the 1956 Revolution.

The NEM's success was seen in the improved quantity and quality of goods. The legalization of household farms and other forms of private enterprise created a second economy—one that operated outside government control, dramatically improving the general economy. This development had significant consequences. First, economic growth greatly strengthened the regime's legitimacy. The party had a social compact with the people—economic freedom in exchange for political discipline. By the mid-1970s, Hungary had the highest standard of living in Central or Eastern Europe. Second, a relatively strong economy allowed Hungary to enter the post-1989 period without the economic cataclysms experienced by most other states in the region.

Political reforms followed economic ones. The parliament was given more power and the local councils gained decision-making authority. Trade unions began to defend workers' rights rather than state interests. Furthermore, the media was allowed to debate political issues as long as they did not question the leading role of the party. A 1983 electoral law allowed multiple candidates for the first time in some electoral districts. By 1985, there were fifty opposition members of parliament, a situation unique in the region. Largely inspired by Hungarian nationalism, these policies helped foster societal consensus, a theme that runs from the beginning of the eighteenth century to the present.

Post-1989

As in Bulgaria, opposition from within the Communist Party led to the fall of Kadar in 1989. The impetus for this event began in 1986, when suppressed demonstrations led to the creation of an intelligentsia assembly, the Hungarian Democratic Forum (HDF). In 1988, this group organized a march of 10,000 people to commemorate the 140th anniversary of the 1848 revolution. This symbolic expression against foreign control quickly turned into a demonstration demanding basic political rights. Numerous groups sprang up to support these demands. They included the Alliance of Free Democrats (AFD) and the Alliance of Young Democrats (AYD). Prewar parties were also resurrected, the most significant being the Independent Smallholders (ISP), the Social Democrats (SDP), and the Christian Democratic People's Party (CDPP). In contrast to Bulgaria and Russia, the Communist Party quickly lost control of the polity. The pluralism of the NEM had undermined its position, forcing the HSWP to abandon the constitutional clause guaranteeing its leading role in society. In 1989, it renamed itself the Hungarian Socialist Party (HSP). This led to a 1989 Roundtable between the HSP and the opposition, laying the framework for political change.

In contrast to negotiations in Bulgaria and Poland, the Roundtable talks in Hungary were not key events as political evolution had been occurring over a number of years.

JOZSEF ANTALL, JR. (1932–1993)

Jozsef Antall, the son of a man who risked his life helping Jews and Poles escape Nazi concentration camps, was introduced to Hungarian politics at a young age. However, he withdrew from politics in 1948 when the communists took power. Antall only wanted to be involved in a democratic government, so he focused on an academic career. In 1967, he completed a Ph.D. program from Eotvos University in Budapest, deliberately writing his dissertation on medical history to avoid interference from the communist authorities. In 1972, he became director of a museum, a post he held until he became prime minister in 1990. Antall made the museum one of the few places in Hungary where non-communist scholarship was allowed.

In 1989, Antall became president of the Democratic Forum, one of the largest opposition parties. Because of his anticommunist credentials, he played a key role in the Roundtable negotiations. During these talks, communists and their opponents discussed ways to foster Hungary's transition from four decades of socialist rule to a multiparty system. In 1990, the Democratic Forum won the country's first free elections and Antall became prime minister. As prime minister, he improved relations with the West and moved Hungary toward a capitalist free market economy.

Antall's timing in Hungarian politics was crucial to his success. Although a lifelong anticommunist, he was actively involved in Hungarian politics only during the last three years of his life, following the weakening of the Soviet Union in the late 1980s. He died of cancer in Budapest in 1993.

In March 1989, 100,000 people protested against the government, demanding democracy, free elections, the withdrawal of Soviet troops from Hungary, and the rehabilitation of Nagy. In August, 2 million workers expressed their discontent with planned price increases. These two events forced the HSP to schedule multiparty elections. On October 23, 1989, the anniversary of the 1956 revolution, the Hungarian republic was proclaimed.

The first free elections since 1945 were held in March 1990. The overwhelming winner, with 43 percent of the seats in the parliament, was the Hungarian Democratic Forum. Together with the Independent Smallholders and the Christian Democrats, the HDF formed the first noncommunist government since 1947. Significantly, the election made Hungary the first multiparty system in the region. In contrast to Bulgaria and Poland, in which political parties were based on simple pro- versus anticommunist platforms, voters in Hungary had a choice of parties with very different policies. Although the reformed Communist Party had achieved a measure of legitimacy, just before the election a scandal known as "Danubegate" cost the HSP electoral support.[13] As a result, it won only 8.5 percent of the vote. In contrast, in the first post-1989 Bulgarian elections, the BSP (ex-communists) won 34 percent of the vote.

After the elections, the National Assembly elected Árpad Goncz of the AFD as president, Gyorgy Szabad of the HDF as chairperson of National Assembly, and Jozsef Antall as prime minister. The government committed itself to democratization and the creation of a market economy. The death of Antall in December 1993 and the May 1994 elections ended the first phase of the transition. In May 1994, Hungary held its second general election. The HSP won a majority of seats in the parliament. Although it did not need their support to form a government, the HSP made the AFD a junior coalition partner. This is the first time in Hungarian history a left-wing government was freely elected. Their victory suggested the idealism of the 1990 election was replaced with a desire to return to the stability of the past. This can be seen in the heavy losses for the leading reform parties. The HSP/AFD alliance allowed the popular Goncz to be relected in 1995.

With the anniversaries of two important historical events,[14] 1996 was the year Hungary started to emerge from the shadows of the past. Domestically, the enactment of difficult reforms led to an improved macroeconomic situation. Externally, as a result of a landmark treaty with Romania—which renounced all territorial claims and pledged to resolve outstanding minority issues—and parliamentary approval for NATO to use Hungary as a staging base for implementing the Bosnian peace accords, the country's image in the West significantly improved.

For most Hungarians, however, 1996 was a year remembered for "continuing economic hardship, political scandals, an increase in extremist rhetoric, growing corruption, and an increasing gap between the nouveau rich and lower classes."[15] These problems led to the success of the Alliance of Young Democrats and the Independent Smallholders' Party in the 1998 parliamentary election. Promising an end to economic hardship, the AYD leader Viktor Orban was selected as prime minister. He has provoked the opposition by centralizing power in the prime minister's office—doubling its budget in 1999—and changing parliamentary rules which normally require the consent of a two-thirds majority. This has led many observers to question whether Orban will be able to complete his four-year term.

INFORMING POLITICAL IDEAS

Although the official political culture was similar in all four states, historical experiences fostered a unique set of Hungarian subcultures. They include a constant struggle against foreign influence, an emphasis on societal consensus, restrictions on the power of the central government, and a desire to be included in the cultural sphere of Western Europe. Although linked to different legacies, these characteristics are deeply ingrained in the Hungarian political consciousness.

Political Culture

Since their arrival in the Carpathian basin, Hungarians have struggled for self-determination. This can be seen in their encounters with the Mongols, the Turks, and the Hapsburgs. Although it was initially an idea shared only by the elites, by the nineteenth century self-determination became part of the national consciousness. In contrast with the other subject nations of the Hapsburg Empire, only the Hungarians were able to achieve equal status with the Austrians. This struggle can also be seen in the postwar era, when recurring demands for economic and political autonomy from the Soviet Union finally exploded in the 1956 revolution.

A closely related feature is societal consensus. Like Poles, Hungarians believe that without internal unity, the country will again fall under foreign domination. Thus most people believe individual needs are much less important than the societal good. Therefore, ideological and political competition, viewed as normal and healthy in the West, is seen as damaging by Hungarians.[16] When polled, Hungarians consistently express greater support for institutions that represent consensus, such as the parliament, the constitutional court, and the military. Institutions embroiled in conflict, such as political parties and trade unions, are far less popular.

The internal equivalent of national self-determination has been a continuing attempt to limit the power of the central government. This policy can be traced back to 1222, when the nobles forced the crown to accept the "Golden Bull." In the contemporary era, this desire can be seen in the new amendments to the Constitution, which provide for local governmental autonomy and individual freedoms.

A final historical goal has been acceptance as part of Western Europe rather than politically "backward" Eastern Europe. Hungary viewed its adoption of Christianity as a move toward Western social and political norms. This can be seen in Hungarian attempts to be accepted as equals to the Austrians in the Hapsburg empire. A contemporary manifestation of this policy can be seen in Hungary's decision to adopt basic Western political values—freedom of the press, multiparty elections, and the rule of law— and Hungary's attempt to join the EU and NATO. The official government policy shows the significance Hungary attaches to being accepted as a West European state:

> We have lived in Europe since the time of St. Stephen, our first king. Europe imbued us with a national sense of identity, but it always signified for us modern currents of thought and a modern system of institutions, an up-to-date structure of government and openness to the world, and so ultimately a constitutional democracy.[17]

Little Traditions

As in other states in the region, communist control after World War II created legacies that can still be seen today. In Hungary, the most significant are the belief that the state should play a key role in solving societal problems, rule by elites, egalitarianism, and the lack of societal norms.

The legacy of the communist-imposed mentality that individual self-reliance is "anti-social" is the commonly held belief that the state will solve societal problems. This belief, which fosters a dependent society, lessening personal responsibility and initiative, has limited the number of people involved in politics. A second legacy is the power of a small elite, which continues to dominate the polity. Although elected, their vision of the future is different from the general population. However, in contrast with the past, since the governing elite can now be changed, it is afraid of the voters. This situation can be seen in the government's initial failure to enact sweeping reforms.

The socialist legacy has also fostered an egalitarian mentality. A large majority of the public think income differentials are too large. They believe that social justice requires a "certain extent" of social equality.[18] As an illustration, 90 percent of the population believes the government should continue to provide health care. Tied with Bulgaria, this was the highest percentage in the region.[19] This view is at odds with the present government policy of creating a market economy based on individual freedom. This belief was a major factor in the success of the HSP in the 1994 elections. Perhaps the most important legacy of the communist regime was the lack of societal norms. Today, Hungary still lacks "the values of honest business and virtues like tolerance, honesty in public debates and consistency of political principles."[20]

These features have directly affected Hungary's political development. In an era of continuing change, political pluralism is associated with economic hardship, not as an opportunity for people to gain control of their own destiny. People have yet to realize that freedom entails responsibilities. Thus, the underpinnings of a civil society and a pluralistic political system are still being created. However, in contrast to Russia, democracy is not in danger. Extremist parties win only a small percentage of the vote and no major party espouses anti-democratic views.

Legitimizing Rationale

As in all states, governmental legitimacy is the result of different factors at different times. In the eighteenth and nineteenth centuries, legitimacy was based on the assertion of Hungarian self-determination within the Hapsburg empire. Between 1948 and 1956, legitimacy was based on the government's adherence to Marxist-Leninist ideology and the creation of a new political order. However, the 1956 revolution showed that political exhortations backed by the threat of punishment for those who did not comply were not enough.

Kadar's introduction of the NEM in 1966 was a tacit admission that legitimacy would be based on living standards rather than communist ideology. Although the NEM fostered economic growth and increased support for the regime, the reforms also showed the weakness of the system. The economic decline in the 1980s increased public discontent, removing the last remnant of the government's legitimacy. Today, legitimacy is based on how well the government enforces the law, guarantees the security of its citizens, and promotes social stability and economic development.

Political Socialization

Education

In contrast to Bulgaria, Poland, and Russia, Hungary started reforming its educational system before the end of the old regime. The Education Act of 1985 guaranteed the independence of schools and the professional autonomy of teachers. Even more sweeping reforms were enacted in 1995. A new national curriculum free of Marxist bias was introduced, and schools were given the right to add a local curriculum.[21] Perhaps the most successful achievements have been the reestablishment of private schools and the creation of bilingual schools to promote the languages of the national minorities.

While economic restructuring has cut formerly generous state funding for education, Hungarian children and their counterparts in most CEE states still manage to consistently outperform American students. In the Third International Math and Science study, six CEE states—including Bulgaria and Hungary—took six of the top fifteen places in both math and science.[22] At least in education, the West can learn something from these less developed states. Finally, while there has been a dramatic increase in enrollment at Hungarian institutions of higher education since 1990, the ratio of those attending is still only 60 percent of the West European average.

Social and Peer groups

Under the old regime, the umbrella organization for political mobilization was the Patriotic People's Front (PPF). The PPF worked through 4,000 committees scattered throughout the country to organize elections, stimulate awareness of public problems, and mobilize individuals and groups in support of state policies. Today, because of budgetary reasons and a lack of interest, the number of social and peer groups has dramatically decreased.

Mass Media

Hungary started liberalizing control of the mass media before other CEE states. In 1988, press censorship laws were relaxed. This was followed by the legalization of private ownership of publications in 1989. By late 1990, most of the newspapers and journals were in private hands.

As in the rest of the region, state subsidies for the print media were progressively reduced, forcing many publishers out of business. In contrast to the numerous papers of the communist regime, in 1996 there were only twelve national and twenty-one regional dailies. Although the government continues to have some influence over the print media through its distribution of newspapers, the print media is generally free of state control. This does not mean they are the guardians of public interest. A report in the English-language *Budapest Business Journal* found that six of the top seven dailies in Hungary regularly accept money for publishing promotion articles without identifying the articles as such.[23] As a result, political scandals are usually not thoroughly pursued by journalists.

In contrast to Poland and Russia, until 1996 the broadcasting media was controlled by the government. A new electronic law ended six years of heated parliamentary debates regarding media legislation. The new law separates the media from party politics and ends the former state monopoly by allowing commercial television and radio stations. This led to the creation of twenty-six commercial television stations and 31 radio stations.[24] In addition, Hungarian Television and Radio was split into three separate public foundations—Hungarian Radio, Hungarian Television, and Duna Television. Each of these organizations is directed and supervised by a governing board comprised of members nominated by political bodies and interest groups.

Although the law had broad parliamentary support, media interest groups opposed it on the grounds that it still allowed excessive political influence over the media.[25] However, since the law provides for a transparent regulation system, the government has been prevented from exerting political pressure on the media. Less controversial, the law also established the rules and conditions for applying for frequencies and licensing private broadcasters and created a Board of Radio and Television. The board is in charge of allocating frequencies formerly owned by the state.

Since the national radio and television channels are still overseen by the state, the broadcast media could still serve as a agent of control. However, this has not been perceived as a problem because the broadcast medium is rated as the most reliable public institution.[26] In addition, its use of numerous Western and international programs make it more of an entertainment medium than a channel for propaganda. Since they control the major information outlets, as in the West the power of the media will continue to grow. They already play a key role in fostering political discussion. As an illustration, in spite of attempts to deal with various issues behind closed doors, the internal battles within the HSP and AFD were made public as of a result of media attention.

Governmental socialization efforts in Hungary were far less successful than in Bulgaria and Russia, yet the regime was far more legitimate. Several uniquely Hungarian features explain this apparent contradiction. First, the introduction of the NEM in 1966 increased living standards and allowed limited political participation, thus increasing the government's legitimacy. Second, after the removal of the Moscow-trained Hungarian communists following Stalin's death in 1953, Hungarian party leaders attempted to increase their autonomy within the Soviet bloc. This move can be seen as a continuation of the historical struggle for self-determination.

Finally, some people attribute the failure of socialization to a "conspiracy of intimacy in a small country, where everyone knows everyone else, knew their mothers and grandmothers, and communicates by allusion that escapes outsiders."[27] This situation fosters a consensual policy and helps explain why many Hungarians saw the regime changes of 1989 not as a revolution, but a continuation of previous reforms. The Hungarian social structure is one of "extended cousinage . . . and if one did business with somebody, one cannot switch promptly to treating him as an enemy."[28] This situation affects political stability. In contrast to many countries, political peace has been maintained in the face of declining living standards.

FORMAL GOVERNMENTAL INSTITUTIONS

The Constitution

In contrast to Bulgaria, Poland, and Russia, Hungary has yet to adopt a new constitution. The current legal structure of the state is based on the Stalinist Constitution of 1949 and a patchwork of amendments introduced in 1971, 1983, and 1989.

In 1988, roundtable talks between representatives of the opposition and the Communist Party were held. Since the opposition was in the minority, they decided that instead of writing a new constitution that would reflect the interests of the status quo, they could accomplish more by changing the most egregious provisions of the old constitution; later, after the communists were removed from power, a new constitution could be adopted. More than a decade after the end of the old regime, however, a new constitution has yet to be adopted. In 1996, after an eighteen-month effort by a five-party Constitutional Commission, the HSP dominated parliament rejected a package of ninety-three amendments that would have formed the basis of a new constitution. It is unlikely the new AYD-ISP government will be able to enact a new constitution since they lack the requisite two-thirds parliamentary majority.

What has prevented the country from adopting a new constitution, which many in the West consider the foundation of a law-based state? First, the idea of constitutionalism, or limits on the government, represents a fundamental change from the communist era. Second, with society polarized, political parties cannot agree on what should be included in a new political covenant. For example, socialists want to include provisions that guarantee social and economic rights, while conservatives want to include only basic political rights, such as freedom of speech. Thus it has proven difficult to create wording that is not too vague but at the same time defines the powers and responsibilities of state bodies. Third, the public itself is leery of a new constitution. They are afraid that like the communists before them, whatever party is in power at the time of the adoption of the new constitution would use it to enshrine its power.[29] According to Professor Attila Agh of Budapest Economics University, the right historical moment has passed and since the present constitution works, there is little public support for changing it.[30]

Constitutional amendments declare the Republic of Hungary to be an independent, democratic state based on the rule of law with all power belonging to the people. Like the American Declaration of Independence, it recognizes human rights as inviolable and stresses that the primary purpose of the state is to safeguard these rights. However, in contrast to the American view that these are inalienable rights, in Hungary they are only protected if specifically violated by a law or government action. The Constitution also guarantees equal rights and protection for public and private property. Uniquely, it recognizes the right of "undertaking [entrepreneuralism] and free economic competition."

The Constitution ensures the supremacy of the National Assembly by vesting it with legislative power and control over the executive. The prime minister and other ministers form the Council of Ministers, which is the principle organ of executive power. Administratively, the Constitution divides the state into self-governing municipalities. Amendments also provide for an independent judiciary to ensure the rule of law and the protection of civil rights. The supremacy of the Constitution has been strengthened by the introduction of a Constitutional Court whose role is to ensure the constitutionality of all laws and executive acts.

Although the Hungarian Constitution is democratic, there are problems that have yet to be addressed. Since it is comprised of amendments written in very different regimes, the powers and responsibilities of various governmental bodies are not clearly defined. For example, the prosecutor general is elected by parliament but is not a member of the government. Therefore, he is not responsible to the government and cannot be removed by it. Situations like this have been a source of tension and instability.

More significantly, the introduction of new amendments has weakened the legitimacy of the Constitution. In contrast to the United States, Hungarians do not view it as a sacred political covenant. This problem is heightened by the ease with which the Constitution can be changed. A two-thirds majority is all that is necessary to amend the highest law of the land. In summary, the fact that Hungary has had to amend a communist-written constitution rather than adopting a new one has continued to be a source of political conflicts.

Regional and Local Government

Under the socialist regime, local government in Hungary was based on a hierarchical system of village, municipal, and county councils that functioned more as agents of state control than as advocates of local interests. In 1990, the National Assembly enacted a law that granted autonomy to local governments.

Hungary today is divided into nineteen counties and the Budapest city region. Although there has been an effort to decentralize power by shifting power to the municipal governments, the counties are still the most important unit of local government. This is the result of numerous factors. First, municipalities are legally responsible for implementing policies created by the county councils. Second, counties have more resources, making the municipalities dependent on them for services. Finally, there are too many small municipalities for any to have any significant power.

Organizationally, each county has a directly elected council that in turn selects a council president. Councils have the power to elect committees and establish local administrative offices. County governments have control over the local economy, education, environmental issues, public health, utilities, fire protection, and the protection of the rights of minorities. To support these activities, councils have the power to levy taxes. However, rampant tax evasion—estimated at over 35 percent—lessens this power.[31] Each county is divided into numerous municipalities that have responsibility for the same services as the county. Significantly, the police are under the Ministry of the Interior and local officials have no control over them.

Organizationally, the local government's structure is similar to the county's. However, in a continuing attempt to decentralize power, a 1994 law provided for the direct election of mayors. Prior to this time, mayors were selected by the local council, which were elected proportionately, with a 5 percent threshold. Thus, like Bulgaria, the mayor is often from a different party than the majority of the local council. This obviously slows policy making. Although the mayor is now elected for a four-year term, she can still be overruled by local council. However, the mayor can only be removed from office through judicial proceedings. The Budapest city government is unique because it is the only territorial government and has more power than county governments. It is comprised of twenty-three districts, each with its own mayor and district council. In addition, there is a mayor and city council that presides over the entire municipality of Budapest. However, any of the twenty-three districts can veto policies they do not agree with. For example, if the city wants to build a new road, it must have the approval of each district through which the road passes.

Although local governments have administrative autonomy and cannot be overruled by the central government, there are several obstacles to independent policy making. First, since the central and county governments provide the bulk of local government funding—over 60 percent—they have a large amount of influence in determining spending priorities.[32] Thus local governments have limited resources with which to help their constituents. Second, since regional and local governments are constitutionally tasked with implementing state policies, local government authority is often reduced to acting as an arm of the state. The power of the central government was increased with the enactment of a law in 1993 that allows it to "check" the management and financial activities of local governments.

Control over local governments is also exercised by presidentially appointed "commissioners of the republic." This new position is similar to the Russian "representative of the president." Commissioners advise and monitor local governments and ensure local laws are constitutional. If necessary, commissioners have the power to take local officials to court. This happened over 800 times to the mayor of Budapest between 1990 and 1994.[33] While Hungarian commissioners were to have merely an advisory role, this example shows the central government has significant influence. Overall, however, local governments in Hungary have more autonomy than their counterparts in Bulgaria or Russia.

The Legislature

The center of governmental power in Hungary is the National Assembly. Unlike its Polish and Russian counterparts, the National Assembly is a unicameral body whose 386 members are elected by universal suffrage for a four-year term of office. It has thirteen standing committees and four special committees. Committee membership varies from eight to twenty-seven members. The Assembly can also form ad hoc committees. In contrast to U.S. congressional committees, Hungarian committees mirror the electoral support of all the parties in the parliament. This also includes the selection of committee chairs.

The National Assembly establishes its own rules and agenda, and its sessions are open to the public. The Assembly has two main constitutional mandates: controlling the government and creating legislation. Other legislative functions include levying taxes, declaring war and states of emergency, ratifying international treaties and electing the President and members of the Constitutional Court. This power is exercised through a variety of formal and informal methods. Since the parliament is the locus of power in the Hungarian polity, there are few limits on its power. However, the National Assembly may not pass laws that violate international law, and its actions are subject to referendums. Most significantly, the Constitutional Court may repeal laws which violate the Constitution.

The Electoral System

To contest a seat in the Assembly, a candidate must be nominated by at least 750 people. Under the old electoral system, only the Communist Party could nominate candidates. Therefore, elections were merely a formality to legitimize the regime. Today, as in Germany and Russia, the electoral scheme is a mixed proportional-pluralist system designed to favor larger parties while still allowing smaller parties opportunities for representation.

During the first round of the election, the country is divided into 176 single-member electoral districts, like those in the United States. However, if no one wins a majority in the first round, a second round of elections for candidates who won more than 15 percent of the vote is held. In the second round, the candidate who wins a plurality wins the seat. Another 152 deputies are selected on a second ballot in which representation is based on a proportional system divided into regional and national lists. To compete in a region, parties must have candidates in one-quarter of all regional electoral districts. Ninety-four deputies are selected from these lists. If a party has candidates on at least seven regional lists, it is eligible to have candidates on the national list from which an additional fifty-eight deputies are selected.

To win any of the proportional seats, a party must win at least 5 percent of the vote. To help ensure party discipline, once elected MPs can only switch parties after spending six months as an independent. Based on their showing in the most recent election, the state provides approximately 65 percent of each party's budget. Private donors contribute the rest. In addition to the money provided by the state, candidates are limited to $2 million in campaign expenditures. The eight largest political parties get limited free access to state radio and television. While parties are required to publish their campaign expenditures within sixty days of the second round of the elections, there is no penalty for noncompliance.

The Presidency

An important new constitutional provision was the establishment of the presidency. This institution was established amid great controversy. Fearful of a strong chief executive reminiscent of the communist regime, many members of parliament opposed its creation. In the end it was decided to create the presidency to symbolize the country's unity and to safeguard the democratic operation of the state. Although the Constitution gave this office very limited powers, the first president, Árpad Goncz, managed to increase its influence. Thus the president's actual role has been a source of contention.

In contrast to Bulgaria, Poland, and Russia, the president is not chosen directly by the people. Rather, he is elected by a two-thirds parliamentary majority for a renewable five-year term. If no candidate receives this majority on the first ballot, the candidate with a majority between the two highest vote-getters on the second ballot becomes president. To remove the president from office, one-fifth of the National Assembly deputies must support a petition to impeach him. Then, in a secret ballot, two-thirds of the Assembly must vote to affirm the petition. The formal powers of the president are derived from his or her status as head of state and are therefore mostly ceremonial. They include convening and dismissing the National Assembly and representing the state internationally.

Even these powers are limited. For example, the president may dissolve the Assembly only if it fails to support the government four times in a single year or if the prime minister designate fails to gain a vote of confidence within forty days of being nominated. The Hungarian president also has very limited veto powers. According to Article 26, the president may exercise either a "constitutional" or a "political" veto. The constitutional veto allows the president to forward a bill to the Constitutional Court for review. A political veto allows the president to return a bill to parliament for reconsideration. The Assembly is then required to vote on the bill for a second time within sixty days. If the bill passes by a simple majority, the president is required to sign it within five days.[34]

The only formal responsibilities that give the president more than symbolic authority are his position as commander-in-chief of the armed forces, the power to appoint state officials—local commissioners, judges, generals, state secretaries—schedule elections, and the right to initiate legislation. Because of constitutional ambiguity, the president's exact powers are subject to interpretation. This has caused tensions between the president and the prime minister. Between 1990 and 1992, Prime Minister Antall and President Goncz fought for control over various areas of the polity, such as deciding which of them would represent Hungary at international conferences. Ultimately, it was decided that both would attend. Another example was the government's plan for military reform that was not supported by the president. The Constitutional Court ruled that although the president was commander-in-chief, the responsibility for managing the armed forces rested with the government.

A key reason for these conflicts lies in the nature of the presidency. Although all major parties agreed the president should have mainly ceremonial powers, as in Bulgaria the selection of an opposition candidate as president fostered a duality of executive power that threatened the executive branch. Overall, then, the Hungarian president has less power than his or her Polish, Russian, or even Bulgarian counterparts. While the Russian and Polish presidents enjoy executive authority similar to that of the strong French presidency, the Hungarian head of state's powers are very limited.

The Executive

As in Bulgaria and other parliamentary democracies, the key executive position in Hungary is that of prime minister, who is the head of government. The prime minister and cabinet are directly responsible to the National Assembly and, in contrast to Russia, are completely independent of the president. This fusion of legislative and executive power has promoted governmental stability and efficiency.[35]

The Council of Ministers is comprised of the prime minister and other ministers. The prime minister nominates ministers, who are formally appointed by the president. In contrast to other parliamentary regimes, ministers are not responsible to the parliament and cannot be removed by it; only the prime minister can appoint or dismiss them. The cabinet is responsible for creating and implementing the state's domestic and foreign policies. To help the government accomplish these tasks, various subcabinets, such as those for economic and national security, have been created. In addition to policy creation and implementation at the state level, the cabinet also influences policy implementation at the local level through its power to annul or modify local administrative acts.

Depending on its size and responsibilities, each ministry has two to four state secretaries.[36] There are two types of state secretaries, political and administrative. The former are political appointees who change with the government. In contrast, administrative secretaries are supposed to be permanent nonpartisan civil servants who oversee the administration of the ministry. However, this division has not been the case in practice. After the 1994 elections, over 50 percent of the administrative secretaries resigned. On average, annual turnover has been approximately 35 percent. Combined with the lack of open recruitment, experience, and nepotism, this situation has been a major impediment to policy formation.

In an effort to enhance centralize power and improve policy making, after the victory of the Alliance of Young Democrats in the 1998 election, Prime Minister Orban created the Office of the Prime Minister. The office, headed by one of Orban's former professors, Istvan Stumpf, duplicates the structure of government, with desks mirroring the ministries, thereby strengthening the power of the prime minister in relation to the bureaucracy. With these changes, "the role of the prime minister will be enlarged to resemble that of the chancellor, along the lines of the German model."[37]

The National Assembly controls the Council of Ministers through a variety of means. First, to be elected prime minister the nominee must have the support of the majority in parliament. Second, to be empowered the cabinet must receive a majority plus one vote in the Assembly. If the government fails to gather a majority, the parliament can nominate a new prime minister. The Assembly also controls the government through its ability to control state finances. The National Assembly has the sole prerogative of approving the state budget. By refusing to accept the budget or requiring its modification, the Assembly can directly influence the direction of governmental policies.

Another parliamentary instrument of control is the ability to call a vote of confidence on government policies. However, as in Germany, the Hungarian parliament must choose a new government before it can remove an old one. This provision, the constructive vote of no confidence, must be called for by at least one-fifth of Assembly members. This procedure leaves the prime minister far less vulnerable than prime ministers in other parliamentary systems, such as Bulgaria and pre-1996 Poland. As a result, the first two governments served their full four-year terms while Bulgaria and Poland respectively had eight and seven government changes between 1989 and 1997.

Other means of controlling the government include delaying the passage of legislation and creating ad hoc commissions. Ad hoc commissions can be created at the request of 20 percent of the MPs. These commissions have wide investigative powers, including inquiries into the actions of the cabinet or individual ministers. As in Bulgaria and Poland, MPs can question members of the Council of Ministers, including the prime minister, at a question hour held weekly. Topics are submitted in advance to the chair of the Assembly, and ministers are required to answer them. If the relevant minister is not present, she must respond at a question hour within two weeks.

Overall however, the limits on the Hungarian government are negligible. While it cannot issue decrees in areas not listed in the Constitution or use a "blocked-vote" procedure—demanding the bill as a whole be voted on, as in France—the stability of the government in a time of economic, political, and social change shows the power and legitimacy of the regime.

The Judiciary

Amendments to the Constitution guarantee the independence of the judiciary. Their main responsibilities are to protect the constitutional order and the rights of citizens and to oversee compliance with the law. Judges are appointed by the president and confirmed by the National Assembly. With the exception of the Constitutional Court, all judges have unlimited tenure; unlike Bulgaria, they can only be removed if they break the law. In an additional attempt to ensure judicial independence, the Constitution forbids judges from engaging in political activity or belonging to a political party. Most judges come from the middle class or intelligentsia. Like the educational and medical professions, because the pay and status of judges are low, over 75 percent are women.

Organizationally justice is administered by the Supreme Court, the Budapest Metropolitan Court, county courts, and district courts. While the Supreme Court ensures equal application of law by all courts, the Constitutional

Court is the most important judicial body. Its fifteen members are selected for a nine-year term. To become a member of the Constitutional Court, a judge has to be nominated by a committee of parliamentary deputies composed of one member from each party in the parliament. Candidates are then elected by a two-thirds vote. As in the United States, to "check" the power of the Court, the legislature controls its budget. The Constitutional Court elects its own president and decides its own rules and agenda. To foster consensus, it may *dismiss* any of its members by a majority vote.

Because the participants in the roundtable discussions were uncertain about their own political futures, they established a powerful independent institution that would prevent any group or institution from usurping power. As a result, the Hungarian Constitutional Court is one of the most powerful courts in Europe.[38] The constitution tasks the Court with protecting the rule of law and safeguarding the separation of powers. Its major functions include protection of the constitution by a review of draft legislation, ex post facto protection of constitutional norms through a review of acts passed by the National Assembly, and interpretation of the constitution. Thus, like the U.S. Supreme Court, the Hungarian Constitutional Court has the power of judicial review. Overall, it is considered one of the main guarantors of the supremacy of the rule of law in Hungary.

Although Bulgaria, Poland, and Russia also have constitutional courts, the Hungarian Constitutional Court is unique. It has been more involved in political questions than its CEE counterparts. Also, in contrast to Russia and Bulgaria, the judicial system in Hungary is accepted as fair and its decisions are implemented. This is because it was not used as a tool of control to the same extent as in the other states. The power of the Court has been enhanced by the lack of a new constitution. Numerous amendments to the old constitution, some vague and incoherent, have forced the Court to become involved in many areas of the polity. Recent Court rulings have examined presidential authority, the powers of local government, electoral laws, and civilian control over the military. One of the most important and controversial rulings of the Court was on the Zetenyi-Takacs law. This law waived the statute of limitations for acts of treason, premeditated murder, and aggravated assault that occurred between December 1944 and May 1990, making possible the prosecution of former communist officials.[39] The Court declared the law unconstitutional because it violated the principle of legal security. Although the Court was criticized by the government for usurping the prerogatives of parliament, this ruling suggests Hungary is well on its way to a law-based regime.

To help ensure Hungarian's new liberties are respected, as in Poland and Russia, an ombudsman for civil rights was created. The ombudsman is elected by a two-thirds parliamentary majority for a six-year term that can be renewed once. In contrast to Russia, where the Human Rights Commissioner can be removed by the president, in Hungary the ombudsman is independent from all other branches of power. Although legally Hungarians have the same freedoms as their Western counterparts, this is not yet the case in practice. In a 1996 report, the ombudsman noted that in violation of the Constitution, police frequently restrict access of detainees to lawyers. In Budapest, only 13 percent of the police-assigned lawyers were allowed to participate in preliminary hearings.[40] In addition, the lack of resources and the failure to enact a comprehensive commercial code and bankruptcy law has led to a backlog of 100,000 cases.

The Bureaucracy

Since economic reforms were initiated before the end of the socialist regime, the Hungarian bureaucracy was not as powerful as its counterparts in the other states. However, it still played a key role in ensuring state control. Therefore, in spite of political changes, former bureaucrats from the old regime continue to maintain a significant degree of influence. Although some high government officials were removed after 1989, as a whole the bureaucracy has not changed. Lamenting the inability of the HDF government to implement policy changes, an HDF leader noted: "We have neither the power nor the alternatives to wipe out the professionals of the former regime. There is no one else to substitute for these people."[41]

To improve the professionalism of the bureaucracy, new laws regulating public servants have been enacted. They provide for the establishment of a nonpartisan career civil service based on professional merit. In addition to the lack of professional bureaucrats, two other factors have contributed to the power of the bureaucracy: continued state control over a significant part of the economy and increasing state involvement in new areas of the polity. As an illustration of state control, health care remains under control of the central government.

Societal changes have also made it necessary to address economic and political problems that were neglected in the past. New entities include the Office of Minorities, the Office of Ethnic Hungarians, the Office of Telecommunications, and others. Thus, between 1990 and 1994, the number of bureaucrats actually increased while the role of the state in the overall polity decreased. Although not as influential as the bureaucrats in France, Germany, and Russia, Hungarian bureaucrats play a key role in the creation and implementation of government policy.

This role is facilitated by the link between the political and the administrative spheres. In contrast to the United States, in a parliamentary regime the bureaucracy is not legally separated from the government. Although this situation facilitates the work of the government, it also allows the bureaucracy to dominate policy formation and execution. This situation is furthered by the similar backgrounds of high-level bureaucrats. Many are recruited from select schools, the most important being the Budapest Law University.[42] As a result, most have similar world views.

The Military

As in Bulgaria, the Hungarian military was a minor actor under the old regime, an implementor rather than a creator of policy. Except for a short period after 1956, the defense minister was not even a member of the Politburo. Military representation in party bodies was the lowest in the region. The Hungarian armed forces served as an adjunct of the Soviet military. Their mission was to defend Hungarian territory until Soviet forces arrived. They were also used as a socialization and indoctrination tool. Therefore, military service was mandatory for all males. Military high schools were the main place where peasant children were prepared for attending university.

Today, the influence of armed forces has been reduced. They are preoccupied with trying to defend their budget and rationalize their existence in an era where there are no significant enemies. This has caused an increase in tension between politicians and professional military leaders. The reformation of the Hungarian military began under the communist government in 1988. By the time the new democratic government took office in 1990, party control over the armed forces had been significantly decreased. Today, the military is undergoing a major transformation that is expected to take at least two decades. The changes are linked to a new national security doctrine.[43]

The first phase of structural reform was completed between 1989 and 1992. In addition to the forced retirement of most senior officers, formerly one of the most privileged groups in the communist regime, there has been a 35 percent reduction in the armed forces—from 155,700 to 100,000 troops. As a result, the Hungarian army is one of the smallest in the region. The next phase of restructuring involves equipment modernization, made difficult by severe budgetary cuts. In comparison to 1989, Hungary's 1993 defense budget was 40 percent less. However, with instability and ongoing conflicts in neighboring states, there is a general consensus military expenditures need to be increased.

One of the first major structural adjustments to the armed forces was the decision—as in Poland—to split the Ministry of Defense into two major parts. The General Staff—where the majority of professional military officers are assigned—was merged with the Army Command. For the first time, control of the armed forces has been vested in the military. This reform reduced the authority of the Defense Ministry, now headed by a civilian, to purely political matters. Since the defense minister is responsible to the prime minister and the army commander to the president, the chain of command is not clear. This issue has major military, political, and constitutional ramifications.

The lack of civilian control over the military is a potential problem because it gives armed forces more influence than their Western counterparts. In Hungary, the General Staff makes and implements plans that are usually approved by the defense minister. This allows little civilian input, analogous to the situation that prevailed in the socialist period. As a result, resources are not spent on research and development but on salaries and personnel expenses. This is partly the result of limited opportunities for civilians to educate themselves about military strategy and doctrine and the armed forces' desire to preserve their monopoly in this area. This situation will change with Hungary's membership in NATO.

THE ELITE

While the HSWP dominated the polity under the old regime, in contrast to Bulgaria, Poland, and Russia, the members of the *nomenklatura* were not the only elite in Hungary. The enactment of economic reforms created another group whose status was determined as much by wealth as by party membership.

By the mid-1980s, the Communist Party's control of society had begun to decline. This was the result of the general liberalization of society connected to the NEM and Soviet support for economic reforms. Reformist party members, supported by pragmatic technocrats, enacted political and economic reforms. In 1989, the New March Front, a group of intellectuals closely connected with the reformist wing of the HSWP, followed the Polish example and held roundtable discussions with dissident groups. After these meetings, the party removed the constitutional clause guaranteeing its monopoly on power.

Notably, the process of change was led by a narrow elite. As in Poland, there is a large division between the intelligentsia and the masses in Hungary. This gap between the political elites and society, the widest in the four states, ensured that the transition was led by a small group, not the general public. Although the Hungarian political elites do not have a uniform political culture, they do share certain tendencies. They do not trust the masses, have a habit of "lecturing society," underestimate their adversaries, and believe they are irreplaceable. As a result, attempts to recruit new elites have been stymied.[44] This situation has significant ramifications.

The Governmental Elite

The end of a ban on opposition groups that had served as de facto political parties opened up the political system in 1989. Today political parties and their intellectual circles dominate the polity. Over 30 percent of MPs have doctorates and 70 percent are university graduates. The largest and most important parties are described here.

The Hungarian Socialist Party (HSP)

The HSP was created at the final meeting of the Hungarian Socialist Workers' Party (the Communist Party) in 1989. Its founding was accompanied by the announcement that it was to be neither the successor of, nor the heir to, the HSWP. The party won the majority of the votes in the 1994 elections—54 percent. Although the party lost power in the 1998 election, it still won the second largest number of votes.

The HSP's platform calls for the creation of a democratic socialist state. This includes expanding social benefits, maintaining governmental control over key sectors of the economy, and establishing a cooperative agricultural system. Its broad constituency includes technocrats and *nomenklatura* from the old regime as well as blue-collar workers. Geographically, it draws most of its support from the northeastern part of the county—the Mishkolc area— where unemployment is high and from the Szeged area. Even though the latter is a university town that would normally support reformist parties, Szeged is unique in that during the nineteenth century, poor workers immigrated there from the north of the country. As a result, a majority of the population are state workers.

As with the other former communist parties in the region, the success of the HSP in the 1994 election was the result of the economic insecurity that accompanied structural changes since 1989. Significantly, its support for economic reforms caused it to lose.

Alliance of Young Democrats (AYD)

Although formally founded in March 1988, like most other contemporary political parties the AYD started as an unofficial organization in the early

---

LASZLO KOVACS (1939–)

Laszlo Kovacs served as Deputy Minister of Foreign Affairs under Gyula Horn in the last years of the communist regime. Between 1990 and 1994, he was a Hungarian Socialist Party (HSP) MP, serving as a member of the Foreign Affairs Committee. After the HSP won the 1994 elections, Horn named his former protege, Kovacs, as Minister of Foreign Affairs. In this position, Kovacs became the chief spokesman for Hungarian membership in the European Union and NATO.

As a result of corruption and economic hardship, the HSP lost the May 1998 election, forcing Horn to resign as head of the party. Not as closely associated with the past, Kovacs was elected to replace Horn as HSP president at a 1998 party meeting. As a result of his effectiveness as Minister of Foreign Affairs, Kovacs is very popular and has support across party lines, age groups and socioeconomic backgrounds. In a February 1998 poll, he was ranked as the second most popular Hungarian politician. If the HSP wins the next election, Kovacs is likely to become prime minister.

1980s. It was established to offer students and young professionals an alternative to the official communist youth group. The AYD supports a mixed economy—public and private property ownership, a multiparty system, minority rights, and a neutral foreign policy. In 1992, the AYD was the most popular party in Hungary, with a platform calling for accelerating economic reforms and promoting foreign investment. However, to broaden its appeal after a disastrous 1994 electoral showing, the party adopted a much more populist program that calls for more social protection, rights for Hungarians abroad, and a more nationalist foreign policy. This platform helped it win the most seats in the 1998 parliamentary elections.

The most distinct feature of the AYD is its supporters. Since it was founded as an opposition movement for youth, the majority of its supporters are students or young professionals. Until 1993, party statutes prohibited people older than thirty-five years from belonging to the party.

Alliance of Free Democrats (AFD)

The AFD was formed in 1988 by radical opponents of the communist regime. Its platform is based on limiting government power, a market economy, and guaranteed individual rights. It also supports the reconstruction of the economy, promotion of free enterprise, cutting the power of the bureaucracy, and agricultural reforms. Geographically, the AFD draws a majority of its support from the larger cities—especially Budapest—and the western counties which have benefitted the most from economic reforms.

In the 1994 election, the party won 18 percent of the vote, slightly less than in 1990. By remaining too long in coalition with the HSP, the AFD suffered the voters wrath in the 1998 elections, losing half of their seats in parliament.

Hungarian Democratic Forum (HDF)

The HDF was founded in 1988 as a forum to promote national consensus. By the summer of 1989, it had gained enough popularity to challenge the HSP. Advocating a gradual transition to a market economy, it won 24.7 percent of the vote in the 1990 election. Its platform emphasized human rights, political pluralism, and the rule of law. Rather than representing one ideological perspective, it appeals to people in the middle of the political spectrum. This includes the rural gentry, some intellectuals, and the emerging middle class. Since these groups are located in various areas of the country, the HDF has no single geographic base.

Despite its previous popularity—between 1990 and 1994 the HDF was the largest party in Hungary—in the 1994 election it won only 9.5 percent of the vote. The HDF's poor electoral showing and a growing division between the party's liberal and nationalist wings caused the party to split in 1996, causing it to lose even more seats in the 1998 election.

Independent Smallholders' Party (ISP)

"God, Homeland, and Family," a reference to traditional Hungarian peasant values, is the motto of the ISP. The oldest of the parliamentary parties, it was formed in 1930 to represent the interests of peasants and small landholders. Banned by the fascist Arrow Cross and later by the communists, the party was revived in 1988. Its platform supports the privatization of state farms, restitution of land to pre-1947 landowners, exclusion of foreigners from owning arable land, and reinstitution of the death penalty. In addition to being vehemently anticommunist, the party is also mildly nationalist. One of its goals is to recreate a "pure" Hungary. Its constituents include rural Hungarians and peasants. Geographically, it draws a majority of its support from the southeastern counties.

In 1990, the ISP won 11.7 percent of the vote. However, internal dissension fostered by the strong personality of ISP leader Jozsef Torgyan caused the party split into four separate Smallholders' parties. In the 1994 election, the largest of the four ISPs, led by Torgyan, won 6.7 percent of the vote. Dissatisfaction with the HSP government and increasing concern for Hungarians abroad made the party the third most popular in the 1998 elections.

Christian Democratic People's Party (CDPP)

Formed in 1944, the CDPP was also banned by the communists. Resurrected before the first election, the CDPP is ideologically similar to other European Christian Democratic parties. It supports a democracy that reflects Christian faith and social justice. Although it claims to be a secular party, it wants to restore the Catholic Church to a prominent position in society. While it favors a market economy, it also wants protection for the underprivileged.

The CDPP's constituency includes industrial workers, religious groups, and pensioners. It won approximately 5 percent of the vote in both the 1990 and 1994 elections. A post-1994 electoral split moved the party further to the right. This had disastrous ramifications as the party failed to win any seats in the 1998 election.

Hungarian Justice and Life Party (HJLP)

The HJLP was founded by Istvan Csurka after he was expelled from the HDF for his extremist views. Csurka has called for the registration of all foreigners and blames Jews, communists, and liberals for hindering Hungary's democratic transition. Like Hitler, he wants increased "living space" for Hungary. Support for these views can be seen in a 50,000-person rally that celebrated Hungary's national day in 1997. In spite of a recent improvement in living standards—which usually decreases nationalist support—in the 1998 election the HJLP won seats in the National Assembly for the first time.

JOZSEF TORGYAN (1932–)

Jozsef Torgyan, a 1955 law school graduate, spent the majority of his life as a lawyer, starting as a junior clerk in the Metropolitan Court in 1957 and retiring from the field in 1990. His political interests led him to join the ISP after it was legalized in 1988. Serving originally as the party's attorney, he was eventually selected as an MP in the 1990 elections and served on the National Assembly's Constitutional and Judicial Committee. In 1991, Torgyan's strong personality and leadership style helped cause ISP to split. In the aftermath of the split, he was selected chairperson and quickly became the head of the ISP parliamentary group.

Since becoming head of the ISP in 1991, Torgyan has remained a controversial figure. He is especially critical and verbose about the West, blaming them for putting too many restrictions on Hungary. Torgyan is also considered a populist whose policies fluctuate with changes in public opinion. The majority of his support comes from the sentiments of right-wing intellectuals and nationalistic voters who are disillusioned with recent changes. In fact, the largest reason for the party's revival after the 1991 party split was his appeal to nationalistic sentiments among the population.

In the future, Torgyan could play a very important role in Hungarian politics. As part of the price of joining the AYD coalition in 1998, the ISP is allowed to nominate their common presidential candidate in 2000. Since Torgyan remains the most important and influential ISP party member, it seems likely that he will be the coalition's candidate in the next presidential election. Thus Torgyan will remain a powerful political figure in the foreseeable future.

1994 Elections

In May 1994, Hungary held its second general election since 1989. The HSP won a majority of seats in the parliament. Their victory was analogous to other electoral outcomes in which the former communist parties regained control of the governments of Bulgaria, Poland, and Russia. Although it did not need their support to form a government, the HSP made the AFD a junior coalition partner. The idealism of the 1990 election was replaced with the desire to return to the stability of the past. As a result, the leading reform parties—the HDF and AYD—both lost heavily.

As in Poland, voter turnout increased slightly—from 65 to 68 percent—between 1990 and 1994. Although the exact reason for this slight increase is unknown, one possible explanation is that voters have learned that their vote counts. The electoral results showed that although certain groups have a predisposition to vote for a certain party, in contrast to Germany, people are not afraid to shift their support. Thus the large shift from right to left showed the weakness of party allegiances and the lack of a political center. This is the result of an evolving party system and voter pragmatism.

FIGURE 3.1   Hungarian Electoral Results—1990, 1994, and 1998

Party	% of votes in			total seats* in		
	1990	1994	1998	1990	1994	1998
Hungarian Democratic Forum (HDF)	24.7	11.7	4.4	164	38	17#
Alliance of Free Democrats (AFD)	21.4	19.7	7.6	92	69	24
Hungarian Socialist Party (HSP)	10.9	33.0	32.9	33	209	134
Independent Smallholders and Civic Party (ISCP)	11.7	8.8	13.2	44	26	48
Christian Democratic People's Party (CDPP)	6.5	7.0	—	21	22	—
Alliance of Young Democrats (AYD)	8.9	7.0	29.5	21	20	148
Agrarian Alliance	—	—	—	1	1	
Party of Hungarian Truth and Life	—	—	3.6	—	—	14#
Joint Candidate	—	—	—	4	1	0
Independent	—	—	.3	6	1	1

Note: Voter turnout (first round): 1990—65.1%
                                       1994—68.9%
                                       1998—56.3%

* The number of seats shown here is the total number of seats from party lists and individual mandates. In 1990, the threshold needed to gain seats from party lists was 4%. In 1994 the threshold was raised to 5%.

These parties did not clear the 5% threshold; their seats are from individual constituencies only.

Source: "Parliamentary Elections in Hungary." http://www.tiszanet.hu/mszp/europeanforum/ elections.html

1998 Election

The 1998 election gives us an insight into the future of the Hungarian polity. While the first vote was against the old regime and the second against economic hardship, the third should have defined the major issues facing the regime. If this is the case, voters are concerned with three issues: corruption, economic hardship, and the plight of Hungarians abroad.

While twenty-six parties contested the election, only six won enough votes to gain representation. The AYD–Hungarian Civic Party coalition won 148 seats, the HSP 134, ISP 48, AFD 24, HDF 17, and HTJP 14. In a somewhat bizarre alliance in which the only policy they have in common is a dislike of the HSP, the center-right AYD-HCP and the Smallholders agreed to form a government. This situation suggests a period of political instability for both Hungary and its neighbors. With numerous policy differences, many Hungarian political analysts believe the coalition will not last its full four-year term.[45] These differences allowed the HSP to win the largest number of votes in the October 1998 local elections. Thus the cohesiveness of the coalition will be central to the success or failure of the new government.

The results of the election suggest a continuing political evolution. First, parties are consolidating into left, right, and center groups. This is a natural development since smaller parties realize they cannot influence policy unless they band together, as seen in the AYD-HCP alliance that helped unite the right side of the political spectrum. Second, as in many other democracies, voters are more concerned about immediate economic hardship than successful macroeconomic and foreign affairs policies. Like the Socialists in 1994, the AYD promised a kinder, gentler reform process. Third, modern campaigning has come to Hungary. Taking a page from the success of the right in Poland, AYD leader Viktor Orban used the media to portray the HSP as the holdovers from the past that were keeping a new generation from taking power. Also, in contrast to other parties whose campaigns were premised on telling people what is good for them, the AYD appealed directly to the populace. Fourth, and perhaps most significant, has been the increase in support for nationalist parties. For the first time, an extremist party (the HJLP) gained parliamentary representation. With large Hungarian minorities in surrounding states, this could be destabilizing development for the region. While the voting turnout dropped from 68 percent in 1994 to 57 percent in 1998, the number of parties involved and the peaceful change in power shows a multiparty political system has become well entrenched.

In contrast to centralized control of parties in Bulgaria, Poland, and Russia, Hungarian parties are dominated by their parliamentary leadership.

VIKTOR ORBAN (1963–)

Viktor Orban first emerged as a key player in Hungarian politics on June 16, 1989. Then a 26-year-old long-haired dissident two years out of university, he addressed a crowd of 300,000 at the ceremonial reinternment of Imre Nagy, who had been executed in the Soviet Union in 1958. Orban was one of the first to speak after the fall of the USSR and openly condemn the "enormous historical mistake of the Soviet Union in 1958."

The first "truly popular, charismatic leader," Orban knew Hungarians were "hungering to fill what they sensed to be a crucial void in national life." He saw the "demographic challenge" that Hungary's population posed to the economy and spoke of tax breaks for children and stressed the family, not the individual, as an economic unit. Orban believed that changing the status quo required a transformation in the mentality of the socialized culture. At the age of 35 a lawyer and leader of the AYD, Orban became prime minister after the 1998 elections. While his populist rhetoric is appealing to the average Hungarian, it is likely to cause problems with neighboring states and slow economic development and integration with the West.

This situation is similar to the "electoral professional model" that is standard in Western Europe. While this situation allows the MPs more policy-making autonomy, it also fosters the perception that politics is the province of the elite. This has limited political involvement, slowing the development of democratic institutions.

Nongovernmental Elites

After 1945, the HSWP eliminated nongovernmental groups not associated with the Communist Party. However, some restrictions were lifted with the implementation of the NEM. The government gave trade unions the right to veto collective contracts but not to take independent action. Since 1989, nongovernmental elite groups have increased in size and influence, thus affecting policy making and implementation. The most influential groups are businesses, criminal organizations, and the Roman Catholic church.

Business groups can be roughly divided into two factions: the old "captains of industry" and the new entrepreneurs. The former group is the most powerful and includes the factory and industrial directors from the old regime. Since the state has only started to develop the legal and administrative apparatus to control the economy, this group has been able to gain a monopoly in certain sectors. Their power has been heightened by their ties with other former members of the *nomenklatura* who have been made advisers and consultants to the HSP government. As in the other states in the region, these links have led to numerous political scandals. In the largest scandal in postcommunist Hungary, a number of top officials, including two former Socialist Industrial and Trade ministers, were accused of using their influence to help companies with links to the HSP obtain contracts in closed ministry tenders. When the opposition initiated a parliamentary probe of the affair, the Socialist minister in charge of the secret services put an eighty-year stamp of secrecy on various documents pertaining to the case.[46] This scandal shows what can happen when an inefficient and unaccountable state administration is combined with economic change.

Although an emerging group of entrepreneurs is starting to challenge the old elite, for the most part this group has eschewed politics to focus on personal gain. However, this situation seems likely to change in the future as they become involved in politics to protect their newly acquired power and influence.

In another regional similarity, the demise of a strong state apparatus and open borders have unleashed a torrent of organized crime. Although not as powerful as their Bulgarian or Russian counterparts, the Hungarian mafia not only "dabbles in traditional rackets such as drugs, prostitution, gambling and extortion, but they have also earned millions of dollars smuggling heating oil, stolen cars, and even nuclear materials."[47] As a result of its central geographical location, Budapest has become a criminal battle ground for Russians, Ukrainians, Albanians, and Hungarians. This situation helped double the number of crimes between 1991 and 1995. During the same period, the police budget dropped by a third. According to official figures, two-thirds of police families live below the poverty line. Unsurprisingly, demoralized police often succumb to bribery and corruption. The police's inability to fight growing corruption and organized crime—blamed for a series of murders and bombings at the end of 1996—prompted the Interior Minister to fire the country's four top police officials.[48]

Another important actor is the Roman Catholic church. With over 70 percent of the population professing to be Roman Catholic, the church has historically played a significant role in the development of the Hungarian polity. Until the end of World War II, the church owned two-thirds of the property in Hungary, including 3,000 schools that educated over half of the country's schoolchildren. After the communist takeover, the property and schools of the Church were confiscated and/or nationalized. In an attempt to strengthen government legitimacy, the government began to give the church more freedom in the 1960s. Nevertheless, an aging Catholic hierarchy and government harassment limited the church's influence. Thus, in contrast to Poland, the Church was not a focal point for opposition to the regime.

The liberalization of society after 1989 and a new generation of church leaders has led to an upsurge in religious participation. Today's Catholic leaders are making a concentrated effort to reenter the public sphere. The church has taken the role of "renewing the country morally, awakening social solidarity, easing the cares of the downtrodden and preserving cultural values."[49] As a result, the church is gaining political clout. This can be seen in an agreement between the Vatican and the HSP government that returned, or provided compensation for, buildings and property seized by the communists. More significantly, the agreement also restored church jurisdiction over its extensive private school network. The concordat also stipulated that church-run schools are eligible for the same subsidies as public schools and allows taxpayers to earmark 1 percent of their tax returns for a church.[50] This situation is not unusual in Europe. In contrast to the United States, in most countries the church and state are not separated. This is the result of a widespread belief that sociopolitical and welfare activities of the church are beneficial to the social order. As an example, because it performs a "public task," the Catholic University—as well as the university of the Hungarian Reformed Church—are financed from the state budget.

In the future it seems likely that church influence will decline as society becomes more secularized. Only about 15 percent of Hungarians identify themselves as ardent followers of any church and only 3 percent of Hungarian children attend a religious school.[51] In addition, the most devoted believers are the rural elderly over 50 years old. There is also a lingering resentment against the church because it was given back its property while other groups had to settle for monetary compensation.

THE GENERAL PUBLIC

In contrast to Western democracies, declining living standards have not fostered an increase in political involvement. This is the result of a commonly held belief that average citizens cannot affect policy and can be seen in the fact that fewer than 5 percent of the population are active members of political parties. This situation is in part the result of too many promises that parties were unable to fulfill. Thus, parties of both the right and left have been discredited. In addition, since people were forced to join a political organization under the old regime, many have decided to abstain from active participation today.

This phenomenon has important implications for the future development of the Hungarian polity. If political parties cannot implement electoral platforms, not only will political apathy increase, but the legitimacy of regime could be questioned. This in turn might allow political opportunists to gain power. For example, Istvan Csurka, the nationalist leader of the Hungarian Justice and Life Party, has gained prominence through his criticism of government policies. By refusing to go into details about his own policy prescriptions, Csurka was able to ride a growing wave of discontent to gain parliamentary representation.

Modes of Influence

As the number of people choosing to become formally involved in politics decreases, less formal means of participation are becoming more popular. One means by which the general public can influence the government is through interest groups.

Since 1989, interest groups have played an increasingly important role in the polity. With over 2.5 million members, trade unions have influenced government decisions by sending representatives to the Council for Reconciliation of Interests. This council brings together government officials, employers, and workers. As a result of such meetings, the government and the largest trade unions signed a social contract to prevent strikes. In return, the government agreed to reduce value-added taxes (VAT), raise the minimum wage, increase pensions, and provide loans to fund scholarships for higher education. The three largest trade unions are allied with major political parties—the National Council of Hungarian Trade Unions with the HSP, the League of Independent Democratic Unions with the AFD, and the National Federation of Workers' Councils with the HDF. These alignments allow them to directly influence the policy-making process.

The most powerful union is the National Council of Hungarian Trade Unions. The successor of the former communist-led National Council of Trade Unions, it won 43 percent of the vote in a countrywide election which allowed people to decide which union would represent them on the new joint union-employer councils that manage health care and pension funds. Trade unions can also indirectly influence the government by organizing strikes and demonstrations. As the deputy secretary of labor grudgingly admitted: "after the taxi driver's strike [in November 1990], the behavior of the government changed slightly."[52] However, since the largest and most influential unions are comprised of state employees, the declining number of state enterprises will weaken the power of the unions in the future.

Another illustration of interest group influence is support for ethnic Magyars outside Hungary's borders. Nationalist groups have used constitutional provisions that recognize Hungary's responsibilities to Magyars living outside Hungary to change government policy. For example, in spite of the government's stated intention to sign a bilateral treaty with Romania, it initially failed as a result of pressure from nationalist groups who wanted guarantees of minority rights included in the treaty.

In addition to voting for political parties, the general public can influence policy by voting in national referendums. To propose a referendum, 100,000 signatures must be gathered. This list is then submitted to the Constitutional Committee in the Parliament, which decides whether or not the referendum violates the Constitution or international treaty obligations and whether it should be held. If a referendum is requested by 200,000 citizens, it is mandatory and the results binding on Parliament. However, since the Constitution cannot be changed as a result of a referendum, only certain issues can be decided. While these provisions enhance governmental stability, they also limit the ability of the electorate to use a referendum to change governmental policy. Thus, voting is one of the few avenues available for the general public to become directly involved in politics.

While the lack of direct interest group involvement might be considered negative in the American context, it is not abnormal or a threat to democracy in most European states. As can be seen in the Hungarian Reconciliation Council, societal interests are usually taken into account informally during the policy-making process.

POLICY MAKING AND IMPLEMENTATION

Prior to 1989, although the National Assembly was the highest constitutional organ of state authority, it held only a few short sessions each year. Its deputies simply enacted policies already decided on by the HSWP leadership. When the Assembly was not in session, authority was vested in the Presidential Council, whose chair was also head of state. Although the council had numerous constitutional prerogatives, since its members could not be appointed to the ministries, the council did not play any role in actual policy making. As in other socialist states, this structure was merely a facade for the real policy maker, the HSWP Politburo and its administrative body, the Secretariat.

Today the government (i.e., the prime minister) is the chief policy maker. Although the Constitution allows the president, parliamentary committees, or any member of parliament to propose legislation, in contrast to Bulgaria the government has been the main initiator of legislation. To date, neither the president nor parliamentary committees have used their power to submit bills. However, some individual members have introduced legislation. For example, an AYD deputy drafted a bill to supplement the privatization law. It was adopted by a large majority, thus correcting the problems with the poorly written privatization law.[53] Generally, party discipline ensures individual MPs do not submit legislation.

There are four phases in policy formulation. First, a bill is written by specialists in the ministry that will have jurisdiction over the enacted law. It then goes to the cabinet for discussion. If the bill is approved by the cabinet, the government submits the bill to parliament. The draft legislation is first sent to the parliamentary Committee of Chairs, a group comprised of all committee chairs that decides which committee the bill will go to. As in Bulgaria, a bill in Hungary is submitted directly to the appropriate committee before it is officially introduced into the Assembly.

In committee the bill is researched, amended, and revised. The committee then decides whether the bill is ready for the first reading or whether it should be sent back to the ministry. The chairperson of the committee has a great deal of influence over the fate of the bill, with the power to allow interest groups and/or individuals to give testimony on a bill. However, in contrast to the United States, Hungarian parliamentary committees cannot shelve or reject a bill or hold public hearings. If a bill is in trouble, it is usually withdrawn for "further study" before a formal committee vote.

When this process is complete, the bill is submitted to the full parliament with the committee's nonbinding opinion on whether or not it should be enacted. MPs receive a copy of the bill at least twenty-one days before the parliamentary debate on the bill. At this first reading, amendments can be proposed. The MPs then vote to either continue debate, reject the bill, or return the bill to committee for revision. If the bill is accepted for further debate, only MPs who have registered prior to the session with the chairman of the parliament may debate. This measure was adopted to restrict debate to those interested specifically in its content. However, cabinet ministers and the chairperson of the committee where the bill originated may speak at any time.

If amendments are added to the original bill, the bill is returned to committee. If a majority of the committee agrees, the amendments are added to the bill. The bill is then returned to the Assembly for its second reading. A vote is held on all amendments supported by the government. However, opposition parties can ask to have any amendment voted on separately. While this process delays the adoption of laws, it also helps prevent vague or poorly written bills from becoming law. If a bill makes it out of committee, it usually becomes law because of the government's majority in the Assembly. A quorum of at least half the MPs must be present for the vote.

After voting on the amendments at the second reading the bill is shelved for a week. During this period, the Constitutional Committee can evaluate the bill to ensure it is constitutional. A final vote is taken on the whole bill, and the draft legislation is sent to the president for endorsement and promulgation. Like the French president, he can either return the bill to the Parliament for reconsideration or send it to the Constitutional Court for review. As in Bulgaria, the president's "veto" only delays implementation of the bill for fifteen days—five if requested by the speaker of Assembly.

Policy-Making Influences

While the formal policy-making process is straightforward, it is only one component of a much larger process. Numerous other factors also have an impact on the development of state policy. Perhaps the most important is the absence or presence of a governmental majority in the National Assembly. The first Hungarian government (1989–1994) was a coalition of the HDF, ISP, and CDPP parties. Disagreements within this coalition illustrate the limitations of a multiparty government. When the MDF and the ISP could not agree on a privatization program, the ISP withdrew from the coalition. If a majority of ISP MPs had not defied their party and continued to support the coalition, the government would have fallen.

A similar problem is the exaggerated influence of small parties that are members of the coalition. Since their withdrawal from the government might cause elections to be held, small parties wield much more influence than their electoral support would suggest. As an illustration, in 1992 the CDPP said it was changing its role within the coalition. Spokespersons declared the party would follow its own policy and play the role of an opposition group within the coalition, reserving the right to criticize government policies and to submit its own draft laws. The CDPP thought this move would allow it to separate itself from the growing dissatisfaction with the government. Since the HDF-led government would fall without its support, there was little the government could do.

Coalition governments also give the parliament more influence than if the government had a one-party majority. During the first government, when the coalition parties disagreed, they left it to the parliament to decide issues on which they could not agree. Although coalition governments incorporate more societal interests, they also complicate and restrict policy making. However, when compared to the Suchocka coalition government in

Poland (1992–1993), the first Hungarian coalition government was able to pass numerous policy initiatives. This was the result of the HDF electoral dominance within the coalition—it had won 43 percent of the vote. In contrast, the Suchocka government was comprised of six parties, all with similar electoral support.

Opposition parties also influence the policy-making process. They can submit draft legislation, amend government bills, and they can also use the floor of the National Assembly as a forum to criticize the government. These roles allow them some influence over the government. More significantly, when bills require a two-thirds majority (e.g., constitutional amendments), opposition parties can have a decisive influence on policy. As an illustration, proposed reforms of the armed forces and police were blocked when the HSP government could not muster the requisite support.

Although the president has no constitutional policy-making role and was envisioned as a neutral figure "above politics," President Goncz has played a very active role in the polity. He influenced government policy by refusing to dismiss the heads of the state-owned radio and television stations as Prime Minister Antall had requested. In addition, at the behest of the opposition, on a number of occasions Goncz submitted legislation passed by the government to the Constitutional Court for review. Overall, however, the Hungarian president—like his or her Bulgarian counterpart—has much less influence in the area of policy making than their Polish or Russian counterparts.

A final state institution involved in policy making is the Constitutional Court. It influences policy in three ways. First, it can set deadlines for the passage of legislation. Second, it defines the powers of various governmental organs. Finally, it considers the constitutionality of laws. In performing these functions, it often becomes involved in political disputes between the government and the president.

Nongovernmental actors also influence policy formulation. After a ministry has drafted a bill and before it goes to the cabinet, "concerned" groups are often asked for their opinion. Groups can also try to persuade MPs to offer amendments to bills during their first parliamentary reading.

Case Study: "Minorities Law"

An examination of the passage of a bill on minorities will help illustrate the policy-making process. As a result of the importance and the sensitivity of the minority issue, the government created a Roundtable on National and Ethnic Minorities. The Roundtable decided the best way to protect minority rights was through legislation.

Several drafts of the bill were written by different institutions and organizations. Three of them originated within the government—in the Ministry of Justice, the Office for National and Ethnic Minorities, and the Secretariat for National and Ethnic Minorities. The Roundtable also proposed its own draft. Representatives from these groups prepared a joint draft that was sent to the Government Codification Committee to ensure it was in accordance with the Constitution and other laws.

The government submitted the bill to the parliament, where it was sent to the National Assembly's Committee on Human Rights, Minorities, and Religious Affairs. Within the committee, discussions and reconciliation of disputed points involved all six parliamentary parties, the Office for National and Ethnic Minorities, and members of the Roundtable. After a consensus was reached, the committee sent the bill to the Assembly for debate and a vote. Since all political parties had been involved in its creation, it was easily approved. Although the minority law represents a unique case in which all major interests reached an agreement, its passage helps illustrate the steps involved in the policy-making process.

Case Study: "The Land Referendum"

Although Hungary was one of the first CEE states to privatize state property, a law that prevented Hungarian businesses and foreigners from owning agricultural land remains in force. To conform with European Union law, the Horn government proposed ending this exclusion. To thwart this move, opponents—which included the farmer's unions, agricultural producers, and opposition political parties—gathered the 200,000 signatures necessary to force a binding, countrywide referendum. Partially as a result of an extensive media campaign, opinion polls showed 75 percent of the population opposed allowing foreigners to own land. To head off this referendum, the government initiated its own land ownership referendum.

On behalf of the opposition political parties, the ombudsman requested that the Constitutional Court determine which referendum had priority. The Court decided unanimously that a citizen referendum has preference over a referendum initiated by the government. This forced the government to hold an urgent debate. To derail the opposition, the government submitted the citizens' referendum to the Parliament's Constitutional Committee to determine its legality. The Committee decided the proposed questions would violate the country's international treaty obligations, specifically the GATT and Hungary's Association Agreement with the EU, and thus recommended the referendum be voided. In a 223 to 62 vote, the National Assembly decided not to hold the referendum.[54] This example shows that in contrast to Russia, both informal and formal actors and structures influence policy making in Hungary.

Policy Implementation

Under the communist regime, although they had no constitutional power, the HSWP Secretariat and individual members of the Politburo were responsible for ensuring party policy was implemented. Obviously, this is no longer the case. Policy implementation now takes place at both the central and local governmental levels, largely free of political oversight. At the state level, ministries are responsible for policy implementation. To perform this function, they issue the necessary regulations, decrees, ordinances, and resolutions to ensure laws are implemented. In addition to the thirteen ministers that comprise the Council of Ministers, there are also ministers without portfolio whose responsibilities reflect key issues such as privatization, relations with international organizations, and the rights of national or ethnic minorities.

Another policy implementor is the state secretaries. These professional, nonpartisan civil servants serve as the executive directors of the ministries. As in the United Kingdom, they are appointed for an indefinite period and are meant to ensure bureaucratic professionalism and continuity. In addition to the ministries, the first two Hungarian governments created additional administrative bodies to create and implement specific policies. Examples include the Office of Taxes and Financial Control, the Hungarian News Agency, Supervision of Consumer Protection, and State Banking Supervision.

The central government also has increasingly numerous field agencies that operate at the regional and county level. Examples include agriculture and water management directorates at the regional level and transportation supervision, labor centers, and land offices at the county level. Finally, local governments also participate in policy implementation. Local administrative functions and implement national policies. In summary, although the Council of Ministers is technically responsible for policy implementation, in practice the bureaucracy and local governments ensure policies are implemented.

While the administrative structure and responsibilities are clearly defined, there are numerous impediments to policy formation. Perhaps the most significant is an ineffective bureaucracy. Since laws usually leave room for interpretation, the bureaucracy is an essential element in policy execution. As in the other states in the region, bureaucratic inefficiency often delays policy implementation. An emerging policy implementation problem is the proliferation of central government agencies. Since they are created on an ad hoc basis, these agencies often have overlapping administrative responsibilities, making it difficult to coordinate policy implementation and ensure bureaucratic accountability.

Policy implementation can also be affected by nongovernmental groups. Under the old regime, people were either organized in mass organizations closely allied with the HSWP or did not participate in public life. As a result, there was no tradition of representing independent interests or exerting influence on the government. Today, new organizations have been created to try to influence policy. For example, a series of meetings between Hungarian minority leaders and Prime Minister Horn influenced the way in which bilateral treaties regarding minority issues with Slovakia, Romania, and Yugoslavia were implemented. In addition to ensuring that governmental policy is enforced, interest groups bring people closer to the actual process of government. Thus as in most countries, actual policy implementation is often a long and continuous struggle.

CONCLUSION

In contrast to Bulgaria, Poland, and Russia, the process of change in Hungary has been one of gradual evolution, not radical change. This is the result of a societal consensus that does not exist in other states in the region. Although a majority of Hungarians are dissatisfied with the economic and political situation, in contrast to many other states they do not question the existence of a civil society, democratic institutions, a market economy, or a law-based state. Therefore, and with Poland a close second, Hungary has made the most progress in the creation of a new polity.

Civil Society

In the ten years since the change in regime, a well-developed civil society has emerged. Citizens have the right to create independent organizations, and there is a free and open media and freedom of assembly and demonstration. Therefore, Freedom House ranks Hungary a 2 in civil rights. As in Bulgaria and Russia, however, since only a small number of people were involved in the transformation, the majority of the population remains politically uninvolved. This is the result of factors that in varying degrees affect all the states in the region. First is the lack of democratic experience or political participation. Second, in an era of declining living standards, people are more concerned with surviving than in becoming involved in politics. Third, numerous corruption scandals have lessened the authority of government.[55]

A more significant problem is the lack of societal responsibility. In a legacy from the past, people still believe the government will solve all their problems. This view is fostered by the patriarchal manner in which the contemporary government operates. It has not done a good job of explaining the necessity of reform or the importance of citizen participation. These are not insurmountable problems and are likely to solve themselves over time.

Democratic Institutions/Political Rights

Along with Poland, Hungary has been the most successful state in creating new political institutions and guaranteeing political rights. Hungary has a democratic, multiparty system with free and fair elections. Nevertheless, as a result of simply adding amendments to the old Constitution rather than drafting a new one that reflects the numerous changes in the polity, the roles and responsibilities of political institutions are not well defined. As an illustration, the Constitution gives five entities—the National Assembly, the president, the Council of National Defense, the government and the Minister of Defense—the authority to "direct the armed forces." As a consequence, many key issues become embroiled in political battles. When this situation is coupled with political divisions in the parliament, a nonelected president has much more influence than his limited constitutional mandate would suggest.

This and other minor problems notwithstanding, Hungary has an open, functioning constitutional system. Thus Freedom House gives Hungary its highest rating (1) in the development of democratic institutions and political rights.

Market Economy

Compared with the other states in the region, Hungarian economic performance has been impressive. Although GDP fell by more than 20 percent between 1989 and 1993, the economy has since posted strong growth rates. As a result of the enactment of economic and painful welfare reforms, Hungary has one of the region's lowest inflation rates and a burgeoning private sector. Thus a market economy is well entrenched and is accepted by most people. The EBRD ranks the Hungarian economy as follows:

1. Privatization and restructuring of enterprises: 3.8
2. Competitiveness and openness of the market: 3.6
3. Ability of financial institutions to collect and channel savings to productive investments: 3.75
4. Extensiveness and effectiveness of legal rules on investment: 4

With a 3.8 average, Hungary has the most market-oriented economy in Central and Eastern Europe.

Rule of Law

As in other CEE states, under the communist regime laws were used to restrict freedom. However, since 1989 only the Czech Republic has made more progress in creating a law-based state. With a 5.18 ranking, Transparency International ranks Hungary 28th in its 52-country survey. This is an improvement on its 4.86 rating in 1996.

Nevertheless, there are still threats to the rule of law. One is the failure of postcommunist governments to change traditional governmental practices. They continue to place political considerations over professional ones in the appointment of key government personnel. As soon as the Horn government took power in 1994, media chiefs quickly dismissed or silenced a number of reporters on the grounds they were politically biased pawns of the former government. The government also appointed new radio and television directors without first reaching an agreement with opposition parties, despite the HSP's insistence on consensus during the previous HDF government. Thus the "return of apparatchiks could be a signal that Hungary's democratic transformation might be losing momentum and that the communist style of client-patron relationships and paternalistic business practices could be revived."[56]

Another threat to the rule of law is the societal frustration accompanying economic hardships. These factors have combined to foster the rise of extremist groups.[57] The electoral success of the HJLP in the 1998 elections suggests that until living standards improve for a larger share of the population, extremist messages will find an audience.

Why has Hungary been so much more successful than Bulgaria and Russia in creating a new polity? One important feature seems to be the previous links and contact with the West. Long before the end of the communist regime, both Hungary and Poland had extensive cultural and economic links with the West. Although with the exception of market economics they had little experience with a civil society, political rights, or the rule of law, at least they had experience with states whose systems were predicated on these ideas.

Another possible explanation is breaking the hold of the previous elite. In contrast to Bulgaria and especially Russia, Hungary has had a much more diverse group of political leaders since the fall of the communist regime. This weakens the influence of the old *nomenklatura,* providing the framework for institutional and economic development.

Partly as a result of Hungary's small size, Hungarians seem to have decided they needed to enact reforms quickly if they wanted to remain economically and politically independent. As noted earlier, freedom from foreign influence has been a dominant theme in the development of the Hungarian state.

International Ramifications

The collapse of CMEA and the Warsaw Pact left Hungary economically and militarily vulnerable. In response, the Hungarian parliament adopted "The Basic Principles of the Security Policy of the Republic of Hungary" in 1993.[58] Significantly, this policy was adopted with the support of all six parliamentary parties. They also agreed that to protect state interests, foreign policy should be bipartisan. This and other documents form the basis for Hungary's major foreign policy goals: integration into Western Europe's political, economic, and military structures; ensuring the rights of Hungarian minorities in neighboring states; regional cooperation; and increasing contacts with former Soviet republics.

Hungary's number one foreign policy priority is to become part of Western Europe. Most people link the creation of a new polity with membership in the EU and NATO. In December 1991, Hungary signed an association agreement with the European Union, becoming the first country in the region to do so. This agreement created a free trade zone and, more important, established the institutional framework for future EU membership. For example, a parliamentary European Community Affairs Committee was created solely to prepare legislative work relating to EU relations and future membership. In addition, a government committee ensures Hungarian legislation is compatible with the 35,000 pages of EU laws. While it is mainly an economic document, the EU agreement facilitated political stability. It also shows the domestic impact of international relations in an interdependent world.

Militarily, after the change in regime Hungary initiated bilateral contacts with NATO countries. In 1992, Hungary permitted the use of its airspace by NATO's AWACS planes monitoring the U.N.-imposed flight ban over Bosnia. In 1994, Hungary became a member of NATO's "Partnership for Peace" program. This program facilitated consultations, joint military operations, and the sharing of information between NATO and the signatory countries. As an illustration, Hungary formed a joint brigade with Italy and Slovenia. Participation in this program lead to Hungary to become—along with the Czech Republic and Poland—the first former Soviet allies to join NATO in 1998.

While this Western-oriented policy has at times been tested by the Horn and Orban governments—they both suggested Hungary renegotiate the terms of its European Union associate membership—there is still widespread societal support for Western integration. This support can be seen in the results of a November 1997 referendum on NATO membership in which 85 percent voted affirmatively.

Another key aspect of Hungarian foreign policy is ensuring the rights of the 3 million ethnic Hungarians living in neighboring states. Hungary has tried to negotiate treaties with its neighbors "to support what it considers to be the legitimate demands of the Magyar minorities."[59] While Hungary has signed treaties guaranteeing minority rights with most of its neighbors—Slovenia, Croatia, Austria and the Ukraine—this issue was a stumbling block in developing economic and political relations with Romania and Slovakia. While a landmark 1996 treaty renouncing all territorial claims and pledging to resolve outstanding minority issues improved relations with Romania, Hungarian-Slovak relations are still strained by this issue.

A third objective of Hungarian foreign policy is to increase regional cooperation. Along with Austria, Czechoslovakia, and Italy, Hungary founded the "Quadragonale" in 1989. Later expanding to nine countries and renamed the Central European Initiative, this organization promoted cooperation through political consultations and economic initiatives among member states. Hungary was also a founding member of the Visegrad Group. This organization, which includes the Czech Republic, Poland, and Slovakia, was created to increase economic cooperation and coordinate efforts to join the EU. Hungary views membership in regional organizations as facilitating European integration, thus strengthening political stability throughout the region.

The final major foreign policy goal is increasing contacts with the independent republics of the former Soviet Union. Within this context, the Ukraine has become one of the pillars of Hungary's foreign policy toward the East.[60] As its immediate neighbor and an important connection with the other republics, Hungary has been quick to sign bilateral agreements which regulate their economic and political relations. It has also concluded culture, economic, minority rights, and security agreements with Russia.

Summary

Hungary has been in the vanguard of economic and political change in Central and Eastern Europe since 1989, peacefully making the transition from a communist to a democratic government. Unlike Bulgaria, Poland, and Russia, partially as a result of reforms initiated before the end of the communist regime, the Hungarian polity has not been plagued by frequent government changes and parliamentary stalemate. The Antall and Horn governments were the only ones in the region to complete their full terms of office. The smooth turnover of power following the death of Antall in 1993 and the election of a new governments in 1994 and 1998 points to the legitimacy of the regime. This legitimacy can also be seen in the notable performance of new democratic institutions and a more open society. Thus, not only does the regime have the support of the majority of the population, it also has the power to act.

Still, Hungary faces some challenges. At times it seems like two countries: an open, economically competitive one that is governed by the rule of law, and one where ties between businesses and the government are murky, civil servants take bribes, and almost everyone evades taxes. This split personality has fostered public alienation and led to significant dissatisfaction with the new regime. This can be seen in a lack of strong party identification, growing support for populist parties, and low voter turnout in parliamentary by-elections, several of which had to be conducted six to eight times before there was enough participation to be legally valid.

As in other former communist states, high expectations accompanying the demise of the old regime have yet to be realized. While this situation will cause problems in short term, it is unlikely they will have a long-term effect. In contrast to Bulgaria and Russia, private entrepreneurs provide a stable economic base in Hungary, limiting political extremism. Yet there is still a remote danger is that an increasingly apathetic public that believes it cannot influence economic or political policy will call into question the value of a pluralistic polity.

In spite of these problems, democratic institutions have been established, market reforms enacted, and political rights guaranteed. The stability of the polity and the societal consensus that guides it show that Hungary is well on its way to creating a modern democratic state.

TIMELINE

1944

December   Dominated by the Hungarian Communist Party (HCP), a provisional government is established in Debrecen.

1945

November   Smallholders' Party wins a majority of seats in parliamentary elections.

1946

February 1   The first democratic regime in Hungarian history, the Hungarian Republic, is declared.

1947

August   Matyas Rakosi becomes First Secretary of the HCP.

1948

June   The Hungarian Communist Party (HCP) and the Social Democratic Party (SDP) merge to create the Hungarian Workers' Party (HWP).

1949

January   Hungary joins the Council for Mutual Economic Assistance (CMEA).

August 20   A Soviet-style constitution is ratified and the country is renamed the Hungarian People's Republic. Sovietization begins.

1952

Rakosi is named prime minister.

1953

July   One of the leaders of the reformist wing of the HCP, Imre Nagy, becomes prime minister. To improve the economy, he initiates the New Economic Course (NEC).

1955

April   Rakosi forces Nagy to resign.

May   Hungary joins the Warsaw Pact.

1956

July 17   Rakosi is forced to resign as First Secretary of the HWP.

October 24   Demonstrations in support of Nagy lead to his reinstatement as prime minister.

October 25   To weaken Nagy's influence, Moscow gets Janos Kadar named First Secretary of the HWP.

November 1   Nagy announces Hungary's withdrawal from theWarsaw Pact and the creation of a new party, the Hungarian Socialist Workers' Party (HSWP).

November 4   The Soviet Union invades Hungary.

November 22	Nagy is captured by Soviet troops, deported to Romania, and later executed.
November 25	Kadar becomes First Secretary of the HSWP and begins a purge of Nagy's supporters.

1968

January	The New Economic Mechanism (NEM), a package of economic reforms, is introduced.

1982

More reforms are initiated. The formation of small private firms is legalized.

1983

New electoral law allows for multiple candidates in some elections.

1988

May	After 32 years in power, Kadar is replaced by Karoly Grosz as head of HSWP. He begins talks with opposition groups on ending the HSWP monopoly on power.

1990

April	In the first free elections since 1945, the Hungarian Democratic Forum (HDF) wins a plurality of seats in the National Assembly and forms a coalition government with the Smallholders and the Christian Democrats.
May	Jozsef Antall, chairman of HDF, becomes prime minister. Árpad Goncz, head of the Alliance of Free Democrats (AFD), is appointed president.
November	Hungary becomes the first Central and Eastern European country to be admitted into the Council of Europe.

1991

February	The Visegrad bloc, a regional trading group, is formed by Hungary, Poland, and Czechoslovakia.

1993

December	Peter Boross replaces Antall as prime minister.

1994

May	As a result of a deteriorating economy, the HDF is defeated in parliamentary elections. The Hungarian Socialist Party (HSP) gains a majority in the parliament.
July	Gyula Horn, former HSWP foreign minister and head of the HSP, becomes prime minister.

1995

February	Hungary signs the Council of Europe's Convention on the Protection of National Minorities.

1996

September   Hungary and Romania sign a landmark treaty normalizing the sta-
                   tus of the 1.6 million ethnic Romanians in Hungary.

1997

July 3   After a meeting of NATO leaders in Madrid, NATO extends an
                   invitation for membership to Hungary along with Poland and the
                   Czech Republic.

1998

May   Running a populist platform that promises an end to economic
                   hardship and portraying the HSP as the hand of the past, the AYD-
                   Hungarian Civic Party coalition wins a plurality in parliamentary
                   elections. AYD leader Viktor Orban becomes prime minister.

1999

February   Hungary joins NATO.

WEB SITES

Hungarian Constitution
http://www.uni-wuerzburg.de/law/hu__indx.html
The 1997 Constitution and other political information.

Prime Minister's Office
http://www.meh/hu/
The prime minister's website, with links to news and various ministries.

The Embassy of the Republic of Hungary in Washington, DC
http://www.hungaryemb.org/
Information on Hungary and links to Hungarian websites. Provided by the
Hungarian embassy in Washington, DC.

Hungarian Home Page
http://www.fsz.bme.hu/hungary/homepage.html
General information about the country, regions, cities, and towns. It also has
cultural information and a directory of Hungarian web sites.

Hungarian News Agency
http://www.mti.hu/mti_demo/homang.htm
Although most information here is fee based, some is free.

The Hungary Page
http://www.hungary.org/~hipcat/
News, history, a list of famous Hungarians, and links to related sites.

HunOR: Hungarian Online Resources from U. of Maryland
http://mineral.umd.edu/hunor/
Comprehensive directory of Hungarian-related web sites

WORKS CITED

Agh, Attila. "The Strength of Hungary's Weak President." *Transition* 13 Dec. 1996: 24–27.
—. "The Year of Polarization." *Magyarorszag politikai evkonyve*. Eds. Kurtan, Sandor, and Vass. Budapest: Demokracia Kutatsok Magyar Kozpontja Alapitvany, 1993: 55.
Andorka, Rudolf. "Institutional Changes and Intellectual Trends in Some Hungarian Social Sciences." *East European Politics and Society* 7 (1993): 74–108.
Bihari, Mihaly. "Political Style and Political Culture in Hungary in the Early 1990s." *Magyarorszag politikai evkonyve*. Eds. Kurtan, Sandor, and Vass. Budapest: Demokracia Kutatsok Magyar Kozpontja Alapitvany, 1993: 65.
Bunce, Valerie, and Maria Csanadi. "Uncertainty in the Transition: Post-Communism in Hungary." *East European Politics and Societies* 1 (1993): 244.
Csepely, Gyorgy, and Antal Orkeny. "From Unjust Equality to Just Inequality." *The New Hungarian Quarterly* 33 (1992): 71–76.
Demszky, Gabor. Mayor of Budapest. Personal interview. 25 June 1995.
Durst, Judith. "The Second Economy Flourishing More Than Ever." *Hungarian Quarterly* 34 (1993): 80.
Geiger, Ferenc. Mayor of the XXIII District of Budapest. Personal interview. 20 June 1995.
Hack, Peter. Member of Parliament (AFD). Personal Interview. 25 June 1998.
—. Personal interview. 22 June 1995.
Hungary. Ministry of Foreign Affairs. *The Hungarian Education System*. Budapest: Ministry of Foreign Affairs, 1996.
—. *The History of Hungary*. Budapest: Ministry of Foreign Affairs, 1996.
—. *Relations between Hungary and the European Union*. Budapest: Ministry of Foreign Affairs, 1995.
—. *The Basic Principles of National Defense in the Republic of Hungary*. Budapest: Ministry of Foreign Affairs, 1993.
—. *Program of the Government of the Republic of Hungary*. Budapest: Ministry of Foreign Affairs, 1992.
Jordan, Michael. "Organized Crime Sets Up Shop at the Crossroads of Europe." *Christian Science Monitor* 17 Dec. 1996: 7.
—. "Now-Secular Hungarians Reluctant to Return Schools to Church." *Christian Science Monitor* 9 Sept. 1996: 7.
Kenez, Peter. "Nationalism on the Rise in Hungary." *The New Leader* 21 Sept.1992: 6–12.
Linz, Juan, and Alfred Stepan. *Problems of Democratic Transition and Consolidation*. Baltimore: John Hopkins UP, 1996.
Oltay, Edith. "The Return of the Former Communists." *Transition* 30 Jan. 1995: 34–37.
—. "Hungary Attempts to Deal with Its Past." *RFL/RL Research Report* 30 April 1993: 6–10.
Reisch, Alfred. "Hungarian-Ukrainian Relations Continue to Develop." *RFE/RL Research Report* 16 Apr. 1993: 22–27.
—. "Hungary's Foreign Policy toward the East." *RFE/RL Research Report* 9 Apr. 1993: 39–48.
—. "Hungary Pursues Integration with the West." *RFE/RL Research Report* 16 March 1993: 36.
—. "Roundtable: Hungary's Parliament in Transition." *RFL/RL Research Report* 4 Dec. 1992: 27–35.

Rueschemeyer, Marilyn. "Ongoing Transformations: Women in the Politics of Post-Communist Societies." *AAASS NewsNet* March 1997: 7–8.

Szabo, Charlie. "Suicides Rise as Downer Season Nears." *Budapest Sun* 19 Dec. 1996–January 8, 1997: A1+.

Szilagyi, Zsofia. "A Year of Scandals and Resignations in Hungary." *Transition* 7 Feb. 1997: 14–16.

—. "Shady Dealings and Slow Privatization Plague Hungarian Media." *Transition* 18 Oct. 1996: 44–45.

Taylor, A.J.P. *The Habsburg Monarchy, 1809–1918*. Chicago: Chicago UP, 1992.

United Nations Development Project. *Human Development Report*. Oxford: Oxford UP, 1997.

Urwin, Peter. "Defeated, Reviving and Restored." *Hungarian Quarterly* 34 (1993): 86.

World Health Organization. *Suicide Statistics*. Geneva: World Health Orgnaization, 1996.

ENDNOTES

1. Marilyn Rueschemeyer, "Ongoing Transformations: Women in the Politics of Postcommunist Societies," *AAASS NewsNet*, March 1997, pp. 7–8.

2. "Suicide Statistics," *World Health Organization*, 1996.

3. "Suicides Rise as Downer Season Nears," *Budapest Sun*, December 19, 1996–January 8, 1997, p. A3.

4. This included cutting maternity leave from two years to four months, eliminating automatic family allowances, ending free medical care, introducing fees for higher education, and raising the retirement age from 55 years for women and 60 for men to 62 years for both men and women. Constitutional Watch, *East European Constitutional Review*, Fall 1996, p. 14.

5. *OMRI Annual Survey: 1995*, p. 38.

6. Szonja Szelenyi, Ivan Szelenyi, and Imre Kovach, "The Fragmented Hungarian Elites: Circulation in Politics, Reproduction in Economy," in Ivan Szelenyi, Edmund Wnuk-Lipinski, and Donald Treiman, eds., "Circulation of Elites? Old and New Elites in Post-Communist Society," unpublished ms. Cited in Juan Linz and Alfred Stepan, *Problems of Democratic Transition and Consolidation* (Baltimore: John Hopkins University Press, 1996), p. 309.

7. United Nations Development Project (UNDP), *Human Development Report* (Oxford: Oxford University Press, 1997).

8. *Relations between Hungary and the European Union* (Budapest: Ministry of Foreign Affairs, 1995).

9. *OMRI Daily Report*, February 19, 1997.

10. A. J. P. Taylor, *The Habsburg Monarchy, 1809–1918* (Chicago: University of Chicago Press, 1992), p. 1.

11. *The History of Hungary* (Budapest: Ministry of Foreign Affairs, 1992).

12. An irredentist foreign policy is dedicated to recovering territory historically or ethnically related to one state but possessed by another.

13. The HSP government was caught tapping telephones and opening the mail of opposition parties.

14. The 1100th anniversary of the settlement of the Carpathian basin by Hungarian tribes and the fortieth anniversary of the unsuccessful 1956 revolution.

15. Zsofia Szilagyi, "A Year of Scandals and Resignations in Hungary," *Transition*, February 7, 1997, p. 14.

16. While observing question hour in the National Assembly, the author was amazed by the level of civility compared to that observed in Bulgaria, Poland, and Russia. My host told me

that Hungarians would never accept the viciousness that characterizes parliamentary questioning in other states.

17. "Program of the Government of the Republic of Hungary," (Budapest: Ministry of Foreign Affairs, 1992).

18. Surveys show that people attribute poverty to unfair distribution and are suspicious of the very rich. See Gyorgy Csepely and Antal Orkeny, "From Unjust Equality to Just Inequality," *The New Hungarian Quarterly* 33, 1992, pp. 71–76.

19. In Poland the percentage was 64 percent and in Russia, 81 percent. Bruszt, 91.

20. Rudolf Andorka, "Institutional Changes and Intellectual Trends in Some Hungarian Social Sciences," *East European Politics and Society* 7, 1993, pp. 74–108.

21. *The Hungarian Education System* (Budapest: Ministry of Foreign Affairs, 1996).

22. *The Economist,* April 2, 1997.

23. Zsofia Szilagyi, "Shady Dealings and Slow Privatization Plague Hungarian Media," *Transition,* October 18, 1996, p. 44.

24. Szilagyi, "Shady Dealings," p. 45.

25. Constitution Watch, *East European Constitutional Review,* Winter 1996, p. 12.

26. Attila Agh, "The Year of Polarization," in Kurtan, Sandor, and Vass, eds., *Magyarorszag politikai evkonyve* (Budapest: Demokracia Kutatsok Magyar Kozpontja Alapitvany, 1993), p. 55.

27. Peter Urwin, "Defeated, Reviving and Restored," *The Hungarian Quarterly* 34, 1993, p. 86.

28. Judit Durst, "The Second Economy Flourishing More Than Ever," *The Hungarian Quarterly* 34, 1993, p. 80.

29. Dr. Peter Hack, chair of the Parliamentary Committee on Constitutional and Judicial Affairs. Personal interview. Budapest, Hungary, June 22, 1995.

30. Personal interview. Budapest, Hungary, June 21, 1998.

31. Ferenc Geiger, mayor of the XXIII District of Budapest. Personal interview. Budapest, Hungary, June 20, 1995.

32. Joachim Hesse, ed., *Administrative Transformation in Central and Eastern Europe* (Oxford: Blackwell Publishers, 1993), p. 85.

33. Dr. Gabor Demszky, mayor of Budapest. Personal interview. Budapest, Hungary, June 25, 1995.

34. Constitutional Watch, *East European Constitutional Review,* Winter 1997, p. 15.

35. While Bulgaria also has a parliamentary regime, its deep political divisions have prevented it sharing this parliamentary attribute.

36. For example, the Environmental Ministry has two secretaries and the Defense Ministry has four.

37. "Constitutional Watch," *East European Constitutional Review,* Summer 1998, p. 14.

38. Attila Agh, "The Strength of Hungary's Weak President," *Transition,* December 13, 1996, p. 26.

39. Edith Oltay, "Hungary Attempts to Deal with Its Past," *RFL/RL Research Report,* April 30, 1993, p. 8.

40. Constitutional Watch, *East European Constitutional Review,* Winter 1997, p. 16.

41. Cited in Valerie Bunce and Maria Csanadi, "Uncertainty in the Transition: Post-Communism in Hungary," *East European Politics and Societies,* Spring 1993, p. 244.

42. In 1994, the chair of the Constitutional Court, the chief prosecutor, and three ministers were all graduates of the Law University.

43. *The Basic Principles of National Defense in the Republic of Hungary* (Budapest: Ministry of Foreign Affairs, 1993).

44. Mihaly Bihari, "Political Style and Political Culture in Hungary in the Early 1990s," in Kurtan, Sandor, and Vass, eds., *Magyarorszag politikai evkonyve* (Budapest: Demokracia Kutatsok Magyar Kozpontja Alapitvany, 1993), p. 65.

45. Agh, interview.

46. Szilagyi, "Scandals," p. 16.

47. "Organized Crime Sets Up Shop at the Crossroads of Europe," *Christian Science Monitor*, December 17, 1996, p. 7.

48. Szilagyi, "Scandals," p. 14.

49. "Program of the Government of the Republic of Hungary."

50. *RFE/RL Newsline*, June 23, 1997.

51. Michael Jordan, "Now-Secular Hungarians Reluctant to Return Schools to Church," *Christian Science Monitor*, September 9, 1996, p. 7.

52. Bunce, p. 271.

53. Alfred Reisch, "Roundtable: Hungary's Parliament in Transition" *RFL/Research Report*, December 4, 1992, p. 31.

54. Constitution Watch, *East European Constitutional Review*, Fall, 1997, pp. 18–19. Peter Hack, Member of Parliament (AFD). Personal interview. Budapest, Hungary, June 25, 1998.

55. In an effort to combat this problem, in 1996 the parliament enacted new conflict-of-interest laws. Among the most comprehensive in the region, these laws prevent MPs from serving on boards or in managerial positions of companies in which state ownership exceeds 10 percent. MPs are also required to disclose their property, income, and business interest within thirty days of the beginning and the end of their terms.

56. Edith Oltay, "The Return of the Former Communists," *Transition*, January 30, 1995, p. 34.

57. Peter Kenez, "Nationalism on the Rise in Hungary," *The New Leader*, September 21, 1992, p. 6.

58. Alfred Reisch, "Hungary Pursues Integration with the West," *RFE/RL Research Report*, March 16, 1993, p. 36.

59. Alfred Reisch, "Hungary's Foreign Policy toward the East," *RFE/RL Research Report* April 9, 1993, p. 39.

60. Alfred Reisch, "Hungarian-Ukrainian Relations Continue to Develop," *RFE/RL Research Report* April 16, 1993, p. 22.

61. A 1997 public opinion poll found 67 percent of the respondents thought living standards were better under the Kadar government. More interesting, 23 percent said there was also more "democracy" in that period. The latter figure is higher than any successor government. *Budapest Nepszava*, February 10, 1997. Cited in *FBIS Daily Report*, February 10, 1997.

4

POLAND

INTRODUCTION

Second only to Russia in size and population, Poland has numerous unique characteristics that differentiate it from its neighbors. Its contemporary political system is the result of a history marked by excessive freedom, authoritarianism, invasions, and foreign domination. Poland has a democratic tradition that goes back to the sixteenth century. Although it was democracy only for the nobility, it was one of the most liberal governments in Europe. The Polish-Lithuanian Commonwealth featured a parliament in which every noble's interests were protected to the point where a decision could be not adopted if a single member objected. Eventually, this excessive freedom weakened the state, causing it to be partitioned by powerful neighbors.

Another democratic experiment followed the First World War. As before, democracy was broadly defined as even the smallest political parties were represented in the parliament. As a consequence of the subsequent instability, Marshal Josef Pilsudski led a coup in 1926, ruling as a virtual dictator until his death in 1935.

Following the demise of the communist regime in 1989, a new democratic system was created. A study of post-1989 political developments will help answer the question of whether the new polity will be able to overcome historical legacies that hinder economic and political development or whether a new period of authoritarianism is merely a matter of time. To date, the results have been mixed. In a break from the centralized communist regime, Poles went to the other extreme—legalized anarchy. As a result, twenty-nine political parties were represented in the 1991 parliament. This situation fostered six changes in government between 1989 and 1994, more than in Bulgaria, Hungary, or Russia. Paradoxically, Poland has made the most progress in transforming its economic system. Within only six years, it

had the highest economic growth rate in Central and Eastern Europe and is the only postsocialist economy that has surpassed its pre-transition GDP.

What explains this situation? First, there has been an almost unanimous agreement on the need to transform society. Despite their diverse views, most political parties agree on the need for economic and political reforms. After taking power in 1993, even the Socialists, in spite of lavish electoral promises, realized they could not afford to stop economic reforms. Another crucial factor is the realization that there is no alternative to cooperation if reforms are to be implemented. An example is the close working relationship between the government and trade unions. This relationship has greatly facilitated the implementation of reforms, leading to impressive economic growth.

The international environment has also influenced political developments in Poland. After the dissolution of the CMEA and the Warsaw Pact in the late 1980s, the state had to find its place in a reconstituted Europe. Poland's desire to become part of Western Europe has thus facilitated its democratic and economic development. Despite spectacular progress, the country faces many problems associated with simultaneously transforming the economic, political, and social foundations of the polity. As a result of its size, its position between East and West, and its bold experiment with "shock therapy," Poland retains a special significance in an examination of the Central and Eastern European landscape.

NATIONAL DATA

Geography

Despite changes across the region, the map of Poland has not changed since the late 1940s. This has been one of the longest periods of continuity in the last two hundred years of Polish history. There have, however, been major changes on the country's borders. Prior to 1989, Poland shared a border with only three states: Czechoslovakia, East Germany, and the Soviet Union. Today, none of these states exists. To the north and east lie three successor states to the USSR: Lithuania, Belarus, and the Russian enclave of Kaliningrad. To the southeast and south, Poland borders the Ukraine, Slovakia, and the Czech Republic. To the west, the Oder and Nysa rivers form the border with Germany. Poland's northern border is a 330–mile (528 kilometer) coastline on the Baltic Sea. The capital, Warsaw, lies in the central lowlands near the country's geographical center. Poland has a total area of 312,683 square kilometers (120,727 square miles), approximately the size of New Mexico.

Poland's geographic location has played an important role in its historical development. Poland is located in the middle of the North European Plain, the dividing line between Eastern and Western Europe. With the exceptions of the Baltic Sea to the north and the Carpathian Mountains to the south, Poland lacks natural boundaries. As a result, its history has been marked by numerous periods of foreign domination. At the end of the eighteenth century, it was partitioned between Austria, Prussia, and Russia and did not regain its independence until after World War I. It was the first of Germany's conquests in 1939 and even after its liberation following World War II, because of its relationship to the Soviet Union, Poland was only nominally independent.

From a historical and cultural perspective, Poland can be divided into seven regions: Wielkpolska (Great Poland), the western part of the country and the region around Poznan; Pomerania, the northwest area around Szczecin; Silesia, the southwest region extending from Wroclaw to Katowice;

Mazovia, the region surrounding Warsaw; Malopolska (Little Poland), the southeast region, including the area around Krakow; the Baltic Coast; and Mazuria, the lake district in the northeast. The largest cities are Warsaw (1.65 million), Lodz (850,000), and Krakow (725,000).

Resources

Poland is well endowed with natural resources. Concentrated in the west and south of the country, they include bituminous coal, sulfur, copper, zinc, and lead. Although Poland is the world's sixth largest producer of coal, it is still a net importer of energy. Other major resources include copper, sulfur, aluminum, cadmium, iron, and zinc. The use of coal as a primary source of energy has led to a very polluted environment. For example, the sulfur dioxide content of the air over Krakow is higher than London's, a city six times as large.[1]

Poland also has a large agricultural sector. Main products include potatoes, sugar beets, wheat, rye, and barley. As a result of forced industrialization after World War II, this part of the economy has remained less developed than its industrialized counterpart.

People

Poland's population has increased steadily since World War II, from 23.6 million in 1945 to 37.9 million in 1993. Like other states in the region, Poland's birth rate has declined since the 1980s. In 1996 it was 45 births per thousand, down from 79 per thousand in 1985. However, in contrast to Bulgaria, Hungary, and Russia, the population continues to increase despite economic hardship. This is the result of a lack of contraceptives and a strong Catholic influence. However, a combination of declining health care facilities and high rates of smoking and drinking have led to a decline in life expectancy. In 1996, it was 67 years for men and 76 years for women. Lung cancer kills half of all Polish men who die before age 65.

As in all other CEE states, Poland's population has become increasingly urbanized. In 1946, only 32 percent of the population lived in cities; by 1988 this figure had increased to 61 percent. However, 40 percent of the population still lives off the land. This is one of the highest percentages in the region and gives them significant political influence. As an illustration, the Polish Peasant Party (PSL) delayed the adoption of a new constitution by their insistence it include the provision that "the family farm is the basis of the rural structure of the Polish state." (Article 23)

A large segment of the urban population is of childbearing age and the cities are continuously growing. Because more middle-aged and elderly people live in the villages, the birth rate there is lower than in the cities. Rural inhabitants are among the most poorly educated and, as a result, have suffered the most from economic reforms. In 1994, 31 percent of all agricultural workers were unemployed.[2] The resulting lack of economic opportunities in these areas has caused a continuing migration to already overcrowded urban centers.

Ethnicity

The tremendous number of casualties in World War II, the loss of the population in the areas annexed to the Soviet Union, the repatriation of Poles from the West, and mass expulsion of non-Poles from Poland have combined to make Poland one of the world's most ethnically homogenous states. More than 98 percent of the population are ethnic Poles. Ukrainians, Byelorussians, Lithuanians, and Germans make up the most significant minority groups, but each constitutes less than 1 percent of the population. As a result of Poland's homogeneity and a traditionally liberal elite, Poland has avoided many of the ethnic tensions that plague other CEE states. The minority issue is now merely a matter of historical sensitivity for Poles.

Class Divisions

Although communism was supposed to produce a society in which everyone was a member of the "working class," this transformation clearly did not occur. As in the other former socialist states, society was divided along educational, vocational, and political lines. These divisions created three de facto classes. On the top was the ruling class of the Polish United Workers' Party (Communist Party) officials. In the middle were the university-educated intelligentsia, white-collar workers, and skilled laborers with a secondary school education. On the bottom were the unskilled manual laborers and the peasantry. The fairness of this system not withstanding, the socialist system fostered an egalitarian society. In 1988, 76 percent of the population identified themselves as members of the middle class. This figure compares with only 52 percent in 1993.[3]

In contemporary postcommunist Poland, these divisions remain more or less intact with two key exceptions: the ruling class has been broadened to include former communists, former dissidents, members of the intelligentsia, and a smattering of others; and a new business class has emerged as a result of the growing private sector.

With the exception of Hungary, in terms of numbers and affluence, the new rich in Poland have done considerably better than their counterparts in other CEE states. Like Hungarians, Poles have long been able to travel abroad. In the 1980s, thousands of Polish traders could be found all over Europe. Thus part of the population learned about market forces. After the regime change, these people used their savings to create new businesses. While this group comprises only a small part of society, it controls a major share of the wealth. In 1994, 10 percent of the population controlled 30 to 40 percent of the wealth. Significantly, the latter percentage is increasing.

As in the other CEE states, the people who have not benefited from reforms can be divided into two groups that represent the vast majority of the population. First are the former privileged members of society, such as economic managers, government workers, and so forth. Since these groups were employed exclusively by the state, they have seen their standard of living drop dramatically as a result of declining state intervention in the economy and continuing inflation.

The second group has been even more severely affected by the regime change. This group includes laborers, workers, peasants, pensioners, invalids, and students—whose educational stipends were cut—and the unemployed. Once favored, these groups have suddenly found themselves at the bottom of the economic order. Miners, for example, were historically considered the vanguard of the working class in Poland's coal-based economy. They were paid better than other workers and had special holidays. After economic reforms, they are now at the bottom of society, both in income and social status. After more than a 22 percent decline in real wages between 1990 and 1994, the World Bank estimates that approximately 15 percent of the population lives below the poverty line.

Their problems have been greatly compounded by the loss of subsidies—food, education, housing, transportation—previously provided by the regime. Popular resentment at the costs of the transition has been aggravated by the widening gap between rich and poor. Declining living standards for the majority of the population and increasing unemployment—polls show 60 percent of the population believe that unemployment is the most important problem facing society—has lead to electoral support for populist parties and those opposed to change.

In summary, the change in regime has led to a more stratified society. As in the United States, education and employment are key determinants of economic status. Significantly, in contrast to Bulgaria, Hungary, and Russia, Poles are generally happy with the economic and political changes. A 1996 poll showed more than 75 percent of the population was content with the new system.[4]

Economics

As with most other CEE states, Poland was a traditionally agrarian country that was industrialized under Soviet direction after World War II. In contrast to the rest of the bloc, most farms—70 percent—remained in private hands. Nevertheless, Poland's agricultural sector is underdeveloped. It employs 26 percent of the population, many as subsistence farmers, but produces only 6.6 percent of GDP. Although most agricultural land is privately owned, the Polish food-processing industry is still largely state owned and has changed little from the old regime. Food-processing plants are small, reflecting the scattered locations of farms, and their condition is rapidly deteriorating because of the lack of private or state investment. Even if the agricultural sector was developed, the Common Agricultural Policy severely limits exports to the European Union.

After the declaration of martial law in 1981, Poland's new military government inaugurated a series of economic reforms. The government ended official production targets and allowed factories to decide for themselves what they would produce and how they would distribute profits. In contrast to Hungary, few companies took advantage of these opportunities. Although given the right to chose how they operated, companies were given neither the incentives—an increased salary—nor the penalties—bankruptcy—that exist in a free market. These limited reforms were unsuccessful and caused living standards to drop further.

The minister of finance in the first postcommunist government, Leszek Balcerowicz, initiated what came to known as "shock therapy." Its goal was a quick transition from a centrally planned economy to a market economy. Its provisions included: removing price supports, withdrawing subsidies from state-owned enterprises, liberalizing foreign trade, devaluing the zloty, and taxing wage increases to try and contain inflation.

"Shock therapy" had an immediate effect. In 1989, coupons regulated the sale of meat in state stores, and goods such as toilet paper, flour, and matches were frequently out of stock. By 1991, the economy had experienced a profound transformation. Vendors crowded the streets, selling everything from fresh produce to imported designer tennis shoes. At the macroeconomic level, shock therapy also lowered inflation and fostered a rapid increase in the GDP. It led to the rapid privatization of certain sectors of the economy; by 1997, the private sector employed 60 percent of Polish workers and produced more than 65 percent of GDP. Thus in contrast to Bulgaria, Hungary, and Russia, which incrementally introduced market reforms, Poland's "shock therapy" was a major success. For example, while inflation was over 16 percent in 1997, it was down significantly from 32 percent in 1994 and 585 percent in 1990. Even at 16 percent, it was still the lowest inflation percentage found among the four states.

Shock therapy also fostered economic growth. Between 1991 and 1998, Poland's economic growth averaged 6 percent a year, faster than other state in Europe, East or West. This growth has led to a higher average monthly wage—$450 in 1996—than that in Bulgaria or Russia. In recognition of its economic performance, Poland joined the Czech Republic and Hungary as members of the Organization for Economic Cooperation and Development (OECD). The first to recover from the slump following communism, Poland has earned the reputation as the "tiger" of former socialist states.

Poland's early adoption of economic reforms also included tough stock exchange regulations. As a result, almost 200 companies were listed on the

---

LESZEK BALCEROWICZ (1947–)

Leszek Balcerowicz is considered one of the most knowledgeable Central and Eastern European transition economists. Born in Lipno, Poland, in 1947, he studied at the Central School of Planning and Statistics in Warsaw, graduating with distinction in 1970. He earned his Ph.D. from the same school in 1975. He also earned an MBA from St. John's University in New York. From 1981 to 1982, Balcerowicz served as deputy Chairman of the Polish Economic Association. Before becoming a member of the Polish government in 1989, he also was a university professor at various institutions and still lectures at the Warsaw School of Economics.

When the Solidarity-led government gained control of Poland in September 1989, Balcerowicz took a leading role in reshaping the policy. Until 1991, he served as the Deputy Prime Minister and Minister of Finance while also acting as the President of the Economic Committee of the Council of Ministers. In these positions, he was able to implement his own plan for Poland's economic transformation from socialism to capitalism.

This plan, later referred to as "shock therapy," made Balcerowicz a household name throughout the region. The policy rapidly liberalized the economy by decontrolling prices, slashing subsidies and removing most import barriers. While this ambitious program was successful at laying the foundation for long-run growth, there were very harsh short-run consequences as the people and economy were forced to rapidly adjust to the new system. This policy caused a dramatic recession which allowed the ex-Communists to win the 1993 parliamentary elections.

After the SLD victory, Balcerowicz worked to rebuild his Democratic Union Party, eventually merging it with the Liberal Democratic Union Congress to create the Freedom Party in 1994. To create a government after their 1997 parliamentary victory, the Solidarity Election Alliance formed a coalition with the Freedom Union. As part of the coalition agreement, Balcerowicz was made Deputy Prime Minister in charge of the economy. From this position, he continues to guide the Polish economy and remains the loudest voice for continuing liberalization in the country.

Warsaw stock exchange in 1998, with a total market capitalization in excess of $10 billion dollars. Not only does this foster foreign investment, but the fact that over half of the investments are held by Poles shows that people have come to accept the features of a market economy.

In spite of numerous successes, Poland has many of the same economic problems of its neighbors. Although many smaller companies have privatized quickly, most of the larger, less efficient enterprises remain in state hands. State-owned companies account for a third of industrial sales and employ more than 40 percent of industrial workers, yet produce only 5 percent of the profits.[5] Examples include coal mining, ship building, and the steel industry. Economically inefficient, these industries cost the government millions of zlotys in subsidies. Nevertheless, the government is reticent to close or privatize them because to do so would increase unemployment. Given the tradition of political activism among workers in these industries, reforms in this area could become a flash point for social unrest.[6]

Other problems associated with economic reforms include unemployment, high inflation, and a significant, albeit shrinking budget deficit. Although down marginally from the previous year, in 1997 unemployment was still over 13 percent. Unemployment is concentrated in certain geographical regions and age groups. For example, in the northeast the unemployment rate in Olsztyn province is over 30 percent, while in Warsaw it is 6 percent. As in other CEE states the official unemployment rate probably overstates the scale of the problem. There is anecdotal evidence of workers signing up for unemployment benefits and working at the same time for private companies. In addition, since employers are required to pay social security benefits of almost 50 percent, there is significant incentive for companies to offer unofficial work.

Trade

Although Poland's trade was oriented toward its socialist allies—in 1985, socialist states accounted for 49 percent of Polish exports and 54 percent of its imports—like Hungary it traded widely with the West. The collapse of the Soviet market and "shock therapy" further shifted Poland's trade patterns from the East to the West. In 1991, Poland signed an association agreement with the European Union. By 1996, 80 percent of Poland's trade was with other Western states, with 69 percent of exports and 64 percent of imports coming or going to the EU. Poland's three largest trading partners are Germany, Russia, and Italy. Significantly, in addition to being a large market for Polish goods, Russia still provides over two-thirds of Poland's natural gas.[7] Poland's trade is also affected by its geographical position. Approximately 10 million "commercial tourists" from Poland's eastern neighbors—Belorussians, Russians, and Ukrainians—visit the country each year.[8]

As a result of a spending binge in the 1970s, in 1990 Poland's debt to the West was, at $48 billion, second only to Russia's. Through deals with Western creditors, the debt was halved by 1992. This cleared the way for international borrowing and foreign investment. Between 1991 and 1996, $5.4 billion was invested in Poland, second only to Hungary per capita. U.S. companies ($1.7 billion), multinational corporations ($871 million), and German companies ($512 million) have been the largest investors.

Although Poland still faces problems, it has dealt with the repercussions of economic reforms more successfully than Bulgaria or Russia. However, the difficulties people experience in their daily lives can be seen in the electoral victory of the former communists in 1993 and the Solidarity Electoral Alliance in 1997.

POLITICAL HISTORY

Polish history has been dominated by a series of weak regimes, powerful neighbors, and many rebellions. It has been invaded twenty-six times in the last three hundred years. Nevertheless, it has been an important actor in Central and Eastern Europe. It introduced the region's first liberal constitution and suffered the most per capita casualties during World War II. More recently, it became the first state to end one-party rule, sparking even more dramatic revolutions in other socialist states.

Before the Twentieth Century

Poland originated as a state in the tenth century, when the Piast dynasty united the lands around Poznan, Gniezno, and Kalisz into Wielkopolska (Great Poland). Mieszko I (963–992) accepted Christianity in 966. This is regarded as the founding date of Poland. Christianity was adopted in order to avoid domination by either Bohemia or the Holy Roman Empire. In 991, Mieszko asked that his realm be placed under the direct protection of the Pope. This act was intended to keep the Polish church free of German control.

The subsequent history of Poland was one of continued expansion under Mieszko and his son, Boleslaw Chrobry (Boleslaw the Brave). Polish kings succeeded each other in a direct line until 1138, when Boleslaw Krzywousty (Boleslaw the Wry-Mouthed) divided the kingdom among his sons. The eldest son was to become Grand Duke and have authority over the other brothers, but in practice each created an independent principality. This division greatly weakened the country, leading to territorial incursions by the Danes and a Mongol invasion in 1241.

After the Mongols were driven out, Prussia—part of contemporary Germany—invaded Poland. Konrad I invited the Teutonic Order, a military/religious order whose territory included parts of contemporary northern Germany and Poland, to help him fight the Prussians. By 1288, the Prussians were conquered, but the Order, which had grown beyond Konrad's control, incorporated some Polish territory into its own state. Since they spoke German, the Teutonic Knights came to be viewed as a German army of occupation. This and subsequent German invasions have fostered a very negative perception of Germans by most Poles.

The inability of the state to remove the Order led to increased autonomy for the nobility. In 1370, Kazimierz Wielki (Casimir the Great) died without a male heir. He was succeeded by his nephew Ludwik Wegierski (Louis I of Hungary), who ruled through regents. Louis' youth and inexperience further strengthened the nobility. In September 1374, he issued the Statute of Kosice, which confirmed "all previous rights and immunities awarded to the nobility by his Polish Piast predecessors . . . and limited all forms of noble service and obligation."[9] Louis' action greatly limited the power of subsequent monarchs.

After Louis' death, the Polish nobility supported Jadwiga, his younger daughter, as the new monarch. Fearing growing Muscovite power, they also favored a union with Lithuania through the marriage of Jadwiga to the Grand Duke of Lithuania, Jagiello. The marriage led in 1385 to the Treaty of Krewo. This treaty united the royal houses of Poland and Lithuania. The most significant external developments of this period were a war against the Teutonic Order and resistance to Turkish and Russian expansion. The Teutonic Knights were defeated at Grunwald in 1410, ending the threat from the West. With Poland's southern borders threatened by the Ottoman Empire, Polish forces joined a large Christian army. Defeated at Varna (Bulgaria) in 1444, Poland's trade links with the Orient were cut. The Turkish threat was negated by a 1553 treaty between Poland and the Ottoman Empire.

To the East, Muscovite forces had been attacking Polish territory since 1500. By the late sixteenth century, both Poles and Lithuanians knew they had to deal with this increasingly powerful threat. A personal union between Poland and Lithuania was therefore no longer sufficient. A Sejm, an assembly of the nobility, was called in Lublin in 1568. It created the Polish-Lithuanian Commonwealth (Rzeczpospolita).

Even with increasing external threats, the power of the nobles continued to increase. King Wladyslaw Jagiello issued a proclamation protecting the nobles' land from confiscation without a court's approval. In 1454, Casimir IV promised not to create an army or impose new taxes without the approval of nobility. Thus, the nobles could block any move that would hurt their interests, often at the expense of state interests. Even the hereditary monarchy became subject to electoral confirmation by the nobility. As a result, the throne was at times given to foreign kings who cared little about Polish interests. In addition, since all nobles had the right to participate in the election of the king, the result was often inconclusive. In 1576, 1587, 1697, and 1733, two kings were simultaneously elected. Their attempts to enforce their claim to the throne resulted in civil wars.

Nevertheless, the principle of unanimity was central to the political life of the Rzeczpospolita, fostering the rise of the practices of liberum veto and confederation. The liberum veto was a practice by which a single noble could reject a bill or stop the work of the Sejm. The results of this practice were disastrous. Between 1697 and 1733, eleven out of twenty sessions of the Sejm were stalemated. Only one Sejm was able to pass any legislation at all. This led to the rise of the Confederation. In practical terms, it was a legal rebellion in which members swore to pursue their grievances until justice was secured. These features greatly weakened the state.

Internal weakness made Poland a tempting target for her neighbors. In 1657, Frederick William of Prussia captured the Duchy of Poznan. To the East, from 1717 onwards the Russians enjoyed a virtual protectorate over Poland. This set the stage for the 1772, 1793, and 1795 partitions of Poland. Russia and Prussia participated in all three partitions and Austria in the first and third ones. After 1795, Poland ceased to exist as a sovereign state. The partitions had a powerful impact on Poles. Distrust and dislike for Germans and Russians were reinforced, and resistance to authority became a patriotic duty.

Hopes for a reborn state were revived in 1807 when Napoleon created the Duchy of Warsaw, an independent Polish state carved out of Prussian-held Polish lands. The duchy became the center of efforts to restore a Polish state. In an attempt to regain their independence, the Poles helped Napoleon invade Russia in 1812. The campaign failed, and the Duchy of Warsaw soon came under Russian control. Nevertheless, the period between 1807 and 1813 was significant. It "redeemed, at least in part, the shame of partition. . . . It reminded Europe that the Polish nation did not accept its loss of independence."[10] This experience served as an inspiration for future generations.

After the defeat of Napoleon in 1815, the Congress of Vienna detached the Grand Duchy of Poznan and the Free City of Krakow from the Duchy of Warsaw. The rest of the territory was renamed the Congress Kingdom of Poland. Although still under Russian jurisdiction, it was given a constitution and autonomy. However, Russia did not respect the kingdom's autonomy. The news that Nicholas I intended to use Polish troops to fight French revolutionaries led to an open revolt in 1830. Although at first the revolt was successful, Russian troops soon regained control. The repressive measures that followed only increased Polish resentment of Russian rule.

In 1863, a group of emigre Poles who had taken advantage of an amnesty to return to Poland initiated an armed rebellion. Militarily weak and disunited, the Poles were again quickly subdued by the Russians. The revolt did, however, have one significant ramification: to gain the sympathy of the Polish peasants, the Russians passed several land reform acts that "finally ended aristocratic domination in Poland and, ironically were to aid future nationalist efforts to unify all Poles."[11]

The insurrections of 1830 and 1863 showed the miserable condition of the peasants. Poor economic and cultural conditions delayed the development of a national consciousness. This can be seen in the passive attitude of the peasantry during the insurrections and the 1846 revolt of the Polish nobles in the Austrian controlled part of Poland (Galacia). During the revolt,

Polish peasants helped Austrian troops against their own nobility. Even today, many peasants feel alienated from the upper classes of society.

The Polish rebellion of 1863 led to the imposition of "Russification," an attempt to force Poles to accept Russian culture and ideology. The University of Warsaw was turned into a Russian university, and a Russian curriculum was imposed on all primary and secondary schools. In their part of Poland, the Germans also attempted to impose their culture. Schools were Germanized, and an 1886 law allowed German peasants to colonize Polish land. As a result, in the eighteenth and nineteenth centuries Poles lacked a common history and experience in political participation.

The Twentieth Century

World War I revived hopes for the reconstruction of an independent Poland. Both the Entente and the Allies tried to secure Polish support with vague promises. In 1916, Emperors William II of Germany and Franz Joseph of Austria-Hungary issued a joint declaration that called for the creation of an autonomous Polish state in the territory taken from Russia, with final borders to be determined later. The Russians appealed to the Poles as early as August 14, 1914, when Grand Duke Nicholas promised the creation of a Poland "free in her religion, language, and autonomy under the scepter of the tsar." Polish hopes were heightened by Woodrow Wilson's declaration that "statesmen everywhere are agreed that there should be a united, independent and autonomous Poland."[12]

During the war, two politicians who would dominate the Polish political scene for the next twenty years came to the fore. The first was Jozef Pilsudski. He was born in "Russian" Poland and joined the socialist movement in 1887. With the advent of the war, Pilsudski was made commander of the First Brigade of the Polish Legions, semiautonomous military units formed in the Austrian territory. His battlefield success against the Russians earned him national prominence. Regarding Russia as Poland's main enemy, Pilsudski tried to maintain good relations with Germany after the war.

Pilsudski's political antagonist was Roman Dmowski. Also born in "Russian" Poland, prior to the war he led the National Democratic Party. Dmowski, who was strongly nationalistic, anti-Semitic, anti-German, and pro-Russian, also had numerous supporters among Western politicians. As a result of his pro-Russian orientation, he disagreed with Pilsudski's foreign policy. Their views also differed on the structure of future political order. Pilsudski, who had little respect for democratic principles, favored a strong executive. In contrast, Dmowski wanted a powerful legislature to control the executive.

The post–World War I peace treaties recreated an independent Polish state. Politically, Dmowski's view prevailed and Poland adopted a parliamentary system. As in Wiemar Germany, the government was weak. No political party ever had, or was expected to have, a majority. This factionalization led to a series of coalition governments, continuous political maneuvering ensured that the coalitions were short lived. This situation led Pilsudski to organize a military coup in 1926. Although the Sejm continued to exist, Pilsudski exercised authority through the army.

Similar to the situation in Hungary, there were three main reasons why democracy failed in Poland during the interwar period. First, with the exception of Silesia, Poland lacked an industrial base. This limited the development of a middle class that has historically been in the forefront of political change. In addition, since the nobility in Poland and Hungary comprised approximately 13 percent of the population,[13] they were much more interested in maintaining the status quo than in creating a democratic polity that might strip them of their privileges. Second, since Poland was underdeveloped, the urban population—which is more politically active than its rural counterpart—was much smaller than in other states in the region. Finally, as a result of their geographic vulnerability and their recent independence, most Poles were more concerned with strengthening the state than creating a pluralistic political order.

The weaknesses of the political system added to the difficulties faced by Poland after the war. Because of the partitions, Poles living in different areas viewed each other with disdain. For example, western Poles saw themselves as the most modern, the best organized, and the hardest working. They viewed their brethren to the east and the south with considerable contempt. In turn, Poles in the latter areas viewed their western neighbors as having lost their Polish national identity, with the result that the western Poles were largely excluded from the government.

The reconstructed Polish state also incorporated a large number of discontented Ukrainians, Lithuanians, and Germans. These minorities were all hostile to the Polish state. The Ukrainians resented the fact that an independent Ukraine had not been created after the war, and the Lithuanians were unhappy the Poles had been given Wilno (Vilnius). After 1933, the Germans in Poland came under the influence of Nazi propaganda. This situation made the process of state building difficult.

On September 1, 1939, Germany attacked Poland, starting World War II. The Poles valiantly resisted but were quickly overwhelmed. In what is sometimes regarded as the fourth partition of Poland, the Molotov-Ribbentrop pact split Poland between Germany and the Soviet Union. German-occupied Poland was called simply the "General Government" and was viewed as a colony to be exploited. At the same time the Soviets occupied the eastern part of Poland. After giving Wilno (Vilnius) to Lithuania, they organized elections in the remaining parts of Poland—which were renamed Western Ukraine and Western Belorussia. In rigged elections, the two areas voted to merge with the Soviet Ukraine and Soviet Belorussia. This annexation led to the deportation of 1.5 million Poles to labor camps in central Asia between 1940 and 1941.

Immediately after Poland was invaded, an underground resistance movement was created. It is important to stress the resistance was directed against both the Germans and the Red Army. This can be seen in the Warsaw uprising. Its goal was to liberate Warsaw from the Germans in order to create a base for the return of the exiled Polish government in London, thus preventing the Soviet Army from entering the city. While the Russians watched from across the Vistula River, the uprising was ruthlessly suppressed by the Germans. The failure of this revolt ended organized anti-German resistance, paving the way for Soviet occupation.

Poland's postwar destiny was decided at the Yalta Conference. While the United States and Great Britain supported the creation of a multiparty government and free elections, under Soviet pressure they eventually abandoned these views. There were several reasons for doing this: the Red Army was already in Poland, Soviet assistance was deemed necessary for a quick victory over Japan, and the participation of the Soviet Union was indispensable for the success of the newly created United Nations. The USSR would not be alienated for Poland's sake. To this day, Poles speak of the West's "betrayal" after World War II.

The early postwar years were difficult for Poland. The country had been devastated by the war and Warsaw was almost completely destroyed. Furthermore, by international agreement, Poland's borders were moved approximately 100 miles westward, with the eastern part of Poland annexed by the USSR. Poland was compensated with German territory in the West. These border changes caused one of the largest population movements in history: Germans were expelled from new Polish territories in the west; Poles were expelled from new Soviet territories in the east; and millions of Poles moved into central Poland or newly vacated areas in the West. Interestingly, although foreign influence has frequently threatened Poland's sovereignty, since it was politically, economically, and militarily linked with the Soviet Union, Poland had a major power guaranteeing its borders for the first time in two hundred years.

Elections held in 1947 were won by the Polish Workers' Party. It later merged with the Polish Socialist Party to form the Polish United Workers' Party, i.e. the communist party. The PUWP pursued a policy of Stalinization from 1948 to 1953. This included the elimination of noncommunist parties, persecution of the Catholic church, agricultural collectivization, nationalization of industry, and government takeover of all independent organizations and the media. Sovietization was reflected in the adoption in the 1952 constitution, which stressed the leading role of the PUWP and "eternal friendship" with the Soviet Union. Nevertheless, the goal of penetrating and controlling

Polish society failed. This can be seen in numerous postwar political confrontations between the population and the regime.

Riots in 1956 brought Wladyslaw Gomulka, a victim of the Stalinist purges, to power. Gomulka promised to create a more "Polish" form of communism. Specifically, he eased pressure on the Church, abandoned collectivization, and dismissed the Soviet marshal who was Poland's Defense Minister. However, he did not enact economic reforms and the economic situation continued to deteriorate, forcing Gomulka to raise heavily subsidized retail prices in 1970. These price increases caused new riots and led to his ouster. The new PUWP General Secretary, Edward Gierek, immediately rescinded the price increases and tried to buy support by importing consumer goods. Although successful in the short run, this policy led to even greater economic problems. When Gierek was forced to raise prices in 1976, the usual pattern of strikes and demonstrations was repeated.

Significantly, the 1976 strikes and the subsequent crackdown by the authorities made workers and intellectuals allies for the first time. In a major political development, the Worker's Defense Committee (KOR) was created. Previously, because of their desire to create a new polity, intellectuals had supported the communists. In addition, Polish intellectuals have traditionally seen themselves as more enlightened than the rest of society. The year 1978 saw two developments that would have significant long-term consequences. First, a small group of workers in the shipyards along the Baltic

---

WLADYSLAW GOMULKA (1905–1982)

Wladyslaw Gomulka was heavily involved in the communist takeover of Poland, emerging from the ranks of the communist partisans to become a deputy premier in 1944. He advocated a "Polish road to socialism," which would allow people to own private property. Because of his radical ideas, Gomulka was removed from office and imprisoned. He was released after Stalin's death in 1953.

In 1956, as Khrushchev began the process of de-Stalinization, communist governments throughout the CEE suffered a crisis of legitimacy. Popular riots led to the removal of the Soviet puppet Boleslav Beirut and the return of Gomulka as First Secretary of the PUWP. Although Gomulka retained traditional communist goals, he liberalized Poland's economy. The most significant of his reforms were the end of persecution of the church, the end of collectivization, and the reinstatement of private property rights.

As a result of economic crisis, Gomulka's regime suffered a loss of legitimacy in the late 1960s. (Significantly, Gomulka was removed from office as he came into it, by countrywide strikes and riots.) In December 1970, he was replaced by Edward Gierek.

LECH WALESA (1943–)

Born into a poor family and trained as an electrician, Lech Walesa became involved in politics while working in the Lenin Shipyards in Gdansk. He helped organize shipyard strikes in 1970 and 1976, subsequently losing his job. In 1980, Walesa returned to head the Interfactory Strike Committee, which organized and led the famous Lenin Shipyard strike. When the government refused to allow workers to strike and join trade unions, a general strike broke out across Poland. The government was forced to yield to the committee's demands, which were encapsulated in the Gdansk Agreement. The Interfactory Strike Committee became Solidarnosc (Solidarity), a national federation of trade unions.

By 1981, Solidarity claimed a membership of over 10 million, approximately a quarter of the entire Polish population. Later that year, Solidarity was banned and its leaders imprisoned after General Jaruzelski declared martial law. Walesa was released a year later and returned to the Lenin shipyards, keeping a low profile on the advice of the Pope. In 1983, he was awarded the Nobel Peace Prize, further increasing Solidarity's power. Walesa participated in the 1989 Roundtable talks between Solidarity and the government, which led to restricted parliamentary elections.

In 1990, Lech Walesa became Poland's first democratically elected president. He guided Poland through its first free parliamentary elections and was instrumental in Poland's transition to a free-market economy. Under his influence, Poland began to pursue membership in NATO and the European Union. Partially because of his strident anticommunist rhetoric, however, Walesa's popularity eventually waned. He ran for reelection in 1995 but was narrowly defeated by Alexander Kwasniewski of the Democratic Left Alliance. He now heads the Lech Walesa Institute, which promotes market economies in Central and Eastern Europe and other developing countries.

Coast created an illegal Committee of Free Trade Unions. One of the founding members was a electrician named Lech Walesa. Also in that year Cardinal Karel Wojtyla of Krakow was elected Pope. Taking the name John Paul II, the Pope's visit to Poland in 1979, in which millions turned out to see him, gave Poles a sense of pride and hope.

Another attempt to raise food prices caused widespread strikes. At the huge Lenin Shipyards in Gdansk, Lech Walesa assumed control of the committee representing 16,000 striking workers. The strikes of 1980 differed from the previous ones in that they took on a political character. Workers demanded the legalization of independent "workers' committees" that would replace the government-controlled trade unions. Riots in July were followed by a government agreement to talk with the representatives of the striking workers.

On August 31, the Gdansk Agreement was signed. The agreement was a unique document that recognized for the first time the need for "new, self-governing trade unions which would become authentic representatives of the working class."[14] The PUWP was essentially admitting that neither it nor the government-controlled trade unions were "authentic representatives" of the workers. On November 10, 1981, the National Committee of Solidarnosc—Solidarity—was registered with the court. This was the first step toward political pluralism in Poland.

In December 1981, Solidarity announced its intention to organize a vote of confidence in the regime. After urgent prodding from Moscow, General Wojciech Jaruzelski—prime minister from February 1981 and general secretary of the PUWP from October 1982—declared martial law and banned Solidarity. A national referendum rejected price increases and dramatically showed the lack of support for the regime. Following years of unrest, in 1988 strikes broke out in Krakow and soon spread to other cities.

Post-1989

In August 1989, the PUWP approved a plan for consultations with non-party groups. Although the government declared it would not talk to "illegal" organizations (i.e., Solidarity) that had been banned during martial law, talks were held between Walesa and Interior Minister Czeslaw Kiszczak. Subsequent roundtable talks among representatives of the church, government, and Solidarity resulted in an unprecedented series of agreements. They included the legalization of Solidarity, the right of free speech and association, free elections, and judicial independence. These talks legitimized the opposition, in effect ending the Party's monopoly on power. In June 1989, the first free elections since 1947 gave Solidarity all of the 161 nonreserved seats in the Sejm and 99 of 100 seats in the Senate. On September 12, Tadeusz Mazowiecki formed a four-party cabinet with only four communists in it. For the first time in the history of the socialist bloc, a noncommunist government was in power.

In January 1990, the PUWP was disbanded. In December 1990, Walesa became the first popularly elected Polish president. He named Jan Bielecki, an economist and businessman, as prime minister of a nonpartisan government of experts. The first completely free parliamentary elections were held in October 1991. Under a complicated system of proportional representation, over thirty-seven parties fielded candidates. Voter turnout was only 43 percent and the vote was divided among twenty-nine parties, with none winning more than 12 percent.[15] This plethora of parties caused a political stalemate that prevented the formation of a government for six weeks. This government was replaced less than five months later.

In May 1993, Sejm delegates representing one of the numerous factions of Solidarity introduced a motion of no confidence in the government.

THE 1989 ROUNDTABLE TALKS

Poland's economic decline in the late 1980s led to countrywide waves of strikes throughout 1989, eventually producing the 1989 roundtable talks between the government and Lech Walesa. During these talks, the PUWP discussed the possibility of sharing power with Solidarity. To get support for crucial economic reforms and to try to preserve communist control, the PUWP agreed to the legalization of Solidarity (which had been banned since 1981), freedom of speech, and partially free elections.

In the 1989 election, two-thirds of seats in the Sejm were allotted to the Communist Party and its allies, while one-third were contested electorally. In the resurrected Senate, 100 electoral seats were contested. In return, the PUWP was allowed to select the first occupant of the newly created presidency. With the exception of one seat, Solidarity won every electoral contest.

For the first time in forty years, Poland's government was headed by a noncommunist. Significantly, this radical change had occurred peacefully, without any bloodshed. Poland was the first CEE country to have a noncommunist government; its transition was seen as a model for other states in the region.

Ironically, this government had been created with the support of Solidarity. As a result of a former minister oversleeping, the government was defeated by one vote, leading Walesa to dissolve the legislature. Significantly, the breakdown of the intellectual-worker alliance, which had made the change in regime possible, caused the democratic government to fall.

The 1993 elections were won by the Democratic Left Alliance (SLD), whose main component was the renamed and reformed PUWP. Other parties on the left were also successful, allowing the SLD to form a coalition government with the Polish Peasant Party (PSL), an ally of the PUWP in the communist era. Significantly, a new electoral law that required parties to clear a 5 percent threshold prevented several parties affiliated with Solidarity from gaining parliamentary representation. The failure of the Solidarity supported governments reflected growing popular concern over declining living standards associated with the economic transition from a centrally planned economy and the plethora of problems facing society. Regardless, "this was a strange turn of events for the country that had created both Solidarity and the first noncommunist government in East and Central Europe."[16]

This trend toward the left continued in 1995. In a close election, the head of the SLD, Alexander Kwasniewski, defeated Lech Walesa. His electoral victory gave the SLD control of both the legislative and executive branches of government. However, this situation did not prevent problems for the SDL. In what many saw as an underhanded attempt by Walesa's supporters to embarrass the new government, in January 1996 Prime Minister Jan Oleksy was forced to resign amid unproven allegations he had been a Soviet KGB informer. Wlodzimiercz Cimoszewicz, a technocrat with no formal party membership, was selected to replace him.

The year 1997 was a milestone for Poland. In May, a new constitution was approved by a referendum. Significantly, only 42 percent of the population bothered to vote, approving the new constitution by a slim (53 percent) majority. In September's parliamentary elections, dominated by a debate over the power and influence of former communists, the parties of the right led by the Solidarity Electoral Alliance regained power with almost a third of the vote. Significantly, this was the best electoral showing by any political party since the change in regime.

INFORMING POLITICAL IDEAS

During the communist era Poland's official political culture was based on the leading role of the Communist Party. In contrast to other CEE states, however, the PUWP was unable to completely overcome the precommunist political culture. As Stalin once said, implementing communism in Poland is "like fitting a cow with a saddle." This was the result of a close and historic relationship between the state, nation, and cultural attributes. Interestingly, some of these factors helped the communists gain power after World War II.

Political Culture

There has always been a close link between the Catholic church and Polish national identity. During the periods of Polish independence, there was little separation between church and state. Church leaders remained strongly loyal to successive regimes and helped them not only in state building, but also in keeping the peasants quiet and diffusing their demands for radical land reform. After Poland was partitioned in the eighteenth century and after World War II, the church became the embodiment of Polish nationalism and identity.

Political traditions have also influenced the political culture. Historically, Polish intellectuals believed they alone had the necessary prerequisites for leadership. They were not interested in mobilizing the support of workers and peasants because they considered these classes inferior. The general public accepted the view that ordinary people, because they lacked the requisite necessary knowledge or experience, should not interfere in politics, and lack of political involvement made them susceptible to manipulation. Thus, a small group of intellectuals have often dominated the polity. This legacy can be seen in the constitutional provision that members of the parliament "shall be representatives of the nation . . . and not bound by any instructions of the electorate." (Article 104)

Other Traditions

Historical experiences have also fostered a unique set of Polish subcultures. They include the struggle against foreign domination, nationalism, chivalry, individual honor, and authoritarianism. Although linked to different historical experiences, these characteristics can still be seen in the political consciousness. As a result of its location between Germany and Russia, Poland has long struggled to maintain its independence. Since they faced almost impossible odds, there is a popular image of Poles engaged in a heroic, almost holy struggle to preserve national values. This struggle against foreign domination fostered the development of chivalry, with an emphasis on individual honor. Even today, most Polish men still greet a woman by bowing and kissing the back of her hand.[17]

Although Polish history is filled with struggles against both external enemies and strong kings, it also has a strong authoritarian streak. As an illustration, Josef Pilsudski's 1926 coup and his creation of an authoritarian regime were widely supported. Support for a strong government can still be seen today. In a 1992 survey, over 33 percent of the population said they would support the suspension of Parliament and political parties—the highest of any country in the survey.[18] These views are the result of political and economic instability as well as the belief that a weak state will be open to foreign influence.

Little Traditions

Just as communist attempts to create a new political order after World War II were thwarted by historical legacies, the reconstruction of the contemporary political order is burdened by historical and communist legacies. In return for a political monopoly, the communists promised a classless society and social and economic equality. This policy had several consequences. First, it reinforced precommunist traditions of state control, support for industry, and an extensive social welfare system. Second, it created an egalitarian mentality. Opinion polls continue to show a large majority of the public thinks income differentials are now too drastic.

As in other CEE states, one of the most important legacies of communism is the lack of morals and norms. Although 60 percent of the workforce is employed in the private sector, they account for only 15 percent of the contributions to the social security fund. In other words, there is large-scale tax evasion. Today, what was once bad—individualism, profit—is now good, and vice versa. The creation or redefinition of values and norms will play a key role in the development of the Polish polity.

Another communist legacy is the lack of a strong work ethic. No matter how hard people worked, they received the same material rewards. Without economic or political incentives, apathy grew. As in other CEE states, these features weakened the regime's legitimacy. This happened more quickly in Poland as a result of Poles' traditional distrust of Russians. As in Hungary, close ties with the USSR cost the ruling party support among the general population.

The combination of forty-five years of political socialization and Polish history has led to an evolving political culture that is based on both individualistic and egalitarian, authoritarian and democratic, and socialist and capitalist features. The competition between these characteristics helps us understand why Poland has had so many governments since 1989.

Legitimizing Rationale

As with the other ruling communist parties, the legitimizing rationale of the PUWP was the creation of a new economic and political order. Thus, when the economy started to deteriorate, the PUWP lost its authority as the "leading and guiding force of society." This in turn led to increasing calls for political reforms. When the Party refused to adhere to these demands, it lost the little legitimacy it had left.

Today, government legitimacy is based on enforcing the laws of the land, guaranteeing the security of its citizens, and promoting social stability and economic development. Significantly, a large portion of the population has yet to accept these features. When asked to identify the most pronounced features of the new regime, people point to capitalism, freedom, anarchy, corruption, and crime. Few say anything about democracy. As a result, a large part of society, particularly the youth, do not respect authority. Most people have yet to realize that "democracy" entails responsibility and following the law, a situation that suggests the definition of democracy in Poland is still developing.

This problem can be seen in the actions of political parties. As in Bulgaria, the new democratic leaders who took over the government could not overcome their personal differences. In a democratic polity, where bargaining and compromise are essential elements of the political process, these attacks are destructive. In both countries, voters expressed their dissatisfaction with the democrats by reelecting ex-communists in the second round of elections following the change in regime.

Political Socialization

Education

Although the Polish educational system under Soviet rule was similar to that of other CEE states, it had the lowest per capita number of university students. As a result, only 6.5 percent of the population have a university degree. This compares to 24 percent in the United States. This low number extends to the rest of the educational system; over 30 percent of the people do not have a secondary education. Two factors explain this situation.

First, because education has traditionally been seen as an intellectual pursuit, most students who pass the difficult university entrance exams come from families with an intellectual background. Another problem is the cost of education. While a university education is "free"—that is, there is no tuition—students from the countryside must pay for accommodation, food, and so forth. In Poland, these costs are more than half the average salary. Thus the percentage of students from small towns and villages (i.e., nonintellectual families), recently dropped to an all-time low of 2 percent.[19] This combination of factors has created a self-perpetuating elite, preventing widespread improvements in socioeconomic status.

Through its large network of schools, the Catholic church has historically played a large role in education. The communists tried to end religious education and foster an atheistic culture. The church was viewed as the enemy of the state since it made people think about issues and values (such as faith in the individual and belief in a supreme being) that were detrimental to the spread of communist ideology. Not surprisingly, the Soviet seizure of Poland's eastern provinces and their use of thousands of Polish citizens as laborers were banned topics.

The contemporary educational system faces numerous problems. Most significant is the lack of money to modernize facilities or improve teacher's salaries. Public spending on education has dropped by 20 percent since 1989.[20] Many teachers, tired of poor salaries, are going into the private sector, where they can quickly double their earnings. Second, although more students are attending universities, many secondary school graduates have chosen to go into business. The lack of a trained elite will cause problems in the future.

In terms of curricular development, civic education, though crucial for the development of a democratic polity, is only starting to be promoted. In 1995, a civics textbook for eighth graders was introduced that emphasized not only theoretical information about democracies, but also practical exposure to democratic institutions. This was an important step, for although students understand a market economy, they do not understand that a democratic system entails responsibility and participation in public life. Other hopeful signs include the rapid proliferation of private schools—over 1,000 in 1995—and some changes in the curriculum to include languages and computer science.

As in Bulgaria and Russia, Poland has yet to fundamentally reform its educational system. Although new subjects have been introduced and ideological courses removed, the old secondary school system—which emphasizes rote memorization rather than critical thinking—remains.

Mass Media

While the communist regime controlled all sources of information, in contrast to other CEE states it allowed some nongovernmental publishing houses—usually affiliated with the church—to exist. Even with church support, publishing a book was an arduous process. First, a list of proposed titles was sent to the Ministry of Culture and the Committee for Religious Affairs. Typically, 50 percent of the requests were rejected. Next, the publisher had to apply for paper from the state. Since there was only a limited amount of paper available for nongovernmental publications, the publishers often had to bargain for paper. After the books were printed they still had to be approved by the local censor before they could be distributed.

This situation has radically changed. Because of Solidarity's experience under the communists, one of the first acts of the new regime was to allow the creation of independent newspapers and radio and television stations. Today 85 percent of the media is in private hands. While there is a vibrant and independent press, similar to the situation in other states in the region, an initial expansion of new journals and newspapers was quickly followed by their consolidation following the end of governmental subsidies. The concentration of many private radio stations and publishing houses limits a free and open media. Since most get their funding from big businesses, their reporting is often biased. In an attempt to limit foreign influence, foreign ownership of newspapers and magazines is capped at 45 percent.

As in the rest of Europe, television has become the primary source of information. In a problem familiar to many people in the United States, the founding of independent television stations has created an entertainment medium and which provides little in the way of news and political analysis. A more important problem is the government's attempt to influence the media. Although the monopolistic Radio and Television Committee was abolished and a supposedly nonpartisan Polish Radio and Television Broadcasting Council was created in 1993, the media has been a hostage to political infighting.

The Broadcasting Council has nine members, three of whom are selected respectively by the Sejm, Senate, and president. This body has wide-ranging powers, including the supervision of programming, the assignment of frequencies and licenses to broadcast, and the allocation of income from license fees.[21] Soon after its creation, the SLD placed its supporters on the supervisory and managing boards of Polish Television (TVP). The director of the most popular television station was fired and programs considered by left-wing politicians to be overtly critical of the communist era were canceled.[22] One head of Polish Television complained that some politicians wanted to turn television into an instrument of "indoctrination."[23]

Another obstacle to a vigorous and independent media is a strict "anti-slander" law. Unique among the four states, Article 270 of the Penal Code prohibits anyone from deriding the Polish nation, its political system, or its principal institutions. Article 273 imposes a prison sentence of up to ten years for anyone who violates this statute. The law has been enforced on several occasions.

FORMAL GOVERNMENTAL INSTITUTIONS

The Constitution

In contrast to other states in the region, Poland has a long constitutional history. Its 1791 constitution was the first in Europe. Nevertheless, a constitution which incorporated the post-1989 changes in the polity was enacted only in 1997. Prior to its enactment, the legal structure of the state was based on the 1952 Stalinist Constitution and the "Little Constitution" of 1992. The "Little Constitution" eliminated some of the most obvious anachronisms of the previous constitutional order, such as the description of Poland as a "Socialist State."

There were numerous reasons for this eight-year delay. First, as in all former socialist states, the idea of constitutionalism, or limits on the government, is new. Second, with a very polarized society, political parties could not agree on what should be included in the new political charter. As in Hungary, the former communists (SLD) wanted to include provisions that guarantee social and economic rights, while moderates wanted to include only basic political rights. Finally, the role of the church in the polity proved to be an extremely contentious issue.

The victory of the left in both parliamentary (1993) and presidential elections (1995) facilitated the adoption of the new constitution. As with most political covenants, it is a compromise document. On one hand, it provides for broad social rights, including social security, a minimum wage, guaranteed free basic health services, and education; on the other, it has provisions that weaken state control, such as legalizing the creation of private schools.

Structurally, legislative powers are shared by the Sejm and Senate; executive power is shared by the president and the Council of Ministers; and judicial power is vested in independent courts. To ensure the supremacy of the rule of law, a Constitutional Tribunal was created. Constitutional changes require a two-thirds vote of the Sejm and an absolute majority in the Senate.

In contrast to Russia, which adopted the French presidential model or Hungary which adopted the German parliamentary model, Poland created a mixed presidential-parliamentary model of government. This was the result of two unique factors. First, because the communists were still in power in 1989, Solidarity had to agree to the creation of a presidency that would allow the PUWP to keep some control over the system, a feature that was incorporated into the new constitution. The mixed model was also a compromise between two competing historical legacies: the tradition of a powerful legislature (the liberum veto); and the realization that a strong parliament had historically made Poland vulnerable to foreign control.

Regional and Local Government

After World War II, the administrative structure was reorganized. Poland was divided into 17 historical regions (voivods), 300 districts (powiaty), and 4,000 municipal (gmina) self-governments. Most regions have a long history, spanning more than four centuries. To weaken local power, in 1973 the number of regions was increased to 49 and many of their powers were transferred to the central ministries and special administrative organs. In addition, the districts were eliminated and the number of municipalities was reduced to 2,500. These changes ensured local governments acted more as agents of state control than as advocates of local interests.

In an attempt to make local government truly representative of local interests, one of the first acts of the Mazowieski government was to end the subordination of local governments to the central government. A constitutional amendment made local governments the "basic form of organization of local public life." The gmina were given increased authority over matters such as primary school education and cultural institutions. However, local government remained financially dependent on the central government.[24] In addition, after winning the parliamentary elections in September 1993, the SLD reversed its predecessor's policy of increasing the autonomy of local governments. It also replaced a large number of voivod governors with SLD members.

The adoption of a new constitution and subsequent legislation have caused one of the biggest administrative changes in any former communist state. The number of voivods was reduced to sixteen, each headed by a governor who is appointed by the prime minister. Governors are responsible for supervising the administration in their area and providing a link between the central and local governments. However, real power belongs to the sejmik, or regional assembly. This popularly elected body controls 30 percent of the income tax and 15 percent of the value-added tax (VAT) raised in their regions. Although the assemblies cannot pass laws, they oversee regional policies such as economic development and the police.[25]

In 1998 legislation reintroduced the powiaty as the intermediate tier of government between the gminas and the voivods. The 320 powiats are governed by district councils, independent of the central government. The councils have assumed most of the tasks that formally belonged to the voivods, including secondary education, health care, roads, and welfare programs. Nevertheless, the most basic unit of local self-government is the 2,489 gminas. They are responsible for "all tasks of local self-government not reserved to other units of local self-government." Although this new structure gives local governments more power than their Bulgarian or Hungarian counterparts, because Poland is not a federal state, they do not enjoy the wide powers given to local governments in the Russian Federation. Nevertheless, this structure should make officials more democratically accountable and lessen corruption.

While local governments have legal autonomy, there are numerous obstacles to independent policy making. First, since the central government still provides the bulk of local government funding, it has a large amount of influence in determining spending priorities. In addition, the state has transferred a number of programs to the municipalities without the requisite financial support. Second, the prime minister, voivod governors, and regional auditors have the authority to overrule decisions made by local authorities. In addition, the Sejm can dissolve any local council if it "flagrantly" violates the Constitution, or in case of "a prolonged lack of efficiency in performing public tasks by the organs of gmina."[26] In summary, it remains to be seen whether the administrative reforms will accomplish their goal of shifting power from the center to the periphery.

The Legislature

Like Russia, Poland has a bicameral parliament. Comprised of the Sejm and the Senate, together they constitute the legislative power of the state. The lower house, the Sejm, is the most powerful. Its 460 deputies are elected for four year terms. With the exception of the Council of Ministers, deputies and senators cannot hold state or government posts.

Organizationally, the Sejm has three major components: the Presidium, the Senior Deputies Caucus, and commissions (committees). There are twenty-four standing commissions which average between thirty and forty members. The Sejm also has the authority to form ad hoc committees. Before the first session of the Sejm, the leaders of the parties meet to decide commission chairs. Although the SLD/PSL government gave the opposition seven committee chairs, there is no legislative provision, as in Bulgaria and Hungary, for them to have any. In addition to evaluating proposed legislation, committees play a role in selecting the government through their questioning of perspective ministers. Although the Sejm is the supreme law-making authority of the state, because of the powers of the president and the government it plays a relatively minor role in policy creation. To date, its main function has been to oversee the government.

The Senate is the upper chamber of the Polish parliament. Disbanded in 1939, the communists resurrected the Senate during the 1989 Roundtable talks in an attempt to pacify the opposition while still dominating the government. The Senate has 100 members and shares legislative and budgetary powers with the Sejm, though any bill rejected by the Senate can be overridden by a two-thirds majority in the Sejm. In this regard, the power of the Senate is similar to the Federation Council in Russia or the House of Lords in Great Britain.

Both the Sejm and the Senate establish their own rules and their sessions are open to the public. In contrast to other CEE states, the Polish parliament operates permanently, with sessions formally ending only with the dissolution of parliament. Meetings of Sejm and Senate are called by their respective presidiums. Normally, the Sejm is convened every two weeks for sessions lasting three days. Unless there is pressing legislation, the first part of the week is usually reserved for deputies' meetings with constituents in their voivod.

The Electoral System

Like Bulgaria, Poland's electoral system was a little different from the Soviet model. To make the regime seem more representative, the Communist Party gave other political parties and groups seats in the Sejm. These included the United Peasant Party, the Democratic Party, and two Catholic groups. However, these groups had no power because they were members of the National Unity Front, which was controlled by the PUWP. The Front sponsored a single list of candidates in each constituency during elections.

As in Hungary and Russia, the contemporary electoral scheme is a mixed proportional-pluralist system designed to favor larger parties while still allowing smaller parties opportunities to gain representation. Of the 460 members elected to the Sejm, 115 are elected from single-seat constituencies and 345 are chosen by proportional representation. In contrast, the Senate's 100 members are elected from single-seat constituencies.

The first free elections since 1925 were held in 1991 under a complicated system of proportional representation. In some electoral districts, voters were faced with as many as thirty-seven candidates for the Sejm and twenty-seven for the Senate.[27] Since the communists had restricted the number of parties, this system was designed to give all parties an equal opportunity to participate. This electoral system allowed twenty-nine parties to gain seats in the Sejm, with none winning more than 13 percent of the total vote. This led to two years of political instability.

To remedy this situation, a new electoral law was passed in 1992. It imposed a 5 percent threshold for individual parties and 8 percent for coalitions. As a bonus to larger parties, parties with over 7 percent of the total vote would proportionally share an additional sixty-nine seats from a national list of candidates drawn up by each party. There is also an electoral provision that exempts national minorities from the 5 percent threshold. In the 1993 parliamentary elections, this new system reduced the number of parties in the Sejm to seven but had the unintended benefit of helping the better-organized parties (i.e., the former communists) win the election.

All parties who win seats in the Sejm are eligible for state subsidies. For each party member in the Sejm, the party gets 60 percent of an average worker's salary, an amount that can be increased or decreased by the presidium of the Sejm. Major parties receive free access to radio and television and the government pays for party offices in all electoral districts during an election. In contrast to the United States, these features weaken the influence of special interests. However, by helping to preserve parliamentary seats for major parties, they make it difficult for parties out of power to gain representation.

Because the electoral system was used as a tool of control under the old regime, it is still viewed more as a political weapon than a democratic tool. This can be seen in the attempted passage of a new law on local elections by the SLD/PSL government in 1994. The law would have placed greater weight on voting for parties rather than specific candidates. As in the national elections, this would have helped the most organized parties. This blatant attempt to politicize local elections was vetoed by President Walesa.

The Presidency

In the interwar period, General Pilsudski created a strong executive presidency. With the enactment of the 1952 constitution, however, Poland joined most other socialist states in creating a collective head of state—the State Council. As a result of the 1989 Roundtable talks, the Council was abolished and the presidency was reestablished. Another provision of the negotiations allowed PUWP General Secretary Jaruzelski to become the first president.

The powers of the Polish president transcend the largely ceremonial powers of his counterparts in parliamentary states such as Bulgaria and Hungary. He is elected by direct popular vote for a five-year term. Since the president is directly elected and is the only nationally elected politician, he has more authority than his Hungarian counterpart, who is elected by the parliament. Although the Polish presidency is not as strong as its Russian counterpart, the Constitution gives the office significant powers. The president is the head of state, commander-in-chief of the armed forces, and nominates the head(s) of the three top judicial bodies—the Constitutional Tribunal, Supreme Court, Chief Administrative Court—and the chief of the General Staff. The president also has the power to ratify international treaties, impose martial law or declare a state of emergency at the request of the Council of Ministers, veto Sejm legislation—which can be overruled by a 3/5 majority vote—and dissolve parliament if it cannot form a government or pass a budget within three months. The president may only be removed from office by impeachment. This requires a two-thirds vote of both houses of parliament, after which the case is tried by the State Tribunal. The president also takes an active role in the formation of the government through his nomination of the prime minister.

While these provisions gave the executive significant power, there are also checks on presidential authority. For example, although the president can issue executive orders, they are limited to certain policy areas. Even then, they must be countersigned by the prime minister. A state of emergency is limited to ninety days, although it may be extended for thirty more days with the consent of the Sejm. While a state of emergency is in place, the Sejm cannot be dissolved and the Constitution cannot be amended.

Numerous observers have compared the powers of the Polish presidency to its powerful French or Russian counterpart. This is a misleading comparison. In contrast to Russia, the Polish cabinet is responsible to the Sejm, not the president. In addition, the authority to order a national referendum in France is the exclusive prerogative of the president, while in Poland a majority vote of the Senate is required. This is an important limitation, for as the de Gaulle period in France showed, referendums can give the president a way to bypass both the government and the parliament.

In summary, the Polish presidency is a unique institution that attempts to fulfill two contradictory goals: to prevent a return to the political instability that has historically dominated the Polish polity and to prevent a return to authoritarian rule.

The Executive

In the communist era, executive authority was officially vested in the Council of Ministers. The Council directed the state administration and the economy. Although today the president shares executive power with the Council of Ministers, the latter body is the main executive authority. Constitutionally it is charged with conducting the internal affairs and the foreign policy of the Republic, drafting the state budget, and managing the governmental administration. As head of Council of Ministers, the prime minister organizes the work of the Council, selects ministers, and directs the activities of the various ministries. The Council has the power to issue regulations with the force of law.

The Sejm controls the Council of Ministers through a variety of means. First, to be elected prime minister, the nominee must have the support of a majority in parliament. Second, to be empowered, the cabinet must receive a majority in a vote of confidence within fourteen days of being nominated. If the cabinet does not receive a majority, the president appoints the prime minister and a cabinet, with a majority vote of the Sejm. Other means of controlling the government include delaying the passage of legislation and creating ad hoc commissions. These commissions have wide investigative powers, including inquiries into the actions of the Cabinet or of individual ministers. Also, as in Bulgaria and Hungary, MPs can question members of the Council of Ministers, including the prime minister.

The most important parliamentary instrument of control is the ability to call a vote of no confidence in the government. In contrast to the legislative bodies of Bulgaria and Hungary, the Sejm can also pass a vote of no confidence in individual ministers. However, no confidence motions cannot be voted on within seven days of being introduced. After a motion of no confidence has been introduced, no subsequent confidence motions can be made for three months. Similar to the Hungarian constructive vote of no confidence, the president can refuse to accept the resignation of the prime minister until a new one is appointed or elected. In summary, even with a majority in the Sejm, the Polish government has limited powers.

The Judiciary

Under the communist regime, the judicial system was politicized and dominated by the communist party. Judges were appointed by the Party and could be dismissed at will. To remedy this situation, the new Constitution guarantees the independence of the judiciary and gives them the power of judicial review. Thus their primary role is to guarantee the "inviolability of the person" and the constitutional order.

To promote judicial independence, judges are forbidden from engaging in political activity or belonging to a political party. Based on the recommendations of an autonomous and self-governing National Council of the Judiciary, judges are appointed by the president, have unlimited tenure, and can only be removed if they break the law. Organizationally, justice is administered by the Constitutional Tribunal, the Tribunal of State, the Supreme Chamber of Control, the Supreme Court, the Commissioner for Citizens' Rights, common courts, and special courts. The Constitutional Tribunal is responsible for ensuring laws and regulations are in conformity with the Constitution. Its fifteen members are elected by the Sejm for a single nine-year term. In a major expansion of its powers, the new constitution no longer allows the Sejm to override Constitutional Tribunal verdicts, greatly increasing the independence of the judiciary.

Unique to the region, Poland created a State Tribunal to prevent high state officeholders from abusing their positions. The Tribunal assesses the constitutionality of acts by the president, prime minister, members of the Council of Ministers, and other senior government officials. Its sixteen members are elected by the Sejm and hold office for the period of the Sejm's term of office. The Supreme Chamber of Control is responsible for controlling the economic, financial, and organizational activities of the state administration to ensure "legality, economic prudence, efficacy and diligence." This body was created to prevent a return to a centralized state. The Supreme Chamber of Control is particularly important today because the Polish bureaucracy is largely unreformed and obstructionist. Like other supreme courts in the area, the Polish court is charged with ensuring the administration of justice and the equal application of law by all courts.

Since the judicial system was used to suppress political opposition and provide a legal facade for state actions, reforming it has been a priority for the new regime. Although structurally the system has been changed, many problems remain. First, judges are not representative of society at large. Most judges are holdovers from the communist era and a majority are women. This is because male lawyers have more opportunities for working outside the judicial system. In addition, since judges are poorly paid, corruption is widespread.

The inefficiency of the legal system is also a major problem. Most courts have a lengthy backlog of cases, the result of a lack of funds and expertise. As an illustration, the investigators examining the Foreign Debt Servicing Fund had to wait for over a year for Finance Ministry officials to produce requested information. This case also involved international finance, an unfamiliar area for state prosecutors, requiring them to bring in expensive consultants. For a ministry that was behind in paying salaries and was unable to pay its telephone and electricity bills, this was an exorbitant cost. Even smaller tasks are not performed efficiently. On average, it takes eighteen months to simply register property deeds in Warsaw.

Another problem has to do with the laws themselves. Since numerous new statutes are needed to reflect economic and political changes, laws have been introduced faster than judicial understanding of them. In addition, since laws are not usually drafted by lawyers, there are numerous contradictions and loopholes within them. This can be seen in the limited protection for private property, a key feature of a system based on the rule of law. Another problem is the lack of experience in the numerous areas that now need regulation. For example, partly because of the lack of precedent and specialists in this area, it took over two years to enact an intellectual property law.

There are also problems with the organization of the courts themselves. The Polish legal system still uses elected lay judges to adjudicate cases. This system was established in the communist era to show the power of the people in the administration of justice. Since many have little or no legal training, not only are their decisions suspect, but they have also been susceptible to political influence and bribes. Perhaps the largest problem, however, is the lack of respect for the rule of law. Jaroslaw Kaczynski, a political opponent of President Walesa, was investigated for illegal business ties. No evidence has been found to show any such ties, but the probing "[seems] to intensify after each new salvo is fired by Kaczynski to the president and to his associates."[28] The Sejm has also passed laws that give the justice minister the right to appoint court chairpersons and influence the organization of the courts' work.

Thus the Polish legal system has numerous historical legacies to overcome. In the last two centuries, prior to 1989 Poland has experienced only six years of a democratic, law-based regime. Even when the country was free of foreign domination, law was used by the noble classes to enshrine their privileges against the rest of society. As a result of these problems, the judicial system is still not accepted as fair and impartial. In other words, the law is still seen as a political tool. After Prime Minister Oleksy was criticized in the press, he asked government prosecutors to investigate the source of the criticism for legal violations. Since this mentality is present at the highest levels of government, it should come as no surprise that average Poles do not respect the law. This attitude leads many to ignore or try to get around the law. As in other CEE states, there is a lingering belief that the law is a tool of the state to restrict people. Thus, the idea of the rule of law is still developing.

Partly as a result of these problems, Poland established a Commissioner for Citizens' Rights. The Commissioner is tasked with "safeguard[ing] the freedoms and rights of persons and citizens." The creation of this position shows the importance Poland attaches to civil rights and liberties. Although the Commissioner has been active, she has not always been effective. In one case, even after the Commissioner issued a report stating that telephone tapping by prosecutors, police, and the Office of State Security constitutes a threat to civil liberties and that prevailing laws governing this practice are not in accord with international standards, the parliament declined to pass a new law regulating this practice.[29] Nevertheless, the Commissioner has had some success. For example, anyone who wanted to buy a car formerly had to pay a deposit in advance and then wait for delivery. The Sejm passed a law stipulating that because of inflation, the amount of deposit was to be increased. After the Commissioner's intervention, a new law was passed to end this practice, thereby preventing an infringement upon property rights.

The Bureaucracy

With the notable exception of agriculture, under the communists all aspects of the polity were under central control. As a result, a huge government bureaucracy was created. Like bureaucracies elsewhere, Poland's was characterized by standard operating procedures, risk aversion, and unresponsiveness. In spite of political changes, bureaucrats from the old regime continue to maintain a large degree of influence over the state. Although high-ranking government officials were removed after 1989, most lower-level bureaucrats remain in place.[30] This is the result of two related factors: the lack of skilled professionals and the lack of resources to train a new cadre of officials. Low wages and poor working conditions have led to numerous cases of corruption. In October 1994, Prime Minister Cimoszewicz accused sixty-nine ranking officials—including three ministers—of having violated the anticorruption law by drawing a supplementary income from sitting on supervisory boards of companies linked to the state.[31]

The power of the bureaucracy continues to be substantial. Three key factors have contributed to this situation: continued state control over sectors of the economy, excessive regulation, and politization. Like other European bureaucracies, because of the parliamentary links between the executive and legislative branches the Polish bureaucracy plays a key role in policy creation and implementation. This role has been enhanced by the continued politization of the civil service. Since the state administration is under the control of the Council of Ministers, it gives the ruling party significant patronage powers. This power was further strengthened by a 1997 "reform" in which the Interior Ministry was expanded into the Interior Affairs and Administration Ministry, taking over some of the local administrative duties. The new law also strengthened the power of the prime minister and increased the chances for patronage by requiring high-ranking government and local officials to offer their resignations when a new government is elected.[32] Even without this law, like the Solidarity government before them, the SLD used the bureaucracy to install its supporters in every available position, from the judiciary to the chairmanships of state-owned insurance companies.[33] These appointments have prevented the emergence of a professional civil service and slowed the creation and implementation of reforms.

While there have been some attempts to reform the bureaucracy, as in Bulgaria and Russia there is still an urgent need for systematic changes and a reduction in the number of bureaucrats.[34] Even more important, Poland's leaders must stop using the state apparatus as a partisan political tool.

The Military

Like other parts of the polity, the Polish military is being transformed. As in Bulgaria, the armed forces, in particular the army, are viewed as the embodiment of the state. As a result of this legacy, as well as the communist desire to have a strong military, the armed forces enjoyed a privileged role in society. In today's pluralistic system, the military must compete with other interest groups for scarce resources. With the general lessening of tensions in Europe, its share of the national budget has been decreasing. However, as in Bulgaria, it enjoys the most public support of any governmental institution.

Two key issues affect the contemporary Polish armed forces: the implementation of a new national security doctrine and civilian control over the military. The new doctrine is predicated on the belief that external threats will no longer be from the West, but from the East; specifically, the unstable situation in the republics of the former Soviet Union. As a result of this new doctrine, troops are being redeployed from the western to the eastern border. At the same time, the military is being cut back from its 1989 strength of 350,000 to 200,000 soldiers. The doctrine also recognized the need for close collaboration with neighboring states and the importance of becoming a member of NATO.

The enactment of this new doctrine is causing numerous problems. First, reducing the armed forces has added to the already high number of unemployed. Second, the military is split over the prospect of joining NATO. Interestingly, polls show older officers are more in favor of joining than younger officers. Since the younger officers will have to implement this policy, this could be a significant policy impediment.

Third, as in Bulgaria and Hungary, change has been impeded by financial limitations. Troop redeployments and the integration of Polish weapons systems with NATO forces requires money the military does not have. In 1989, military spending equaled 8.9 percent of GDP. In 1994, it was down to 2.1 percent. According to independent analysts, this is not even enough to prevent the army's "technical degradation."[35] These problems, compounded with decreasing living standards for the formerly privileged officer class, will increase military frustration with the new regime. If conditions deteriorate enough, it is conceivable the military might become involved in politics. Precedents include Pilsudski's 1926 coup and the declaration of martial law in 1981. Although remote—there is no military officer with Pilsudski's popularity and a military government would lack external support—the likelihood of military intervention is higher than in Hungary or Russia.

The second major aspect of military reform is enhancing civilian control over the military. Enshrining civilian control is one of the basic principles of a democratic state. Although institutional reforms have been enacted, there is still some ambiguity about the chain of command. For example, while the president can appoint and dismiss the chief of the General Staff, the defense minister answers to the prime minister. Since this ambiguity was the result of constitutional compromise, it will be difficult to overcome. The dismissal of the chief-of-staff in March 1997, allegedly for resisting the authority of the civilian minister of defense, shows the degree of resistance to this policy.[36] Constitutional ambiguity allows the military to play a larger role in the polity than in Western states.

THE ELITE

As a result of Poland's unique history, and in marked contrast to their regional counterparts, Polish Communists were never able to completely dominate society. This can be seen in their tolerance of private farming and the Catholic church as well as the existence of numerous dissident groups. As in Hungary, by the 1980s the power of the Party had been drastically reduced. Its weakness can be seen in the use of the military rather than civilian security organs to declare martial law in 1981. The ending of the Party's monopoly on power in 1989 signaled the rebirth of pluralistic politics. Today governmental and nongovernmental elites struggle for power and influence.

The Governmental Elite

As in Bulgaria, Polish political parties can be roughly divided into two groups: those with roots in the communist period and those without. Even within these categories there is a plethora of ideological positions. This factionalization has caused parties to fragment, which until recently fostered political instability.

The most significant determinants of Polish political affiliation are economic beliefs, geography, religion, and education. Economically, voters are divided almost equally between supporters of a market economy, opponents to it, and supporters of a mixed state/market system. As would be expected, people who have been hurt most by the new system are the most hostile to it. They include pensioners, peasants, and unskilled workers. In contrast, supporters of a market economy are mostly younger people, those with an advanced education, and those who live in urban areas. Geographically, people who live in the former German and Austrian partitions, which are more industrialized and urban than the Russian partition, are more educated and consequently tend to vote for the new parties. These areas also have a higher voting turnout, 10 to 15 percent above the countrywide average. The intensity of personal religious convictions also has a major influence in political affiliation. Devout Catholics are vehemently anticommunist and against a strong state. This section examines how these societal splits are reflected in the political parties.

The Democratic Left Alliance (SLD)

The SLD, Poland's largest political organization, is a coalition of twenty-eight groups and organizations, most of which have their roots in the communist era. Of all the postcommunist parties in Central and Eastern Europe, the SLD is probably the most democratic and inclusive, covering the gamut from free marketeers to unreconstructed communists. While one would expect such a diverse group to suffer from political infighting, the societal divide between communists and anticommunists fosters unity.

Like any professional political organization, the platform of the party has changed with the times. In 1993, it stressed an active state role in the economy—that is, subsidized state industries and wages, limited privatization, and increased social benefits to lessen economic inequalities. In contrast, the 1997 platform called for a "lasting and stable democracy, an efficient and open economy, and a just and united society." Even though the rightist SEA won a plurality in the 1997 parliamentary election, the SLD increased its percentage of the vote. This is partly the result of the SLD's superior use of resources and organization. In contrast to other parties, they made sure that local offices in every electoral district were equipped with telephones, faxes, and the like.

Its broad constituency includes former *nomenklatura* as well as the unemployed, blue-collar workers, elderly, and people with a secondary education or less. With the exception of the *nomenklatura*, the SLD represents those on the margins of society. These people have grown weary of the economic instability that has accompanied structural changes since 1989 and associate socialist programs with pre-1989 economic stability. Although they have support throughout the country, the SLD has been especially popular in areas of high unemployment (e.g., Silesia), in small and medium towns, and in western Poland.

The Polish Peasant Party (PSL)

The Polish Peasant Party is the successor of the United Peasant Party, a communist front party that supposedly represented the peasants during the communist era. Between 1993 and 1997, the PSL was junior partner in the SLD government. The PSL's platform promises state funds for agriculture, guaranteed prices for farm produce, and high tariffs to protect farmers from foreign competition. While the PSL pays lip service to the idea of a free market, its programs favor state ownership of major industries as well as state intervention in the economy.

The PSL draws most of its support from poorly educated farmers who want the continuation of expensive agricultural subsidies. Geographically, they are strongest in the old Russian partition—the most backward economically—and in the central part of the country, such as the Plotsk region, where peasants were never collectivized. Because of its unified constituency, Poland's large peasant population, and the fragmentation of parties on the right, the PSL has much more political influence than its counterparts in other CEE states. This can be seen in the selection of its leader as prime minister in 1993. In a dramatic shift, the party lost more than half of its electoral support in the 1997 election. More than any other party, the PSL was hurt by the creation of the SEA. With the conservative and religious parties now united, the traditionally conservative rural population returned to their natural voting inclination.

The Freedom Union (FU)

Although created through the merging of the Democratic Union and the Liberal Democratic Congress in 1994, the FU traces its history to the 1989 Roundtable talks. During the talks, its leaders served as advisors to Solidarity. Like the SLD, the FU represents a wide political spectrum, albeit to the right of center. The party platform supports market reforms, free trade and privatization. The FU is also committed to social justice, political tolerance, and a "moral role" for the church. Because most of its members are well educated—47 percent have university degrees—it is often viewed as the party of the intelligentsia. Most FU supporters live in the large cities—

Warsaw and Krakow—and in the western part of the country, along the prosperous German border.

Non-Party Bloc to Support Reforms (BBWR)

The BBWR, or the Bloc, was founded by President Lech Walesa in 1993. Officially, the BBWR was created to unite various segments of the population who are normally not politically active and to lessen parliamentary and societal conflict. However, it is generally accepted that Walesa created the bloc to prevent the former communists from regaining power and to serve as a personal political vehicle. Thus the BBWR is similar to Jozef Pilsudski's Nonparty Bloc to Cooperate with the Government, which was established to support his authoritarian rule in 1927.

The Bloc lacks a concrete platform, although it does support some market reforms. While it draws some support from blue-collar workers, middle-aged people with a higher education, and the church, the largest group of supporters are traditionalists who are anticommunist and anti-Russian. They believe Poland's salvation lies in the creation of a stronger executive. Geographically, the Bloc is most influential in Gdansk—Walesa's hometown—and the Tatra mountains. Partially as a result of an undefined platform, the BBWR won only 5.4 percent of the vote in the 1993 elections. It ceased to exist as an independent party when it became part of the Solidarity Electoral Alliance in 1997.

Confederation for an Independent Poland (KPN)

This party was founded in the 1970s as an anticommunist opposition movement. Although the party remains anticommunist, it has remade itself into a populist party. As a result, it appeals to skilled workers and young people—mostly men, anticommunists, anti-Solidarity, urban voters—in other words, the people most afraid of losing their economic position. Geographically, its strongest support is in Silesia. Although it won 5.8 percent of the vote in 1993 and 7.5 percent in 1991, the KPN failed to clear the electoral threshold in 1997.

Union of Labor (UP)

An offshoot of Solidarity, the UP is Poland's social democratic party. Its supporters include clerks, people with a secondary education, young women who are pro-choice, and anti-clerics. It is one of three parties, along with the SLD and PSL, whose percentage of votes increased between 1991 and 1993. In the 1997 election, the UP barely failed to clear the 5 percent electoral threshold.

Movement of Poland's Reconstruction (ROP)

Founded after the 1995 presidential election by former prime minister Jan Olszewski, this party appeals to disaffected. Their strength is the result of a nationalist populist program that blames Poland's problems on the former *nomenklatura*'s control over business and politics. Support for this view can be seen in their 5.6 share of the vote in the 1997 election.

Solidarity Electoral Action (SEA)

This coalition was founded in 1996 to unite right-wing parties that separately failed to win the 5 percent of the vote necessary to enter parliament in the 1993 election. Since it is an amalgamation of thirty-seven parties and movements ranging from Thatcherite liberals to peasants, the party's platform is broad on generalities and short on details. Seemingly contradictory, Marian Krzaklewski, the leader of the SEA, has promised to overhaul public services and create a more equitable society while at the same time ensuring economic growth. The alliance also stresses pro-family and traditional values.

The coalition's core supporters are Catholic nationalists, populists, and blue-collar workers united by a common dislike of the ex-communists, whom they accuse of "stealing" the revolution. While this alliance allowed the SEA to take power in 1997, it is doubtful their dislike of the communists will be enough to hold the disparate factions together. As an illustration, complaining that the government was not following the provisions of the SEA manifesto, less than a year after the election one of the SEA members— the Confederation for an Independent Poland-Patriotic Camp—threaten to withdraw from the alliance.[37]

MARIAN KRZAKLEWSKI (1950–)

Marian Krzaklewski, holder of a Ph.D. in computer science, became active in politics when he joined the Solidarity movement in 1980. Rising quickly through the ranks, he was elected head of the movement in 1991. After electoral loss to the former communists in 1993 because of in-fighting between parties on the right, he realized the only way to regain power was to unite them. Under the banner of the Solidarity Electoral Alliance, Krzaklewski consolidated the anticommunists opposed to the SLD government. By 1996, a reinvigorated Solidarity had increased its popular support to nearly 20 percent, and a year later it won a plurality in the 1997 elections.

Known as an excellent organizer and strong leader, Krzaklewski has been the driving force behind the reemergence of the right. His platform represents disillusionment with the new system and opposition to the old. Krzaklewski believes the Roman Catholic church should occupy a prominent role in Polish society and is against the free market reforms proposed by the left. He uses populist political tactics and anticommunist sentiment to rally voters. As a result of his success in unifying center-right parties, Krzaklewski is viewed by many as a likely presidential candidate in 2000.

National German Party (MN)

Although they received only 0.7 percent of the vote, because of the minority electoral provision, this party won four seats in the 1993 elections. In addition to protecting minority rights, the MN advocates closer economic ties with Germany. As a result, it draws most of its support from the old German partition—Opole, Katowice, and Czestochowa.

1993 Parliamentary Elections

Contested for the first time under the new election law, the 1993 elections radically changed the composition of the Sejm. Although twenty parties won votes, only seven passed the threshold for representation. The elections were an undisputed victory for the left. Although they won only 35 percent of the vote, the new electoral system gave them over two-thirds of the seats in both the Sejm and the Senate. Respectively, the SLD won 171 seats in the Sejm and the PSL 132. The largest opposition party, the Freedom Union, won only 10.6 percent of the vote, giving it seventy-four seats. Compared to the 1991 election, support for the Solidarity-linked parties dropped from 50 to 40 percent. The overwhelming success of the leftist parties can be attributed to the fragmentation of parties on the right, the ability of the socialists to mobilize their own supporters, and voters tired of suffering the hardships associated with economic reform. The success of the left was analogous to the electoral outcomes in Bulgaria, Hungary, and Russia. However, in contrast to those states, the electoral turnout—52 percent—was significantly higher than the 43 percent turnout in the 1991 parliamentary elections. Nevertheless, this is still the lowest of the four states.

While many people were alarmed by the prospect of communists again running the country, there was a benefit to this new political alignment. With only two parties controlling the government, Poland had some much-needed political stability. In its first months in office, the new government continued economic reforms, albeit more slowly. Because of its dependence on international sources of funding, the socialists had few other options.

1995 Presidential Elections

In a close election, the head of the SLD, Alexander Kwasniewski, defeated incumbent Lech Walesa by a 52–48 percent margin. Voter turnout was 68 percent. The election showed the continued polarization of the Polish polity. The big cities, rural areas, and the south and east voted for Walesa, while the towns and the north and west backed Kwasniewski. Because of the left's electoral success in 1993 and 1995, almost half the population are not represented in the parliament or the presidency.

Significantly, the left did not win the election as much as the right lost it. Kwasniewski portrayed himself as a new politician, modeling his campaign on President Clinton's. He also played down his past with the slogan "Let's

---

ALEXANDER KWASNIEWSKI (1955–)

President Kwasniewski began his political career by joining the ruling Polish United Workers' Party (Communist Party) when he was an undergraduate at Gdansk University. Rising slowly through the party ranks, he was appointed Minister of Youth in 1985. During the 1989 Roundtable talks with Solidarity, Kwasniewski served as one of the Communist representatives. Two years later, he was elected as a MP for the SLD, a social democratic party comprised mostly of former Communists. He worked hard to create a new image of the party as a responsible, pro-reform force, sensitive to human needs, especially in the face of the poverty and unemployment brought on by market reforms. Taking over as a leader of the SLD, Kwasniewski led it to victory in the 1993 parliamentary elections. Not satisfied with being the party leader, he began a concerted effort to capture the presidency.

His appeal to the voters stemmed from both his image and his message of reform. In contrast to the sharp tongue and poor syntax of his predecessor, the neatly dressed, media friendly Kwasniewski ran as the candidate who would lead Poland into the next century. He pledged compromise and political peace after six years of turbulent reforms. This led to his election as president in 1995. Since taking power, Kwasniewski has been a voice of moderation, supporting membership in NATO and the EU. Although once a critic of market economics, he now supports market reforms. Overall, Kwasniewski has been instrumental in integrating Poland with the west and fostering continuing economic and political reforms.

Choose the Future." In contrast, Walesa ran a negative campaign based on the simple message that a vote for the SLD was a vote for returning to the past. This message, combined with poor public speaking skills, did not resonate with an electorate tired of societal confrontation.

After the results of the vote were announced, 600,000 letters were sent to the Supreme Court demanding the election be annulled because Kwasniewski had made misleading campaign statements about his educational and financial background. This mass protest showed not only the ability of the right to mobilize a half a million people in a few days, but also the great divide in the polity.

1997 Parliamentary Elections

As in Hungary, the victory of the left fostered political cooperation among the parties on the right. Unifying under the banner of Solidarity and boosted by the common perception that the ex-communist elite has profited more than anyone else from Poland's change in regime, they won almost a third of the vote. This was the best electoral showing by any group since the new regime was created. Since the SEA is a coalition of thirty-seven parties domi-nated by a trade union, the longevity of the government is in doubt. Within a year of the election, defections had reduced the number of SEA Sejm seats from 201 to 187. As a result, the SEA/FU governing coalition's majority fell from thirty-one to seventeen seats.

Interestingly, the two most successful parties—the SLD and the SEA—ran on platforms that would curb inflation, cut unemployment, speed priva-tization, and continue efforts to gain membership in the EU and NATO. Thus, in contrast to Bulgaria and Russia, the election showed an emerging societal consensus. However, the election also showed the defining issue in Polish politics continues to be whether or not one was a communist. This deep divide limits the ability of the parties to fulfill their campaign promises and increases public apathy. On a positive note, 6,600 candidates competed

FIGURE 4.1   Sejm Electoral Results—1991, 1993, and 1997

Party	% of votes in			total seats* in		
	1991	1993	1997	1991	1993	1997
Democratic Left Alliance (SLD)	12.0	20.4	27.1	60	171	164
Polish Peasant Party (PSL)	8.7	15.4	7.3	50	132	27
Democratic Union (UD)	12.3	10.6	—	62	74	—
Union of Labor (UP)	2.1	7.3	—	4	41	—
Confederation for an Independent Poland (KPN)	7.5	5.8	—	51	22	—
Nonparty Bloc to Support Reforms (BBWR)	—	5.4	—	—	16	—
German Minority	1.7	.7	—	7	4	—
"Fatherland" Catholic Election Committee	9.8	6.4	—	53	—	—
Solidarity#	5.1	4.9	33.8	27	—	210
Freedom Union (FU)$	—	—	13.4	—	—	60
Center Alliance	8.7	4.4	—	44	—	—
Liberal Democratic Congress	7.5	4.0	—	37	—	—
Polish Peasant Party—Peasant Alliance	5.5	2.4	—	28	—	—
Others	19.1	12.3	—	44	—	—

Note: Voter turnout: 1991—43%
                        1993—52%
                        1997—48%

* In 1993, a 5% threshold to gain seats in the Sejm was enacted.

Solidarity formed an alliance with a number of smaller parties following the 1993 elections to form the Solidarity Election Action (AWS) party. After its 1997 win, it was renamed the Social Movement for Solidarity Electoral Action.

$ The Freedom Union was created in 1994 as a result of the merging Democratic Union and Liberal Democratic Congress.

Sources: Jan de Weydenthal, "Poland: Personal, Political Clashes Make Solidarity Victory Shaky," *RFE/RL* http://www.rferl.org/nca/features/1997/09/F.RU.970925151234.html, and Louis Vinton, "Poland Goes Left," *RFE/RL Research Report,* 8 October 1993.

for the 460 Sejm seats and the turnout was 59 percent, 7 percent higher than in the 1993 parliamentary elections.

Nongovernmental Elites

Since 1989, nongovernmental elite groups have increased in size and influence, affecting both policy making and implementation. Two of the most influential groups are the former *nomenklatura* and the Roman Catholic church.

Although its economy is growing, Poland's transition has not been without problems. The privatization of state property has allowed the former *nomenklatura* to gain control over it, allowing them to exchange their status of a political elite under socialism for the status of an economic elite under capitalism.[38] Although this group is now in competition with an emerging class of entrepreneurs, the later group has so far ignored the political process to focus on personal profit. However, as in Russia, it seems likely that in the future they will become involved in politics in order to protect their economic status.

Historically, the most important nongovernment actor has been the Catholic church. With over 90 percent of the population professing to be Catholic, the church has played a significant role in the development of the Polish polity. For most of the nineteenth century, when Poland ceased to exist as a state, the church led the struggle to preserve Polish language and culture. After Poland was reconstituted as a state following World War I, the church and state were closely linked. During the communist era, and although the government tried to eliminate its influence, the church became the rallying point for opposition to the regime. Its historic role gave the church an unprecedented degree of autonomy. The church remained the moral authority for the people, creating an uneasy coexistence between an authoritarian system that controlled society and the church that greatly influenced it.

Today the church is unique among interest groups in Poland. This is the result of history and laws that give certain rights to the church. As a result of the 1989 "Relationship of the State to the Catholic Church in Poland Act," the Catholic church is a legal entity. This agreement also gave the church priority in obtaining publishing and broadcasting space; the right to perform religious instruction in schools, the military, and prisons; and tax breaks. Most important, it allowed the church to recover estates and property confiscated under the communists. These features have given it a tremendous amount of influence.

The church also exercises influence through unofficial links with political parties. Although the Pope has discouraged the church's official involvement in politics, certain parties have made sure their platforms conform to the views of the church. Their influence can be seen in such unpopular laws as the ban on abortion and the restoration of religious instruction in schools.[39] As a result, many Poles think the church meddles too much in politics. This

CARDINAL STEFAN WYSZYNSKI (1901–)

Ordained in 1924 and selected as a cardinal in 1952, Stefan Wyszynski has been called the "Primate of the Millennium." After pursuing his education in Warsaw, Lomza, Wloclawek, Lublin, France, Italy, and Belgium, Wyszynski founded the Christian Workers' University in 1935. He fled Poland just in time to avoid being sent to the concentration camps, but returned in 1945 and established a seminary. The following year he was selected as a bishop.

Wyszynski signed a coexistence agreement with the communists, but he refused to condone the state's persecution of the people. In 1953, the year after he was elevated to cardinal, Wyszynski was put under house arrest for refusing to discipline priests who acted against the government. Three years later, he was released and began working with Wladyslaw Gomulka to defuse tension over the relationship between church and state. In return for religious education in state schools, Wyszynski agreed to give the government veto power over the appointment of high-ranking church officials. Wyszynski's relationship with Gomulka's successor, Edward Gierek, was not as strong. However, the uneasy truce between the Catholic church and the communist government continued, with Wyszynski publicly endorsing the government but at the same time supporting opposition groups such as Solidarity.

Wyszynski had a large impact on the relationship between the church and state in Poland. He was instrumental in preserving the power of the church at the expense of the government. This allowed Poland to maintain a civil society and links with the Western world while still under communist rule.

can be seen in the 1993 parliamentary elections and the 1995 presidential victory of the former communist Alexander Kwasniewski, despite strong church efforts against him.

Church-state relations in Poland have been the source of great controversy since 1989. Even though the system has changed, the church has tried to continue its previous societal role. As an illustration, Catholic bishops tried to get "moral values" enshrined in the new constitution and, instead of a strict separation of church and state, argued for an "independent and autonomous" relationship.[40] This has led to an ongoing debate about the role of the church in the polity, with public opinion increasingly in favor of ending the privileged position of the church. A January 1993 poll showed 59 percent of the respondents considered the influence of the Catholic church on the political and social life as excessive.[41] The societal split regarding the role of religion can be seen in the five-year delay in ratifying a treaty with the Vatican that regulates Poland's relations with the church.

While the church has considerable contemporary influence—three separate passages in the preamble of the new constitution refer to God and the "Christian heritage of the Nation"—it is likely that the power of the church will wane. Although 90 percent of the population is Catholic, only 60 percent attend church regularly. Since the largest group of practitioners is over 50, this percentage is likely to decrease in the future.

THE GENERAL PUBLIC

After the communists came to power, all political parties and formations not controlled by the PUWP were outlawed, leading most Poles to forsake political involvement. Polls conducted in the 1980s showed that a majority of the population was more interested in economic growth than political participation.[42] Thus the only time large segments of the population became "politically" involved was over economic issues. Significantly, every leadership change—1956, 1970, 1981, 1989—was the direct result of economic protests.

While a majority of the population was politically apathetic, segments of the Polish intelligentsia continued to fight the regime. This can be seen in the illegal creation of a Polish chapter of Amnesty International and the Confederation of Independent Poland. By the mid-1980s, there were over 2,000 regular *samizdat*—self-published and prohibited—publications in Poland, more than in other CEE state. The inability of the security forces to eradicate these groups, combined with growing economic problems, gradually undermined the legitimacy of the regime.

The culmination of these trends put Poland in the forefront of democratic change, setting off a chain reaction in the rest of the region. As in other CEE states, Poland's initial movement toward democracy was characterized by public euphoria and a willingness to participate in the political process. However, as low electoral turnout indicates, this no longer seems to be the case. What has caused the return to political apathy? First, most people still do not view the government as "their own." The legacy of the communist "us versus them" mentality is still prevalent. Most people do not think their participation makes a difference. This belief is compounded by the widespread perception that politicians are opportunists.[43] Not surprisingly, these perceptions have caused many people to abstain from political involvement. Finally, there is a lack of government credibility. High societal expectations in 1990 were dashed as the Solidarity government did not tell the people about upcoming economic hardships. This factor should become less significant with continuing economic growth.

Poles also have a tradition of involvement outside politics. Although the country was officially atheist, there were over 15,000 functioning churches; and in a socialized economy, 75 percent of the farmland was in private hands. Thus, in certain areas large sections of the population were outside of the control of the state. Thus people influenced state policy without the danger of being politically active. These traditions reinforce the contemporary disdain for politics. In a 1994 poll, 70 percent of Poles said it is better not to be involved in politics, the highest negative response in the region.[44] As a result, politics seem irrelevant to average people. In particular, youth are anti-politics and anti-state. This attitude could have detrimental consequences in the future because it might question the need for a pluralistic society.

Political Recruitment

As in other democracies, the primary way in which Poles can influence the political system is by joining political parties. However, the common perceptions that politicians are corrupt and that politics is a dirty business have kept most people from joining. As a result, only 2 percent of the population are members of political parties.

Negative perceptions of politicians are reinforced by the numerous "leftovers" from the communist period. Out of the twenty-one ministers who took office following the 1993 elections, sixteen had either been members of the PUWP or the United Peasant Party. Because membership in the PUWP or one of its front parties was a prerequisite to formal political involvement, many leaders of the center and right parties also have links with the previous regime. This situation has important implications for the future development of the Polish polity. If people fail to vote or join political parties, the legitimacy of the new democratic regime might be questioned.

Modes of Influence

A history of government repression, contemporary public apathy, and numerous fragmented and ineffective political parties have all combined to limit the public's political influence. However, as the number of people choosing to become formally involved in politics decreases, less formal means of participation are becoming more popular. One means by which the general public can influence the government is through interest groups. Since 1989, interest groups have played an increasingly important role in both directly and indirectly influencing policy decisions.

It is difficult to overstate the importance of trade unions in Poland's postwar history. Three of the four communist leaders were replaced following worker discontent. Although during most of the communist period workers were grouped into official unions that supported the regime, during the 1980s several independent trade unions emerged, the most important of which was Solidarity. Between 1980 and 1981, 11 million people, out of a workforce of 16 million, joined Solidarity. This level of support threatened governmental control, culminating in the banning of Solidarity and the declaration of martial law in 1981. While this move temporarily weakened Solidarity, increasing economic problems in the late 1980s again brought

Solidarity into the political arena. Its leaders played a key role in the Round-table talks that led to the end of the communist regime.

Post-1989 changes in the polity have greatly weakened Solidarity. What had been a unified workers' movement has dissolved into numerous, and in some cases competing, factions. Today four countrywide industrial unions operate alongside seventeen other major independent industrial branch unions and three agriculture unions. The National Alliance of Trade Unions (OPZZ), the successor of its communist-era namesake, is the largest union, with approximately 4 million members and 61 parliamentary deputies. Solidarity still has over 2 million members but has lost many to spinoffs such as the Christian Trade Union Solidarity and Solidarity 80 (500,000). Other unions include the Free Miners' Union (300,000 members) and the National Teachers' Union. Economic changes have made Solidarity, once the bitter opponent of the communist regime, tacit allies with the ex-communists in opposing job-threatening economic reforms.

In recognition of the importance of Solidarity in ending the communist regime, Poland has numerous legal provisions that give unions political influence. First, the labor code guarantees workers the right to join a union. As a result, over 80 percent of the workforce has joined a union—in contrast, only 13 percent of the workforce is unionized in the United States. As in Germany, workers' councils by law must be involved in the decision-making process at both state and private companies.

Trade unions also influence the polity through their ability to organize strikes and demonstrations. As a result of increasing economic hardship, the number of strikes has increased. Several strikes took place in 1996, including actions by coal miners and doctors. Nevertheless, trade union influence has declined with the change in regime. This is primarily the result of two factors. First, the common purpose—that is, getting rid of the communists—that kept Solidarity united under the old regime is gone. Second, and more significant, was the end of cooperation among various societal groups. Solidarity represented the first time in Polish history that intellectuals, students, and workers worked together. Previous revolts against communist rule were always led by one group or another, but they never truly joined forces until the creation of Solidarity. Therefore, it was only natural that this "unholy alliance" would end. Unfortunately, an opportunity to overcome historical animosities has been lost, lessening the degree of societal consensus, a phenomenon that can be seen in the rise of numerous political parties. This situation has been intensified by the personal animosities of leading politicians. Worried that he had become marginalized, Lech Walesa got Solidarity to support his 1990 bid for the presidency. This act greatly politicized the union, accelerating its fragmentation.

The lack of social consensus has led to the creation of interest groups and other quasipolitical groups. Party X, a militant anti-immigrant group, was created to support previously unknown political emigre businessman

Stanislaw Tyminski's 1991 bid for the presidency. This group has been blamed for attacks on Jewish and other minority groups. Although the influence of extremist groups is limited, their existence indicates discontent with the current state of affairs. Interestingly, groups that played a large role in the past, such as the Church and trade unions, have discredited themselves by continuing to involve themselves in politics. In one case (without discussion in the Sejm), the Church was able to get the government to issue an administrative order mandating that religion be taught in schools. Like the old regime, policy in this case was enacted by administrative fiat, not political debate.

The public as a whole has gained limited political influence. In addition to voting for political parties, the public can influence policy through referendums. To call for a vote on a referendum, 500,000 signatures must be submitted to the Sejm speaker. Although the final decision on holding a referendum lies with the president or Parliament, the result of a referendum is binding if more than half of the number of eligible voters participate. While the cynicism and apathy of the communist period has given way to more meaningful participation, a significant proportion of the population has yet to become politically active. Encouragingly, some movement is occurring at the grassroots level. Although groups are mostly concerned with local issues such as trash pickup, phone installations, and neighborhood associations, their creation suggests people are starting to realize that they can affect the polity. This is significant because such groups are the genesis of a civil society.

POLICY MAKING AND IMPLEMENTATION

Based on the Soviet model, the official policy-making structure of the Polish People's Republic was a facade for the real decision maker, the politburo of the PUWP. As in the other CEE states, the Communist Party both created and implemented policy through an interlocking directorate of party and state officials. Thus the policy-making process took place behind closed doors at the PUWP headquarters and involved only a small number of people. The end of the communist monopoly on power brought significant changes to the policy-making process. As the result of institutional ambiguity and numerous new actors, policy making has become much more complicated and is now the outcome of bargaining, compromise, or stalemate among various governmental and nongovernmental actors.

In contrast to the parliamentary systems in Bulgaria and Hungary, Poland's mixed presidential/parliamentary system diffuses policy-making authority. The Constitution identifies both the president and the Council of Ministers as institutions of executive power. It allows Sejm Deputies, senators, the president of the Republic, and the Council of Ministers to initiate legislation. Nevertheless, to date approximately 60 percent of draft legislation has come from the Council of Ministers.

There are five stages of policy formulation. First, a bill is usually written by specialists in the ministry that will oversee its implementation. The bill then goes to the Council of Ministers for approval. In contrast to other CEE states, before the draft legislation is sent from the government to the Sejm, parliamentary rules state that the government must "present the results of consultations and public discussions and include various opinions." This allows various groups to comment on the proposed legislation. The bill is then introduced into the Sejm for its first reading. At this point, the bill is either rejected, examined by the Sejm and sent to the relevant committee, or sent directly to committee. Polish committees have limited influence on legislation. This is a result of several factors. First, committee discussions of draft legislation take place only after its first reading, in which the basic form of the bill is already determined. In contrast, the Bulgarian and Hungarian parliaments consider bills only after they are first discussed in committees. This gives committees in the latter states more influence over legislation. Also in contrast to Bulgaria and Hungary, there is no constitutional provision that requires committees to reflect the strength of the various parties in the Sejm. Since the government usually has a majority in parliament, most governmental bills are approved at committee level without major changes.

Finally, while Sejm committees may discuss bills and introduce changes to the initial version, if the sponsor—usually the cabinet—disagrees with the amendments, the bill is taken out of the committee and discussed by the whole Sejm. As in the British House of Commons, these parliamentary rules speed up adoption of legislation since they concentrate the power in the hands of the majority party and the executive. However, they also limit the independence of committees.

After discussing a bill, the committee sends it to the whole Sejm for a second reading. Committee reports are presented and proposed changes debated. If no changes are proposed, the bill is given a third—final—reading and voted on. If the bill receives a simple majority, with a quorum of at least half of the deputies present, it is sent to the Senate. If amendments are added, the bill is returned to committee, where the amendments are evaluated. The bill then returns to the Sejm for a third reading where the amendments, if any, are voted upon.

After the bill is introduced, the Senate has thirty days to adopt or reject the bill or propose amendments. If the Senate does not act within thirty days, the legislation is considered passed. If the Senate amends or rejects the bill, the Sejm may overrule the Senate by a simple majority. Unlike other bicameral legislatures, such as Germany and the United States, in which disagreements between the two houses are reconciled in a joint committee, this is not the case in Poland. As in Russia, the upper house has the power only to delay legislation, not defeat it.

The draft legislation is sent to the president, who has three options: sign the bill, veto it, or send it to the Constitutional Tribunal for a ruling on its constitutionality. If the president vetoes the bill, it is returned to the appropriate Sejm committee for reconsideration. The Sejm then decides to either revise the bill or with a three-fifths vote, override the presidential veto. If the president or a group of fifty MPs refers the bill to the Constitutional Tribunal and it is judged constitutional, he must sign it. These provisions ensure that neither the president nor the government abuses its powers.

As in Bulgaria, the government can also declare a bill urgent, speeding its adoption. If a bill is declared urgent, the Senate has to act within fourteen days rather than the normal thirty and the president must act within seven days rather than twenty-one. Because of parliamentary instability and the urgent need for introducing economic and political reforms, this prerogative was used extensively between 1990 and 1993.

Policy-Making Obstacles

As a result of the mixed parliamentary/presidential system and the lack of societal consensus, there are significant obstacles to policy making. The first is the lack of experienced politicians. By occupation, the largest group in the 1993–1997 Sejm are farmers—13 percent. In contrast, lawyers and legal specialists comprised only 4 percent of the membership. While this situation might be applauded in the United States, it slows policy making. Inexperience is not only limited to the Sejm. Many bills have had to be redrafted because of a lack of expertise in the various ministries. A related problem is the sheer number of laws that need to be enacted in order to reflect the changed polity. These obstacles make it difficult to evaluate and enact policy.

Institutional ambiguities also slow policy making. An example is conflicting jurisdiction over national security and foreign policy. Although the Constitution gives the cabinet the authority to "ensure the internal security of the State and public order [and] ensure the external security of the State" (Article 146), it also states that the president shall safeguard the sovereignty and security of the state as well as the inviolability and integrity of its territory (Article 126). While the Constitution tries to resolve this ambiguity by stating that the president of the Republic shall cooperate with the prime minister . . . in respect to foreign policy (Article 133), this general statement is no substitute for specific constitutional guidelines.

Since the first four postcommunist governments and the president were supported by Solidarity, constitutional ambiguity was not an issue. This situation changed with the parliamentary victory of the left in 1993. Forced to "cohabit" with a president from another political party, the new government stated its desire to change the way foreign policy and security policy were formulated. A member of the PPL noted that "although [Foreign Minister] Skubiszewski's style of policy making has been well-received, his links to the president created 'uncertainty' about who made foreign policy decisions." Another member of the governing coalition was even blunter: "It is necessary to change the situation in which the foreign minister is subordinated both to the president and the prime minister ... which results in an actual doubling of policy."[45]

Overall, however, the most important policy-making obstacle is the polarized political arena. The lack of societal consensus has amplified the effect of other policy impediments.

Policy-Making Influences

While the formal policy-making process is relatively straightforward, it is only one part of a much larger process. There are numerous governmental and nongovernmental actors who have had an impact on state policy.

Governmental Actors

The most important factor influencing policy making is the absence of a clear governmental majority in the Sejm. The first postcommunist governments show the combined problems of a weak parliamentary majority and weak party discipline. Comprised of up to seven parties, these coalitions had little control over their membership. Since their withdrawal from the government might cause elections to be held, small parties wielded much more influence than their electoral support would suggest. In May 1993, a small offshoot of Solidarity that had previously supported the government introduced a no-confidence motion that led to the collapse of the Suchocka government, forcing new elections. Although coalition governments incorporate more societal interests, they can also complicate and limit policy making. This limitation is no longer important since the new electoral law allowed both the SLD/PSL alliance and the SEA to win absolute majorities in the 1993 and 1997 parliamentary elections. Their success consolidated government support in the parliament and expedited the policy-making process.

Although unusual, the Sejm as a whole can also affect policy formulation by its refusal to support cabinet proposals. As an illustration, in March 1993 the Sejm rejected an important government-sponsored economic plan dealing with privatization of large-scale enterprises.[46] Opposition parties also influence the policy-making process. They can submit draft legislation and, through the committees, attempt to amend government bills. They can also use the floor of the Sejm as a forum to criticize the government. More significantly, when bills require a larger majority—two-thirds for constitutional amendments and three-fifths to overturn a presidential veto—opposition parties can have a decisive influence on policy.

Two other state institutions play a role in policy formulation. In addition to the ability to introduce legislation, the president can influence policy through his ability to veto legislation and by forwarding legislation passed by the Sejm to the Constitutional Tribunal for review. The president can also use the presidency as a bully pulpit. According to the Constitution, he can "deliver a message to the Sejm, to the Senate or to the National Assembly [which] shall not be a subject of debate" (Article 140).

The Constitutional Tribunal also influences policy by defining the powers of various governmental organs and considering the constitutionality of laws. While its past influence was limited by the parliament's ability to overrule its decisions, the removal of this provision from the new Constitution should allow it to play a more important role in the future.

Nongovernmental actors

In contrast to other CEE states, interest groups have played a significant role in the policy-making process. This can be seen in their sponsorship of numerous bills. Most interests try to influence the policy-making process through direct contacts (i.e. lobbying) with the main policy makers. Another avenue of interest group involvement is through their participation in governmental councils or commissions. As an illustration, the Suchocka government offered Solidarity a consulting role in the preparation of the 1994 budget. As in Bulgaria and Hungary, a commission in which the government, trade unions, and employers hold regular meetings has been created. Through consultations, the government tries to gain support for its polices.

As in France, Polish interest groups are often linked to political parties. For example, the OPZZ was the second largest force within the 1993 SLD coalition, winning 61 of the SLD's 171 Sejm seats and giving the union a crucial voice in the legislature. Its power was demonstrated by the fact that the first piece of draft legislation submitted to the new Sejm was sponsored by OPZZ deputies. This situation has benefits and drawbacks. On the negative side, all interests (e.g., minorities, foreigners) are not equally represented. Close cooperation between trade unions and the government has also limited the ability of the workers to wield traditional weapons such as collective bargaining and strikes. On the positive side, the almost direct involvement of interest groups provides for more societal participation in government. As a result of globalization and democratization, interest groups will become increasingly powerful.

As noted earlier, the church also influences policy making. Because it is somewhere between an interest group and a state institution, the church occupies a special place in the Polish polity. While it has been careful not to identify with any one political group or candidate, several parties in Poland have received explicit support from the church. The church also has official contacts with the government through the Governmental-Episcopal Commission.[47]

Public opinion, measured mainly at the ballot and opinion polls, also influences policy creation. The electorate's preferences drastically changed the ideological makeup of the regime by electing a rightist, then a leftist, then another rightist government. In this way, the public shapes the general directions of policy formulation.

External variables and institutions also influence the polity. For example, the large Polish national debt and loan agreements signed with the International Monetary Fund limit the ability of government to enact economic policies that would increase the budget deficit or the rate of inflation.

The number of actors summarizes the complexity of the policy-making process. The constitutional framework is straightforward: parties present platforms, people vote, and winning parties form a Cabinet that introduces the laws necessary to fulfill their program. However, reality is not so simple. The 1997 elections produced a government with a solid parliamentary majority. Yet policy options were constrained by the requirements of external forces and the fact that any retreat from market reforms would lessen the economic freedom people had come to take for granted. Thus whatever policies a government adopts, it faces numerous difficulties implementing them.

Case Study: "Law on Local-Government Restructuring"

Since the transition, the restructuring of local governments has been a perennial political issue. Under the communist regime, Poland's seventeen historical regions were eliminated and forty-nine new ones created. This reorganization ensured that local governments acted more as agents of state control than as advocates of local interests. As we saw earlier, one of the first acts of the Mazowieski government was to end the subordination of local governments to the central government. Until 1998, however, a political stalemate prevented the requisite organizational changes. Both the SLD and PSL opposed reforms as they would lose power and influence in rural areas where they were strong.[48] In contrast, parties on the right—the SEA and FU—wanted to lessen the number of administrative regions and transfer power and responsibility to them. Not only would this help foster the creation of a civil society by decentralizing power, it would also reduce administrative costs. One of their first acts after their electoral victory in 1997 was to introduce legislation to enact these reforms.

The bill called for the creation of twelve regions and the reintroduction of the powiat as an intermediate tier of government between the viovod and the gmina. A variety of groups opposed these reforms. Local governments did not support the bill because many of them would be consolidated or eliminated. For the reasons already noted, the SLD and PSL also opposed the bill. In what commentators suggested was an attempt to mobilize antigovernment sentiment with an eye on the upcoming local and presidential elections, President Kwasniewski also opposed the legislation. Attempts to reconcile these differences by the speaker of the Sejm and talks between the president and prime minister were unsuccessful. Vetoing the SEA/FU bill, Kwasniewski announced he would only accept the number of regions supported by all Sejm factions, including the opposition SLD and PSL.[49] An attempt to override his veto failed.

Two weeks after the veto, following extensive negotiations between the president, the government, and the parliamentary opposition, a compromise was reached. It provided for the creation of sixteen rather than twelve regions. Four days later, the bill was adopted by the parliament and the president signed it into law. In addition to showing us that a parliamentary majority does ensure the enactment of policy in a mixed presidential/parliamentary system of government, this example also shows us that in contrast to other states in the region, the vast majority of politicians accept the need for political reforms.

Policy Implementation

After a law is adopted, it must be put into effect. Thus the success of the new policy depends largely on the actors who implement it. Although the central governmental bureaucracy was responsible for implementation under the communist regime, the PUWP Secretariat ensured that policy was actually put into effect.

Today, while the government is still responsible for policy implementation, actual enactment takes place at both the state and local levels, largely free of political oversight. While the administrative structure and responsibilities are clearly defined, there are still impediments to policy implementation. First, reminiscent of the communist regime, is the politization of the bureaucracy. As noted earlier, the central government controls both national and regional bureaucracy through the URM office. Since the head of the URM appoints regional leaders, this position gives him a strong patronage tool. In 1993, the new SLD/PSL government declared that in addition to "professional qualifications, the voivods should generally be affiliated with the dominant party."[50] This policy politicizes the civil service, causing it to be viewed as a political instrument rather than an impartial state body.

Another impediment is an ineffectual bureaucracy. Since laws usually leave room for interpretation, bureaucratic interpretation has a large role in policy execution. Thus an unstable polity, weak political oversight, and the need for many new laws have combined to make the Polish bureaucracy a major obstacle to change. This can be seen in the "crippling lack of coordination between the government ministries and an epidemic of buck-passing." Various ministries put off decisions for years while covering up their inaction with excuses like, "The case is being examined." In terms of coordination between the different levels of government, "clerks in regional offices often do not learn of regulatory changes for months after they have been made and then often act according to political considerations. Poles in business complain that officials who appear immobile are often just waiting for a bribe."[51] This situation has profound ramifications for policy implementation. An inefficient bureaucracy hinders everything from tax collection to creation of new businesses. This situation fosters disillusionment with the government, lessening its legitimacy and confidence in the system. It only adds to the general frustration which has accompanied the change in regime.

Perhaps the greatest obstacle to policy implementation is the lack of individual involvement. Under the old regime, people were either organized in PUWP mass organizations or did not participate in public life. As a result, people are not used to questioning the state. For example, in contrast to the United States, Polish environmentalists would not sue the government to ensure an environmental law is being enforced. In conclusion, actual policy implementation in a period of societal transformation is often difficult.

CONCLUSION

Ten years after the end of the communist regime, Poland has made significant progress in the creation of a new polity. While it faces problems similar to all states in the region, the early enactment of economic reforms has fostered the creation of a civil society and democratic institutions, making Poland a model for other states in the region.

Civil Society

Like Hungary, Poland has a well-developed civil society. As many as 20,000 nongovernmental organizations, including professional, political, cultural, ecological, and single-issue groups and associations are operating in Poland.[52] There is also free and open media and freedom of assembly and demonstration. As a result, Freedom House ranks Poland a 2 in civil rights.

Democratic Institutions/Political Rights

Although Poles are becoming increasingly dissatisfied with the political and economic situation, they do not question the existence of democratic institutions and free and fair elections. This can be seen in the seven uneventful changes of government since 1989. In contrast to Russia, the major actors in Poland accept the new pluralistic system. However, this does not mean the institutional framework of the state is without problems.

The adoption of a new constitution has not ended the friction between the executive and legislative branches that results from both having strong independent powers. This condition is the result of a lack of democratic experience and a bitterly divided polity. Although the major parties agree on the broad outlines of policy (i.e., a market economy and integration with the West), they have yet to reach political agreement on such contentious issues as the separation of powers, the responsibilities of various state bodies, and the role of the church. This can be seen in the 1997 electoral campaign in which the Solidarity Electoral Alliance called for changes in the "Bolshevik" constitution because it failed to ban abortions and does not state that "natural law" is higher than human-made law.

This and other minor problems notwithstanding, Poland has an open, functioning, constitutional system. Thus Freedom House gives Poland its highest rating (1) in the development of democratic institutions and political rights.

Market Economy

As a result of "shock therapy," Poland has overcome its post-1989 transitional economic recession. It has one of the fastest-growing economies in Europe and is the only CEE country that has surpassed its 1990 GDP. In spite of the fact that the great majority of Poles support economic and political changes, as in other CEE states a significant percentage long for the security of the past. For all its evils, the old system provided a sense of security that the new system does not. This belief is partially the result of a general lack of understanding of how the old system worked. For example, since there were no direct taxes, people did not realize that 43 percent of their salaries went to fund the health care system. The lack of knowledge about the previous system does not lessen the challenge of how to sustain economic growth while mitigating its social costs. As any Western politician would agree, it is very difficult to balance public expectations and sound fiscal policies. How the government resolves this dilemma will test the flexibility of the new system.

This situation not withstanding, the early enactment of economic reforms has moved Poland rapidly down the path to a market economy. The EBRD ranks the Polish economy as follows:

1. Privatization and restructuring of enterprises: 3.6
2. Competitiveness and openness of the market: 3.5
3. Ability of financial institutions to collect and channel savings to productive investments: 3.25
4. Extensiveness and effectiveness of legal rules on investment: 4.1

Although Poland's 3.6 average is slightly less than Hungary's 3.8, it does not take into account how much more developed the Hungarian economy was in 1989. Thus Poland has had the fastest economic development in the region.

Rule of Law

In comparison to the situation in Bulgaria and Russia, the rule of law is much more developed in Poland. However, as a result of problems noted earlier, the judiciary is not wholly free of governmental influence and people are not equal before the law. Thus Poland ranks slightly behind Hungary in the creation of a law-based state. With a 5.08 ranking, Transparency International ranks Poland 29th in its 52-country survey. This is a slight decline from its 5.57 rating in 1996.

What explains this decline? One major reason is lack of a new legal code. The failure to enact a code that takes into account the numerous changes in the polity since 1989 has created a legal vacuum in certain spheres and left whole areas of political life unregulated and dependent on improvisation. This has allowed corruption to flourish. For example, in 1995 dozens of Polish policemen were arrested for using police computers to trace cars whose insurance had expired, then tipping off thieves who stole them and ransomed them back to their owners. Although the Constitution strengthens the power of the judiciary, without a new legal code, the latter will be unable to completely fulfill its constitutional mandate of guaranteeing "the freedom and rights of citizens."

Why has Poland been so successful in creating a new polity? Like the Hungarians, Poles have had extensive contact with Western Europe and the United States—Chicago is commonly known as the second largest Polish city—and see themselves as culturally part of the West. This perception led to a societal consensus regarding the need for economic and political reforms.

Another explanation is the fear of an increasing unstable Russia. With continuing economic and political problems in their powerful next door neighbor, many Poles realize the necessity of implementing reforms. In addition, Poles are much more optimistic about the future than Russians who are still mired in the past.[53]

International Ramifications

As in the rest of the region, the demise of the CMEA and the Warsaw Pact left Poland in a economic, political, and security vacuum. Like Hungary, Poland has looked to the West to fill these voids. Its foreign policy goals are centered around membership in the European Union and NATO. Politicians from across the political spectrum believe inclusion in these bodies will be defining events in Poland's transition.

In another similarity with Hungary, Poland's membership in these organizations is largely dependent on events outside of its control. For example, domestic economic problems in the EU have resulted in the imposition of protectionist measures against Polish and other CEE states' exports. In 1996, 60 percent of Poland's trade deficit was with EU countries. Although Poland became an "associate" member of the EU in 1994 and was selected as one of five CEE states to begin integration talks for full membership, current EU policy adversely affects Polish exports and domestic production. Membership in the EU will also have a high domestic political cost as the economy must be drastically changed. This includes privatizing more state industries, closing inefficient coal mines, and modernizing farms that employ over 25 percent of the population.

The attempted August 1991 Moscow coup and the October 1993 storming of parliament were seen by many Poles as a threat to their newly regained sovereignty. Against strong Russian resistance, the Czech Republic, Hungary, and Poland were the first former socialist states to be included in NATO. The disagreement with Russia over NATO expansion points to a key dilemma facing Poland: how to integrate itself with Western economic and military structures while not offending its powerful neighbor. To offset Russia's opposition to its Western policy, Poland has improved relations with their common neighbors, the Ukraine and Belorussia.

Although Poland will not be full a member of the EU for a number of years, Poland's desire to join them has forced it to start adjusting its political and economic standards to conform to this organization. This makes it more difficult for governments to use economic and social policies for domestic political ends. While there has been a societal consensus on Poland's foreign policy, a majority of the population supports a change in emphasis away from simply imitating the West. Above all, they want "Poland to be Polish."

Summary

Although Poland was the first Central or Eastern European state to break with communism, by 1992 it was close to economic and political collapse. The first three postcommunist governments each lasted less than nine months and most Poles watched their living standards drastically decline. Economic collapse and/or a return to an authoritarian regime were distinct possibilities.

By 1994, everything had changed. The economy was growing rapidly, and more than half of it was in private hands. Although the successor to the PUWP won the 1993 parliamentary and 1995 presidential elections, the return of the left to power occurred within constitutional guidelines. The method of governing has also been transformed. The former regime's monopoly of power has ended and a decentralized democratic system based on checks and balances has begun to emerge. In contrast to the past, the government has treated its opponents fairly. Even the most extreme nationalist groups, such as the Self-Defense Party and Party X, have been allowed to contest elections. These actions have greatly increased the legitimacy of the regime.

Another sign of democratic legitimacy can be seen in the use of legal measures, rather than violence, to challenge government policies. For example, although over a million people signed a petition to hold a national referendum on a new law that restricted abortions, the church managed to block it. Instead of taking to the streets, most people took their revenge at the ballot box by supporting "pro-choice" parties in the 1993 elections. This example illustrates how the new Polish democracy has been able to "contain, if not alleviate public dissatisfaction."[54] As a result, the Polish polity is stable. The government has managed to face and contain public dissatisfaction and at the same time adhere to basic democratic principles. Poland's post-1989 experience shows there is a strong correlation between the degree of societal consensus and the effectiveness of economic and political reforms.

If economic growth and stability are considered basic criteria for evaluating the performance of a polity, then Poland is a success. Successful macroeconomic developments have given Poland the fastest-growing economy in Europe. Nevertheless, there are still obstacles to be overcome. First, deteriorating living standards have started to erode the broad consensus that has been the driving force behind the post-1989 transition. As a result, governmental legitimacy in the future will depend in large measure on whether it is able to increase economic security.

Even more alarming is the lack of competing political visions of Poland's future. Instead of offering competing visions of economic development or national interest that people are most concerned about, the main parties are more interested in determining who did what in the communist regime.[55] After returning to power in 1997, the SEA introduced a bill that would ban ex-communists for five to ten years from numerous public posts, ranging from cabinet ministers and judges to managers of state-owned companies. Thus many politicians place their own interests above societal interests. This has led to the unusual situation in which the former communists support the establishment of a Western market economy while the right supports policies that would limit Western influence and preserve the socialist welfare system.

This situation has many negative consequences. First is the weakening of centrist parties such as the Freedom Union, which played a key role in the economic and political transformation.[56] Second, the political divide has fostered the creation of small dissident parties, further fragmenting the political scene. Finally, since the main parties are against, rather than for, something, it is likely people will continue to avoid political involvement. Poland already has the lowest voter turnout among the states in this book, weakening the authority of the regime and perhaps setting the stage for future problems. These problems notwithstanding, the foundations of a civil society are in place, democratic institutions have been established, market reforms initiated, and political rights guaranteed. Like Italy, Poland's economy continues to grow in spite of an erratic political system. Although this slows the pace of change, the stability of the polity shows that Poland, like Hungary, is well on its way to creating a democratic polity.

TIMELINE

1944

July	The communist-dominated Polish Committee of Liberation is formed in Lublin.
Summer	The USSR invades Poland.

1945

January	The USSR recognizes the "Lublin Government" as the provisional government of Poland.
February	At the Yalta Conference, the Allies extend recognition to the "Lublin Government," after it forms a coalition with the London government in exile and other noncommunist groups.

1947

January	As a result of fraudulent elections, the Communist Party gains control of the legislature. Sovietization begins.
December	The Polish United Workers Party (PUWP) is created with the merger of the Polish Socialist Party (PSP) and its leftist allies.

1948

September	"Local Communist" Wladyslaw Gomulka, first secretary of the Communist Party, is replaced by "Moscovite" Boleslav Bierut.

1949

January	Poland joins the Council for Mutual Economic Assistance (CMEA). To help ensure Polish loyalty, Soviet Marshal Konstantine Rokossovsky is made defense minister.

1951

Gomulka is imprisoned.

1952

A Soviet-style constitution is ratified and the Republic of Poland is renamed the Polish People's Republic. The government launches farm collectivization, takes control of industry, and starts an antireligion campaign.

1953

September	Cardinal Wyszynski, head of the Polish Roman Catholic Church, is imprisoned.

1956

March 12	Bierut dies of a heart attack and is replaced by Edward Ochab.
June	Widespread discontent with Soviet influence and governmental repression leads to antigovernment riots in Poznan.
October	Gomulka is freed from prison and is reinstalled as head of the PUWP. He ends collectivization and eases the antireligion campaign.
October 28	Cardinal Wyszynski is released from prison. Defense Minister Rokossovsky is removed from office.

1968

March	Students protest against suppression of intellectual freedom.

1970

December	After a 30 percent price increase in food, workers in Gdansk go on strike. People demand better living conditions and political reforms. Gomulka is forced to resign and is replaced by Edward Gierek.

1976
Government announces big increases in food prices; riots ensue.

1978
Cardinal Karol Wojtyla, archbishop of Krakow, is elected pope of the Roman Catholic Church. Taking the name of John Paul II, he became the first Polish pope in history.

1980
Gdansk becomes the center of a national strike. Workers demand higher wages and the right to free trade unions.

September Gierek is forced to resign. Stanislaw Kania becomes head of PUWP.
November Led by Lech Walesa, Solidarity, an organization of free trade unions, is recognized by the government.

1981
October Kania is replaced by Wojciech Jaruzelski, an army general.
December Jaruzelski imposes martial law. Solidarity is banned and Walesa and hundreds of union leaders are imprisoned.

1982
Walesa and other union leaders are released.

1983
July Martial law is suspended.
Lech Walesa receives the Noble Peace Prize.

1989
After a series of negotiations, Solidarity is legalized and allowed to compete in parliamentary elections.
August Parliament elects Wojciech Jaruzelski president and appoints Tadeusz Mazowiecki, a Solidarity leader, prime minister.

1990
January The "Shock Therapy" reform program, directed by finance minister Leszak Balcerowicz, is enacted. The PUWP is dissolved.
June Solidarity splits into competing factions.
November Mazowiecki, Walesa, and Stanislaw Tyminski run for the presidency.
December Walesa wins the presidential election and becomes the first non-communist leader since 1944.

1991
October Parliamentary elections.
Mazowiecki's Democratic Union, the intellectual faction of Solidarity, gains a majority in both the Sejm and the Senate.
Jan Olszewski is selected prime minister.

1992
February The Catholic Church gets parliament to pass an anti-abortion law.
May Olszewski resigns after his economic program is rejected by the Sejm.

| | Final accord on the withdrawal of Russian troops from Poland is signed. |
| August | Hanna Suchocka is selected as prime minister. |

1993

| October | Parliamentary elections: a coalition of the Democratic Left Alliance (former PUWP) and the Polish Peasant Party, a former Communist front party, win a majority of seats in the Sejm and the Senate. Waldemar Pawlak is selected prime minister. |

1995

| November | In a close election, Aleksander Kwasniewski is elected president, defeating Lech Walesa. |
| | Jozef Oleksy is selected prime minister. |

1996

| January | Prime Minister Oleksy resigns after being accused by Walesa's party of spying for Moscow. |
| February | Wlodzimierz Cimoszewicz becomes prime minister. |

1997

May 25	A national referendum is held to approve a new constitution. Less than 40 percent of the voters turn out, but the Constitution is approved by about 57 percent. This constitution replaces the communist constitution of 1952.
July 3	NATO extends an invitation for membership to Poland, Hungary, and the Czech Republic.
September	Parliamentary elections: The party Solidarity Election Action wins a majority, with the Democratic Left Alliance close behind.

1998

| October | The SLD, routed in 1997 parliamentary elections, wins the most seats in nine of the country's sixteen regional parliaments. |

WEB SITES

Polish Constitution
http://www.uni-wuerzburg.de/law/pl__indx.html
The 1952, 1993, and 1997 Polish constitutions and other political information.

The Sejm of the Republic of Poland
http://www.sejm.gov.pl/english.html
The website of the lower house of the Polish parliament. Includes information on all aspects of Polish politics.

Poland
http://www.poland-embassy.org.uk/
Political, economic, and cultural links from the Polish embassy in London, UK.

The Official Website of Poland
http://poland.pl/
Information on Polish politics, economics, culture, geography, tourism, and other matters. Links to the president's website.

Inside Poland
http://www.insidepoland.com.pl/
A very comprehensive website of every aspect of Polish politics, economics, and culture.

PolishWorld
http://www.polishworld.com/
A Polish search engine, including links to Polish news sources.

The Warsaw Voice
http://www.warsawvoice.com.pl/
A weekly English-language newspaper for foreigners living in Poland.

WORKS CITED

Banks, Arthur S., ed. *Political Handbook of the World 1992*. Birmingham: CSA Publications, 1992.

Battiata, Mary. "In Poland Red Tape Knows No Ideology: Bureaucratic Tangles Still Daunting, Despite Communism's Demise." *Washington Post* 23 Feb. 1992: A22.

Curry, Jane L. "Which Way Is Right?" *Transitions* October 1997: 74–79.

Daniszewski, John. "Polish Parliament Rejects Privatization Plan." *Washington Post* 19 March 1993: C3.

Davies, Norman. *God's Playground: A History of Poland*. 2 vols. New York: Columbia UP, 1982.

de Weydenthal, Jan B. "Polish Foreign Policy after the Elections." *RFE/RL Research Report* 15 Oct. 1993: 17–20.

—. "Troubled Polish-Russian Economic Relations." *RFE/RL Research Report* 2 July 1993: 31–33.

"Feeling Perkier." *Economist* 2 March 1996: 48–49.

Feusi, Alois. "End of the Line in Warsaw." *Swiss Review of World Affairs* Nov. 1994: 8–9.

Gieysztor, Alexander, et al. *History of Poland*. 2nd ed. Warsaw: Polish Scientific Publishers, 1970.

Jordan, Michael. "Ticket to NATO: No Sass from Top Brass." *Christian Science Monitor* 22 May 1997: 1.

Karpinski, Jacob. "With the Left Fully in Charge, the Polish Right Prepares for 1997." *Transition* 7 Feb. 1997: 17–19.

—. "Polish Ruling Parties Assert Control over Television." *Transition* 18 Oct. 1996: 51–54.

Karski, Jan. *The Great Powers and Poland 1919–1945*. Lanham: University Press of America, 1985.

Kramer, John. "The Environmental Crisis in Eastern Europe." *Slavic Review* 2 (1993): 204.

Krol, Marcin. "Measuring the Costs of a 'Free' Education." *Transitions* Sept. 1997: 82–83.

Kurczewski, Jacek. "Poland's Perpetually New Middle Class." *Transition* 21 March 1997: 22–25.

Magill, Frank. *Great Events from History.* Modern European Series. 3 vols. Englewood Cliffs: Salem Press, 1979.

Maksymiuk, Jan. RFE/RL Political Analyst. Personal interview. 22 July 1998.

Mason, David. *Poland.* Unpublished manuscript, 1996.

Nelson, Harold, ed. *Poland: A Country Study.* Washington: GPO, 1983.

"The New Poland." *Global Affairs* Spring 1992: 139–141.

"On Hold." *The Economist* 20 Feb. 1999: 62–63.

O'Rourke, Breffni, and Chris Klimiuk. "New Polish Government to Face Urgent Economic Tasks." *RFE/RL Daily Report* (25 Sept. 1997): 2 pp. Online. Internet.

Poland. Parliament. "Ustawa o samorzadzie terytorialnym." *Dziennik Ustaw* no. 16. Warsaw: 1998.

"Poland's Devolutionary Battleground." *The Economist* 7 Feb. 1998: 53.

Rose, Richard, and Christian Haerpfer. "New Democracies between State and Market: A Baseline Report of Public Opinion." *Studies in Public Policy* [Glasgow: University of Strathclyde] 204 (1992).

Sabbat-Swidlicka, Anna. "Church and State in Poland." *RFE/RL Research Report* 2 April 1993: 47–50.

—. "Toward the Rule of Law: Poland." *RFE/RL Research Report* 3 July 1992: 16–24.

Slay, Ben. "Poland: The Role of Managers in Privatization." *RFE/RL Research Report* 19 March 1993: 52–56.

"Televisual Coup." *The Economist* 16 Aug. 1997: 39–40.

"Unfinished Business." *The Economist* 20 Sept.1997: 23–25.

Vinton, Louisa. "Poland Strives to Meet NATO Standards." *RFE/RL News Brief* 24–28 Jan. 1994: 17.

—. "Outsider Parties and the Political Process in Poland." *RFE/RL Research Report* 21 Jan. 1994: 14.

—. "Poland's New Government: Continuity or Reversal?" *RFE/RL Research Report* 19 Nov. 1993: 1–7.

ENDNOTES

1. John Kramer, "The Environmental Crisis in Eastern Europe," *Slavic Review,* Summer 1993, p. 204.

2. Alois Feusi, "End of the Line in Warsaw," *Swiss Review of World Affairs,* November 1994, p. 9.

3. Jacek Kurczewski, "Poland's Perpetually New Middle Class," *Transition,* March 21, 1997, p. 22.

4. The corresponding figures are 23 percent in Bulgaria, 27 percent in Hungary, and 32 percent in Russia. "New Democracies Barometer IV," Paul Lazarsfeld Society, Vienna. Cited in *The Economist,* March 2, 1996, p. 48.

5. "On Hold," *The Economist,* February 20, 1999, p. 62.

6. Breffni O'Rourke and Chris Klimiuk, "New Polish Government to Face Urgent Economic Tasks," *RFE/RL Daily Report,* September 25, 1997.

7. Jan B. de Weydenthal, "Troubled Polish-Russian Economic Relations," *RFE/RL Research Report,* July 2, 1993, p. 32.

8. Jacob Karpinski, "With the Left Fully in Charge, the Polish Right Prepares for 1997," *Transition*, February 7, 1997, p. 19.

9. Norman Davies, *God's Playground: A History of Poland*, vol 1, p. 111 (New York: Columbia UP, 1982).

10. Alexander Gieysztor et al., *History of Poland*, 2nd ed. (Warsaw: Polish Scientific Publishers, 1970), p. 358.

11. Frank Magill, *Great Events from History. Modern European Series*, vol. 2 (Englewood Cliffs: Salem Press, 1979), p. 149.

12. Jan Karski, *The Great Powers and Poland 1919–1945* (Lanham: University Press of America, 1985), p. 7.

13. This was one of the highest percentages in Europe, much larger than the 2 percent of the French population who angered Parisians enough to launch the French Revolution.

14. Arthur S. Banks, ed., *Political Handbook of the World 1992* (Birmingham: CSA Publications, 1992).

15. One of the more colorful parties, the Polish Beer Lovers' Party, won 3.3 percent of the votes and 16 seats in the Sejm.

16. David Mason, *Poland*, unpublished manuscript, p. 14.

17. Ibid., p. 18.

18. Richard Rose and Christian Haerpfer, "New Democracies between State and Market: A Baseline Report of Public Opinion," *Studies in Public Policy*, no. 204 (Glasgow: University of Strathclyde, Centre for the Study of Public Policy, 1992).

19. Marcin Krol, "Measuring the Costs of a 'Free' Education, *Transitions*, September 1997, p. 82.

20. *The Economist*, September 20, 1997, p. 25.

21. John Downing, *Internationalizing Media Theory* (London: Sage Publications, 1996), p. 144.

22. Jakob Karpinski, "Polish Ruling Parties Assert Control over Television," *Transition*, October 18, 1996, p. 51.

23. *RFE/RL Daily Report*, December 15, 1994.

24. Constitution Watch, *East European Constitutional Review*, Spring 1998, p. 21.

25. *The Economist*, February 7, 1998, p. 53.

26. Parliament of the Republic of Poland, "Ustawa o samorzadzie terytorialnym," *Dziennik Ustaw*, no. 16, p. 206.

27. Mason, "Poland," p. 13.

28. Anna Sabbat-Swidlicka, "Toward the Rule of Law: Poland," *RFE/RL Research Report*, July 3, 1992, p. 16.

29. Constitutional Watch, *East European Constitutional Review*, Fall 1996, p. 19.

30. One foreign investor described Poland's bureaucracy as "thousands of non-educated older people sitting in dirty dark offices with only one thing left—a stamp." Cited in *The Economist*, September 20, 1997, p. 25.

31. *RFE/RL Daily Report*, October 27, 1994.

32. Jacob Karpinski, "With the Left Fully in Charge, the Polish Right Prepares for 1997," *Transition*, February 7, 1997, p. 18.

33. *The Economist*, August 16, 1997, p. 40.

34. For example, a civil service "reform" that made it almost impossible to dismiss employees until their retirement age and requires seven years of experience for certain civil service jobs actually favors those connected with the old regime. Constitutional Watch, *East European Constitutional Review*, Fall 1997, p. 32.

35. Louisa Vinton, "Poland Strives to Meet NATO Standards," *RFE/RL News Brief*, January 24–28, 1994, p. 17.

36. Michael Jordan, "Ticket to NATO: No Sass from Top Brass," *Christian Science Monitor*, May 22, 1997, p. 1.

37. *RFE/RL Newsline,* April 28, 1998.

38. Ben Slay, "Poland: The Role of Managers in Privatization," *RFE/RL Research Report,* March 19, 1993, p. 52.

39. "The New Poland," *Global Affairs,* Spring 1992, pp. 139–141.

40. *RFE/RL Daily Report,* October 25, 1994.

41. Anna Sabbat-Swidlicka, "Church and State in Poland," *RFE/RL Research Report,* April 2, 1993, p. 50.

42. Harold Nelson, ed., *Poland: A Country Study.* (Washington: GPO, 1983), p. 135.

43. Asked whether politicians get involved in politics only to make money, Poland had the highest negative response—64 percent. This compared with 42 percent in Bulgaria, 45 percent in Hungary, and 58 percent in Russia. Bruszt, p. 91.

44. Corresponding responses were 50 percent in Bulgaria, 41 percent in Hungary, and 54 percent in Russia. Ibid., p. 90.

45. Jan B. de Weydenthal, "Polish Foreign Policy after the Elections," *RFE/RL Research Report,* October 15, 1993, p. 18.

46. John Daniszewski, "Polish Parliament Rejects Privatization Plan," *Washington Post,* March 19, 1993, p. C3.

47. Anna Sabbat-Swidlicka, "Church and State in Poland," *RFE/RL Research Report,* April 2, 1993, p. 47.

48. Jan Maksymiuk, RFE/RL Political Analyst. Personal interview. July 23, 1998, Prague, Czech Republic.

49. Constitutional Watch, *East European Constitutional Review,* Summer 1998, p. 25.

50. Louise Vinton, "Poland's New Government: Continuity or Reversal?" *RFE/RL Research Report,* November 19, 1993, p. 7.

51. Mary Battiata, "In Poland Red Tape Knows No Ideology: Bureaucratic Tangles Still Daunting, Despite Communism's Demise," *Washington Post,* February 23, 1992, p. A22.

52. Freedom House, p. 327.

53. Jan Maksymiuk, RFE/RL Political Analyst. Personal interview. July 22, 1998. Prague, Czech Republic.

54. Louisa Vinton, "Outsider Parties and the Political Process in Poland," *RFE/RL Research Report,* January 21, 1994, p. 14.

55. Although President Kwasniewski usually has approval ratings over 50 percent, many Poles refuse to reconcile themselves to his victory. When Kwasniewski was sworn in 1995, Walesa refused to attend the ceremony.

56. Jane L. Curry, "Which Way Is Right?" *Transitions,* October 1997, p. 75.

CONCLUSION

Now that we have examined Bulgarian, Hungarian, Polish, and Russian polities, what conclusions can we draw? This section looks at some of the similarities and differences among the states, the reasons for them, and how they affect the transition to a law-based state with a civil society, democratic institutions, and a market economy. Finally, we take a look at the future of the region.

SIMILARITIES

The imposition of the Soviet economic and political system explains the numerous similarities between states in the region.

Political Similarities

One striking similarity throughout the region is a lack of political participation. Following the initial euphoria that accompanied the end of the communist regimes, people in all these countries have grown increasingly apathetic. This apathy can be seen in declining electoral participation. The decline is the result of three main factors: communist legacies, evolving political values, and the insecurity associated with rapid change.

As might be expected, the heavy hand of Soviet socialist development has left numerous destructive legacies. For at least forty-five years, the people of Central and Eastern Europe were ruled by arbitrary and powerful regimes that allowed no opposition or representation outside the ruling party. No institutions existed that could check the power of the party. All public organizations served the state, not their members. Therefore, people grew up with the belief that they could not influence the government. When asked in 1992 whether they thought they could influence governmental decisions, positive responses ranged from a high of 18 percent in Hungary to a low of 5 percent in Poland.[1] In comparison, the average in Western democracies is 70 percent. This situation is in large part the result of political immaturity and the failure of people to take responsibility for their lives. In other words, people have yet to make the transformation from subjects to citizens.

Interestingly, Hungary and Poland have a lower voter turnout than Bulgaria or Russia do. Since these two states are more economically and politically advanced than Bulgaria and Russia, this situation seems contradictory. At first glance it suggests a lack of regime legitimacy, but lack of political participation can also be viewed as a positive development, reflecting the emergence of a broad political consensus and the creation of nongovernmental groups that allow people to try to solve their own problems—that is, a civil society. In other words, decline in political participation may be a measure of the institutionalization of democracy rather than a threat to it.[2]

Another commonality is the lack of underlying political values. Under the old regime, even though they were often distorted, there was a common set of political norms. Almost overnight they changed, with good—communism—becoming bad and bad—capitalism—becoming good. Today values are still developing. This has created a moral crisis. Values have to relearned and norms created.[3] This is difficult in any situation, let alone one surrounded by economic and political upheaval.

This situation has numerous ramifications. First, in this critical period of political development, elections have been fought on the basis of being against something rather than for something. Thus the larger societal questions, such as what type of political system should be created, have yet to be addressed. For example, the issue that dominated most of the first elections after the fall of the old regime was being for or against the communists; the second, being for or against economic reforms. In other words, every election implies that simple negativism is a legitimate and useful political posture for the whole polity. This attitude has caused large governmental swings and a weakened opposition. It is a situation that stifles political competition, slowing democratic development.

Finally, lack of political participation has allowed the old elites to maintain their hold on power. This lessens the legitimacy of the regime since people see little difference from the old regime and in turn fosters even more apathy, decreasing confidence in the new political institutions.

Social Similarities

Under the old system, the state dominated society, controlling everything from industry to social services. With the gradual lessening of state control, countries in the region are being forced to restructure their social systems. This task is compounded by the huge budget deficits that greatly limit previously generous state-subsidized social services. Many benefits, such as child care, health care, subsidized housing and food, are either being eliminated or sharply cut back.

The move from free, universal social services has deprived a significant proportion of the population of coverage. Since the state no longer provides these services, the burden has been shifted to individuals and families. The removal of housing and food subsidies has resulted in a drastic loss of income for people on a fixed income, such as pensioners and the unemployed, forcing them into poverty. This has contributed to an increasing mortality and crime rates.

Economic changes have also affected medical care. Since 1990, infant mortality has increased dramatically throughout the region. In Russia, approximately 10 percent of children starting school are not healthy.[4] This situation has led to a decline in birth rates since families are reticent to have children in these conditions. A declining population means even fewer workers to support the elderly in the future.

The end of state subsidies for industry and the privatization of parts of the economy has created another problem familiar to many in the West: unemployment. However, unlike in the West, there are no efficient institutions or financing mechanisms for dealing with unemployment. As a group, women have been affected most because they are usually the first to be laid off. Thus the formerly high rate of female participation in the workforce has been greatly reduced, lessening the number of households with two incomes.

Attempts to overcome these problems have been limited by the legacy of the past and the slowness with which reforms were implemented. Under the old system, people took social benefits for granted, paying only a nominal fee for housing, health care, food, and so forth. To lessen societal unrest, the governments in all four states have tried to continue some of the old subsidies. To pay for these programs, states have been forced for the first time to impose direct taxes. In Poland, for example, the social security tax alone is 45 percent. Since people never had to "pay" taxes under the old regime, they try to avoid them. Most dramatically illustrated in Russia, this tax dodging decreases governmental revenues, lessening the amount of money that can be given to those most affected by change. A vicious circle is created in which high tax rates cause tax avoidance, fostering the need for higher rates, which leads to even more avoidance. Even when reforms were initiated, they were either not explained to the public or they were introduced haphazardly, undermining their effect.

Although some groups have benefited from the end of state control, the economic burden of the transition has fallen on the most vulnerable—pensioners, the unemployed, unskilled manual workers, people with a limited education, state employees, and certain ethnic groups. This has led to increasing social stratification. As wages, social security benefits, and the availability of social services deteriorate, poverty increases, fueling public impatience with reforms and undermining the legitimacy of the new regimes. Even though all the countries in the region are now experiencing economic growth, with the exception of Poland no country in Central and Eastern Europe has returned to its 1989 GDP. Thus people have yet to see a direct correlation between improved economic performance and their own situation.[5]

In the current economic climate, governments can neither eliminate the old system nor create a new one. This paralysis has slowed the development of market economies, pluralistic political systems, and the rule of law. Significantly, just as social programs are being cut and living standards decrease, people have been given political rights that they can use to try to protect their economic status. This pressure puts tremendous demands on the regimes, prolonging their transitions.

Summary

Not surprisingly, these conditions have had similar repercussions in the countries under examination. Across the region, many people feel a sense of national humiliation and want to find a scapegoat. They feel threatened by economic dislocations that have allowed some to become fabulously rich while leaving others more impoverished than before. This has put a tremendous strain on society and allowed the former communists to return to power.[6] Because they still have little experience with the tensions inherent in democratic politics and free market economies, some people are increasingly susceptible to the appeals of those who would combine a nationalist message of revenge with socialist promises of economic security. While varying in degree, this "red-brown" coalition between the old communist *nomenklatura* and the new nationalists can be seen throughout the region.[7] Notably, similar social problems fueled the rise of national socialism in Germany in the 1930s.

These problems are compounded by the weakness of new political institutions. Since the state apparatus under the communists was all encompassing, the change in regime has had a dramatic effect on the polity. For example, throughout the region, crime has drastically increased and police efficiency has fallen. The breakdown of law and order has forced people to look for other means to solve their problems and to rely on "connections" or ways to circumvent the law. Since the government is weak and the police no longer omnipotent, a vacuum has been created in which people have neither a sense of personal responsibility nor civic solidarity. Like the situation in southern Italy, these conditions have fostered the growth of local "mafias." Ten years after CEE states started down the path of change, continuing instability makes it difficult for reformers to build support for the necessary, but difficult economic, political, and social reforms. This can be seen in the electoral success of ex-communists in Bulgaria, Hungary, Poland, and Russia between 1993 and 1995 as well as the electoral success of the anticommunists between 1996 and 1998.

Nevertheless, with the exception of Russia, politics in the region have started to gravitate toward the center. Each election narrows the differences between political parties. For example, although center-right coalitions have recently taken power, the countries' commitment to market reforms, democracy, and EU membership will be largely unaffected. This is the result of increasing voter maturity and, more important, global economic integration. Worried by the economic platform of the AYD party, the Hungarian stock market dropped 17 percent after their electoral victory in the May 1998 election. Because multinational companies produce two-thirds of the country's exports and are the driving motor of the economy, the day after the election AYD leader Viktor Orban went to the Hungarian stock exchange to try and reassure investors.

DIFFERENCES[8]

More interesting than the similarities among the former socialist states in Central and Eastern Europe are the differences. As we have seen, there is a growing economic and political gap between Bulgaria and Russia and their former allies Hungary and Poland. What explains these differences? While the scope of this book is limited, some observations can be made.

Historical Differences

Although each state has responded differently to the post-1989 environment, all share historical legacies that have affected their transition. In contrast to Americans, who use the phrase, "That's history," to describe something as gone and forgotten, history permeates the region. As J. F. Brown notes:

> "The past weighs heavily on East Europe—the pre-communist as well as the communist. The latter needs to be overcome; so do some aspects of the former; others need coming to terms with; practically none can ever be recaptured. But the pre-communist past is vague and impressionistic. The communist past is focused and immediately relevant to the issues of today.[9]

Russia emerged from Mongol domination having learned the lesson that a large empire can only be held together through coercion and violence. Thus the Tsars tolerated little opposition to their rule. In contrast to Western Europe, the ideas of popular sovereignty and universal suffrage, prominent components of the Enlightenment, were never accepted in Russia. Although the Ottoman Empire was not as repressive as its Russian counterpart, its control of Bulgaria for five hundred years retarded the emergence of a politically active population. Thus both Bulgaria and Russia lack a culture of civic involvement, the rule of law, and societal consensus on domestic and foreign policy.

Significantly, because of Bulgaria's conservative society, there is no tradition of dissent and therefore little opposition to the communist regime. In contrast, there were numerous dissident groups in the Soviet Union. Thus, while the Russian opposition since 1989 has had a well-defined program of economic and political changes, until 1997 the opposition in Bulgaria was driven only by parochial disputes and an anticommunist message that offered no clear alternative path of development. Thus in some ways, Bulgaria is even less politically developed than Russia.

Compared to Bulgarians and Russians, Hungarians and Poles have a long history of political participation. This can be seen in the nobility's selection of the king in Poland and the acceptance of the Golden Bull in Hungary. In a sense, Hungary and Poland are merely resurrecting what they had before, while Bulgaria and Russia are creating fundamentally new political systems.

Differences in Economic Reform

Differing only in degree, the legacy of the Soviet economic model was similar for all the states in the region: bankrupt factories making shoddy goods nobody wanted, intrusive bureaucracies filled with underpaid and corrupt officials, and a financial sector that existed only because of state intervention. One of the most urgent tasks facing the countries in the region was to turn this mess into a functioning market economy.

This common legacy notwithstanding, Hungary and Poland have been far more successful than Bulgaria and Russia in creating market economies. As a Polish specialist at Deutsche Bank Research notes, there are two main routes to a market economy: creating the right economic and political conditions for individuals to start their own business ventures and privatizing existing state-owned enterprises.[10] As we have seen, Bulgaria and Russia have done little in either area.

LOOKING AHEAD

Our examination of selected states in Central and Eastern Europe has shown that many factors influence economic, political, and social development. Therefore, it was naive to think the creation of a new polity would be quick and easy.

The key to understanding the ongoing transition in the region lies in the link between economics and politics. People in the former communist countries still expect a great deal from government, especially in terms of economic security. In a time of upheaval, political legitimacy and stability are largely dependent on the success of the governments in alleviating economic uncertainty. At the same time, tough economic decisions cannot be made by governments that lack popular support. Although most people understand the necessity of reforms, they differ vastly in their position on the scope and speed of implementing them. Therefore, at least in the short run, economic stability will continue to be a key variable in the development of a new polity. As an illustration, the early enactment of reforms and the resulting economic growth have greatly aided Poland's transition.

The demise of the Soviet Union and the corresponding end of the political chasm in Europe were greeted with euphoria. Most people believed the repudiation of authoritarianism and a centrally planned economy and the acceptance of Western economic and political systems in Central and Eastern European states would initiate a new era in European prosperity. As we have seen, this optimism is not yet justified. For some states, it will take many years before the conditions needed to create a civil society, democratic institutions, a market economy, and the rule of law are firmly in place. This process is made even more difficult by the fact that these features are all intimately connected. For example, economic reforms have impoverished a large part of the population, increasing crime. Responding to societal demands, police have resorted to extrajudicial measures to solve this problem. While popular, these measures weaken support for the rule of law.

States in the region have been trying to do in five to ten years what took many decades in the West. As a result, a growing percentage of the population has concluded that emulating the West is not possible or desirable, leading many observers to predict a return of authoritarian regimes to the region. Because of a lack of constitutional safeguards and the fragility of the new systems, this group thinks that if law and order and economic security become larger public concerns, governments might limit individual and institutional freedoms. While conceivable, the likelihood of this scenario is exaggerated. Although the military and security organs could easily take over, why would their control be any more efficient or successful than that of the communists?

For the second time in fifty years, the states of Central and Eastern Europe must build a new polity. The first was imposed by force; the new one must come through persuasion. Although this will be an arduous process because of the heavy hand of history, the success of some states shows that nothing is predetermined and that culture and legacies of the past can be overcome. At some point, facing the future will take precedence over the comfort of the past.

The development of the new polities in Central and Eastern Europe is very interesting because it gives us insight into many of the transitional problems new regimes all over the world face and, more important, how they can be solved. What are these lessens? First, as Bulgaria and Russia show, incremental change is the most difficult. Second, in order to strenghten the authority and legitimacy of the regime, it is important that the burden of change be shared by all of society, not simply the poor. Third, politicians must do a good job "selling" reforms. They have to convince the population not only that change is necessary, but that it will be painful. Finally, without societal consensus, the state will lack the stability needed to enact reforms.[11]

Movement in this direction can be seen in the fact that the number of interest groups is growing, economic reforms continue to be enacted, democratic institutions have been created, and legal rights are being strengthened. A telling illustration can be seen in the electoral success of the former communist parties. Although many in the West saw this as a setback, the reformed communist coalitions accepted the democratic rules of the game in the way they acquired power—through elections—and how they ruled. Just as important, they were accepted as the legitimate winners by the parties they defeated.

With the exception of Russia, after a decade of pain and populism, with the worst of the transition behind them, voters and parties seem to be moving to a less volatile phase of transition. As the history of the West shows, democracy has to be learned and the road is bumpy. The states of Central and Eastern Europe are advancing at different speeds, but they are advancing.

ENDNOTES

1. Laszlo Bruszt, *Political Culture and Economic Orientations in Central and East Europe during the Transition to Democracy, 1990–1992* (Berlin: Wissenschaftszcentrum Fur Suzialfurschung, 1993), p. 91.

2. Paul Goble, "When Politics Isn't the Answer," *RFE/RL Newsline,* May 15, 1998.

3. As Ken Jowitt has noted, Leninism has left its imprint on the collective psyche, generating behavior patterns that will continue to affect public perceptions and actions, even if only in a residual way. See Kenneth Jowitt, "The Leninist Legacy," in Ivo Banac, ed., *Eastern Europe in the 1990's* (Ithaca, NY: Cornell University Press, 1991).

4. Pestoff, p. 294.

5. Emoke Lengyel and Antal Toth, "Public Opinions in Central and Eastern Europe on the Economy of the Region and on European Integration," in Kurtan, Sandor, and Vass, eds., *Magyarorszag politikai evkonyve* (Budapest: Demokracia Kutatsok Magyar Kozpontja Alapitvany, 1993), p. 640.

6. Note that the term "former communists" has a limited political application. Ex-communists are a very mixed group. For example, the Hungarian Socialist Party pursued economic policies that would make Ronald Reagan smile, while Russian communists continue to advocate a return to centralized planning.

7. Paul Goble, "New National Socialist Threat," *RFE/RL Newsline,* June 26, 1998.

8. The author would like to thank Antal Dizstl, Counsellor at the Hungarian Embassy in Sofia, for his insights, which are incorporated in the following observations.

9. J. F. Brown, *Hopes and Shadows: Eastern Europe after Communism* (Durham: Duke University Press, 1994), p. 45.

10. Cited in Breffni O'Rourke and Chris Klimiuk, "Polish Government to Face Urgent Economic Tasks," *RFE/RL Newsline,* September 25, 1997.

11. Assen Agov, Chairman of the Bulgarian Foreign Affairs Committee. Personal interview. July 29, 1998, Sofia, Bulgaria.

Appendix

STATISTICS

TABLE A.1 Military Figures

	1985		1990		1994	
Country	Armed Forces in Thousands	Armed Forces per 1,000 People	Armed Forces in Thousands	Armed Forces per 1,000 People	Armed Forces in Thousands	Armed Forces per 1,000 People
Bulgaria	189	21.2	129	14.4	80	9.1
Hungary	117	11.0	94	9.1	60	5.8
Poland	439	11.8	313	8.2	255	6.6
USSR/Russia	3,900	14.0	3,400	11.7	1,395	9.3
United States	2,244	9.4	2,181	8.7	1,715	6.6

Source: Daniel Gallik, ed., *World Military Expenditures and Arms Transfers 1995* (Washington, D.C.: U.S. Arms Control and Disarmament Agency, 1996).

TABLE A.2   Birth and Death Rates

	Bulgaria	Hungary	Poland	USSR/Russia	U.S.
Crude birth rate 1984 (per 1,000)	—	13.5	19.5	18–20	15
Crude birth rate 1991	13.0	11.7	14.1	17.3	14.6
Crude birth rate 1996	8.3	10.7	11.9	10.9	14.8
Crude death rate 1984 (per 1,000)	—	13.5	9.5	10	9
Crude death rate 1991	11.6	12.6	9.3	10.3	8.7
Crude death rate 1996	13.6	15.1	10.1	16.3	8.8
Life expectancy 1980	71.3	70	71	67.1	74
Life expectancy 1991	72.7	71.6	72.9	69.8	75.7
Life expectancy 1996	71	69	72.1	63.2	76
Infant mortality rate 1980 (per 1,000 live births)	20	23	21	22	10.8
Infant mortality rate 1991	12.5	14	12.4	22	10.3
Infant mortality rate 1996	15.7	12.3	12.4	24.7	6.7

Source: Marlita A. Reddy, ed., *Statistical Abstract of the World* (New York: Gale Research, 1985, 1990, 1996).

TABLE A.3   Population Information

	Bulgaria	Hungary	Poland	Russia	U.S.
Area and Population					
Area (sq mi)	42,683	35,653	117,571	6,659,250	3,615,105
Population 1980 (in millions)	8.8	10.7	35.5	139	227.7
Population 1990	8.9	10.3	38	148	250
Population 1996	8.6	10	39	148.1	266
Population per sq mi 1996	202	281	329	22	75
Population Density					
Urban population 1980 (% of total)	61	57	58	70	74
Urban population 1994 (% of total)	70	64	64	73	76
Population Growth Rates					
1971–80	.4	.4	.9	.9	.9
1981–90	-.2	-.3	.7	.6	1
1991–94	-.8	-.3	.3	0	.9

Source: Marlita A. Reddy, ed., *Statistical Abstract of the World* (New York: Gale Research, 1985, 1990, 1996); The World Bank, *From Plan to Market World Development Report 1996* (New York: Oxford University Press, 1996).

TABLE A.4   Education

	Bulgaria	Hungary	Poland	USSR/Russia	U.S.
Primary Education					
Enrollment ratio 1980	—	96	100	—	100
Enrollment ratio 1992	—	89	98	—	100
Secondary School Enrollment					
(% of age group) 1980	84	69	77	96	94
(% of age group) 1993	68	82	84	88	98
Postsecondary Education[a]					
Enrollment ratio 1980	—	12.9	17.6	—	58
Enrollment ratio 1992	—	15.3	23	—	81.6

[a]Third-level enrollment includes college and university enrollment and technical and vocational education beyond the high school level. There is considerable variation in reporting from country to country.

Source: Secondary school data from The World Bank, *From Plan to Market World Development Report 1996* (New York: Oxford University Press, 1996); postsecondary school data from *Digest of Education Statistics 1995* (Washington, D.C.: U.S. Department of Health, Education, and Welfare, Education Division, National Center for Education Statistics, 1996).

TABLE A.5   Media

	Bulgaria	Hungary	Poland	USSR/Russia	U.S.
Newspaper circulation (copies per 1,000 pop.) 1979	234	242	237	396	282
Newspaper circulation 1988	267	273	184	474	259
Newspaper circulation 1992	164	282	159	387	236
TV sets per 1,000 population 1981	187	262	228	306	631
TV sets per 1,000 population 1989	249	409	292	323	814
TV sets per 1,000 population 1995	260	427	298	372	816

Source: Marlita A. Reddy, ed., *Statistical Abstract of the World* (New York: Gale Research, 1996).

TABLE A.6 Economic Data

	Bulgaria	Hungary	Poland	USSR/Russia	U.S.
GNP (1994)					
(constant US$ 1994 in billions)					
1985	55	70.2	19.2	—	541.3
1990	50	69.6	18.1	88.6	619.7
1994	37.3	64.1	20.6	78	672.7
GNP per capita (1996 in US dollars)					
at PPP exchange rates					
1985	6,154	6,593	5,182	10,140	22,700
1990	5,622	6,721	4,769	10,180	24,790
1996	4,239	6,213	5,336	5,216	25,810
Debt and Inflation					
Total External Debt 1980 in					
billions of US dollars	.4	9.7	8.9	4.5	737
Total External Debt 1996 in					
billions of US dollars	9.6	27.6	40.4	125	5,181
Inflation (1990	22	29	586	5.6	3.7
Inflation (1992)	82	22.9	43	1358	4.0
Inflation (1995)	62.1	28.2	27.8	190.2	2.5
Unemployment Rates					
1988	1.7	1.7	—	—	5.5
1990	11.7	8.5	11.8	0.08	6.9
1997	12.5	10	13.6	9.3	4.5
Imports and Exports (1996) in					
billions of US dollars					
Export	4.8	14.2	24.4	88.2	625.1
Import	4.6	16.8	32.6	65.1	795.3

Source: GNP data: Daniel Gallik, ed., *World Military Expenditures and Arms Transfers 1995* (Washington, D.C.: U.S. Arms Control and Disarmament Agency, 1996); debt and inflation: World Bank, *From Plan to Market World Development Report 1996* (New York: Oxford University Press, 1996); unemployment: International Monetary Fund, *World Economic Outlook: A Survey by the Staff of the International Monetary Fund.* (Washington, DC: IMF, May 1996); imports and exports: International Monetary Fund, *Direction of Trade Statistics Yearbook 1996* (Washington, DC: 1996), *Statistical Yearbook 1993* (New York: United Nations Publication, 1995), *Statistical Abstract of the United States, 1996: The National Data Book* (Washington, DC: U.S. Department of Commerce, 1996); Transition Report: 1997 (London: European Bank for Reconstruction and Development, 1998).

INDEX